RATS
IN THE
GRAIN

RATS IN THE GRAIN

The Dirty Tricks and Trials of

Archer Daniels Midland

James B. Lieber

FOUR WALLS EIGHT WINDOWS
New York | London

This book is dedicated to my mother and father for a lifetime of love and support.

© 2000 by James B. Lieber

Published in the United States by
Four Walls Eight Windows
30 West 14th Street, room 503
New York, NY 10011
http://www.fourwallseightwindows.com

U.K. offices:

Four Walls Eight Windows/Turnaround
Unit 3 Olympia Trading Estate
Coburg Road, Wood Green
London N22 6T2

Library of Congress Cataloging-in-Publication Data

Lieber, James B
    Rats in the grain : the dirty tricks and trials of Archer Daniels Midland / by James B. Lieber.
        p.   cm.
    Includes bibliographical references and index.
    ISBN 1-56858-141-6
    1. Archer Daniels Midland Company. 2. Food industry and trade—
    Corrupt practices—United States. I. Title.
hd9009.a73 l53 2000
364.16'8'0973—dc21

                                                                99-058568

Printed in the Canada
10 9 8 7 6 5 4 3 2

Interior design by Terry Bain

It is not from the benevolence of the brewer,
the butcher, or the baker that we expect our dinner.
—Adam Smith, The Wealth of Nations, *1776*

"The competitor is our friend and the customer is our enemy."
—Unofficial ADM motto, attributed to Dwayne O. Andreas in FBI files

ACKNOWLEDGMENTS

Many people helped make this project possible. In particular I would like to recognize the contributions of: Richard Abrams, Kenneth Adams, Jack Bray, Paul Brinkmann, Tara Burghart, Greg Burns, John Connor, Anthony D'Angelo, Steve Delany, Fritz Dujour, Phil Edney, Jock Ferguson, Albrecht Funk, Martin Glotzer, Jim Griffin, Alan Guebert, Linda Heflebower, Carol Hoech, David Hoech, George Hoech, Nick Hollis, John Kelson, Scott Lassar, Tom Lieber, James K. Lindsay, Richard Lindsay, James McKown, Nancy Millman, Nell Minow, Russell Mochiber, Patrick Mullen, Jim Mutchnick, John Nicol, Lafell Peterson, Cari Anne Rehm, Sharon Reynolds, Randy Samborn, Lynn Sarko, John Stebbins, Bill Walker, Reid Weingarten, Ron Weiss, Alex Whitacre, Ginger Whitacre, Mark Whitacre, Ann Yahner, and Robert Zaideman.

I received invaluable document collection, preparation, and manuscript support from Ruth Hart, John Kimmell, and Tracey Mathis. Cleo Stearns furnished a useful working bibliography at the beginning of the project. Without the talents and dedication of April Boyer, including her skill with electronic data, much of this book would not have been possible including the analysis of an 8,000-page court transcript, and the appendices at the back of the book on other ADM cases and ADM's political contributions. These appendices as well as the ones on the cast of characters and the time line are intended as ready references for the reader.

I also would like to thank my editor, JillEllyn Riley, and the staff of Four Walls Eight Windows for their judgment and courage. Independent publishers are as necessary to the functioning of an open society as are independent writers and independent book sellers. There were others who helped with this project and asked to remain anonymous whose input is also greatly appreciated.

Finally, I want to thank my wife Margie who makes my writing life possible.

CONTENTS

PREFACE

In the summer of 1995, an extraordinary case broke. Federal agents searched the headquarters of Archer Daniels Midland Company, commonly known as ADM, and charged the company with fixing markets worldwide.

ADM was not just any company. For decades its political influence was unrivalled among American businesses. Showered with federal largesse, it had become the number one recipient of corporate welfare.

The bust of ADM initially won the attention of an army of reporters. Most asked the same question: did the government have the will to take on this commercial behemoth with whom it was inextricably intertwined?

Within a month of the raid, the shape of the story shifted seismically. The whistleblower, a complex figure, possibly mentally ill, was discredited and publicly pilloried. Much of the media grew uncomfortable and slipped away. For the most part, the bad news about ADM was replaced by the familiar "Supermarket to the World" commercials about feeding the hungry and pumping vitamins into the rest of us that supported public radio news broadcasts and Sunday morning political talk shows.

A handful of writers and reporters stuck with the case despite, or perhaps, because of the odd turn of events. As a lawyer, I wondered if the legal process and especially its fire and iron—public trial by jury—could deliver justice. Or, would it be compromised like other institutions that ADM rubbed up against, including Congress, regulatory bodies, and the White House?

In a tabloid culture, trials of gruesome crimes generate the most news. Searing tragedies for those involved, they become diverting gladiatorial spectacles for the rest of us. But bloodless white-collar trials say more about the way the world works, and it is my personal bias that it makes sense to pay more attention to them.

This is not a view shared by most in media. Early on, my agent approached Court TV about the possibility of my covering the trial while I wrote the book. She was told the case was "not slutty enough" for the cable audience. Nevertheless, I continued to follow it for the next three years, including attending the momentous Chicago federal trial that spanned the summer of 1998. The proceedings afforded a rare keyhole view of the usually unseen and unseemly workings of world markets. Ironically, a small part of the case actually would involve prostitutes used tactically in industrial espionage.

This was not a simple story to cover. Famous for shaping its own message and putting off all but the most servile reporters, ADM was no help. The Department of Justice seemed highly conflicted. On one hand, it divulged a deluge of mainly innocuous documents. On the other, it stood and continues to stand on secrecy to restrict access to matters of public concern. In time, I came to understand that the simultaneous providing and withholding of information represented a government at odds with itself. One part wanted the law to run its course notwithstanding the power of the accused. Another sought to protect ADM and do its bidding.

Whether the final results favor whistleblowers or wrongdoers, deter or tolerate price-fixing, and ultimately enhance or mock the law, are hard questions that remain for the reader.

PART I THE RAID

THE MOLE

On June 21, 1995, FBI Special Agent Brian Shepard appeared before a federal magistrate in Urbana, Illinois. Shepard had come from Decatur, about forty miles west, where he ran a one-man FBI office, a satellite of the regional headquarters in Springfield. As usual, when Shepard asked for a search warrant, the proceedings were closed to the public. If word of a warrant leaked out before it was served, the evidence could be gone before the agents arrived. Most warrants targeted cash, crack, drug paraphernalia, stolen goods, or weapons. But this time Shepard wasn't trolling for ordinary contraband.

Of average height, the middle-aged agent wore a suit off-the-rack that hung loosely on his lean frame. He had a weathered face, high cheek bones, and soft, straight, graying brown hair that spilled over his forehead. He handed his affidavit to the magistrate. In a clear, measured, high-toned drawl, he made out the case for the search. The magistrate looked up from the paperwork. Obviously, this wasn't routine.

Shepard's affidavit also differed from most. It was not based on a tip from an anonymous informant. Though highly detailed and spanning over two-and-a-half years of clandestine surveillance of organized criminal activity, it did not rely on the work of a FBI agent who had gone undercover. Moreover, the organization under scrutiny was not a drug gang, child pornography ring, consumer fraud racket, or the mafia. Rather, it was ADM, the region's dominant corporation and one of the largest and most powerful in the country, producing a raft of food, feed, and fuel additives.

Shepard's "cooperating witness," Mark Whitacre, also was not a disgruntled employee in a stalled career. Referred to as "CW" in the warrant, he was president of ADM's BioProducts division, a new and already profitable unit on which ADM was staking much of its future. Though only thirty-eight, Whitacre had reached ADM's inner circle and had become a corporate vice president. Recently, he had been named by a stock analyst as the leading candidate to succeed ADM's president James Randall, seventy-one, who was thought to be nearing retirement. ADM had distributed the analyst's report to its shareholders.

Whitacre had no perceptible economic needs. He lived in high style in the baronial former residence of the company's legendary chairman and chief executive officer Dwayne O. Andreas, seventy-seven, who had ruled ADM for almost three decades. Conventional wisdom held that once Andreas passed from the scene his son Michael Andreas, forty-six, would take the reins. Known as Mick, the younger Andreas already held the position of vice chairman and oversaw day-to-day operations. He and Whitacre were friends. It was expected that the two would follow smoothly in the footsteps of Dwayne Andreas and James Randall to form an effective tandem at the top of the organization.

According to Shepard, Whitacre long had been spying on and informing against the chairman's son. The executive also had given evidence against other top rung managers including Terrence Wilson, president of ADM's corn processing division. Besides mail and wire fraud, the alleged crimes involved setting up international price-fixing cartels to rig world markets in three commodities. One was lysine, an amino acid used to promote growth in pigs, poultry, and cattle. The others were citric acid, the all-purpose flavoring and preservative used in foods and detergents, and high fructose corn syrup (HFCS), the major sweetener of soft drinks.

Shepard's affidavit spelled out how ADM had set up phony trade associations with its competitors. Then the company arranged conferences of the groups often in far-flung venues.

Shepard called the organizations "facades." Each conference had an "official" meeting where innocuous matters were discussed and an "unofficial" behind-the-scenes session for price fixing. Shepard's affidavit was brutally honest about the credibility of his cooperating witness:

> To the extent that this Affidavit contains information provided by the CW which is not corroborated by tape recordings and surveillance by the FBI, I believe the information is reliable. Before the CW received a letter granting use immunity, he made admissions against his own penal interest by disclosing the existence of the conspiracies to fix prices and allocate sales volumes or customers. The CW is willing to testify under oath to the information supplied.
>
> Nevertheless, the CW has not always been truthful in his statements to the

FBI. He initially provided some false and misleading information to the FBI. The CW has since provided information about price-fixing and volume-allocation schemes that I believe is reliable. As noted, much of that information is corroborated by tape recordings of conspiratorial meetings and conversations and surveillance by the FBI.

Whitacre had no criminal record or apparent motive to lie. Plus, the conspirators' conduct was preserved on hundreds of hours of tapes that Whitacre had recorded with concealed equipment provided by the FBI. The magistrate signed the warrant. The raid of ADM's headquarters focused international media attention on the price-fixing scandal in Decatur.

Previously the central Illinois town had been known for its association with Lincoln. In May 1860, it hosted the Illinois Republican Convention that nominated him for president. A month later, the Republican National Convention in Chicago named Lincoln as its candidate on the third ballot after his cousin John Hanks and close friend Richard Oglesby—a Decaturite who would become a Civil War general, Illinois governor and senator—returned from an abandoned homestead outside of Decatur with fence rails that were piled on the speaker's platform. The delegates were told that the wood had been split by Lincoln thirty years before. The candidate rode the "rail splitter" legend into the White House.

Earlier, Decatur had not been so lucky for Lincoln. In March 1830, three generations of the Thomas Lincoln family including Abe, 22, arrived from Indiana. The first night they camped in a corner of the town square. Then they cleared a ten-acre site on the Sangaman River eight miles away. The river's name comes from *sangama* an Indian word meaning plenty of food, an allusion to the bounty of the rich well-watered local prairie. The young Lincoln helped his family break ground, plant corn, and build a barn, cabin, and smokehouse.

The Decatur experience soured when the family came down with "ague," probably malaria. They moved again the following March and started over in Springfield. Seven years later, Lincoln began returning to Decatur, the Macon County seat, to handle cases as a circuit riding attorney.

Decatur still trades on the Lincoln legend. The old circuit court, renamed the Lincoln Courthouse, is a spare clapboard box on a snippet of park. The Sangaman River homestead has been vandalized practically beyond recognition.

Tourism in any event seems unlikely in this tough town of about 90,000, with its round-the-clock clangor of trains and trucks, many emblazoned with the molecule in a diamond-shaped leaf insignia of ADM. Mountainous dun-colored mills

with nests of pipes, winking aircraft warning lights, and steaming plumes dominate the urban landscape. The sticky sweet and sour stench of enzymes brewing
corn starch is overpowering.

The town, which locals sometimes call "da crater," seems to have more than its
share of convenience stores, used car lots, and scruffy bars. Because Illinois is the
number one soybean state and Decatur is the soy processing capital, there are numerous businesses with such names as the Soy City Motel, Soy City Electric, and Soy
City Tire. There is a small, spiffy financial district, but little else seems new here.

At the edge of the mills sits ADM's six-story administration building. The second floor "war room" contains the terminals, screens, and clatter of over a hundred in-house buyers and sellers of commodities in world markets. On the top floor
is the upper level management suite, an island of relative calm, soft lighting, and
plush carpets that resembles an art museum. During the 1980s, Dwayne Andreas
became taken with the quality of laser-enhanced topographically correct repro-
ductions of classic paintings that could be picked for about $1,500. Executives and
visitors walking these corridors saw the spitting images of Van Gogh's *Starry Night
over the Rhône*, Monet's *The Artist's Garden at Giverney*, Pisarro's *Boulevard Montmartre*,
and, one particularly relevant fake, Grant Wood's *Dinner for Threshers*, which por-
trays fatigued farm hands in their overalls at a table heaped with food. Other walls
bore mementos and pictures of the senior Andreas with famous friends, including
Presidents Truman, Kennedy, Bush, and Reagan; Chief Justice Warren Burger; Ex-
Canadian Prime Minister Brian Mulroney; Mother Theresa; General Secretary Gorbachev; and President Yeltsin.

At midnight on June 27, 1995, approximately seventy FBI agents conducted the
raid. They hit the administration building and seized carloads of documents from
management files. They fanned into the suburbs and invaded the homes of ADM
executives, whom they interrogated.

The event, which quickly became known locally as "Gestapo Night," also
included visiting Mark Whitacre's residence in Moweaqua, Illinois, about fifteen
miles south of Decatur. He lived in a sprawling colonial mansion with thick columns,
manicured grounds, a pool, a stable with horses, corral, and bridle paths. Dwayne
Andreas, the prior owner, had retained a pricey grove of black walnut trees at the
edge of the property. The FBI's purpose in "tossing" Whitacre's office was to provide him with a measure of protective coloring. It did not want its mole outed yet.
It hoped that he would hear evidence or comments by his colleagues in reaction
to the raid.

No stranger to crisis, the company rarely made a move without deploying either or both of its Washington law firms. One was Williams & Connolly, the capital's premier purveyor of hardball litigation tactics. The firm was famous for gaining outstanding results for notorious clients in desperate jams, including Teamsters Jimmy Hoffa, Iran-Contra figure Oliver North, former Texas Governor John Connally, and would-be Reagan assassin John Hinckley, Jr. More recently, it took on the representation of President Clinton during the Lewinsky scandal and impeachment trial and with typical aggressiveness turned defense to offense by accusing the special prosecutor of ethical and grand jury lapses.

At Williams & Connolly, Dwayne Andreas had had a personal relationship with Edward Bennett Williams, the brilliant trial lawyer who had won him an acquittal in a Watergate criminal case twenty-one years earlier. After Williams died, the lead partner at the firm on ADM business became Aubrey Daniel, III, a steely, slash-and-burn tactician who earlier in his career successfully prosecuted Lt. William Calley for his role in the My Lai massacre of civilians during the Vietnam War.

The other Washington law firm was Akin Gump Hauer & Feld, which in its way was as prominent as Williams & Connolly. Its way was lobbying, writing legislation, cultivating politicians and officials and performing high-level errands. Its leaders were Robert Strauss, seventy-seven, the former Democratic National Chairman and Ambassador to the Soviet Union, and his protegé Vernon Jordan, the former head of the Urban League and a confidante of President Clinton.

Squads of lawyers from the two firms descended on Decatur on the morning of June 28, 1995. Each attorney was assigned to an ADM employee thought to be a possible target of the government. Because the company still had no idea of Whitacre's role, it provided him with John Dowd of Akin Gump.

A lawyer's approach in a situation where both a corporate client and an employee potentially are in trouble is delicate. Does the lawyer's allegiance run first to the company or to the individual? The meaning of Dowd's role may not have been clarified to Whitacre. At any rate, the executive whose cover was precarious decided that he had become Dowd's client and had entered into a solid confidential relationship with the attorney. During their discussion the day following the raid, Whitacre decided to come clean about his government activities.

Dowd apparently saw their relationship differently. Immediately, he exposed Whitacre to ADM. Later when Whitacre accused Dowd of violating the attorney-client privilege, the Washington lawyer insisted that Whitacre had authorized him to tell the company.

The results of a raid based on Whitacre's inside information were dramatic. ADM stock, one of Wall Street's enduring stars, began to tumble, based on market worries that the company's worth had been falsely inflated by price fixing. In the same vein, some ADM shareholders believed that they had been misled as to the values of their holdings and filed numerous class-action suits against management.

ADM took another solid punch a week after the raid when Howard Buffett, a vice president and company spokesman, resigned. Buffett was the son of Warren Buffett, America's most successful post-war investor and second richest man after Bill Gates. At ADM, Howard Buffett became a reliable public voice for ADM's policies, including federal subsidies for gasohol (made with corn-based ethanol), heavy funding and lobbying of politicians, and opening up Cuba and Vietnam for trade. Now Buffett refused to spin or justify ADM's conduct.

Buffett's resignation took ADM completely by surprise. It responded by angrily banning him from the premises on July 10, 1999. The company had no backup ready to replace him as an officer or board member. Now Buffett shied from the press. Though in time ADM's criminal complicity would be proven, no other manager besides Buffett would resign in protest.

Unlike Buffett, Whitacre at first willingly cooperated with the media that swarmed him. Tall and blond, he favored expensively tailored double-breasted suits and bold silk ties. His fair complexion, soft features, and large eyes behind horn-rimmed glasses gave him a studious bearing and more than a slight resemblance to another celebrated whistleblower/turncoat—John Dean, Nixon's renegade White House lawyer. Whitacre's speech was sincere, staccato, and slightly compulsive. He seemed to need to get the ADM matter off his chest, but it apparently pained him to give information harmful to his colleagues and the company. To the press, he mentioned fearing for his family, which had been receiving threatening late-night calls. His children had endured schoolyard taunts about their father being an FBI snitch and questions about whether the family would go into the federal witness protection program. He wondered aloud in interviews if it would have been better simply to leave the company three and a half years before instead of spying for the government.

The son of a GM dealer, Whitacre grew up in an upper-middle-class family in Morrow, Ohio, about thirty miles north of Cincinnati. In high school, he began dating his pert, vivacious, future wife Ginger Gilbert and was president of his senior class.

He went to Ohio State in 1975 with the notion of becoming a veterinarian but decided to aim for a lucrative career blending science and business. He finished an honors program in animal science and received a bachelors and masters degree in just four years. Only two years later, he emerged with a doctorate from Cornell in nutritional biochemistry. At graduate school, he distinguished himself with hard work and such high energy that his fellow students half jokingly tried to keep him away from the office coffeepot.

His first job involved research at Ralston Purina in St. Louis. He stayed less than a year before receiving an offer in 1984 from Degussa, a German chemicals firm. Degussa intensively trained him in German for which he had keen aptitude, both oral and written. The company made him a technical sales representative and moved him to Germany in 1985. His assignments caused him to travel widely in Europe and Asia.

At Degussa, Whitacre rose to the directorship of applied technology and moved in 1988 to the company's US headquarters at Teterboro, New Jersey. In America, he was promoted again to vice president. His large house in Warwick, New York, often served as the lodgings for the company's visiting German brass. It was rumored that Whitacre could become the first non-German to head the company's American branch.

In 1989, ADM decided to enter the lysine business. As was its practice, Decatur sought a joint venture to avoid the delay in hitting the market that would be caused by building its own facility.

Because of Degussa's extensive amino acid experience, ADM approached the company. ADM brought a lot to the proposed marriage: capital, clout, and above all its vaunted "river of dextrose." A byproduct of corn processing, dextrose is the basic raw material from which lysine is extracted.

Whitacre had been restless in Teterboro. Usually he arrived early, finished his work in a few hours, and spent the rest of the day bouncing around the office and the plant searching for ideas. At thirty-two, he found himself across the bargaining table from ADM, as Degussa's lead negotiator. He saw a company dissimilar from his own. ADM was lean, unbureaucratic, dynamic, and quick to seize a new direction.

Ultimately, Degussa rejected the joint venture opportunity, but Whitacre accepted an offer from ADM in October 1989. He would be president of a new division then called Biochem Products.

Whitacre was happy to move back to the Midwest and for three years ecstatic about ADM. The company soon changed the name of the division to BioProducts and rapidly pumped $150 million into it. Whitacre supervised the building of the world's largest lysine plant and recruited the best sales and technical talent worldwide. In the process, he hired some of his old Degussa friends whose lives or at least lifestyles he changed with hefty bonuses and salary increases. They would become his devoted inner circle.

ADM had big plans for BioProducts, which in addition to lysine would produce other amino acids, bacitracin, ascorbic acid (vitamin C), lactic acid, monosodium glutamate (MSG), and vitamin E. The company hoped to generate a third of its earnings from the division by 1997. Because of his experience travelling abroad for Degussa, ADM also put him in charge of expansion into Southeast Asia.

Not only was Whitacre busy but he appreciated the nimble, decisive can-do atmosphere at ADM. He reported directly to Mick Andreas. The huge lysine plant, with an annual output capacity of 250 million pounds, went from blue prints to production within less than a year and a half, an astonishing feat. The facility, which looked like an indoor stadium, opened in February 1991.

At the time, lysine was selling for about $1.30 per pound. ADM started a price war in order to win market share. When the price hit 60 cents, the operation was not even paying off the building costs. According to Whitacre, "we were losing money, a few million dollars a month. Production costs were high because we were just getting started."

This sorry state was not regarded by ADM as permanent but only as stage one. As Whitacre put it, stage two started when Mick Andreas and James Randall, the ADM president, put him in touch with Terry Wilson the president of the corn processing division. Not especially popular among employees, Wilson, a gruff, bearish man with forearms like hams, silver hair, and metallic glasses, was the subject of office rumors about price-fixing. He put Whitacre at ease about losing money and said it was time to meet with the major competitors, which were two Japanese firms, Kyowa Hakko Kogyo and Ajinomoto.

Whitacre told his FBI handlers that Wilson previously had set up a conspiracy to fix prices in citric acid. According to Whitacre, Wilson and Mick Andreas convinced the Japanese that it was time for everyone to climb out of the red in lysine. The way to do it was by raising prices collectively and carefully dividing up the market.

Whitacre reported that ADM even had a price-fixing motto: "The competitor is our friend and the customer is our enemy." The phrase stood modern capitalism on its head. Whitacre promised that it "turned up lots of times on the tapes" he secretly made of the meetings. "Terry used to say it, and Mick would say it. It was our philosophy. . . . There are tapes of Mick Andreas quoting his father as always saying this."

From the first, the government declined all requests to release the tapes under the Freedom of Information Act, because they were evidence in an ongoing criminal investigation. ADM also early developed a militant strategy to prevent any disclosures of the tapes, but portions leaked out.

After his exposure, Whitacre publicly recounted how he became an informant wearing a wire and at times carrying a tiny recording device implanted in his briefcase. He claimed that in 1992, when price-fixing was being discussed with the Japanese but before it actually began, lysine batches in the ADM plant came out spoiled.

There was a suspicion of sabotage by engineers from the Japanese competitors, who had visited the Decatur facility. Eventually sabotage was ruled out. Before it was, Dwayne Andreas became concerned, and ADM called a contact at the CIA who referred the case to the FBI. This resulted in the invitation of Brian Shepard to the plant. Among others, Shepard approached Whitacre who allowed the FBI to tap his home phone and agreed to spy. One of the ironies of the case is that the FBI initially contacted Whitacre about matters unrelated to price-fixing.

In 1995, Whitacre insisted that he was not threatened by the government. "The FBI never forced me to do anything." He wanted to do the right thing because "from the beginning, I wasn't comfortable with the idea of price-fixing, not only because it's illegal but because I also believe it's the wrong way to do business."

Brian Shepard also was a significant part of the equation for Whitacre. "I don't know. I just really trusted the guy. If it were another kind of guy, I might not have told him. He was really trustworthy and I found it a real relief to talk to him. . . . We really hit it off well."

For the most part, Whitacre charmed the press, which did not probe the inconsistencies in his stories. For example, Whitacre always maintained that Dwayne Andreas was in on the price-fixing scheme. If so, why did he alert the CIA about alleged sabotage and later invite the FBI on site? If the competitor truly was the friend, why would such a friend even be suspected of sabotage? Above all, why really did Whitacre cooperate with the government? No similar tugs of conscience had disturbed him during school or in prior jobs. He was not known for making ethical stands or for doing anything to put his meteoric career at risk.

Whitacre fast was becoming a folk hero of American business. A pariah at ADM, he found himself at the center of the largest antitrust probe in American history and in the pages of the *New York Times, Wall Street Journal, Time, Newsweek,* and *Barrons. Fortune* devoted a cover piece and extensive space to Whitacre's first-person account: "My Life as a Corporate Mole for the FBI." Residents of Moweaqua, from the barber to the police chief, told television that Whitacre and his wife Ginger were model citizens, parents, and philanthropists. The couple was especially concerned with the plight of poor children. They organized toy drives and invited local kids to play on their grounds. *Time* described Whitacre as practically a "second son" to Dwayne Andreas. Reporters, editors, and readers warmed to the story of a man who had everything and seemingly put it all at risk as a covert operative for the FBI in order to protect free enterprise.

Some media pundits wondered if ADM could survive. There were bound to be more shareholder cases, plus endless class-action antitrust suits with crippling "treble" damages, as well as the bloodletting of the company's leadership in criminal court. As for ADM, it had not been sitting on its hands. On July 21, 1995, to buttress its stock price which had plunged 15 percent since the raid, it announced it would repurchase 20 million shares.

The company's enormous and in some ways ominous influence began to be felt. Some long-distance callers to WAND-TV in Decatur, which had recently run a lengthy Whitacre interview, were patched through without their permission to ADM security. Neither the station nor the company offered any public explanation beyond suggesting that the phone lines in central Illinois had gotten crossed. Some of the callers later complained of continuing irregularities with their own lines or being watched.

After an ABC television investigative reporter parked briefly on a public street in Dwayne Andreas' neighborhood, he was questioned by police. The journalist did not return to Decatur. ADM's reaction to Whitacre was predictable. At first, the company shunned him and gave him nothing to do. Having a known whistle-blower on site makes managers uncomfortable. By the second week in July, ADM had barred Whitacre from the premises, although it kept him on the payroll. Whitacre's lawyer James Epstein of Chicago told the media he expected ADM "to invent some pretext to fire Mark."

ADM put Whitacre's past under a microscope. The first matter the company came up with was relatively minor "résumé fraud." ADM said Whitacre had mis-characterized himself as a PhD in biochemistry. Although Whitacre had won a PhD from Cornell, it was in the field of nutritional biochemistry, a somewhat less rig-orous science. Then ADM announced that Whitacre had faked having an MBA from Northwestern University's elite Kellogg School of Management when he suc-cessfully submitted his name for nomination to the board of trustees at Decatur's Milliken University. In fact, Whitacre held an MBA from Kensington University, a correspondence school in California.

Whitacre seemed shaken by the MBA revelation. After being banned from ADM, he took his family on a vacation. Now, from the road in Kentucky, he began call-ing the Decatur media. He rambled on air to WAND-TV that he had no idea "where the item on Northwestern came from." He suggested ADM itself. "I do know that there's a lot of press releases and different things that go out and different analysts we talk with and sometimes our degrees go and get overinflated."

He added that the close personal scrutiny "almost feels like you are running for politics." He continued to assert his integrity telling a Chicago paper, "when this is over, I believe there will be a place for me in American business. Someone will still want to hire an honest person."

After a week it became clear that the credentials flap had failed to damage Whitacre. It simply paled in comparison with the worldwide corporate scam he had alleged.

ADM, however, continued to dig. Soon it accused him of conventional graft. In July, the company discovered that Whitacre had authorized payments based on dummy invoices from nonexistent European companies. The checks then found their way into Swiss and Cayman Islands bank accounts controlled by Whitacre and three of his ADM cohorts, two of whom had come from Degussa.

On August 8, 1995, ADM announced that the scheme had defrauded it of at least $2.5 million. The company fired Whitacre and his fellow alleged embezzlers and sought their indictments. A federal grand jury had been investigating price-fixing at ADM and its competitors. Now one was formed in central Illinois to target fraud by executives, including the famous informer.

Later ADM calculated that the wire transfers totalled more than $9 million. It refused to explain why standard audit techniques had failed to detect the scheme before Whitacre blew the whistle on the company.

For a time, Whitacre continued to fight brashly. He publicly insisted that he merely had partaken of an insidious off-the-books bonus plan for upper management. The extra cash came with significant strings: if an executive displeased ADM, it could expose him for tax evasion. He argued that this is what had happened to him but strenuously denied that he had stolen anything. ADM ridiculed the notion of under the table bonuses and painted him as a thief.

The government now had a problem on its hands. Overnight, Whitacre had gone from an altruistic whistleblowing witness to something like a soiled mafia snitch, neck deep in crime. In fact, the FBI had a bigger headache with Whitacre than with the organized crime turncoat because the latter usually had been granted full immunity from prosecution in exchange for his testimony. At the beginning of his tour of duty as a spy, Whitacre had signed a narrow agreement with the government. It barred charges against him for any acts of price-fixing he committed before and during his cooperation with the FBI, so long as they were revealed to Brian Shepard or other agents. It forbade him to commit additional crimes. Most of the offshore transfers had occurred after Whitacre had started wearing a wire.

Caught off-guard, the FBI and Justice Department prosecutors knew that they would be accused of giving Whitacre a license to steal if they broadened his immunity. Their case could go off the rails. But failing to protect him meant that he could cease to cooperate and refuse to testify against ADM at an eventual antitrust trial.

Whitacre desperately pressed for a deal. On August 2, 1995, he met with federal agents, confessed his role in the overseas payments ring, and explored a guilty plea to tax evasion and mail fraud, which leaked to the press. It was rejected.

The following day, he and his lawyer tried to rekindle an earlier conversation about the economic consequences of his informing. During his two-and-a-half years undercover, he had received no payments, but there had been talk about what would happen if ADM discovered and fired him. Under such circumstances, Whitacre wanted the government to buy his home and pay his salary until he could become re-established. During his service to the FBI, no agreement had been nailed down. Now that his fears had come true, the government was not willing to continue the discussion.

On August 6, 1995, Whitacre began writing suicide notes. One was to the *Wall Street Journal*. It stressed the wire transfers: "regarding overseas accounts and kickbacks, and overseas payments to some employees, dig deep. It's there! They give it; then use it against you when you are the enemy."

The government began weighing whether it could make the case without Whitacre. Prosecutors who listened to the audio tapes and watched the video tapes found them compelling. There was a possibility that they alone could induce a guilty plea from ADM. But, ADM was a tough company that could not be expected to plead guilty.

A jury also could be expected to be impressed by the tapes. However, in some high profile trials, taped evidence had not been enough to carry the prosecution. Although seemingly caught dead-to-rights on video, John Z. DeLorean, the high-level automotive executive, had been acquitted of cocaine dealing, and Marion Barry, the former mayor of Washington, had been convicted only of a minor charge.

The antitrust prosecutor and FBI resolved to try to "flip" additional witnesses against ADM. By now the Justice Department through grand jury subpoenas had seized records from a host of companies involved in manufacturing lysine, citric acid, and high fructose. They included, in addition to ADM, Kyowa Hakko Kogyo and Ajinomoto of Japan, Sewon of Korea, CPC International, Inc., England's Tate & Lyle PLC (owner of ADM's crosstown rival A.E. Staley), and Haarmann & Reimer, a division of Germany's Bayer A.G. White-collar prosecution experience dictated that not all of these companies would stonewall the government, and that at least some of their executives would testify in exchange for immunity.

On August 8, 1995, Whitacre called the caretaker of his pool and grounds and told him not to come in early the following day. The next morning, Whitacre went into his garage and closed the door. After getting into his daughter's BMW convertible, he used the car phone to bid a final goodbye to his wife. The message was recorded by their answering machine while she slept. Then Whitacre turned on the motor. When the gardener arrived, he braved the exhaust fumes to reach Whitacre, drove him out of the garage, and shook him awake.

Whitacre, who credited the man with saving his life, was spirited to a hospital in Chicago. He stayed for a week and emerged with a diagnosis of manic depression. The suicide attempt was seen by some as an admission of guilt to theft. Questions also arose about whether Whitacre had faked the gassing in order to arouse sympathy, to obtain better treatment from the government, or even to get ADM off his back.

The facts of the event were strange enough to stimulate a series of articles in the *Echo*, an obscure journal for forensic psychiatrists, which were passed among prosecutors and agents on the case. The articles pointed out several oddities. In the first place, Whitacre had been found unconscious in the backseat of the BMW. In most known attempts of this type, the person sits in the front. But more important, Whitacre did not seem to have carbon monoxide poisoning. Otherwise, he could not have been roused to consciousness by mere shaking. Several factors explain this. Carbon monoxide emissions have been reduced substantially in late model cars. Also, the car was not parked in a confined space but in Whitacre's six-car garage. In addition, before getting in the backseat, he reportedly had lowered the BMW's rag top. It seems likely that Whitacre, as a large-animal scientist, was versed in physiology and could have calculated his odds and shut his eyes all the while waiting to be discovered.

The psychiatrist analyzing the case also doubted the diagnosis of bipolar disease. While Whitacre had demonstrated remarkable peaks of high energy in his work, there were no similarly reported valleys of depression or documented lapses of judgment (before the alleged embezzlement scheme) during his schooling, work, or relationships that typify the mental illness.

On the other hand, the suicide attempt seemed credible given the strain of his situation. For almost three years, Whitacre had led a double life. The hours at his corporate post, which included working out the kinks in a costly start-up venture plus constant travel, were formidable. His FBI activities amounted to a virtual second job in terms of planning, taping, and travelling, as well as debriefing sessions usually at night with his government handlers.

His home life deteriorated. His wife and three children—sons aged 8 and 15, and a daughter 16—were aware of his snitching. Communication with his wife became strained for the first time in their marriage. He spent less time with his children and worried what they thought when they saw the wire when he took off his coat at night. Above all, the stress of informing on people who were his friends at ADM soon started tearing him apart as evidenced by his efforts to back away from the FBI.

Internal government files uncovered years later revealed that Whitacre had begun threatening suicide to the FBI not long after he started spying on ADM. An FBI log entry from November 18, 1992 noted:

> Source advised that source had been very distraught and had been working under intense pressure during the last couple of weeks. Source advised that everyone of source's superiors at Archer Daniels Midland (ADM), Decatur, Illinois, were turning against source. . . . Source said source felt that everything was against source.

Source advised that source had brought biochemical books home and was researching the lethal doses of various chemicals as source was considering committing suicide. Source said that source had been an upbeat person all of source's life but that the last couple of weeks source has been very depressed.

Though his handlers perceived the mole's depressed and erratic behavior, they forbade him from seeing a psychiatrist or psychologist for fear that his secret activities would stop or be leaked. The abrupt termination of Whitacre's career, his alleged betrayal by a lawyer, his outing as a spy and money launderer, and fear of jail caused mounting anguish without an end in sight. Those who knew him do not doubt that he wanted to die.

The stock analysts now questioned Whitacre's credibility, his sanity, and whether he could do any lasting damage to his former employer. By mid-August, ADM shares were trading at over seventeen dollars and had been restored to the value before his revelations.

Whitacre seemed to bounce back quickly. By fall, he had rented a suite in a suburban Chicago office park as the president of a biotech start-up firm that was attempting to bring new Chinese blood testing kits into the US medical market. Whitacre said that lithium made him feel better and boasted that soon his new company would have a private placement of its stock.

Whitacre also attempted to better his legal situation by continuing to inform to the government. He alleged other illegal activities at ADM. His efforts did not catch ADM off-guard.

The company was famous for its influence in Washington over Congress, federal agencies, and even the White House. It had no special clout with law enforcement in Chicago. Now it prevailed upon the Department of Justice to base all investigations involving ADM, except for the antitrust cases, in Washington, DC. The new attorneys in charge of the embezzlement probe would be attached to the fraud section, a part of the Justice Department's criminal division.

The shift in headquarters was ironic because all of the alleged fraud, money laundering, and related crimes were initiated in Decatur. Nothing was alleged to have occurred in Washington. The justification for the move was the accusation made by ADM's lawyers from Williams & Connolly that the Illinois FBI agents had aided or condoned Whitacre's bogus invoice scheme.

The advantages of the move for ADM were undeniable. Soon a "Chinese Wall" was built between the Justice personnel working on the antitrust case in Chicago and the fraud officials in Washington. Key Illinois operatives, such as Brian Shepard and Chicago federal prosecutor Scott Lassar, who knew ADM well, were removed from the fraud loop. Through its prestigious beltway law firms, ADM also exercised far more influence over the Department of Justice in Washington than it did in Chicago, where in fact some prosecutors in the US Attorney's Office regarded the lobbyist lawyers with contempt.

Deputy Attorney General Mary Spearing, chief of the fraud section, and her deputies Don Mackay and James Nixon came to Chicago for a meeting with Whitacre on September 5, 1995. They were joined by FBI agents Anthony D'Angelo, Michael Bassett, and Edward Herbst. The so-called proffer session took place at the offices of Whitacre's lawyers James Epstein and Robert Zaideman, who both were present. Chicago federal prosecutors Scott Lassar and James Griffin, who headed the antitrust case, made the introductions and departed within five minutes.

For hours Whitacre revealed the minutiae of the fraud scheme, transaction by transaction, check by check. He identified each participant and account, foreign and domestic, and insisted that all of the bonuses had been approved by James Randall or Mick Andreas. He believed himself guilty of failing to pay taxes but not of theft or embezzlement.

Whitacre also outlined a widespread pattern of corporate misconduct. It included the misappropriation of technologies necessary to produce such products as antibiotics, amino acids, and vitamins. The general ploy was to bribe another company's worker to steal secret material from his plant and bring it to ADM. In addition, Whitacre accused Randall and ADM director of security Mark Cheviron of hiring prostitutes to pry information out of employees at a competitor's lysine plant in Eddyville, Iowa.

He accused ADM officials of self-dealing by inducing the company to lease their real estate and pay top rates, personal use of corporate air craft, environmental offenses, pervasive campaign finance violations, electronic bugging of competitors, and cocaine trafficking.

With his attorneys by his side, Whitacre made charges involving the company that could have taken federal investigators and grand juries months if not years to unravel, much as the antitrust conspiracy had. But ADM's attorneys from Williams & Connolly were even more active. They pushed the Justice Department hard to drop the antitrust case due to the alleged misconduct by Whitacre's FBI handlers. In this they were unsuccessful. But they were highly effective in lobbying the fraud section of the Justice Department to limit its probe to bogus invoicing involving Whitacre and his subordinates and to wrap up the investigation quickly.

The fruits of ADM's inside-the-beltway strategy became apparent. In October 1995, not one but two Justice Department spokespersons, John Russell and Carl Stern, informed the *New York Times*, *Wall Street Journal*, *Chicago Tribune* and other media that ADM was not "the target or subject" of any investigation by the criminal division. Stern told *Fortune* that in order to win the favorable ruling, ADM's attorneys from Williams & Connolly successfully had lobbied senior Justice officials just below the level of the attorney general.

At the same time that Stern's bosses gave him the green light to release the information, the ADM publicity department began advising journalists to call Justice for a comment. The result was very good copy for ADM. The off-the-books bonus scheme was portrayed as an aberrational scandal with Whitacre as its ringleader rather than as part of a wider corporate pattern. *Fortune* aptly called its piece "ADM takes the Justice Department for a Spin."

The resulting flap about ADM's manipulation of Justice soon led its spokespeople to issue a caveat. While ADM was off the hook for fraud and related offenses, individual corporate employees still could be the subjects of investigations. By late 1995, Whitacre correctly perceived that only he and his underlings were being scrutinized, which led him to grow increasingly despondent.

In March 1996, he made a claim on WAND-TV of abduction. Unknown men in suits had thrown him into the back of a brown sedan. It had no license plate or operable door locks. The men drove him around for half an hour telling him to shut up about ADM. Then they pushed him out on the street. The story was not verifiable. Shortly after the interview, he moved with his family to Chapel Hill, North Carolina.

THE SPECIAL COMMITTEE
AND THE GADFLY

". . . Dwayne [Andreas] doesn't know who he's up against."
—David Hoech

Despite Whitacre's seeming demise, ADM was far from out of the woods. Indictments were expected. The government, shareholders, and buyers of price-rigged commodities all would make serious claims. Terry Wilson's alleged remark that "the customer is the enemy" was becoming as notorious in the nineties as Leona Helmsley's "only the little people pay taxes" was in the eighties.

The response to management's purported misconduct now fell to ADM's board of directors. However, the board was known for being allied with management. In fact, ten of its seventeen members were present or former ADM officials. Four directors were Andreases including Dwayne, Mick, Lowell, (Dwayne's brother and a retired ADM president), and Martin (Dwayne's nephew and a senior vice president focused on high fructose corn syrup). In an era of increasingly activist independent boards, the ADM body seemed archaic and hamstrung. It was too large to be effective. The Andreas family collectively owned only about 7 percent of the shares, but it ran ADM like a mom-and-pop grocery.

The board was a reliable rubber stamp for its chairman. Dwayne's son and alter ego Mick had been notified that he was the target of the federal antitrust probe and could be indicted. Mick also was a director. Could the board take an objective position on behalf of the shareholders if it meant siding against Mick and thus against Dwayne?

In order to mount its defense, ADM took a page out of its book of political tactics. When the company fought for key political issues such as ethanol and sugar subsidies, it often did not do so directly. Instead of being up-front in the struggle, ADM would back or act through a trade group or farmers' lobby. The tactic allowed ADM's position to seem more broad-based, less self-interested, and at times even objective.

Dwayne suggested something similar to mute the criticism of the board, the company, and the family. The public response to the crisis, including dealing with the government, would be turned over to a special independent committee of the board. It would be made up of the "outside" directors who did not work at ADM and were not Andreases.

The directors included Brian Mulroney, ex-prime minister of Canada; Marguerite "Happy" Rockefeller, widow of Governor Nelson Rockefeller; F. Ross Johnson, the former chairman of RJR Nabisco; Ray A. Goldberg, a Harvard professor of agribusiness; Gaylord O. Coan, president of Goldkist, a Georgia farmers' cooperative, who had replaced Howard Buffett on the board; John H. Daniels, a former ADM CEO and member of one of the firm's founding families; H.D. Hale, a retired ADM executive; John Vanier, the brother-in-law of an ADM executive; and Shreve H. Archer, Jr., the descendent of another founder and father of the company's current treasurer.

The special committee hired its own law firm, New York's Simpson Thatcher & Bartlett. Its senior partner was Cyrus Vance, secretary of state under Jimmy Carter. With its selections, ADM had sent a message. It was still so powerful that it would be shielded by a head of state, Mulroney, and a secretary of state, Vance. The outside directors group did not immediately instill confidence in their independence. Like other board members, they were beholden to the Andreas regime for profits and perks. For a meeting every other month and some modest committee work, a director could earn $100,000 per year, over twice the going rate at most big companies. No one ever had had to perform the most fundamental and difficult responsibility of a director, which is firing the CEO.

The backgrounds of some committee members raised immediate doubts about whether they could function independently. Shreve Archer and John Daniels, board members respectively since 1948 and 1957, were completely enamored of the chairman. As a retiree living in Arizona, Archer stated, "Having been actively involved with Dwayne Andreas has been the most stimulating experience of my life. How do you describe one of the most brilliant minds in the world?"

Aging socialite Happy Rockefeller hardly could be expected to defy Andreas, a former political associate of her husband. After Governor Rockefeller died, his widow had sealed off half of their New York apartment for Andreas, who became her across-the-wall neighbor. A dutiful attendee at board meetings, she credited Andreas with giving her the opportunity to meet such luminaries as Mother Theresa and Gorbachev.

Harvard Business School Professor Ray Goldberg probably had the longest-standing family ties to Andreas. A half century before, Goldberg's father Max, a grain trader from North Dakota, had served as one of Andreas' most influential tutors on commodities markets. When Ray Goldberg was young, he, in turn, regarded Andreas as a mentor. In 1990, the professor had nominated Andreas to be president of the International Agribusiness Association.

Perhaps the least auspicious outside director was Canadian F. Ross Johnson. The former CEO of RJR Nabisco, he was the only member of the board with Fortune 500 experience beyond ADM. While CEO of RJR Nabisco, Johnson had tried to take over the company in a management leveraged buyout. Johnson triggered a bidding war won by raiders Kohlberg Kravis & Roberts. Johnson was deposed, but he made a fortune in the buyout. The emerging corporation was saddled with huge debt, which caused it to spin off businesses. After Johnson left RJR, his longtime friend and golf partner Dwayne Andreas offered him a seat on the ADM board.

Johnson's lack of attention to detail had become glaring during the RJR takeover attempt. Now he was put on the audit committee of the ADM board and became its chairman. Because of its fiscal oversight, the committee was the only board unit required by the New York Stock Exchange. It was the audit committee's ultimate responsibility and one in which it failed to prevent large phony bills from being paid.

As a member of the outside directors, Johnson would be negotiating with the government. On September 13, 1995, he showed questionable judgment by mocking the FBI in a speech at Emory University Business School in Atlanta.

> I happen to be fortunate to be the chairman of the audit committee of Archer Daniels Midland. It's an incredibly successful, great company. You know, it's the old story. Everything's going well, we all think it's great, and then things become a problem. And this certainly looks like a problem.
>
> It's a pretty exciting experience when you find that one of your top division presidents has been recording everything you've said for 2 1/2 years. . . . It's a mystery. . . . Start out with the idea that this guy was the boy scout and went to the FBI one day and said, you know: "Hark, hark. These terrible people are thinking about fixing prices." . . . It just never happens that way. . . . It turned out . . . that the FBI . . . have got some good scumbags in there too—it's almost a criminal mentality.

Johnson's fellow Canadian, Brian Mulroney, would become the leader of the outside directors. The lantern-jawed Tory had governed Canada from 1984 to 1993. He lead the nation into the North American Free Trade Agreement (NAFTA), attempted to placate French separatists by putting them in his cabinet, and tried to make special accommodations for Quebec in Canada's constitution. These measures, however, were rejected by provincial legislatures. He was perceived as close to US business interests, including ADM, which has major processing operations in Canada. He was personally friendly with Andreas who sometimes informally advised him. At one point, Mulroney blocked the merger of two Canadian mills, which allowed ADM to acquire one. His regime endured an economic slowdown, dissatisfaction with NAFTA, and persistent scandal allegations. By the end of his second term his popularity fell to 17 percent, the lowest in Canadian history.

After leaving office, Mulroney practiced law in Montreal. A proud capable man, he was also a superb negotiator. He initially played a public role at ADM's stockholders meeting in October 1995, the first following the raid. The annual affair held in a high school at the edge of Decatur usually had the regimented feel of "Eastern Europe under communism," as one regular attendee put it. As usual, most of the shareholders were white, gray-haired, Republicans from the upper Midwest. Some were dressed up. Others came in ball caps, orange and blue Illini jackets, and white socks. These were Dwayne Andreas' people. He had helped them prosper. They weren't the problems for ADM's leadership. Public employee and union pension funds controlled the largest bloc of ADM stock, about 12 percent. In 1995, the California Public Employees' Retirement System (CALPERS), one of the nation's and ADM's largest shareholders, rated the Fortune 300 industrial companies on governance and gave ADM a rare "F." At the annual meeting, CALPERS and two similar funds from Florida and New Jersey were sponsoring a motion against re-electing the present directors.

A trim 5'4" bantam with lively eyes, black hair, and thick brows, Andreas, was known for conducting the annual meeting like a well-rehearsed orchestra. But in 1995, he chafed over questions from the floor about price fixing, Whitacre, and his son. "I am completely outraged at the cloud that has been cast over this great corporation, unblemished through seventy years of business. Throughout my life, I have spoken frankly and honestly to my partners and shareholders, and I am certainly not going to change now." Tiring of accusations from an official of the Carpenters Union Pension Fund, Andreas cut off the speaker's microphone. The man protested that Andreas was not running the meeting according to Roberts' Rules of Order. "This is my meeting," snapped the chairman. "I make the rules."

Mulroney was able to rescue the event with remarks that he delivered in a humble, low-key fashion. Regarding the special committee of independent directors, he assured the audience that, "None of us sought this assignment, and we accepted it solely out of a sense of duty to the shareholders." The committee "met on seven occasions at Dwayne Andreas' request to direct the company's response to the litigation." He revealed surprisingly that they had sat down with Whitacre and his lawyer, whom they tried to convince to meet with Williams & Connolly, but failed. He admitted that grand juries still were looking into possible antitrust violations at ADM but that "no company personnel have been charged in connection with crimes." He apologized for not being able to be completely forthcoming:

> This has left us in a difficult situation. On the one hand, we are being pressed to provide information, and on the other, legal counsels advise that, with pending litigation, it would be irresponsible of us and a disservice to the company and its shareholders to publicly discuss these issues in any greater detail.
>
> We assure you that the special committee will act decisively and responsibly if it concludes that any activity has taken place that is illegal, unethical or damaging to the best interests of the company and its shareholders.

Mulroney swore to the crowd that Whitacre's fraudulent wire transfers had been investigated three times to determine if they were part of an authorized conspiracy to reward executives under the table. The three investigations had been conducted by the audit committee, by the accounting firm Ernst & Young, and by the federal government. All agreed that Whitacre had accomplished the scheme without the company's approval. Finally, he reported that that morning Dwayne Andreas had initiated the creation of a committee on corporate governance to design a truly independent board. Mulroney would cochair the committee with Professor Ray Goldberg. They would submit a report within three months.

ADM General Counsel Richard Reising rose to speak. A longtime Decaturite not considered glamorous like an Andreas, he was widely trusted and considered a voice of reason by local investors. Reising assured those in the bleachers that "the Department of Justice has confirmed that there is no credible evidence that Mr. Whitacre's thefts were part of a plan by ADM to funnel compensation to its executives." For Reising to have misrepresented this critical fact in a setting with shareholders would have constituted securities fraud. The statement amounted to strong support for the charge that the Justice Department's investigation of ADM had been exceedingly brief. In time, questions arose about whether there had been any investigation at all besides the probe of Whitacre and a handful of his subordinates.

The remarks by Mulroney and Reising took the wind out of the sails of the initiative by the institutional investors to remove the board. The directors were re-elected by 80 percent of the shares. For a company that was used to lockstep unanimity, this was a wake-up call but not a revolution.

In January 1996, the board announced that it unanimously had accepted the report of the governance committee. The recommendations included that the board would be reduced to twelve members. Most important, the majority would be independent. These directors could not have business or professional relationships with ADM and could not be former employees or family members of top management.

Board compensation would be brought in line with other major corporations, approximately $40,000 per year. Health and retirement benefits no longer would be provided to directors. At least half of a board member's compensation would be paid in stock in order to marry him or her to shareholder interests. Board members no longer could serve after seventy. Ray Goldberg and Happy Rockefeller would be stepping down. Goldberg lauded the new structure. "This makes ADM consistent with the best governance procedures of all the major corporations in the United States."

Four insiders also announced that they would give up their seats: Mick Andreas, his cousin Martin, president James Randall, and H.D. Hale, the president of ADM Milling. Dwayne Andreas vowed that he had no intention of retiring but would be willing to give up one of his jobs as CEO while remaining chairman. He professed that his health was good. "I am going to stay on as long as they want me to, maybe two or three more years."

Terry Wilson now resigned. Mick Andreas went on an indefinite leave of absence from his position as vice chairman but would draw his full salary.

The dissatisfaction of the institutional investors had been a great danger to ADM. If they had pulled out, the stock would have plunged. In early 1996 their objections melted away. CALPERS deemed the board reorganization with its independent majority as "a most significant event that is a victory for institutional investors and all shareholders." Of course, it did not hurt that annual sales had risen 11 percent to $12.67 billion and earnings per share had jumped from .57 cents to $1.55.

Little internal opposition remained. But there was something called the ADM Shareholders' Watch Committee. Beginning on July 17, 1995, it put out a newsletter that was faxed to the company's officers, directors, lawyers, accountants, and many of the employees. It also found its way into the offices of journalists, prosecutors, and politicians. The *Watch Letter,* as it became known, infuriated Dwayne Andreas and other top managers. On days when it arrived in Decatur, secretaries were sent scurrying to the fax machines to yank the sheet out before it could be copied and read by other employees.

The *Watch Letter* was replete with literary references from Burke, Churchill, Emerson, Lincoln, Shakespeare, Patrick Henry, Thomas Paine, and Proverbs. Bursting with barbed invective, it railed against the "Andreas Crime Family." It referred to chairman Dwayne Andreas and the members of the board as "a pimp and his stable of whores." The *Watch Letter* purported to represent ADM's "50,000 shareholders, a sleeping giant," whom it intended to rouse. It claimed to be running "Operation Thousand Eyes," with "moles inside every division of ADM." It targeted all manner of alleged waste and abuse including free private use by top executives of the corporate jet, bribes to foreign leaders especially in Mexico and

Indonesia, and payoffs to highway officials to induce them to ignore ADM's over-weight transports, as well as the use of prostitutes to gather information from competitors. It reserved special ire for Williams & Connolly, whom it accused of bleeding the shareholders with rates approaching $1,000 per hour and bills that it said the firm padded by sending as many as five lawyers to a deposition. It accused the lawyers of protecting Dwayne and Mick Andreas rather than the company.

The *Watch Letter* was not without humor. It reported that Dwayne Andreas had broken a plate in anger in the corporate dining room. He was accused of "playing frisbee with the shareholders' china." It maintained that Dwayne and Mick Andreas, Terry Wilson, and James Randall all belonged in "Club Fed." It referred to the group as the "gang of four."

Sometimes the *Watch Letter* went over the top as when it likened Dwayne Andreas to Hitler. Sometimes it printed rumors, but often it hit the mark. Sometimes it opened old wounds as when it published that an Archer family member once had committed a hit-and-run in Decatur without being charged because of a payoff with ADM money.

The *Watch Letter* raised a number of disturbing theories especially about the Department of Justice's fraud investigation that had rejected Mark Whitacre's claim that the overseas wire transfers amounted to a scheme of secret bonuses approved by top management, including president James Randall. The *Watch Letter* questioned why an embezzlement case in Decatur was being handled by the Justice Department in Washington, DC, rather than by the US Attorney's office in Illinois. Its answer was that officials in Washington would be more receptive to Williams & Connolly and to limiting the probe to Whitacre and his underlings.

The *Watch Letter* was the first to print that an FBI agent assigned to the fraud investigation was Michael D. Bassett. In March 1987, using the alias "Michael McLaughlin," Bassett had gone to work as an ADM clerk in the Chicago Board of Trade's treasury bond pit. The cover and training that ADM had provided to him had been approved by Dwayne Andreas. As part of "Operation Sourmash," Bassett participated in key arrests and convictions of traders in a high-publicity sting. Now out of the thousands of FBI agents in the US, it was Bassett who was assigned to investigate fraud at the company that had assisted him so significantly almost a decade earlier and that still had the same leadership. The Justice Department's only explanation for this assignment was that Bassett was highly qualified for the new task and that his "assignment was coincidental." The *Watch Letter* maintained that ADM had picked its own investigator.

The Shareholders' Watch also seemed to have had access to the tapes made by Whitacre or to the information on them. Periodically, it would print summaries of the taped price-fixing meetings.

For example, the *Watch Letter* described a session in Hawaii between ADM and foreign lysine producers. The *Watch Letter* alleged that Terry Wilson showed the gathering of mainly Japanese executives charts on fixing prices in the citric acid markets while saying that the same scheme could be used for lysine. Wilson described how important it was for each member of the conspiracy to remain in step on price and production in order for the conspiracy to succeed. In describing how serious a breach would be regarded, the *Watch Letter* said, "he turned his index finger under as if it had been cut off," a Yakuza (Japanese organized crime) warning.

The *Watch Letter* also described a Los Angeles meeting, reportedly videotaped by the FBI, where Mick Andreas was described as having displayed price-fixing charts to the Japanese and "told them that ADM had been fixing prices for over twenty years and is well-experienced in this area and not to worry."

The government and ADM strictly controlled the issuance of the tapes. As evidence in an ongoing law enforcement investigation, they were not released in response to requests under the federal Freedom of Information Act. A critical part of Williams & Connolly's service to ADM was attempting to keep the tapes secret. However, they were given to the special committee of the board once they entered into guilty plea negotiations with the government.

A federal judge in Springfield, Illinois, who was handling about twenty class-action civil suits distributed some of the tapes, over ADM's objection, to plaintiffs' lawyers under the severest confidentiality controls. Any attorney who disclosed the contents of the tapes could expect to be held in contempt and possibly disbarred. One of the lawyers who had been given the recordings explained why such strictness had been imposed. "It's very much like Watergate. Nixon could govern, until it became known what was on the tapes—the obscenity, money, and hatred, and a pattern of criminality. When that came out he was finished. These [ADM] tapes are disgraceful. If they ever come out, the leadership is finished." Now it seemed that the copies of the tapes or transcripts could have been leaked to the writer of the *Watch Letters*.

Each of the letters was signed by the *Lamet Vov*, two Hebrew letters with sounds corresponding to *l* and *v*. This never was explained in the text; nor was the significance in Jewish mysticism. Due to their positions in the Hebrew alphabet, the sum of the two letters is thirty-six. In the Talmud, a *Lamet Vov* is an extremely righteous person disguised by ignorance and poverty, who emerges to avert disaster and persecution. In each generation, there are at least thirty-six of these figures.

The use of the nom de plume was arcane but interesting. In truth, the writer did not completely hide his identity. It would have been impossible because he was constantly on his phone from Florida gathering and spreading information. In the early phases of his work, he had asked sources to keep his name and phone number from ADM. He said that board member Ray Goldberg finally blew his cover to the company.

It turned out that the *Lamet Vov* was David Hoech (pronounced Hake), then fifty-six, the holder of two shares of ADM stock. He lived with his wife, Carol, fifty-five, in a pleasant Fort Lauderdale condominium complex.

A bull-chested six-footer, Hoech was perhaps thirty pounds overweight, though he remained solid and powerful-looking. He had tight steel gray curls and dark eyes that put everybody on trial. Both in speech and presence, he projected toughness, although he could be gentle with family and friends. His voice had aspects of the resolute rasp of John Wayne and the slow menace of Peter Lorre. Basically self-educated, he was a massive reader and book lionizer. He spouted literary references as avidly in speech as he did in writing.

Carole Hoech, a short spunky blonde with a warm twinkle in her eye, was his partner in all things, including the firm Global Consultants, Inc. It was the second marriage for both Hoechs, who were close to each other's children and grandchildren.

Both Hoechs were raised in St. Louis. Carole was the daughter of Frank Nykiel, the late chairman and CEO of Chromalloy, a large diversified public company with metals, transportation, textiles, and petroleum services businesses. Famous for his probity, Nykiel felt that his $800,000 salary was enough during the 1980s and refused the expense account perks and freebies available to someone in his position. *Forbes* once called him a "white knight" for turning the company around.

Also a towering figure, David Hoech's father George was a staunch Republican and a Baptist minister. The descendent of abolitionists, he was a steadfast proponent of civil rights. A stickler for the law, he even refused to allow bingo in his church.

Not surprisingly the son rebelled. After graduating from high school, he signed up for Vietnam as an airborne medic, where he was dropped both behind enemy lines and into the China Sea, "kicking sharks" in order to rescue pilots. He recalled the war as a period of close camaraderie and occasional bar fights. Eventually he turned against the war. The whole Vietnamese experience was central in his consciousness. Photographs of his buddies during the war and at reunions at the Wall in Washington were proudly displayed among his mementos.

After his discharge in 1966, Hoech moved to Japan, married a Japanese woman, and became fluent in the language. While there, he caught the consumer electronics wave and grew wealthy by distributing products in the United States, Southeast Asia, and elsewhere. He also became close to the small Jewish community in Tokyo, mainly Americans and Israelis in business, and once held a Passover Seder for fifty in his office. Around the same time, he became aware of his mother's Jewish ancestry and learned about the religion—hence, the moniker *Lamet Vov*.

In 1982, he moved back to St. Louis. With his cultural and language skills (he also knew some Korean and Mandarin), he was able to establish himself as a consultant to Asian companies, including Japanese firms building plants in the United States. In addition, he positioned himself to advise American clients in markets with Far East competitors.

In the late 1980s and early 1990s, his work moved into agribusiness. Among others, he advised Cargill, America's largest private company, Japan's Kyowa Hakko Kogyo and its American branch Bioyowa, based near St. Louis, as well as A.E. Staley, ADM's Decatur neighbor.

Hoech's stock in trade was information. He was very good at gathering it from his client's rivals through the conventional means of press clippings, financial reports, etc., and the unconventional, although always legal means, of cultivating and listening to the employees of competitors. As the eighties turned into the nineties, Hoech spent a good deal of time in Decatur finding out what ADM was up to and trying unsuccessfully to add it to his client list. During this period, he befriended Mark Whitacre and others at the company. He bought a couple shares so he could receive stockholder's information and attend annual meetings.

He did not like ADM's air and water pollution and industrial accidents. "ADM's not a good corporate citizen," he said. But above all, he disliked "Dwayne's arrogance," and the political influence and economic clout held by the Andreas family for whom he felt the corporation worked rather than the other way around. "To be an Andreas in Decatur is like being a royal in Buckingham Palace."

A proponent of free markets, Hoech was angered but not surprised by the allegations of price-fixing involving ADM. After the scandal broke, Whitacre's close friends, including Howard Buffet, distanced themselves from the mole. Hoech remained by his side. His regard for Whitacre as a whistleblower did not blind Hoech to the false invoice scheme. "I told Mark, you're over twenty-one and that was shareholders' money." By the same token, he saw Whitacre's graft as part of an approved pattern of corporate corruption.

After Whitacre exposed ADM, the media mobbed the story, touting it as a David and Goliath parable. After the exposer was exposed, the press drifted away. Good versus evil inside a multinational corporation was front-page news. Greed versus greed was buried in the business section, if it made the paper at all.

Hoech refused to let the story die. He maintained intense relations over the next three years with reporters from the *New York Times*, *Wall Street Journal*, *Bloomberg*, *Chicago Tribune*, and *Decatur Herald-Review*. He supplied them with leads that they often followed and sometimes with ADM or government documents, including tape transcripts. Some reporters questioned his motivation, and at times his sanity, but most kept coming back for more. Hoech never let the case get out of the news or relaxed his pressure on ADM. Generally, he was good for a high-minded sound bite. "The law prostituted," he would say, "brings on chaos, and chaos brings on dictatorship. Democracy functions best when people stand up. That's all I'm doing. People call me and say you don't know who you're up against. I say Dwayne doesn't know who he's up against."

He relentlessly attacked elements of the government that he believed were catering to ADM's influence. When President Clinton flew to Nixon's funeral with Dwayne Andreas, Hoech widely disseminated the news. When Andreas gave $10,000 to Clinton's impeachment defense fund at the height of the price-fixing scandal, Hoech cried foul.

At times, the FBI threatened him with prosecution, usually for obstruction of justice based upon his contacts with Whitacre and other witnesses. Hoech maintained that he simply wanted the government to do its job, and he was helping it, or at least keeping its back straight. He never was charged with any crime.

Hoech achieved some significant coups. He played a role in "delivering" Whitacre to *Fortune,* resulting in a landmark series on whistleblowing at ADM that included Whitacre's memoir of spying. Hoech infuriated his former clients at Cargill by disseminating information about that company being involved in price-fixing with ADM, although Cargill was not prosecuted.

After Whitacre's disgrace, everyone following the antitrust case knew that the prosecution could crash and burn unless other witnesses came forward. As it happened, Hoech had been a consultant to Japan's Kyowa Hakko Kogyo Corporation, a named coconspirator. Also he had known one of its alleged price-fixing executives, Masaru Yamamoto, for over a decade.

In early January 1996, Hoech wrote an impassioned three-page letter urging Yamamoto to "make a deal with DOJ for immunity first for yourself and second to try to protect the company." Hoech anticipated the argument that Dwayne Andreas' fabled political influence would get rid of the problem. "Yes, ADM is trying to tell people that Dwayne is taking care of this mess, and it will be only a large fine, and the case will be dismissed. In your position I would want to believe this. Do not even entertain the idea as you will be deceiving yourself as it is all propaganda."

Hoech appealed to the Japanese both practically and spiritually. If Yamamoto and his company came clean and worked for justice, then customers would stay with them. But matters would go downhill, if Kyowa and its executive chose to shield ADM and were perceived as outlaws. The evidence was compelling:

> The tapes are very devastating, and this information will flow over into the Japanese news media. I cannot stop this as ADM is so arrogant, and this will be a high-profile case. The FBI, Whitacre, and yourself know what was discussed,

but remember that any conversations you had between Whitacre and yourself were recorded for the past three years, including such places as Paris, Atlanta, room #6010 in Chicago, breakfast in Hong Kong, and all telephone conversations and meetings.

Gently Hoech suggested that Yamamoto go about "righting yourself" in order to find "inner peace." Solace could be taken from the fact that, "you are the victim not the victimizer; that is ADM." Hoech asked Yamamoto to "please accept my advice and thoughts as one friend to another who has looked at this mess from every angle." The writer urged his correspondent to act in accordance with the highest principles:

> Confucius said, "Those who know the truth are not equal to those who love it, and those who love it are not equal to those who live it." You are a man of integrity who can hold your head high. Freeing yourself and taking the lead in your situation will protect you against further harm to yourself and those around you.

Shortly after the letter, Hoech's advice was heeded, and Yamamoto began to cooperate with the US government. The Justice Department did not give him complete immunity, but allowed him to plead guilty in exchange for no jail time and a fifty-thousand-dollar fine. Because he was the first to make a deal, he would receive the lowest fine. Hoech said Yamamoto also convinced other Japanese to work for the prosecution.

In early 1996 the *Watch Letter* also attracted attention in the market. Dain Bosworth, a respected Minneapolis brokerage house that had advised buying ADM stock less than a year before and touted Mick Andreas and Whitacre as its future leaders, issued a "sell" bulletin to its investors. Dain worried about the *Watch Letter*'s allegations that ADM had covered up the Archer hit-and-run, that Dwayne Andreas had instigated the firing of A.E. Staley's CEO Larry Cunningham because Cunningham refused to fix prices, that ADM was deploying private investigators to discredit and intimidate people, and that the Decatur company was engaging in foreign bribery.

Dain called these "serious accusations." While it did not vouch that they were true, it was "especially struck by the naming of names, dates, and places," and "subsequent 'authentication' of some of the data via articles in the news media." In addition, the investment house questioned some of ADM's business "fundamentals" as well as the "darkening clouds regarding the price-fixing investigation."

Infuriated by the piece, ADM hired Williams & Connolly to grill the Dain analyst who had written it at a deposition. The transcript has been sealed. The lawyer reportedly asked over a hundred questions focusing on David Hoech.

Hoech also fought a protracted battle with the *New York Times*. In 1996 he supplied *Times* reporter Kurt Eichenwald with a document pertaining to Mark Whitacre's move to North Carolina. A copy got into the hands of Williams & Connolly, which filed it for ADM in court in Illinois. Then stranger things started to happen. Williams & Connolly retracted the document from the court in order to remove the fax "tell-tale" at the top of the page that listed a phone number at the *Times*.

Hoech caught wind of the filing, retraction, erasure, and refiling. In an emotional taped call he accused Eichenwald of betraying him as a source and carrying water for ADM. The reporter denied the charge shouting, "Somebody's trying to set me up."

Adam Liptak, a lawyer at the *Times*, became involved. In a letter, Liptak admitted to Hoech that the number at the top of the document belonged to a fax machine at the newspaper. "You have concluded from these facts, not unreasonably, that the *Times* faxed the document to ADM." However, Liptak assured that the fax machine in question "has been disabled so that it cannot send outgoing faxes." Plus, he insisted that even fax sending machines at the *Times* "do not print their numbers on documents." The lawyer finished by telling Hoech, "If you came across additional information on how this phone number came to be reflected on this document, I would be eager to hear it."

Hoech said he no longer cared much about the purloined document. "I just wish they wouldn't lie to me."

Hoech also conducted guerilla lobbying of the directors. Somehow he found everyone's private line, home phone, vacation home phone and fax. He passed the numbers out freely to reporters.

He gave ADM people a chance to return his calls. If they did not, he called them at home at 2 AM and told them they should have. Or he left a message, "You talk to me or I'll be in your face tomorrow." They believed him and often called back.

Sometimes he scared people, although his threats could be seen as jests. Once he left word for Ray Goldberg to call him back or else he would "come up there to Harvard and duct tape you to your chair in front of the classroom." Goldberg then spoke with him.

Mainly, in 1996 he waged a campaign through the *Watch Letter* about the type of punishment that should be meted out in the antitrust case. Because the tapes were so compelling, he never doubted that ADM would plead guilty. He feared that the company would pay a fat fine to prevent Mick Andreas from going to jail. Such a penalty, he felt, could exceed two hundred million dollars and perhaps reach half a billion. "It doesn't matter to Dwayne. It's only shareholders' money."

ADM did not take kindly to Hoech's activism. The corporation used its lawsuit against Whitacre (to recover embezzled funds) as a vehicle to subpoena all of Hoech's financial records as well as those of his business, his wife, his ex-wife, his brothers, and his sister. To date, he and his wife have spent in excess of $160,000 on running their campaign against ADM and paying legal fees. Their consulting business has dried up.

After taking on ADM the Hoechs complained of being followed and threatened. Some anonymous callers referred to ADM. The Hoechs have said that they eventually will sue ADM for harassment and harm to their business. In one recent threat recorded on their answering machine, the calm male voice intoned, "We hear you're willing to settle with ADM—settle for a bullet between your eyes."

In most respects, the Hoech's immaculate, sun-washed apartment resembled homes of other well-healed senior Floridians. But there were differences. The walk-in closet was a repository of ADM documents and cassette tapes of Hoech's conversations with the corporation's executives, government officials, and reporters. Hoech added that a larger "archive" existed at an undisclosed location in the Midwest.

Security was tight. The lobby was monitored through cable television. Loaded handguns and a pistol grip shotgun were discretely placed out of view, but within ready reach under sofas and behind doors. Carole Hoech also carried a small automatic in her purse at all times.

Why have they done it? Various charges have been flung at the Hoechs, including that they were working for a competitor of ADM, or helping hidden would-be investors who wanted the stock price to go down. But, the Hoechs and their financial and tax records have been examined up and down, and nothing untoward has materialized. Asked why they have turned their lives upside down over ADM, Hoech says, "Because Dwayne's no better than a street pimp. He and his people in Washington think the masses are asses."

SKIRMISHING

"This is the beginning of the end for the internal culture and practices and management of ADM."
—Kenneth Adams

Hoech was right about the corporate guilty plea. After the special committee of independent directors absorbed the damaging impact of the audio and video tapes, it weighed the logic of cutting a deal with the government for ADM to plead guilty to the price-fixing of lysine and citric acid. At a minimum, in the plea agreement the government would be willing to compromise on the size of the fine.

One problem was that a guilty plea could "run wild" in the civil cases. Juries handling the class actions would learn that ADM had been convicted of a crime. This fact would produce a plaintiff's verdict against the company because the burden of proof in civil cases is a "preponderance of the evidence" standard, which is far lower than the criminal "beyond a reasonable doubt" test. The jury's knowledge that ADM's behavior was so deviant as to be admittedly criminal almost certainly would pump any damage award to its full potential. Another reason for ADM to settle the civil cases early was to keep the audio and video tapes from coming out in pretrial proceedings or depositions.

Williams & Connolly, led by Aubrey Daniel, was given the task of resolving the civil matters. Daniel knew that many plaintiffs' class-action lawyers would be inclined to settle early, before they had much time or money invested in a case. He had enough money available to make it worth their while. By April 1996, ADM was ready to settle the lysine suit involving 600 plaintiffs, mainly feed, poultry, and livestock companies, for $25 million. Two Japanese coconspirator companies, Ajinomoto and Kyowa Hakko, were each willing to kick in $10 million.

The Chicago federal court had held an auction among lawyers to see who would represent the class plaintiffs least expensively. A Philadelphia firm was the low bidder. It was willing to take a 15 percent contingency. The firm had little time or money in the case. Now it very much wanted to settle for 15 percent of $45 million.

Analysts called ADM's proposed settlement a slap on the wrist and upgraded the stock. A study performed at Purdue University showed that the probable domestic market injury from price manipulation of lysine was between $165 and $180 million. If tripled, as the antitrust laws specify, that would yield about a $500 million award. ADM and the Japanese companies were paying less than ten cents on the dollar.

Media criticism of the settlement grew. The judge, at one point, accused ADM of stonewalling the court by not providing its own candid evaluation of the damage. When Aubrey Daniel declined to furnish the information based on attorney-client privilege, the court postponed the resolution. At the later "fairness" hearing —a procedure to determine if the proposal justly compensated the victims—the judge heard strenuous objections from plaintiffs but nonetheless approved the settlement. Some well-heeled plaintiffs, such as Continental Grain, elected to "opt out" and pursue their claims individually.

But it did not take a half-billion-dollar case to put Aubrey Daniel's team in motion. Quietly, a case developed in Kansas City about the deaths of cows from eating a tainted ADM cottonseed-based feed containing too much of a naturally occurring poisonous pigment called gossypol. The felled cattle had been worth about $35,000. The ranchers through their attorney, a young law firm associate named James McKown, demanded $50,000 but were willing to negotiate. For over a year McKown had waged a competent and conservative case. He did not sound alarms about the uncertain effects of the pigment on humans, such as possible reproductive sterility from gossypol that entered the human food chain through meat. Still ADM did not budge.

In mid-1996, the ranchers added a significant wrinkle: Mark Whitacre was willing to testify, and he had interesting things to say. He knew ADM's chief witness, Gerald Weigel, a supervisor who also had worked at ADM's BioProducts division. In an affidavit, Whitacre revealed that Weigel had inflated his credentials under oath—he did not have a doctorate as he had testified. The information gave credence to Whitacre's earlier statement that others at ADM had puffed their credentials. In the Kansas City case, a jury also could infer that Weigel did not have sufficient advanced scientific training to vouch for the safety of the feed.

Whitacre swore that ADM had known the feed was dangerous for years but had continued to sell it consistent with its philosophy that "the customer is the enemy." Whitacre's affidavit also was packed with allegations that had nothing to do with the feed case but were calculated to sting ADM. He laid out the price-fixing scheme and swore that it had the approval of Dwayne Andreas and James Randall.

He maintained that ADM had stolen technology from Cargill by bribing one of its employees and sought to acquire proprietary lysine data from Heartland Lysine by using prostitutes. He wrote that James Randall's nickname for Mick Andreas was "the cocaine kid."

Whitacre added that when ADM wanted secret citric acid technology, it gave $150,000 to a Cargill employee to quit and bring it to ADM. In order to obtain lysine data from the Heartland subsidiary of Ajinomoto, ADM security had hatched a plot using prostitutes.

ADM did not charge Whitacre with perjury. Instead, Aubrey Daniel came to Kansas City in September. McKown was surprised to see a partner from a Washington firm personally attend to a small case in the Midwest. The young lawyer was impressed with Daniel's skills but sensed something ominous about having ADM's top gun on the opposite side. For instance, before a deposition, strong-arm types emerged who insisted upon frisking the ranchers' lawyer for weapons. When McKown tried to call a Decatur TV station in order to request a video tape of its interview with Whitacre, he was put through to ADM security without explanation. The feed case was beginning to seem like something out of *The Firm*.

ADM also filed a curious affidavit in Kansas City. This one originally had been written in 1995 by FBI Agent Michael Bassett for obscure proceedings in the banking system of the Cayman Islands. The document laid out all the false invoices and wire transfers involving Whitacre. The use of papers from a secretive off-shore financial haven again seemed more akin to Grisham than to routine Missouri practice. The Bassett affidavit, of course, had nothing to do with dead cows and everything to do with discrediting Whitacre.

The savvy McKown, who never had expected to see a Washington heavyweight (as opposed to a local counsel for ADM), the FBI, and offshore banking in his cow case, could put two and two together. He knew that all the extra attention meant that ADM would pay. In early October, Aubrey Daniel offered the ranchers $105,000, three times their actual losses and twice as much as their lawyer had demanded. They took the money, and the case went away as did the threat of Whitacre testifying in the trial.

In the summer and fall of 1996, other legal problems came to a head. ADM settled its major antitrust class action for fixing the price of citric acid. The $35 million settlement was almost as favorable to the corporation as was the resolution of the lysine class. The company also agreed to pay $30 million to shareholders whose stock had fallen as a result of the scandal.

The lysine criminal case likewise steamed forward. Three companies pled guilty to conspiring to fix the price and allocate sales volumes of the amino acid from June 1992 through June 1995. An executive from each also entered a guilty plea. All agreed to cooperate with the government against ADM. Those making the deals included the Ajinomoto Company of Tokyo and Kanji Mimoto, its former feed-additives manager; Kyowa Hakko Kogyo, also of Tokyo, and Masaru Yamamoto, its former general manager of agricultural products; and Sewon America Inc., a division of Seoul's Sewon Company, and Jhom Su Kim, the former president of its US unit. Mimoto and Kim were fined $75,000 a piece. Yamamoto forfeited $50,000.

Kenneth Adams, a lawyer whose clients had rejected the lysine class-action settlement, insisted, "This is the beginning of the end for the internal culture and practices and management of ADM."

With the announcement that the lysine conspirators had folded and were cooperating, ADM stock dropped 62 1/2 cents to $17.75. Plea negotiations accelerated between the government and the independent directors. Early press coverage included leaks that ADM, with $2 billion in cash and marketable securities on hand, was exploring whether it could pay a massive fine, perhaps $400 million, to keep the chairman's son from going to jail.

On October 15, 1996, Aubrey Daniel appeared in federal court in Chicago. Since the hearing began at 12:10 it was lightly attended. A compact stylish man with leathery skin, heavily lidded eyes, and the stillness of a predator lizard, Daniel seemed very much in control. He was accompanied by his partner Barry Simon. Their client was Archer Daniels Midland, but they flanked ADM controller Steven Mills, whom the special committee had designated as the corporation's representative.

The government and Mills earlier had signed a seventeen-page proposed agreement that required court approval. The gist of the deal was that ADM would plead guilty to two antitrust counts and pay a combined fine of $100 million. Seventy million was for fixing the price and sales volume of lysine. Thirty million punished similar anticompetitive behavior involving citric acid. In exchange for cooperation in ongoing federal investigations and trials, the government would give immunity to ADM and its employees for prior crimes, including price fixing in the larger high fructose corn syrup (HFCS) market and for stealing technology from other companies. There were two exceptions. Mick Andreas and Terry Wilson were not covered by the agreement. The government was preparing their indictments.

Daniel told federal judge Ruben Castillo that Mills could answer any questions the court might have about ADM's responsibility. Castillo, who previously had accepted the guilty pleas of the Japanese, had to be assured that the plea was entered knowingly. After prosecutors summarized the evidence of guilt, the judge asked Mills if he agreed. The studiously bespectacled accountant grew uncomfortable.

Mills: Well, I have no personal knowledge of these facts, but the company does not dispute the facts as presented.

J. Castillo: And in your own words on behalf of the company, what do you
think it is that the company did here?

Mills: Well, it's been accused of meeting with competitors and setting
prices and volumes of selling lysine.

J. Castillo: And did the company do that?

Mills: Again, I don't have any personal knowledge of those facts, but the
company doesn't dispute the facts.

J. Castillo: In your investigation into these matters as the designee of
the special committee, does it show that the company did participate
in these actions?

Mills: Yes, sir.

Castillo conducted parallel questioning about citric acid and got similar answers
from Mills. Above all, the judge had to rule out outside deals and pressures in order
to accept the plea. This was very important. ADM was a famously effective special interest. The judge had to be clear that the punishment announced in open
court was not being softened or reduced by other government officials in a back-
room deal. Castillo asked, "Have any promises or agreements been made to the
company?" He meant besides those contained in the agreement that the controller
had signed.

"No," said Mills emphatically.

Finished with Mills, Castillo heard from Phillip Warren, the federal antitrust
prosecutor based in San Francisco who had overseen the citric acid investigation
and grand jury. ADM was pleading guilty only to criminal activity from June 1993
through June 1995. The "volume of affected commerce" during the conspiracy
period was $350 million. Under the federal sentencing guidelines, the fine for a cor-
poration participating in this much economic harm ranged from $112 to $224 million. Warren however moved for a "downward departure" to $30 million based on
"substantial cooperation" in the ongoing citric probe. ADM, which reviled Whitacre
for snitching on it, now was informing on other companies.

Castillo did not look happy with the discount but would "not at this point upset
the apple cart." He called it a "sad day for corporate America because ultimately
the consuming public are the victims of these types of conspiracies." He ended
the twenty-minute session by declaring that "the simple message of today's proceeding is that no American company is above the law, and if a hundred million
dollars doesn't send that message, then I don't think there's a number on God's
earth that I can set that would send that message, and so that will be the sentence
of the Court."

In the wake of the plea, the Department of Justice in Washington held the type of high-level press conference it reserves for major victories. The assistant director of the FBI, head of the antitrust division, and US Attorney for the Northern District of Illinois, all heaped praise on each other for mutual cooperation.

Attorney General Janet Reno outlined the national significance of the case.

> Archer Daniels Midland Company has agreed to plead guilty and pay a $100 million criminal fine, the largest criminal antitrust fine ever, for its role in two international criminal conspiracies to fix the price of lysine, a feed additive used to ensure the proper growth of livestock, and citric acid, a flavor additive and preservative found in soft drinks, processed foods, detergents and other products.
>
> Because of these illegal actions, feed companies, poultry and swine producers, and ultimately America's farmers, paid millions more to buy the lysine additive. Also, manufacturers of soft drinks, processed foods, detergents and other materials, paid millions more to buy the citric-acid addictive, which ultimately caused consumers to pay more for those products.

James Burns, the United States Attorney for the Northern District of Illinois, assured the press that a Chicago grand jury was continuing to investigate price-fixing. "ADM employees and officials from top to bottom are under a commitment to cooperate with us and with the grand jury. . . . And, they will be in a fishbowl and under a microscope, and that is exactly what we are going to expect in that cooperation."

The Washington press corps fired questions at the panelists. Some of the answers did not satisfy it. The deal did not require ADM to pay restitution to victims of antitrust crimes; the tapes would not be released under the Freedom of Information Act; and, in fact, the corporation's cooperation would not be from "top to bottom." Neither James Randall, nor Dwayne Andreas, would be required to submit to interviews by the Justice Department. The department would not comment on the reasons for the exclusion, which had developed in confidential plea negotiations. From this point on, the government would be hounded with allegations of a cover-up.

Some investors expressed outrage that ADM had committed crimes, and now the company had to make amends from its treasury. CALPERS objected that "shareholders assets are being squandered." Its spokeswoman Patricia Macht offered, "Dwayne obviously should go. It's a lot like an apple—if it's blemished on the outside, it's rotten at the core."

Most of Wall Street was not nearly as finicky. It instantly totaled up the profit ADM had made by fixing the prices of lysine and citric acid, which came to roughly $300 million. The company had paid a $100 million fine and $90 million in the civil cases. The government had agreed not to punish price-fixing in the far larger, nearly $3 billion, high fructose corn syrup market that ADM dominated with nearly a one-third share.

On the news of the largest antitrust fine in history, Wall Street rewarded ADM with double-the-usual volume of trading and an 1 ⅛ rise in its share price to $21.75, its all-time high. "The scarlet letter has been removed," crowed John McMillan of Prudential Securities.

Even David Hoech conceded that the independent directors led by Mulroney had done their job. They had refused to sacrifice shareholder value to protect Mick Andreas or Terry Wilson. On December 3, 1996, the pair and Mark Whitacre were indicted in Chicago for fixing the price of lysine.

The indictments of Andreas and Wilson long had been expected. Charging Whitacre was a surprise. After all he had brought the matter to light, his activities in the conspiracy were sanctioned and monitored by the government, and they had nothing to do with embezzlement. The government's retort was that by breaking his cooperation agreement, he had lost his immunity.

From a tactical standpoint, the government's decision to prosecute Whitacre made sense. In civil depositions lately, he had been taking the Fifth Amendment, and he could be expected to continue the pattern of silence during a trial. The early pre-trial sparring between Andreas' and Wilson's attorneys and the government showed that these defendants intended to point their fingers at Whitacre. They would maintain that he was the true price-fixer. They were, as one of their lawyers put it, the "honorable businessmen who did their best to help ADM break the Japanese strangle hold on the lysine market."

The government, of course, did not agree but feared under certain circumstances that a jury could. A problem could arise for the prosecution if Whitacre were not a defendant. Then the jury could interpret his silence as evidence of guilt. In short, if Andreas and Wilson accused Whitacre of running the antitrust scam apart from them, and he failed to reply in court, then the jury could draw an inference against him. On this basis alone, the others could go free.

However, if Whitacre were a defendant, then the jury would be firmly instructed that it could not hold his silence against him. Putting aside the ethics of trying the person who had made the case, logic favored charging him. Perhaps hoping to cultivate Whitacre, the defense played up his peculiar plight. "'Unusual' isn't the word that comes to mind. It's 'unprecedented,'" said Reid Weingarten, Wilson's attorney. "I was a prosecutor for twelve years, and I've never known of an informant who worked for the government for three years to be prosecuted."

Whitacre had not thrived in North Carolina. Due to the criminal allegations against him, he had been forced to step down as an officer of Biomar, which anticipated going public. But, he continued to work for a subsidiary of the company called Clintech, which intended to stay private. He no longer lived in grand style but owned a small home in Chapel Hill.

In the fall of 1996, he and his wife filed for bankruptcy protection in Winston-Salem. The petition was highly unusual as it listed assets of $9.3 million and liabilities of $1.25 million. But $7.5 million of the assets, obviously the gains from the fake invoices, were frozen in foreign and domestic bank accounts by the federal government.

The couple disclosed monthly living expenses of $10,837. This included $3,000.00 in legal fees. Their monthly income totaled $10,150. That was less than half of their 1996 earnings, which equalled $268,000 for the year. That was way down from 1995, his last year at ADM when his income from legal and illegal sources reached $3.95 million.

A relentless learner, Whitacre was closing in on his law degree from Kensington University in California, the source of his controversial MBA. Also, he had become active in two weekly Bible study groups involving business people in the Research Triangle Area of North Carolina. Perhaps with good reason, his children did not seem to share his business ambitions. His daughter, a recent high school graduate, was a fast-food worker who wanted to be a teacher. His elder son, a senior, aspired to be a carpenter.

Although Whitacre already had declared bankruptcy, in the fall ADM also sued him in Decatur for $30 million, including the $9.5 million he had taken. Whitacre made a counterclaim for at least $700,000 for wrongful discharge. He insisted that the wire transfers were just a "pretext" to fire him. The real reason was his work for the FBI.

As a result of the lawsuit, private investigators and ADM attorneys began interviewing, and in some cases deposing, Whitacre and his wife's families, friends, and associates. Many felt harassed. Whitacre and his wife also complained of threatening calls and being followed.

His legal problems mounted in January 15, 1997, when the fraud section of the Department of Justice filed criminal charges against him in Urbana. The indictment contained forty-five counts, including transportation of stolen property, money laundering, conspiracy, wire fraud, and tax evasion. He could receive the maximum twenty-year sentence and a $20-million fine. Nevertheless, the court allowed him to remain free without posting a bond, based on his promise to appear.

In January 1997, Whitacre filed a new lawsuit in Urbana claiming himself the victim of civil rights violations. The defendant was Brian Shepard, his former FBI handler. The court papers accused Shepard of regularly threatening Whitacre with incarceration, hitting him with a "hard-sided brief case," denying him access to a lawyer, and preventing him from seeing a psychiatrist, which had contributed to his earlier suicide attempt.

The suit had potential to explode in the government's criminal antitrust case. Whitacre alleged that Shepard had ordered him to destroy tapes favorable to ADM. In a criminal case, there is little worse that law enforcement can do than shred exculpatory evidence.

Because of Whitacre's earlier praise of Shepard, the claim raised doubts. To allay them, Whitacre came forth with documents purporting to show that he had discussed misconduct by Shepard as early as 1995. One was a letter from his psychiatrist that mentioned mistreatment by the agent. However, the letterhead did not match the psychiatrist's, and it contained an incorrect area code. Whitacre also had a copy of a 1995 fax detailing FBI abuse to his former lawyer James Epstein. Epstein tactfully said he would publicly discuss the validity of the fax if his ex-client would permit it. In a tearful interview with the *New York Times*, Whitacre admitted that both documents were false. He had destroyed his own credibility. Why? Now he was hospitalized as a psychiatric patient in North Carolina. He emerged with a higher dosage of lithium but stuck with his story that Shepard had directed the destruction of evidence.

Whitacre's undercover work and the tapes that came of it continued to bear fruit for law enforcement. On January 29, 1997, Haarmann & Reimer, a New Jersey-based subsidiary of Germany's Bayer, pleaded guilty to a price-fixing conspiracy involving citric acid. After its own guilty plea, ADM had cooperated against Haarmann, which now would testify against others. Haarmann agreed to pay a $50 million fine, second only to ADM's.

As with lysine, the citric scheme was highly developed. The executives involved termed themselves "masters" or "sherpas" depending on their levels of responsibility in the conspiracy. Haarmann also participated in the settlement of a citric acid class action for $94 million. Despite Whitacre's turnabout, ADM still faced major unsettled civil cases among plaintiffs who had chosen not to become members of the lysine, citric, and high fructose classes, preferring to wage individual battles.

The first of the major cases of this type hit in June 1997. Kraft, Quaker Oats, Proctor & Gamble, and Shreiber Foods, four major buyers of citric acid, sued ADM, Haarmann & Riemer, Hoffman-La Roche, and Austria's Jungbunzlauer for conspiracy to overcharge for the product. The alleged damages were $350 million before tripling, so it was potentially a billion-dollar case.

A federal judge in Peoria was handling the high fructose class action. The defendants included A. E. Staley, CPC, Cargill, and ADM, which had the largest market share and the most to lose. In mid-June, the judge allowed the tapes made by Whitacre to be distributed on a restricted basis to the class attorneys.

The scandal also took its toll on leadership. On April 17, 1997, Dwayne

Andreas officially retired as chief executive but retained his position as board chairman. Without the crisis, he would have stayed on or been replaced by his son. Now his nephew G. Allen Andreas became CEO. Some critics understandably saw little change. As Ann Yerger, director of the Council of Institutional Investors, put it, "It is always a little suspicious when a relative of the chief executive gets named as the replacement."

A lawyer, Allen Andreas, 54, had run ADM's European operations. Also over the past year, he had been the company's main face to the financial community, and he had a rapport with it. Most observers believed that it would take some time for him to come up to speed in the hurly-burly trading and deal-making environment of Decatur; and that Dwayne would continue to run the company for the foreseeable future.

Allen Andreas' reputation received a blow in mid-1997 when the European Union raided offices over which he had presided in England in order to gather evidence of price-fixing of amino acids on world markets. Wall Street reacted by dropping the ADM share price 87.5 cents to $21.00. Allen Andreas also raised eyebrows by pledging to bring his cousin Mick back into the company upon his expected acquittal. The fact that Mick, who never stopped drawing his $1.3-million salary, had presided over operations during an admitted criminal conspiracy apparently did not disturb the new chief executive. Also, Mick may have never stopped working. Some people who dealt with ADM reported that he continued to do business for the company but from an office in downtown Decatur.

Another Andreas, Dwayne's brother Lowell, resigned from the ADM board in 1997. Many investors had hoped for an independent replacement. The board named Andrew Young, the former mayor of Atlanta and ambassador to the United Nations, who was an old friend of Dwayne Andreas and also in the chairman's circle of condo neighbors at the Sea View Hotel, which Andreas owned in Florida.

Another member of the old guard, James Randall, stepped down on June 23, 1997. Whitacre had implicated Randall in the price-fixing scandal and also had accused him of misappropriating technology and authorizing the false overseas payments. As for ADM, it maintained that Whitacre had photocopied Randall's signature on the approval forms, called Authorizations for Expenditures or AFE's.

Two weeks later, federal judge Harold Baker in Urbana, Illinois, approved the settlements of seventeen shareholder derivative actions. The defendants, past and present members of the ADM board, agreed to pay $8 million to resolve all the cases. Covered by insurance, the sum was not extraordinary, but the settlement also decreed a reform. From now on only directors who had joined the board after the price-fixing scandal could nominate new directors. As a result, Robert Strauss, Dwayne Andreas' lawyer and confidante, was forced from his perch as chairman of the nominating committee.

As for Whitacre, he could no longer hope to be the president or even a board member of any public company. On October 10, 1997, he appeared in a federal courtroom to plead guilty to thirty-seven counts in his indictment for taking $9.5 million from ADM. He was pasty, exhausted, and had lost about ten pounds since his court appearance the prior winter. Judge Baker asked him if he wanted to go forward with the plea. Speaking in a calm voice that had lost its characteristic rapid blurt, Whitacre said "very much, your honor." He had reviewed the plea document "for many hours." Judge Baker inquired about his mental and physical condition. Whitacre matter of factly responded that he saw a psychiatrist for manic depression, took lithium, and felt very well. The judge accepted the plea and allowed Whitacre to return again to Chapel Hill, based on his assurance that he would appear for sentencing.

David Hoech had been Whitacre's sounding board during the decision about whether to plead. "You can't beat income tax evasion. Why go through the exercise? He needs to get on with his life. That's what he said to me."

The criminal trial of Andreas and Wilson also threatened to damage the corporation with its disclosures. In the fall of 1997, as the criminal case entered a period of intense pretrial sparring, ADM remained very much a corporation under siege.

REVENGE

"His [Whitacre's] crimes flowed from garden variety venality and greed."
— *Judge Harold Baker*

It was an ugly courtroom, large, windowless and too brilliantly lit by a ceiling that was a vast field of fluorescents. The light glinted off the furniture surfaces, even though they were mostly brown, which made the room feel tight. In fact, the court was crowded—not with spectators but with attorneys.

The government had two sets of lawyers. One group was from the US Attorney's Office and the other was from the Chicago office of the antitrust division. Next to the jury box, they ringed a table as if they were having a conference. Mick Andreas' lawyers and staff sat at another table. Terry Wilson's team took up their own table. Though a defendant, Mark Whitacre did not have a team or a table. In the pretrial days, he did not want to come to Chicago, much less to court, unless he had an order to appear. His present lawyer, Bill "T-Bone" Walker, a tall beefy man in his forties with a baby face, sat in the gallery. When the judge had a question for him, he rose from his seat and delivered the answer in a friendly twang. He came from Granite City, Illinois, a depressed downstate river town, and he didn't seem altogether comfortable on the twenty-second floor of the federal monolith in Chicago.

The judge was a petite African-American woman with unwrinkled skin, short black hair, and oval eyes. Her name was Blanche Manning. She was sixty-four but looked forty-four. She had spent most of her career as a state trial and appeals court judge and initially seemed slightly diffident about her ability to handle a long, contentious federal antitrust case. She sat beneath a bronze bas relief of an American eagle assembled from harsh metallic shapes. The thin vertical lines that covered its shield looked exactly like a bar code, a constant reminder that this case was about price-fixing.

Because of Judge Manning's perceived lack of experience, the prosecutors had tried to make an end run around her. When her name had been drawn by lottery for the assignment, the US Attorney had moved to send the case to Judge Ruben Castillo, the stern jurist who had been seasoned by handling the Japanese and ADM corporate guilty pleas.

The defense loudly accused the prosecutor of blatant judge shopping, which it was. Judge Manning, who refused to get off the case, would have known that the government had challenged her capabilities. She did not seem to hold that against the prosecutors, though at times she seemed indulgent of the high-powered defense lawyers.

ADM had paid for the representation of both defendants. It soon became apparent that no expense would be spared. Jack Bray, fifty-seven, represented Mick Andreas. A partner based in the Washington office of King & Spalding, he was one of the capital's most accomplished litigators and was equally at home in criminal or civil cases. With his well-tailored suits, gunmetal gray hair, and sonorous voice, he seemed the image of a trial lawyer. Always freshly barbered and usually in the midst of a long complicated case, he tended to measure trials in terms of the number of haircuts required. The Andreas trial was expected to last two to three months, which could mean a dozen trims.

For a trial horse, he had an unusual subspecialty as a tax lawyer. He was extremely good at explaining complicated economic and financial matters in court. A law review editor at St. Louis University, Bray had been recruited by the Department of Justice during the civil rights era. Going into private practice during Watergate, he had become the lawyer to Gordon Strachan, H.R. Haldeman's protegé.

As the consummate professional, Bray usually liked and was liked by his opponents. He could see and try both sides of a hard case. He once offered that he would have been as happy to handle either the prosecution or the defense in the ADM case. The real point for him was to be before a jury. In court, he seemed unflappable, courteous, well-spoken, and ready for anything. Jurors would see him as the calm point in a storm and would rely on him for the truth.

Like Bray, Reid Weingarten, forty-eight, Terry Wilson's lawyer, had a Justice Department background and now worked in a large Washington firm, Steptoe & Johnson. Physically, Weingarten was Bray's antithesis. Instead of every hair in place, Weingarten had a corona of unruly curls. His suits were rumpled and his tie often askew. He had a big toothy grin and sleepy hooded eyes that came alive during argument or the examination of a witness.

Weingarten had been a long-haired philosophy major and radical at Cornell in the sixties. He attended Dickinson, a small law school in Pennsylvania where he also tended bar. Traces of the early nonconformist still crept through in his trial work. In court, he was impassioned, tenacious, and readily used the slang and gestures of everyday people. He had excellent rapport with juries, which probably had been developed as a deputy district attorney in Harrisburg, Pennsylvania.

Then he had served as a trial lawyer with the Department of Justice's Public Integrity Section where he acquired expertise in combatting judicial corruption. As a member of the Iran-Contra independent counsel's team, he had prosecuted Major General Richard Secord.

In private practice he had become the white-collar defense lawyer of the hour in Washington, DC. His numerous high-profile cases put him on the cover of the *National Law Journal* in December 1997. His recent clients had included two cabinet members, Mike Espy and the late Ron Brown, ex-Teamsters president Ron Carey, and Yah Lin Trie, the alleged influence peddler for the Chinese government.

Bray and Weingarten had different styles and appearances but during the pre-trial phase of the case, they presented a solidly unified defense. It stressed attacking Whitacre and the FBI. Andreas and Wilson would stand together.

The government would be represented by Scott Lassar, the US Attorney for the Northern District of Illinois. It was unusual for an actual US Attorney to take the lead in a major case. Mainly trial work was handled by assistants, while the chief focused on policy and administration. During his service as an assistant federal prosecutor, Lassar had developed the criminal case against ADM that led to the guilty plea and fine. It seemed natural for him to continue with the individual prosecutions once he had been promoted to the office's top job.

Some questioned his dedication to see the job through. In early 1997 he applied for an open federal judgeship. The criticism was somewhat unfair. With the gridlock between the Republican Senate and Democratic White House, it often took years to broker and confirm judicial nominations. Speedy trials, on the other hand, were mandated for criminal cases. At the time there was no reason for Lassar not to believe that he could wrap up the case before taking the bench. As it happened, he made the list of three finalists but did not receive the nomination.

Some consolation came in August 1997 when President Clinton nominated him to be US Attorney. A gaunt, angular man with a helmet of prematurely gray hair, Lassar, forty-seven, stayed lean with a regimen of tennis and jogging. He had an offbeat sense of humor and privately referred to ADM as "price-fixer to the world." He had graduated from Oberlin and Northwestern Law School but mocked credentials by hanging only his junior high diploma in his office.

After law school, he started working in the US Attorney's office. It was the only job he had applied for, and he loved it. He was allowed to develop as a public corruption prosecutor. He tried cases including bid-rigging, extortion by public officials, and judicial corruption. He prosecuted frauds involving taxes, immigration, bankruptcies, commodities trading, and drug testing. He tried and convicted police officers for beating a man in custody.

During a stint in private practice, he won seven-figure verdicts for plaintiffs in complex securities and trade secrets cases. He also served as an arbitrator for the National Futures Association, resolving transactional disputes in that complex market. It was a strong background for investigating and prosecuting white-collar crime, especially in agribusiness.

Lassar was not as prepossessing as Bray or as dynamic as Weingarten, but he was massively prepared. He also exuded a strong sense of morality. The law firms of Bray and Weingarten had slick promotional materials that sold success on every page. In his word-processed trial history—this is very unusual in a market driven profession—he listed convictions (wins) as well as acquittals (losses). In the courtroom, Lassar came off as a balanced advocate who believed in his case, not as a rogue prosecutor willing to win at all costs.

Lassar described the ADM scandal as full of "plot twists." After so many of these, and probably with more to come, he held three firm beliefs about the case. First, Brian Shepard would not destroy evidence. The FBI agent was a man who could not abide injustice, much less create it. Lassar recalled a trip that he and Shepard made to Hong Kong in 1996 to meet with Japanese witnesses because the Japanese government refused to allow the interviews on Japanese soil. From afar on a crowded street, Shepard saw a man beating a woman and ran to intervene. The police arrived at the same time, so the agent had not been involved in the scuffle. Lassar was struck by how Shepard's reflexive response was not blunted by being in a foreign country where he did not speak the language.

Second, based on his experience and the series in the *Echo*, he believed Whitacre was a "sociopath" and frequent liar rather than a manic depressive. Lassar did not expect Whitacre to testify at the trial but would not be surprised by "anything he does."

Third, regardless of what the defense was saying, the tapes compellingly presented the guilt of Andreas and Wilson. Although the defense attorneys had put different spins on the contents to a press that hadn't heard them, this would fail in front of a jury. A technical problem involved figuring out how to get the tapes into evidence at trial without Whitacre to introduce them. Lassar believed that the tapes could be "self-authenticating" if introduced by others. People besides Whitacre could identify the voices. Without cooperation from the government's former star witness, the process sounded difficult but doable.

The defense attorneys continued to spin their versions of the tapes for public consumption. The recordings, they maintained, proved their clients' innocence and Whitacre's guilt. At the same time, they filed motions to keep the tapes from ever coming before the jury. To the judge, they insisted that Whitacre had been too mentally ill to consent to wear a wire, plus he had not been supervised properly by the FBI.

Judge Manning rejected the arguments. Cooperating witnesses often were not paragons of mental health and stability. The government had to be able to make use of evidence from whatever source. Whitacre had not been so impaired that he could not function normally in his life or job, and there was no proof that bipolar disease had destroyed his will. Plus, the FBI's records seemed to reflect reasonable supervision.

Surprisingly, the defense now tried to suppress evidence from another ADM executive, a vice president named Barrie Cox. At ADM, Cox had worked under Terry Wilson in the citric acid business. Recently, Cox had testified before a grand jury with a grant of immunity. At this point, Cox's testimony still remained under seal with the rest of the grand jury proceedings. Nevertheless, it was intriguing that another corporate officer besides Whitacre had informed against the defendants.

Judge Manning also denied this motion to suppress. The ADM corporate guilty plea specifically provided that other ADM officials besides Whitacre would have to cooperate with the government.

Taking a cue from Whitacre's civil rights complaint against Brian Shepard, the defense now made its most serious motion to suppress. It claimed that the tapes in existence represented a partial set because Shepard had ordered the destruction of those favorable to the accused. Moreover, the defense argued that many of the recordings that remained had been tampered with by Whitacre. Therefore, *all* the tapes should be kept out of the trial. Taking the allegations seriously, Judge Manning held hearings during eight days in November and December 1997. Mick Andreas and Terry Wilson now came to court. Whitacre remained in North Carolina until he received a subpoena to testify.

The mood at the defense tables was upbeat and confident, at times even festive. Occasionally Mick Andreas would turn to wave at a well-wisher. During breaks he would joke and chat with a circle of family and friends, seeming to hold court himself. The resemblance to his father was striking, but the son was a more physically commanding version: deeper voiced, broader, stronger, and taller. In fact, Mick looked like Dwayne on lysine.

Terry Wilson, a big, raw boned, white-haired man, looked like a prosperous prairie farmer. Equally relaxed, he seemed somewhat less gregarious than Mick. During breaks he would run out for a smoke and sometimes demonstrated his golf swing to admirers in the hall.

Brian Shepard seemed distinctly uncomfortable. Obviously pained by the accusations against him, he took the stand. He firmly denied ever ordering the destruction of evidence. He was proud of the FBI's investigation of ADM, which he'd dubbed Operation Harvest King, and received the 1997 Attorney General's Award from Janet Reno for his work.

Under Jack Bray's dignified but pointed cross-examination, Shepard had to make several admissions. He had allowed Whitacre to keep tapes he had recorded for up to thirteen days, which would have given him time to doctor them. He knew that Whitacre sometimes lied. He sensed that the mole had some mental problems.

On his cross, Weingarten pushed the matter further. Shepard, he learned, had consulted with the FBI's Behavioral Sciences Unit in Quantico, Virginia. This was the famous team that profiled serial killers and dangerous fugitives. But Shepard had made no report of his contact with the group and could not recall its advice. "Is it typical in the FBI," asked Weingarten, "that you call the Behavioral Sciences Unit and you have a little chat, they have a little chat back, and there's no record made?" Shepard replied, "I don't know what typical is when dealing with the Behavioral Science Unit."

Weingarten got Shepard to admit that Whitacre sat for two polygraph tests. The defense lawyer tried to bring out that the informant had not passed the tests. His voice rising with outrage, Weingarten asked, "And he busted them both, did he not?" Scott Lassar made an objection. Judge Manning sustained it. Polygraph results are not admissible. But Weingarten had made his point. The FBI had continued to use Whitacre. They knew he was untruthful.

What was more important involved the subject of the polygraphs. In 1992, when batches of lysine were spoiling, ADM feared sabotage. Ironically, this allegation rather than any evidence of price-fixing first attracted FBI attention to ADM.

According to Shepard, Whitacre had ratcheted the allegation up a notch. He claimed to ADM and the FBI that the sabotage was part of a Japanese extortion scheme. If ADM put $10 million in a Swiss bank then the problem would stop. Shepard also revealed that Whitacre maintained that the Japanese had threatened his daughter. After he failed his second polygraph, he admitted to the FBI and ADM that he had lied. The Japanese extortion scheme was a fiction.

It was also a "hinge fact" in the sense that its inferences could swing both ways. Plainly, it supported the defense. As Weingarten put it, "If this agent turned him loose, knowing he was a criminal, knowing that he was a liar, knowing that he had a predisposition to fabricate evidence, and just ignored it, that's extremely relevant." Whitacre's scheme to get $10 million into a Swiss bank in 1992 also dovetailed with his wire transfers worth $9.5 million.

On a more subtle level, Lassar took equal comfort from the earlier discovered misconduct. Like the FBI, ADM was aware of Whitacre's false extortion scheme but *had not fired him*. Why? The inference the government hoped the jury would draw was that Whitacre was too deeply involved in helping to set up the lucrative price-fixing racket at that time to be let go. Plus, ADM may have feared that if Whitacre reacted angrily to being fired, he would expose criminality in the company.

The false extortion scheme also provided a clue to the mystery of why a young man on top of the corporate world would risk everything for the FBI. A logical explanation might be that the government now had two crimes over Whitacre's head: extortion and lying to a federal agent. People routinely cooperate with law enforcement to avoid prosecution.

Another possible reason arose from the testimony of Rusty Williams, Whitacre's groundskeeper, who had rescued him from the carbon monoxide fumes. A wiry, fair-haired man in his thirties, Williams took care of Whitacre's "estate, painting, lawn care, whatever he needed done." The base salary was $1,300 a month. Whitacre threw in a pickup truck and a house on the grounds for Williams and his family. Williams also received cash gifts. "Not long after I started working for him, Mr. Whitacre gave me $7,000 to pay off some debts." As the two men became close, Whitacre often discussed business. The owner said "he could be a billionaire by age 50."

In 1992, Whitacre showed his briefcase with the recorder in its false bottom to Williams. When the investigation became public in June 1995 and Whitacre was in the limelight, he explained his role to his groundskeeper. According to Williams, Whitacre "called himself 014 because he was twice as smart as 007."

Terry Wilson's local Illinois counsel, Kristina Anderson, asked the witness if Whitacre had said anything to him following the 1995 raid. "Yes, ma'am," Williams answered, "that when this was done that Mick Andreas, Mr. Randall, and Mr. Wilson would be in prison, and that Mr. Dwayne Andreas' hold on ADM would be quite shaken, and that he would, Mr. Whitacre would, be at the helm of ADM."

The defense called Mark Whitacre to the stand. It intended to show that under government direction, he had selectively recorded to avoid material favorable to ADM, tampered with some tapes, and destroyed others.

Bill Walker told the court that he had advised his client to take the Fifth. "But Dr. Whitacre, a PhD from Cornell at age twenty-three, he's going to do what he wants. Like Mr. Shepard, I can't see into Dr. Whitacre's mind."

The defense began asking Whitacre a barrage of questions. After it became clear that he would not answer any, the judge excused him. One of the questions which Whitacre declined sought the whereabouts of his wife. The defense had been unable to find or subpoena her. Judge Manning declared a recess of several weeks partly in order to give the defense another chance.

When court re-convened in mid-December 1997, Whitacre's wife Ginger was on the stand. A bright-eyed woman with thick chestnut hair, she gave her address, admitted to being married to Whitacre for eighteen and a half years and said, "I invoke the Fifth Amendment" in response to everything else. Each time frustration crossed her brow, as if she badly wanted to be helpful. Then she would force a brave smile and wait for the next question from the defense attorneys.

The questions were ominous. Did she listen to the tapes with Mark and her parents? Did she send five shoe boxes full of tapes to David Hoech in Florida? Did she sign false income tax forms with her husband? Was she aware of his embezzling? Weren't some overseas bank accounts where the stolen funds went also in her name?

Back in October, Mark Whitacre had thrown in the towel and pleaded guilty to thirty-seven counts in Urbana. People still wondered why. But Ginger Whitacre's testimony, or rather its absence, furnished a plausible explanation: Whitacre took the full weight so that his wife would not be charged.

Having been subpoenaed, David Hoech also took the stand. He described himself as "a consultant in the Pacific rim area in international business." Otherwise, he took the Fifth Amendment to all questions.

The defense wanted to probe whether Ginger Whitacre had sent Hoech five shoe boxes. According to the questions that Hoech refused to answer, the boxes contained copies of tapes Whitacre made as a mole, plus other recordings that Whitacre supposedly made of conversations between Shepard and himself without the FBI agent's permission. In these, Shepard allegedly ordered Whitacre to discard tapes favorable to Mick Andreas and Terry Wilson. The defense had obtained the transcript of a recent telephone call between Whitacre and Hoech, that Hoech allegedly had recorded. In court, Mark Hulkower, a lawyer on Wilson's team, brandished the transcript and asked Hoech, "Isn't it a fact that the following discussion takes place?" Then he began to read:

> *Whitacre:* I'll tell you what I was calling you about, Dave. I sure hate to call you on a Sunday like this. Sorry to call you on a Sunday, but I—
> *Hoech:* No problem, no problem.
> *Whitacre:* The main reason I called you was, is, those tapes Ginger sent you early July of 19, last year, '95.
> *Hoech:* What about them?
> *Whitacre:* Well, I wanted to get them—well, what about if I wanted to get them right away? There were several tapes in that, copies of the stuff I made for the Justice Department. There was also a bunch of micro cassettes I had in one of the boxes of, uh, me and Brian Shepard.
> *Hoech:* Yeah, wasn't he a piece of shit.
> *Whitacre:* The tapes, you didn't destroy those, did you?
> *Hoech:* Yeah, Mark, I got rid of everything. Hey, you know, I'm fifty-six years

old, and I don't want to get my ass in trouble with the government. You know if I'd have had those tapes when they came down and subpoenaed me in April, man, we'd have all been fucked.

The attorney continued to read from the telephone transcript:

Whitacre: You know, one of the main things, Dave, I want to talk to you about face-to-face was the, if you're up here, was to talk to you about those tapes.
Hoech: Mark, there ain't no tapes. I destroyed all those tapes last year. I told you if they were there, I'd have had them out the other day. You know, this thing got so messy last year, right?
Whitacre: Yeah, but I can't imagine you'd destroy 'em.
Hoech: Well, you gotta goddamn imagine that's the way.
Whitacre: Damnit, Dave, I need those, I need those Brian Shepard tapes.
Hoech: Well, I don't have 'em, Mark. You know, I thought maybe you kept some back the way you were talking, when I told you I'd get rid of all of them, you know, I mean.
Whitacre: Dave, he must have meant that I was going down.
Hoech: I know it, but, Mark, I wouldn't let you go down if I had the tapes. You know me better than that. You know—
Whitacre: I just can't see you doing this unless you really got worried about something.
Hoech: Well, I did. I told you, goddamnit, when I got rid of 'em."

When it became clear that Hoech would say nothing about the call, Weingarten asked the government to give Hoech immunity from prosecution so he could testify. If Hoech actually had destroyed tapes knowing they were evidence in an investigation, then he could be guilty of obstruction of justice. But in private conversations, he told people that he had none of the mole tapes and had never destroyed any. Plus, he never had heard any tapes of Shepard telling Whitacre to get rid of recordings favorable to ADM. He even had written a letter to this effect to Judge Manning. The call with Whitacre seemed to be an elaborate charade. At least that is what Scott Lassar believed. Why Hoech had engaged in it remained a mystery.

Judge Manning wanted to give Hoech immunity to testify but admitted that as a judge she lacked the authority. Only the prosecutor had it. Scott Lassar's cocounsel from the antitrust division, Jim Griffin, told the court that the government would not extend immunity to Hoech "because we don't think he's credible, and we only give immunity to witnesses who are truthful." This explanation seemed thin in light of the numerous times the government has sponsored the testimony of mafia informants, jailhouse snitches, and other shady characters, and it plainly failed to satisfy Judge Manning. But unlike Hoech, witnesses given immunity do not ordinarily push prosecutors to do their jobs or scream about a cover-up.

In order to buttress its lack of belief in Hoech's truthfulness, the government presented another FBI witness, Michael Bassett, who plainly detested Hoech. He was the former undercover operative who had masqueraded years before as an ADM clerk during the sting at the Chicago Board of Trade. As a result, in his newsletter Hoech had accused the agent of a conflict of interest. Bassett, a thin, sallow-faced man with a thatch of light brown hair and matching mustache, now worked as a special agent in the Albany office.

During the FBI's investigation of purported fraud at ADM, Bassett was still in Chicago and was assigned to the case. He traveled to Florida to meet with Hoech at his home in 1996. Interestingly, Bassett did not go with a search warrant, which seemed to show that the agent did not believe he would find tapes. In court, Bassett took issue with Hoech's *Shareholder's Watch Letters* calling them "unfriendly and unflattering" to ADM. He revealed that Hoech had "three shares of stock in the company and was a consultant to ADM competitors." His goal seemed to be to show that Hoech would give biased testimony if given immunity.

Bassett said Hoech offered to provide him with current ADM employees who could corroborate Whitacre's tales of fraud in ADM, but Hoech never came up with names. "He has zero credibility," said Bassett. The agent believed that Hoech could be prosecuted for making the telephone tape with Whitacre. To him, obstruction had occurred if Hoech had destroyed evidence or if the tape was an act to throw off law enforcement. "Either way you cut that tape, he's got a problem."

A bevy of additional FBI agents testified on behalf of the government to explain its procedures for surreptitiously recording conversations. Finally, the defense presented its expert on audio tapes, James B. Reams. From Virginia, Reams was a heavyset former FBI agent who wore aviator glasses and spoke with a gracious tidewater lilt. Earlier, he had performed tape analysis for Judge Sirica during Watergate. More recently, he had analyzed recordings in the Texaco racial discrimination case.

Reams testified that ADM's attorneys had given him a $50,000 state-of-the-art piece of equipment to analyze all of the audio tapes that Whitacre had made for the FBI. He expected to receive about $500,000 for the entire assignment. So far he had examined 95 out of 220 Whitacre tapes. He was not yet ready to write a report or give a final opinion. He said that preliminarily his findings were consistent with some tape tampering. Reams's testimony was highly unusual. He was an expert but had not offered an expert opinion. He merely had provided a vague preview or teaser, as part of the defense strategy to shape media and public opinion before trial against Whitacre and the FBI. The government had a tape expert, too, but saw no reason to present him to rebut a nonopinion.

After all that she had heard, Judge Manning seemed to stress one issue, the failure to give immunity to Hoech. "I'm deeply concerned about how the government is proceeding." She announced that she was considering options, including dismissing the case or keeping out the tapes, as a result. The latter substantially would raise the odds of acquittal. It would also mean that the tapes would not be seen and heard by the public until the trial and all appeals had run their course, an outcome which ADM fervently desired.

David Hoech was the potential scapegoat for this situation. The self-styled political guerrilla had been ADM's most strident foe and Whitacre's closest ally. The prosecution could be fatally damaged for lack of his testimony but would not give him immunity in order to receive it.

Afterwards Hoech seethed about the hearing. Prior to it, he had told Hulkower that the Whitacres had given him no tapes. Nevertheless, the lawyer called him to the stand in the hope that Hoech would say that he heard a cassette of Brian Shepard ordering Whitacre to destroy evidence. Hoech made an ethics complaint to the bar association of the District of Columbia accusing Hulkower of attempting to mislead the court by representing falsely that the lawyer would be able to present Hoech's testimony. The bar ultimately dismissed the matter.

Also, Hoech scored Bassett's conduct. The FBI agent was "Dwayne's handpicked stooge." Hoech insisted Bassett's testimony was false from the number of shares of stock—Hoech had two not three—to the allegation that Hoech had not cooperated. Hoech argued that it was Bassett who had not followed up and had not investigated any alleged crimes at ADM besides those attributed to Whitacre and his clutch of subordinates.

In early 1998, the government made clear that it was pursing Whitacre with hammer and tongs. A sign of the hardened approach came during the sentencing of Reinhard Richter.

A German national, Richter, forty-six, had befriended Whitacre when they both worked at Degussa. When Whitacre was tapped by ADM, he brought Richter along. Fluent in Spanish, Richter would become president of ADM Mexico.

In 1995, the government identified Richter as part of the fraud ring. He had allowed Whitacre to park stolen funds in his Texas bank account. According to Whitacre, ADM president James Randall had approved a scheme to give Richter an off-the-books bonus of $190,000 using fake invoices. Allegedly Randall had made a comment that Richter could use the money to buy a Ferrari, which Randall, a Ferrari-owner, knew would cost about $190,000.

The sentence dictated by federal guidelines for Richter's infractions could include incarceration for up to fifteen–twenty-one months, full restitution, and a $50,000 fine. In 1997, when Richter pled guilty, it became known that he was cooperating with the government against Whitacre. After leaving ADM, Richter had remained in Mexico.

On January 30, 1998, he arrived in the Urbana, Illinois, federal courthouse for sentencing accompanied by nationally prominent defense attorney Gerald Goldstein of San Antonio, Texas. Before the hearing, the lawyers from the fraud section chatted amiably with Goldstein, who accepted a subpoena for his client to return to testify against his ex-colleagues. Judge Harold Baker, who was handling the fraud cases took the bench, scanned the presentence investigation (PSI) report from the federal probation office, and announced that the PSI included a "downward departure" recommendation from the government. Baker asked Goldstein if he had any objection to the PSI's finding. "I'm not sure," laughed the lawyer, "that I could argue myself into a better position."

The judge then asked Richter to come forward. A dark-haired man with a trim goatee who wore a gray business suit, Richter looked like the personification of a suave European manager. His face turned beet red as he approached the bench. As he composed himself to make a statement, his complexion drained back to normal color. He spoke in almost accentless English. "I am very proud to have worked for ADM. It's a great company. I'm very sorry I got into this problem. I didn't have the strength to resist." That was all. He said nothing about Randall.

Judge Baker imposed a sentence of one year of nonreporting probation and a $25,000 fine. If Richter traveled out of Mexico, he simply would have to alert the probation office.

Afterwards, I tried unsuccessfully to speak with Richter. Gerald Goldstein, who had done an effective job for his client in negotiating with the fraud section for its assent to minimal punishment, was willing to talk briefly.

> Reinhard and several of his friends worked for Degussa. Mark [Whitacre] got them their jobs, hired them, and was responsible for maintaining their relationship with ADM, and he would remind them of that. He was a Machiavellian pied piper who brought them dream careers that were fun. These guys were all extremely well paid—my client probably made six or seven hundred thousand. Going to work at ADM was the best thing that ever happened to him.
>
> My client felt a compulsion that if he did not do what Whitacre wanted, he would lose his job. I think they all felt that.

Goldstein insisted that Richter made no profit from the scam. It was all "basically Mark's money" and had just passed through his client's account. We began to discuss Whitacre's long-standing allegation that his client had received an under-the-table signing bonus that Randall had said Richter could use to buy a Ferrari. "Mark Whitacre is unable to leave well enough alone," said Goldstein. "Then he gets his tit in a wringer." Goldstein was emphatic that there was no bonus. "My client never got anything." Then he added, "there is some truth to the remark [by Randall] that my client now could buy a Ferrari." But he assured me it was said in a "purely social context," meaning at a party, and did not represent any misconduct by the ADM president.

Mark Whitacre was scheduled for sentencing in the same Urbana courtroom in the late afternoon of Thursday, February 26, 1998. In order to proceed, Judge Baker had returned from New York where his brother-in-law had had a stroke. By noon it was apparent that Whitacre would not show. The small courthouse, crowded with reporters, was abuzz with a rumor that the defendant had attempted suicide.

Most of the reporters and lawyers went to lunch at the 1950s-style diner across the plaza from the courthouse. I sat two tables away from the fraud section group, which had flown three lawyers from Washington for the sentencing. It was not a complex matter and could have been handled by one.

I didn't attempt to overhear their conversation, but they were in high spirits, and some of it rose above the general clatter of the place. In particular, Whitacre's latest attempt to kill himself was the source of joking and laughter. Also, they spoke constantly about Aubrey Daniel, whom they obviously knew well. It was Aubrey this and Aubrey that, and how much do you think Aubrey makes an hour? Was it $750, $850 or more? Clearly they were in awe of ADM's barracuda.

At 2:30 PM the court convened. Usually genteel, Judge Baker seemed testy. Bill Walker informed him that his client had attempted suicide that morning. The attorney said Whitacre would be able to appear the following day. Walker offered to travel to North Carolina and bring him up to court. The attorney had just spoken to Whitacre's psychiatrist, who said that the defendant "was competent and had no medical problem" that would prevent him from being sentenced.

The judge shot a hard look at Walker, "I find it unacceptable to have you bring him back." Donald Mackay, the fraud section attorney, asked for an arrest warrant calling the defendant "a flight risk and possibly a danger to himself." The judge seemed to grow angrier. Whitacre was "in violation of release by an act of his own hand." Baker revoked bail and directed the US marshals to take custody of Whitacre.

Two days before, David and Carole Hoech had received a package from Whitacre. It contained a sealed letter. On the envelope were instructions not to open it until the afternoon of the twenty-sixth. It contained a suicide note:

Dear David & Carol,

I am really sorry that we were unable to get together this winter. I really have enjoyed your friendship and support these past three years. You guys sure know how to go into battle against a mighty foe.

A lot of things have been happening the past couple of months. It ended up that the sentencing became one of the least of my worries. As you know through Bible study, the degree programs, and the support of my family, I was very prepared for it. However, ADM continues to harass with lawsuits against siblings, my parents, etc. Even my daughter has been served a notice for a deposition. You know how that is from your own subpoenas. This is ridiculous. Someone, we assume ADM, even called today to make a threat. Tanya [his daughter] answered the phone and motioned for Ginger to get on also. The threat basically stated that even after sentencing ADM would do anything they could to get to me through the harassment of my wife, children, parents, and other family members. It is obvious that they are backed into a corner to go to such lengths to scare innocent children.

I am now five and a half years into this case and when it seems to come to an end for me, it seems to continue for others that are close to me. Therefore, I have been doing some very deep thinking and came to the conclusion that there was only one thing to do in order to give my family freedom.

I hope that you understand the sacrifice I made for my family. I have been married to Ginger for 19 years and been with her for 25 years. She has been the best thing in my life and have grown even closer over the past couple of years. My kids are the greatest and I love them with all of my heart. These four months without working has been a blessing and were filled with wonderful memories.

Selfish suicide is labeled a sin in the Bible. However, the Bible makes it clear that sometimes one has to sacrifice their own life to give life and freedom to others. This is what I am doing for my family.

Take care of yourself and God Bless You! Please keep an eye on Ginger and the kids for me during these tough times. I pray that things will clear up for them very soon.

David, my advice to you is to go out and enjoy your life and leave this crap alone! They are not worth the effort and only others seem to suffer, not them.

Take care my friend! I hope to see you one day in a more peaceful place where justice does prevail.

The letter was signed by "Mark E. Whitacre." The use of his full name in a last note to close friends suggests that Whitacre had hoped for a wider distribution.

Soon portions of the letter were carried in newspapers. It also appeared in its entirety in the *Corporate Crime Reporter*, a Washington newsletter.

In his package to the Hoechs, Whitacre also enclosed an affidavit notarized on February 22, 1998, which had been filed in the Urbana federal court. It had been drafted a month before his latest suicide attempt and was meant for consideration by his sentencing judge. Whitacre obviously intended to impress the court with his scholarship and ambition. He laid out his education in great detail.

> I received a Bachelor of Science Degree Cum Laude in Animal Science from Ohio State University in December, 1979. Also in December, 1979 I received a Masters of Science Degree with distinction in an Honor's Combined BS/MS Program at Ohio State University. The BS/MS degrees were received in four years instead of the average of six years which is typical. I received a Doctorate Degree (PhD) in Nutritional Biochemistry from Cornell University in May, 1983 in 23 months instead of the average three–four years that are required. I received a Masters of Business Administration (MBA) from Kensington University in May of 1994. Since that point I received a Juris Doctorate (JD-Law degree) from Kensington University in October, 1997. My GPAs out of a possible 4.0 are BS-3.65; MS-3.9; PhD-3.6; MBA-3.8; and JD-3.1.

He went on to explain that he had been accepted into a master of laws (LLM) program at Northwestern California University at Sacramento, which would allow him to take the bar exam in that state. He had "also started since November 1997 a three-year program for a PhD in Psychology." Then he delineated his remarkable career:

> It involves an extensive background in International Business in top executive positions. I also have almost four years experience living in Europe (W. Germany) and many years experience being responsible for business in SE Asia. Over the past two years, my most recent experience involved being CEO/President of a biotech company in Chapel Hill, North Carolina, and CEO/President of one of its sister companies. From November, 1989 to August 7, 1995 I was employed at Archer Daniels Midland Co. (A Fortune 50 company). For most of my employment I was President of the ADM BioProducts Division of the company. This was one of the fastest growing divisions of the company with over $1.5 billion invested (became largest Biochem Company in the world). In October, 1992 I was promoted to Corporate Vice President (Corporate Officer) of the company in addition to being President of the BioProducts Division. This gave me added responsibility over SE Asia acquisitions and joint ventures.

As an exhibit to the affidavit, he included the March 1995 Dain Bosworth bulletin because of its conclusion that "I was expected to be the next president of ADM and the CEO's son was expected to be the next CEO." Whitacre outlined his service as an informant to the government from November 4, 1992 to August 7, 1995:

> While working undercover for the FBI, I recorded hundreds of audio and video tapes. These tapes were turned over to the FBI. As a result of this investigation, ADM has already plead (sic) guilty and paid the largest fine in history of $100 million. Several other companies have also plead guilty (sic) and paid multimillion dollar fines. I was told by some officials of the government that the evidence that I provided was the most ever in any white-collar crime in history.

One could question the judgment of a felon who pled guilty to thirty-seven counts and then took a self-laudatory tone about his achievements. But at least his jobs and degrees were real, as was the impact of his informing.

Then Whitacre went into his high-wire act. He wrote that he admitted to the charges because "I take full responsibility for my actions that led up to the Plea Agreement of October 10, 1997." Yet, he called the funds he sent abroad "under-the-table payments" and part of "a company scheme and not my invention." He stressed, "the fact that my attorneys have filed a suit against ADM in that the money was given to me and not theft." The contradiction was maddening to the government. He was "taking full responsibility" but insisted he hadn't taken anything.

Whitacre also had a surprise for Rusty Williams, his former groundskeeper. Williams had testified in the fall during Judge Manning's suppression hearing to his boss' "014" scheme to dethrone the Andreases and become a billionaire CEO. The testimony, if brought into evidence, would not cause the jury at the Chicago price-fixing trial to view Whitacre warmly. Also the introduction of such a motive could damage Whitacre's chances in his civil suit against ADM.

In his affidavit, Whitacre wrote that he had given Williams about $113,000 in cash payments, plus a $30,000 truck, and a $50,000 house "that we let Rusty use for free during these 4+ years. . . . However, Rusty told me several times that he did not include any of these payments, truck, and house on his yearly taxes. He even mentioned that his tax consultant was not comfortable to do his taxes because of this. I held back on this because Rusty has been such a good friend. However, my attorneys have stressed that everything needs to be laid out before sentencing."

Why was he busting Rusty Williams for tax fraud? Perhaps it was because Whitacre was angry about his former helper's testimony. Regardless of his motives, the affidavit raised new questions about Whitacre's first suicide attempt. If Williams had truly rescued Whitacre, then the survivor probably would have been forever grateful. The normal reaction would not be to harm him. On the other hand, if Whitacre simply had used Williams as a pawn, then there would be no reason for lifelong gratitude. Or perhaps Whitacre really had wanted to die, still did, and saw Williams as impeding his wish.

The biggest surprise in the affidavit involved Brian Shepard. Whitacre confessed that the FBI agent had never instructed him to destroy any tapes favorable to ADM. He swore that he had turned in every

> original tape of ADM and its competitors to the FBI with no exceptions. Furthermore, no tapes were altered at anytime. No tapes were ever rewound and started over as ADM has claimed. Whenever a tape was started it continued in a fashion without ever rewinding. The FBI machines provided to me did not have rewinding or playing capabilities. However, some of the tapes were copied by me but without ever altering the original tape.
>
> The only reason why I claimed that Agent Brian Shepard told me to destroy selected tapes is due to the fact that a good friend of mine (currently an ADM executive) convinced me that he would be able to stop all the ADM civil suits (Urbana, Switzerland, civil suits against my wife, parents, sister-in-law, brother-in-law, etc) and all the harassment of my family. He further told me that he would be able to recover my stock options (approx. $1.5 million) as stated in my counter-suit against ADM. Even though I claimed this about Brian Shepard stating to destroy the tapes ADM did not change their strategy as they promised. This person advised me to use only nondetectable phone cards and to use only pay phones in order to protect him from ADM scrutiny.

The Justice Department rejoiced about the recantation because it vindicated Shepard. Plus, it undermined a plank in the Andreas and Wilson motions to suppress the tapes in Judge Manning's court. The story about the unnamed "good friend" within ADM being the germ of the effort to smear Shepard was vintage Whitacre. On one hand, it was bizarre. On the other, it possessed certain intriguing aspects of plausibility.

The existence of a "good friend" who could make good things happen for Whitacre seemed to explain two other previously inexplicable "plot twists." One was the staged phone call between Whitacre and Hoech where they discussed Shepard's goal of getting rid of evidence favorable to ADM.

The other involved ADM. In the spring of 1997, not long after Whitacre sued Shepard, ADM quietly dropped its Swiss case against Whitacre. Some of the Swiss funds were not transferred back to this country but remained in his accounts. Another step would have to be taken before Whitacre gained access to these funds. ADM would have to unfreeze the accounts. It never did.

On Wednesday, March 5, 1998, the court staff in Urbana had to set up extra chairs in Judge Baker's small courtroom. Whispering, the crowd wondered about what Whitacre would look like after his second suicide attempt and how much time he would get for his crimes.

Whitacre's family and friends had been alarmed by the fact that he had been held in the Decatur jail rather than in a facility nearer to Urbana. Whitacre was not popular in the ADM company town. Had he been locked up there to scare him or to teach him a lesson? If so, it did not show. He entered through a security port flanked by two marshals. He looked well, perhaps a bit chunky. In his navy suit, white on white shirt, and muted crimson tie, he could have been any aging yuppie with stock options and a mortgage or two. Before court convened, he smiled politely at familiar faces and huddled with his lawyers.

The sentencing would not be typical. No family members would speak about the defendant's excellence as a husband or father. No community groups would talk about his tireless volunteering. No minister would describe the quality of his faith. Whitacre would address the court directly or through Walker.

Judge Baker invited the defense to present any objections to the presentence investigation (PSI) prepared by the US Probation Office. Bill Walker was concerned about the report and the long sentence of 133 to 188 months it recommended. Predictably, the probation office and federal prosecutors had been put off by Whitacre's effort to "take full responsibility" while continuing to claim he was given secret bonuses. Walker argued vigorously that Whitacre had pled guilty to spare the government the expense of a trial and was prepared to take his punishment.

Then Walker dropped a bomb. "They say the bonus plan is not true. But Dr. Whitacre has a right to hold onto his beliefs. The government knows good and well that the bonus plan exists. They've heard the tape about it between Mick Andreas and Dr. Whitacre in March of 1994." Then Walker stated the razor-thin distinction on which Whitacre relied and upon which he ultimately hoped to build his lawsuit against ADM. Whitacre had been given the money with the knowledge of the highest officials at ADM, but he was guilty of taking it from "the shareholders who are the living body of the corporation."

As Walker switched into a new subject, he seemed distinctly uncomfortable. Bowing his head for a moment, he sighed, straightened, and then dealt with an assertion in the PSI that Whitacre had forged yet another document, a memorandum in Walker's name on the lawyer's letterhead. The memo was written to the Justice Department. According to Walker, the fake document protested the government's refusal to give Ginger Whitacre immunity from prosecution. Walker tried to justify the new forgery. The memo accurately summarized discussions between himself and the government that subsequently had been communicated to Whitacre. "The text is not in error. The text is not wrong." Then shaking his head in wonder, he added, "It's even written as I would have wrote [sic] it. . . . It's not false. Dr. Whitacre was trying to protect his wife from being prosecuted." However, the lawyer's argument that Whitacre should be forgiven for the new forgery because it used the same language that Walker would have used and was an effort to protect the defendant's wife from prosecution failed to move the court.

Walker also objected to a portion of the PSI, which stated that Whitacre recently had ceased to cooperate with the government. As specified in his guilty plea agreement, Whitacre was supposed to give information against his underlings in the wire and tax fraud scheme.

In an interview with prosecutors in February 1998, Whitacre had not satisfied the government with his answers about Sid Hulse, one of his ex-aides under indictment. In effect, Whitacre was claiming that Hulse's off-the-books payments had been approved by ADM, and so Hulse was not involved in fraud. Now Hulse was having qualms about pleading guilty and threatening to put the government through two trials—one for tax evasion in Atlanta and another for fraud and conspiracy in Urbana. Hence, the probation office wanted to increase Whitacre's sentence, because it felt Whitacre was withholding his cooperation. "Your Honor," implored Walker, "this court should not punish Whitacre for saying that others are not involved." The real issue of cooperation, he reminded the court, related to his client's two and half years as an undercover agent in the antitrust investigation of ADM.

Donald B. Mackay, attorney for the Department of Justice's fraud section, now stood to address the objections. A short, blond, pallid man with mild manners out of court, Mackay now turned into an iron advocate for maximum incarceration. "I take strong exception to some of the remarks of Bill Walker." Mackay wanted the court to understand and dismiss Whitacre's role in the antitrust investigation as "totally irrelevant to this case." He made a point to call the defendant Mr. Whitacre rather than Dr. Whitacre as Walker had. He caustically noted that "Mr. Whitacre is a defendant in that price-fixing case," as opposed to a blameless whistleblower. The notion that Whitacre deserved a "downward adjustment" in sentence length for accepting responsibility appalled Mackay. The defendant "treated us to baseless fabrications that his thefts were an off-the-books bonus plan approved by upper management at ADM. In the strongest terms, on behalf of the United States, I denounce those representations. There is not a shred of evidence that would give support to Mr. Whitacre's public pronouncements."

Regarding the alleged recording of a conversation between Whitacre and Mick Andreas about illegal bonuses, Mackay stormed "such a tape does not exist." Nor had any conversation on the subject been recorded by Whitacre. He castigated Whitacre for "going out of his way to vilify James Randall. He sought to enlist the aid of Reinhard Richter to put out a false story that Randall had approved the bonuses." The court should not allow Whitacre "to peddle that type of defamation. He has repeatedly made false accusations of wrongdoing by others. . . . This man has made a mockery of acceptance of responsibility."

Mackay could not fathom why Whitacre had forged a memo on his attorney's stationery. He insisted that Ginger Whitacre had not been threatened with prosecution. "I cannot read Mr. Whitacre's mind." The prosecutor derided the latest suicide attempt. "There is a suspicion by local police in North Carolina that this was a staged event." To Mackay, it also constituted "a further attempt to hide behind others to avoid responsibility."

Judge Baker told Whitacre to come forward. As her husband approached the bench, Ginger Whitacre, her face streaked with tears, silently mouthed, "I love you." The judge asked Whitacre if he wished to say anything. Half-crying himself, Whitacre said, "Yes, Your Honor. I'm here to take full responsibility for my actions. I want to make that clear. I'd like to apologize to a lot of people in this room and a lot of people not in this room. Mostly, Your Honor, I'm here to accept my punishment."

Judge Baker seemed wary of Whitacre. Ordinarily, he dealt directly, almost conversationally, with the people he had to sentence. Now in a quiet tone, he spoke of Whitacre in the third person rather than addressing him directly:

> To observe that Mr. Whitacre is not the usual felon who comes before this court is a gross understatement. The usual felon is a byproduct of Jim Crowism, segregation, and our society's chemical dependency. These individuals, usually in their mid-twenties, lack opportunities for education, employment or success. They rarely come from intact families. Mr. Whitacre comes from an intact family. He had every opportunity for success and capitalized on those opportunities. He has a PhD, a JD and an MBA. His success was meteoric. He was president of a division and a corporate vice president at ADM. It is not inconceivable that in due course he could have become CEO. But interlaced with his success is a tale of mendacity, deceit, coercion, and theft. His crimes flowed from garden variety venality and greed.

The judge expressed doubts about the suicide attempt. He found "no clear connection between Mr. Whitacre's bipolar disorder and his criminal conduct. At times he displays what could easily be described as sociopathic conduct. It is difficult to know when Mr. Whitacre is lying and when he is being truthful."

The judge sentenced Whitacre to nine years of incarceration, which could be reduced by 15 percent with good behavior. The term would begin with a period of evaluation in a federal prison hospital in Minnesota or Missouri. Afterwards, the judge recommended that the convict be assigned to the prison at Butner, North Carolina, so he could be near his family. In addition, Whitacre immediately would have to pay $11,403,698 in restitution, which included the stolen $9,538,694, plus 5 percent interest. All the money was already accounted for and impounded, so that was not expected to be a problem. Baker instructed him to assign any of the accounts still in his name over to ADM.

Bill Walker stood to protest. In October, the government had induced his client's guilty plea by agreeing to recommend a six-and-a-half to eight-year sentence. Now the government had reneged by recommending up to 188 months, which obviously had affected the court's decision.

The large weary man began thinking out loud. "In the Seventh Circuit [which includes Illinois] my client's only remedy is to withdraw his guilty plea." The idea that Whitacre would go to trial electrified the crowded gallery. "But if he does that," the lawyer continued, "and he gets convicted, then he could get a twenty-year sentence." Walker rejected his own idea of retracting the plea and went back to his table.

To many observers, it was more surprising that the antitrust division of the Justice Department had never shown up at the sentencing. Whitacre was a felon, but he had handed the division its biggest case in history, which stimulated a new awareness about price-fixing. In December, Gary Spratling, the chief of criminal enforcement in the division, said he expected a representative to speak at Whitacre's sentencing. Later, I learned that the strict agreement of separation between the antitrust division and fraud section had prevented antitrust from playing any role in the fraud case, much as it would keep fraud out of the upcoming antitrust trial. If someone from the government had outlined Whitacre's cooperation, his sentence could have been cut in half. As it stood, Whitacre got nine years for conspiring to swindle $9 million. Wilson and Mick Andreas faced a maximum of three years if convicted for conspiring to steal about that much per month from the lysine market over two years. Something was out of balance, amiss. Wilson, Andreas, and Whitacre all were middle-aged executives charged with white-collar crimes. None had prior records. Yet, the Justice Department was seeking the harsher sanction for the local fraud rather than the worldwide scam. David Hoech argued that Justice was doing ADM's bidding by demolishing Whitacre, the whistleblower, so that others would not come forward. The severe treatment of Whitacre favored ADM. In time the government identified forty-nine executives who participated in the price fixing conspiracy. None voluntarily cooperated with the prosecution of the company, Wilson, or Andreas.

After court, Bill Walker and Don Mackay held separate press conferences. Walker said his client would not appeal the sentence. "We were looking at 188 months when we walked in. So 108 isn't a bad result. We thank Judge Baker."

Walker reported on Whitacre's suicide attempt. "His doctor said it was real. There was too much carbon monoxide in Mark's system for it not to be. He tried with two hoses. First with a plastic hose from the pool. But the hot exhaust cracked it. Then he got a garden hose. His daughter found him."

Don Mackay said, "I thought it was a very fair sentence. We're not going to appeal it." He asserted that ADM had cooperated fully with the fraud investigation, which had been very thorough. These were points that later would be challenged by the FBI and its files of the probe. He described Whitacre as the ringleader of the racket who had received kickbacks from the others involved and thus was deserving of the most serious sentence.

He was asked where Whitacre had learned to make wire transfers and use the Swiss banking system. He said he didn't know. He was asked why ADM's audit controls missed the phony transfers for over two years and then suddenly discovered the wrongdoing after Whitacre was exposed as the mole. "Just blind luck," he said. He claimed the discovery was made by an ADM lawyer working on a patent infringement suit. Who was that? "I can't tell you," he smiled. He reiterated that all the money from the fraud had been accounted for. As for the spy tapes that Whitacre had recorded (including the one from March 1994 about which Walker intriguingly alleged to Judge Baker that Mick Andreas had acknowledged the off-the-books bonus system), Mackay admitted that he had not listened to any of them.

After the jailing of the whistleblower on Wednesday, March 4, 1998, ADM made a strong move against the gadfly. On Saturday, March 7, Williams & Connolly served David Hoech's lawyer John Kelso with papers it was filing in a Florida federal court to compel Hoech to turn over all of his and his company's financial records.

This was not a new effort by ADM. It began seeking Hoech's papers the previous year. What was distinctly new was ADM's justification. Williams & Connolly told the Florida court that all of the bogus bonus money was not accounted for and that Hoech might have some of it, despite Mackay's public statements to the contrary.

Previously, an ADM attorney had confessed to Kelso that Hoech's propaganda had stung the corporation. But the retaliatory strike was brazen for two reasons.

First, as they later admitted, neither ADM nor its lawyers had any basis for suggesting that Hoech took any money. Ordinarily, recklessly and falsely accusing a person of a crime is slanderous, but by using its high-priced legal guns to make the slur in court, ADM achieved immunity from a defamation suit. ADM's goal plainly was to harm Hoech's reputation in his backyard by making him seem like a thief.

Upon receiving the court papers, Kelso, a lawyer with a large Miami firm, wrote to Donald Mackay at the Justice Department asking him to clear up the mess based on his earlier statements. Mackay did not respond but another fraud section attorney, James Nixon, replied that the government "has not accounted for all funds" and "cannot confirm whether or not Mr. Hoech received any proceeds."

A week after the sentencing, Mackay told a Bloomberg reporter that "there was never any indication to us that Hoech received any unlawful funds."

The Florida federal judge handling the matter decreed that it "appears that ADM simply seeks to rummage through the bank records in hopes of identifying something useful." In May, the judge partially granted Hoech's motion to quash and limited the scope of the subpoena. Hoech had won the round. With renewed fervor he ripped the alliance between Williams & Connolly and the Justice Department and published that "the Fraud Office is lying for ADM, again." But his reputation was in ribbons and he would receive no further consulting work. On the brink of the Andreas and Wilson trial, ADM had shown that it would square debts, attack in court, and did not expect the government to block its way.

Before the trial, ADM also lost a decision in Delaware. Ajinomoto had sued for patent infringement of a bacterial strain capable of producing an amino acid called threonine, used in animal feeds. The result supported Whitacre's allegation that ADM had misappropriated biotechnologies besides lysine. But the Delaware ruling also foreshadowed a problem in the upcoming criminal trial. Would a jury believe that the defendants had conspired with Ajinomoto executives to fix the lysine market at the same time that ADM was cheating the Japanese?

PART II THE ROOTS

FROM ANDY'S FEED TO THE "SUPERMARKET TO THE WORLD"

*"The key to our success is to have enough plans
to invest our money the day we make it."*
—Dwayne O. Andreas

The history of ADM is really the marriage of two stories. One is the rise of a good but unexceptional midwestern seed processing company. The other is the saga of the Andreas family, a prosperous but not enormously wealthy Iowa clan. The synergy of the two resulted in a combination of wealth and power many orders of magnitude greater than their sum. Unlike most corporate monoliths, ADM never became faceless. Rather, in a way that it is all but unprecedented, the huge, modern, publicly traded company placed its control, identity, and destiny in the hands of one family.

In 1878, an Ohioan named John Daniels began commercially crushing flax seeds into linseed oil. It was not a revolutionary step. The yellowish drying fluid present in paint and varnish, linseed oil had been used since the time of Egyptians. But Daniels expanded production to a new level. In 1902, he moved the operation to Minneapolis and named it the Daniels Linseed Company. Much of the new plant's output was linseed cake, an animal feed. The following year, Charles Archer, the scion of a family that had been crushing flax since 1830, joined the firm that became known as Archer Daniels Linseed. They were a straitlaced penny-pinching pair who shared a spartan office and addressed one another as Mr. Archer and Mr. Daniels.

Unlike many founders, they knew their limitations and hired a professional manager, Samuel Mairs. He trimmed costs and implemented a philosophy of "year-round profits at low margins." Mairs put the company consistently in the black, enabling it to acquire processing firms including Midland Linseed, which resulted in the incorporation of Archer Daniels Midland in 1923. During the decade of the twenties it grew to nine mills and became the nation's leading producer of linseed oil, which it sold in numerous grades to manufacturers of soap, ink, paint, and varnish.

The company also built grain elevators on the Minneapolis riverfront. In 1927, it began a streak of paying dividends that lasted almost four decades. Archer and Daniels died in the early 1930s. Charles Archer's son Shreve became president and led the company profitably through the Depression. ADM acquired Commander Larrabee, a flour company with mills in Minnesota, Missouri, and Kansas. It also started crushing soybeans in Decatur, Illinois.

Historically, grain processors ran quite conservative businesses. ADM fit the mold with one exception. While most millers did not want to tamper with nature's bounty, Sam Mairs believed that agricultural products could be enhanced through chemistry. ADM broke with the industry by opening a research lab. The company adopted a slogan considered shocking at the time: "Creating New Values from America's Harvests."

During the 1930s, ADM came up with two breakthroughs. It developed edible soy protein. Also, it found a way to extract lecithin, a food and candy emulsifier, from soy oil. Through aggressive marketing, ADM's oils began to show up in drugs and brake fluids. The company sold compounds for paint drying, hardening, and glossing; made paper out of flax; processed whale oil into perfume; and listed assets of almost $23 million by the end of the 1930s.

A lull during World War II was followed by a resurgence between 1946-1949 when sales rose almost 300 precent. Bank debt was erased. ADM became the nation's number one soybean processor and climbed to fourth in flour milling. Conservative management continued to plow profits back into research and development.

In 1952, when ADM celebrated its fiftieth anniversary, it produced over 700 items. It served the food, feed, printing, gasoline, leather, ceramics, rubber, pharmaceuticals, and defense industries and owned plants in South America, Mexico, Holland, and Belgium. It had a whaling station in Peru (which closed in 1967) that killed and harvested two thousand animals a year mainly for cosmetics and automatic transmission fluid. Its castor oil was much in demand as an aircraft lubricant, and it had come into America's kitchens with a now-forgotten cake mix called Airy Fairy.

In 1959, Shreve Archer died and was succeeded by Thomas Daniels, also the son of a founder. A polo-playing Yale graduate who had done a stint in the foreign service, Daniels looked to lead the company into another prosperous decade.

In the early 1960s, ADM purchased new storage facilities and expanded grain processing. It widened its lead in soy protein, which promised to become a major meat extender and substitute. However, ADM's chemical operation lagged, and the company was buffeted by unstable commodities prices. Net earnings fell from $75 million in 1963 to $60 million in 1964 and then to $50 million in 1965, when for the first time the company canceled its dividend.

By now John H. Daniels, Thomas' son, was president of ADM. With director Shreve Archer, Jr., leader of the company's other dynastic wing, he invited the brothers Dwayne and Lowell Andreas to buy a large block of stock and essentially take control of operations.

The Andreas brothers had grown up on a farm near Lisbon, Iowa. In all, there were five sons and a daughter. Their parents, Reuben and Lydia Andreas, were industrious and self-sufficient Mennonites. In 1927, Reuben bought a grain elevator out of bankruptcy and began selling feeds that he and his sons mixed by hand from alfalfa, corn, soy, oats, and molasses. They called the business Andy's Feeds.

The fourth of the five brothers, Dwayne was short, dark, and wiry. He had a smile that could light up a room and a silver tongue that led his family to hope he would become a Mennonite preacher. On the farm he did his chores, including milking cows and slopping hogs, but preferred swapping yarns with the salesmen at the feed business. In school he was known as a scrappy guard on the basketball team and something of a rebel. When the coach got fired, Dwayne went on strike, and he was suspended to the chagrin of his father, who had prospered and become president of the school board. He was suspended again for turning in a book report on *Brave New World* by Aldous Huxley, which was considered scandalous by school officials.

After graduating from high school in 1934, he married, fathered a daughter, and attended Wheaton College, which trained ministers including Billy Graham. In less than two years, he had left the marriage, dropped out of college, and returned to the family business to head its sales effort.

The farm grossed over a million dollars at the height of the Depression. In 1936, it changed its name to Honeymead and moved to larger facilities in Cedar Rapids. The following year, at nineteen, Dwayne learned to fly and bought a plane to make sales calls on distant farmers. Sometimes he landed in fields where horse-drawn teams were plowing. Once, he crashed after flying into telephone wires but emerged unhurt.

In 1938, he convinced his father to expand into grain processing. Honeymead built the first soybean oil plant in the country. It also began to pelletize feeds. Even the smallest poultry pellets were known for being substantial enough not to be scattered by barnyard breezes. As Dwayne continued to sell and run the company's transportation arm, which included forty-five vehicles and a rail yard, his younger brother Lowell headed processing.

Dwayne also learned the arcane science of grain trading mainly from experts who sometimes happened to be Jewish. In an era of rampant isolationism and anti-Semitism in the rural Midwest, Andreas was free of prejudice and seemed genuinely to like the Jewish businessmen, a few of whom became his mentors. He became a patron of Jewish charitable organizations. Later, he would back racial harmony efforts, including Martin Luther King's Southern Christian Leadership Conference (SCLC), world hunger fighting initiatives, and a wide range of politicians and campaigns.

After Pearl Harbor, Dwayne won a draft deferment to support his young child. With his brother Lowell in the army, Dwayne ran Honeymead during the war years. In 1945, believing that he would finally be called up, the family sold 60 percent of Honeymead to Cargill, the grain trading and processing giant. Dwayne personally made about $1.5 million from the sale. He was twenty-seven.

World War II ended before Dwayne could be drafted. Cargill hired him as a manager. He rose to vice president in charge of soybeans and linseed oil. In 1948, he hired a brilliant twenty-year-old chemical engineer named James Randall, and the pair entered a long productive partnership.

In Minneapolis, Dwayne won a reputation as a freewheeling bachelor who roved the town in a Cadillac with a telephone on board, quite a novelty in the post-war years. In 1947, he met and married Inez Snyder, a petite blonde who was studying philosophy at the University of Minnesota and had a five-year-old daughter, Terry, from a previous marriage. Like Dwayne, Inez and Terry would become significant philanthropists. Inez's interests included education and politics. As an adult, Terry led an activist organization based in Cambridge, Massachusetts, that focused on international environmental issues such as rain forest depletion. Sally, Dwayne's daughter by his Catholic first wife, became devoted to Catholic charities and especially to the mission of Mother Theresa.

In 1948, he and Inez also had their only child, Michael Andreas. A bright, practical boy, Mick did not share his sisters' idealistic or spiritual bents. In Sunday school, he once defined a prophet as "what's left after you've paid your expenses." Later, he surprised no one by being the child who followed his father into the business.

In 1952, Dwayne left Cargill, which bought him out again, this time for $400,000. His initial investment of $1,500 in Honeymead had yielded nearly $2 million.

When the Andreases initially sold control of Honeymead to Cargill, they did not sell the name. Lowell had run the remains of Honeymead while Dwayne was at Cargill. Now they built up the company again. Its major facility was a soybean crushing plant in Mankato, Minnesota. Some doubted whether Honeymead could sell the huge output of its mill. But, the brothers negotiated highly favorable railroad rates, found markets abroad, and the operation thrived.

In 1960, the Andreases sold Honeymead again. This time the buyer was the Grain Terminal Association (GTA), the soybean business of a 100,000–member farmer's cooperative. The brothers made $10 million in the sale. Dwayne and Lowell were brought on to run GTA. Their contract gave them a share of GTA's substantial profits and made them seriously wealthy men.

In 1966, ADM was drifting. Its earnings had moved south for three years, and it no longer paid a dividend. ADM made the Andreas brothers an offer they couldn't refuse: the ability to buy 100,000 shares representing 6 percent of the company's equity at half of its book value.

Two other Andreas brothers had also prospered. Albert, who had given Honeymead its name long ago, was a grain trader with substantial cement interests. Glen Allen was a banker in Iowa. The eldest brother, Osborne, had left Andy's Feeds to play piano, teach English, and write books on Henry James and Joseph Conrad. On the brink of being tried for stock fraud in 1967 at the age of sixty-four, he committed suicide. Lenore, the only Andreas sister, was a Florida housewife who died in 1969.

The presence of Dwayne and Lowell Andreas on the board of the old-line, blue-blood ADM company scandalized some in the upper rungs of Minneapolis society. However, for the next three decades, an Archer and a Daniels would continue to sit on the board and usually on the executive committee.

Dwayne's behavior also raised eyebrows. He was at once secretive and flamboyant. Among his first acts was firing ADM's twenty-seven-member public relations department and placing the account with an outside agency. He began a career-long habit of personally approving advertising, especially the famous and sometimes high-brow spots for "The Supermarket to the World" that ran on political talk shows. "Sunday morning," wrote Michael Kinsley in the *New Republic*, "is dominated by a mysterious company that is virtually unknown except for its public affairs commercials."

Andreas also entertained lavishly. One party at his large lake house is still talked about by locals because he gave every guest a color television when black and white sets were the norm. He seemed to cultivate a Gatsbyish persona of wealth and influence and like Gatsby he was gone—in this case from Minnesota—before he was understood. By the end of the 1960s, he had transferred the headquarters to Decatur, Illinois, where the company processed soybeans. Decatur presented a better opportunity for the massive physical growth that he contemplated. Also it was farther from the prying eyes of big city media.

From his first day, Andreas revolutionized ADM. He saw the company's weaknesses and shed them. In 1967, he sold its flagging chemical business to Ashland Oil. He had a strong sense of the future. That same year he bought Fleishman Malting, which gave ADM a profitable toehold in the expanding beverage market.

In 1968, his power was formalized when he became chairman of the board and chief executive officer. His brother Lowell became president. Because of Dwayne's fondness for running things from the background, some observers thought the position was temporary and that he would soon recede from the spotlight. In fact, he would hold the reins for three decades.

In 1968, Dwayne won James Randall away from Cargill, where he had become the technical director. Andreas gave Randall an unprecedented opportunity to plan and run production in what would be the nation's biggest processing complex. Randall's reputation grew as he became the pre-eminent plant builder in agribusiness. If ADM sensed a market, Randall could hit it in a hurry with a turnkey facility cranking out high-grade products.

Randall succeeded Lowell Andreas as ADM's president in 1975. The survivor of a hard-scrabble childhood on a Wisconsin farm, he flaunted his wealth with luxury vehicles including his Ferrari, a rarity in Decatur. Also, his tendency to slash the work force gained him the nickname "Neutron Jim." But he stood fast for quality and favored bringing bright people into the company including numerous PhD's from top graduate programs, one of whom would be Mark Whitacre.

Dwayne Andreas was especially farsighted about soybeans. When he joined ADM, he noted its scientific lead over its competitors. He intended to use the advantage in the market as consumers demanded more protein.

Scientists at ADM wanted to develop an edible 100 percent protein product. Andreas favored a less expensive process, which produced a fifty percent blend called Textured Vegetable Protein (TVP). The chairman naturally prevailed. Afterwards he would say "Hell hath no fury like a scientist scorned."

The market responded well to TVP. In order to meet demand, ADM built a plant complex in Decatur to turn out all kinds of edible soy. By 1973, the plant's production had doubled. ADM still could not meet demand, and profit margins were high. Decatur expanded its facilities. ADM also built new TVP plants in Europe and South America. In the meantime, soy oil became the leading cooking oil.

In the early 1970s, ADM purchased Corn Sweetener Inc. Its product lines included corn oil, glutens (sticky fibers), caramel coloring, and, most important, high fructose corn syrup (HFCS), which promised to be as profitable as soy. Net earnings reached $117 million in 1973, more than twice what they had been when the company offered the Andreases the wheel. The shareholders were delighted. They did not seem to mind when Dwayne Andreas placed other Andreases in high positions heading divisions of ADM and on the board. By the 1980s there were four or five Andreas among the sixteen directors: Dwayne; Lowell, who headed the company's bank in Minneapolis; Michael, Dwayne's son; and Dwayne's older brother Albert; who sat on the board from 1972-1985 and initially ran the corn sweetener division. When Albert stepped down at seventy-eight, his son Martin succeeded him as head of sweeteners and on the board. During the decade, Dwayne's nephew G. Allen Andreas (his eventual successor) served as treasurer and later led European operations. There were so many Andreases in positions of power that Dwayne made a conscious decision not to carry the pictures of the directors and officers in the company's annual reports in order to prevent shareholders from becoming apprehensive about nepotism.

ADM rocketed through most of the 1980s. In 1981, it bought the Columbian Peanut Company and became the number one peanut sheller in the United States. In 1986, it acquired Growmark, a huge midwestern grain marketing and river terminal cooperative.

Energy and environmental policy also favored ADM, which became the world's leading producer of ethanol or grain alcohol. As a gasoline additive, corn-based ethanol claimed to reduce carbon monoxide emissions. Also, during an era when fuel was being deleaded, the product was found to raise octane levels.

ADM correctly foresaw that beverage giants including Coke, Pepsi, and Royal Crown would substitute HFCS for more expensive cane sugar. Its wet milling operation in Decatur, the largest in the world, could churn out the corn sweetener and ethanol interchangeably. The complex worked round the clock. By the end of the decade, overall sales reached $7.9 billion.

ADM's management also won praise. *Forbes* reported that the return on capital investment at ADM between 1984-1990 was 9.1 percent versus 6.8 percent at Cargill. In 1990, ADM ranked fifty-seventh on the Fortune 500 list, topping such household names as Borden, Campbell's Soup, and Heinz, companies that had previously dwarfed it.

In fact, ADM had become much bigger than its balance sheet reflected. During the 1980s, it acquired a 50 percent partnership in Alfred C. Toepfer International, often called ACTI. Toepfer was a global trading firm based in Hamburg with loading docks, elevators, and trading agents around the world as well as European and Asian mills. Its other half was owned by a consortium of fourteen cooperatives representing about 2 million farmers in the United States, Canada, the Netherlands, Germany, and France. The American co-ops included such well-known brands as Agway, Gold Kist, and Land O'Lakes. ACTI merchandised about 9 percent of the world's grain and 35 percent of all feeds.

The founder of ACTI, Alfred Toepfer was a legendary grain merchant whom Dwayne Andreas had met while still working at Cargill. During the encounter, the young Andreas brashly joked, "I may be the only man in captivity who can run your business when you retire." In 1983, at the age of eighty-eight, Toepfer joined the ADM Board and Mick Andreas, his father's heir apparent, became a director of ACTI.

The partnership in ACTI made ADM less of a domestic company and more of an international one. It now had a greater capacity to buy raw materials worldwide due to its relationship with the foreign co-ops who were partners. ADM also insulated itself from the hard dollar woes facing many American industries in the 1980s, which made its products competitive abroad.

Perhaps above all ACTI positioned ADM to take advantage of the lucrative and increasingly borderless European common market. ADM took a major stride in this direction by buying and developing the Europoort, a massive manmade peninsula that juts into the river mouth at Rotterdam and looks like a star base. Crisscrossed with transport, refining, and milling facilities, it also includes the world's largest soybean processing complex. It is difficult to quantify the dollar gain from ACTI. Another anomaly of ADM's annual report is that it does not list ACTI income in its balance sheet. Occasionally, however, ADM will issue a glowing and vague statement, such as this one from the 1993 report: "The partnership has over two million members and the combined revenues of the cooperatives, ADM, and Toepfer exceeds $70 billion (US)."

In the early 1990s, ADM got a boost from the Iraqi invasion of Kuwait, which stimulated ethanol sales. ADM had 70 percent of the US market. The company's balance sheet was strong, prompting *Fortune* to run "On How the Money Grows at ADM." The company seemed immune from the recession of the period. It plowed profits into modernizing plants. A total of $1.4 billion was spent to bring new production facilities on stream. The corporate dividend was low, only ten cents per share. But, Dwayne Andreas had no trouble justifying it to shareholders. "The key to our success is to have enough plans to invest our money the day we make it."

The company was not only rich, it was flexible and creative. It understood market nuances and responded to them. ADM anticipated surging demands for pasta; poultry; low calorie sweeteners; pet foods; processed vegetarian meals; high-fiber foods; hydroponic vegetables; farm-bred fish; degradable plastics made with starches; cattle feeds conducive to meat with less fat; canola oil; veggie burgers; biological as opposed to chemical insecticides; and high protein foods, such as soy milk that did not require refrigeration for consumption mainly in underdeveloped countries. ADM's co-generation power plants cleanly burned used tires and high sulfur midwestern coal. Its publicized campaigns to rationalize futures markets also have been lauded. It continued to grow economically and technologically. Its annual sales now top $16 billion. According to its 1999 annual report, it has about 355 processing plants, 500 grain elevators, 2,250 barges, 13,000 railroad cars, and over 100 oceangoing ships. Everyday its plants are serviced by 15,000 trucks. It is the number one transportation buyer in the United States, and its home base in Decatur is the largest agricultural plant complex in the world.

It remains the world leader in the processing of corn, America's biggest cash crop, and an international force in a host of other grains. In fact, no company in the world processes more oil seeds, produces more soy protein or ethanol, or rivals ADM's overall grain fermentation business.

Its advertising rings with indictments of world hunger and bursts with plans to quell it. Its annual reports read like *Prevention Magazine* when describing the company's major commitment to producing health enhancers that it calls "nutraceuticals" including antioxidants such as vitamins C and E, choline-rich granular lecithin that boosts memory and may fight Alzheimer's disease, soy isoflavones that strengthen the immunity to disease, and complex sugars called oligosaccharides that may prevent colon cancer. In many ways, it was an admirable if enigmatic company, not an operation that one might expect to see raided by the FBI and ensnarled in criminal cases. So what went wrong?

ADM: POLITICS, MONEY, AND TROUBLE

"[W]hen it comes to agriculture there is no such thing as a free market."
—Dwayne O. Andreas

Among the most political of companies, ADM makes its influence felt in myriad ways from lobbying through trade associations to providing direct and "soft money" contributions in electoral campaigns to its pervasive commercials on the Sunday morning talk shows watched and performed on by policymakers. However, for three decades its most effective leverage was applied by Dwayne Andreas, a political as well as sales genius enormously skilled at listening, speaking, stroking, partying, and paying in the corridors of power. Probably no one since the trust chieftains of the late nineteenth and early twentieth centuries has drawn more on the connection between business and politics or done as much to cultivate governments and officials.

In 1990, *Fortune* called agribusiness "the most manipulated industry on the planet" and calculated that governments of the industrialized countries annually pump a quarter of a trillion dollars into subsidies, quotas, and set-asides of fertile land. "How the hell," argued Dwayne Andreas, "could you run a business like mine if you don't have communications with the people who make the decisions?" To that end, ADM has sought constant contact in the White House, in Congress, in state houses, in foreign capitals, and at the United Nations. In the case of the latter, in 1962 ADM, on a tip from then-UN Ambassador Adlai Stevenson, purchased a suite in New York's Waldorf Towers next to the official residence of the United States' Mission, which allowed Andreas to befriend every American UN ambassador from Stevenson to ex-Atlanta mayor Andrew Young, who became an ADM board member, to George Bush. It also provided ADM with access to foreign diplomats whose countries could be convinced to import grain or to invite American companies to build processing plants.

The fascination with politics not only emboldened Andreas and later ADM but led them to the edge of acceptable behavior and sometimes beyond it. In fact, his political bent cost him his first high perch in corporate agribusiness. Then a brash young vice president at Cargill, Andreas became intrigued by the Soviet Union and its potential markets.

In particular, he hoped to sell off vegetable oil to the Soviets. In 1952, at the peak of the Korean War, he used contacts in Washington to obtain a rare visa for travel to a trade fair in Moscow. Cargill, however, refused to give Andreas permission to attend. When he went anyway, attached to a French delegation, Cargill asked for and obtained his resignation.

Despite his reduced stature in the agribusiness world (he was back at Honeymead), Andreas managed to gain access to President Eisenhower. In a private meeting, the two discussed the goal of selling food to the Soviets. According to Andreas, the president offered, "I'm for selling them anything they can't shoot back." So were the American farmers who had significant surpluses on their hands throughout the fifties. But the issue of feeding the enemy stirred emotions. A famous headline of the era blared: "No Butter for Boris." Understandably, Andreas worried about the reaction of Senator Joseph McCarthy, the anticommunist demagogue. However, Vice President Nixon, the senator's ally, reminded Andreas that McCarthy came from Wisconsin, a farm state. In fact, McCarthy promised Andreas not to blast trade with Russia so long as it included his constituents' dairy products.

Soon the administration and farmers wanted to broaden sales to the rest of Eastern Europe. Eisenhower believed that less political friction would result if Democrats (rather than Republicans), businessmen, and the Catholic Church publicly took the lead on food exports. In 1954, he induced Senator Humphrey of Minnesota to make a trip to Poland and the Vatican regarding the opening of Iron Curtain markets. Recognizing Andreas' sales skills, the president also asked him to join the junket, which proved successful in large measure because of the chemistry between the two Minnesotans.

While still at Cargill in 1945, Andreas met Hubert Humphrey but made little impression on the liberal Minneapolis mayor. Three years later, Humphrey ran for the Senate. Andreas got a strong reaction from the candidate by leaving $1,000, then a huge contribution, with a campaign staffer who later recalled, "Hubert was aghast and wanted to know: who is this guy?" Soon Humphrey and Andreas became fast friends and traveling companions. They would take eighty trips together during the next twenty-five years.

Their wives and children also became close. Andreas chose Humphrey as godfather to his son Mick. As teens, Mick and Humphrey's son Douglas served as Senate pages together. As vice president in 1965, Humphrey named Andreas to handle his blind trust, a portfolio set up without a public official's specific knowledge so it does not appear that he favors companies whose stock he holds.

Andreas became a major contributor to Humphrey's state and national campaigns and introduced the senator to a stream of wealthy donors in agribusiness and other industries. In addition, he gave Humphrey a lakeside vacation home outright. Andreas endowed a $10,000 prize for civil liberties in Humphrey's name and made the senator the first recipient. Also, while neighbors in Minnesota, the two scheduled a regular golf game. Avid about the sport, Andreas played well. Humphrey disliked the game and hacked erratically. During their rounds, the pair often bet a hundred dollars a hole, hefty stakes in the fifties. Somehow Andreas managed to lose a lot. Of course, Humphrey's winnings did not have to be reported as political contributions.

In turn, the senator doted on his friend. When Andreas wanted a bigger base than the Honeymead family business, Humphrey's connections to the GTA cooperative proved useful to Andreas. GTA bought Honeymead and installed him as executive vice president. Due to the strong Democratic Farm-Labor Party roots and anti-laissez fair outlook of the co-op, the installation of the high-rolling entrepreneur seemed incongruous to some Minnesotans. Andreas' eventual $10 million buyout by GTA coupled with the earlier Cargill settlement formed the basis for the stake that he later would use to take over ADM.

In the fifties and sixties, Humphrey took Andreas on official foreign trips, in particular to leftist and developing nations, billing his friend "an advisor to the Department of Agriculture and specialist in the problems of Public Law 480," the Agricultural Trade Development and Assistance Act of 1954. Generally known as the Food for Peace program, P.L. 480 obligated the US Treasury to guarantee payments for food exports when foreign buyers defaulted. Enormously popular with domestic agribusiness, Food for Peace became mired in controversy. It eased hunger in some of the world's most destitute areas. But in some countries the program undermined farmers who could not compete against imported food at near-giveaway prices, stopped coming to market, and occasionally rioted. Food for Peace also delayed and frustrated land reform, indigenous investment, and rational pricing, as in India during the fifties and sixties when widespread wheat dumping bankrupted thousands of farmers. At times the program became blind to its original purpose, as when it shipped foods that were not accepted in local cultures or insisted that a country absorb a locally plentiful grain or risk being cut off from the program altogether. Regardless, Andreas and Humphrey profited. Domestic agribusiness, including Andreas' companies, shipped a flood of food abroad. Andreas educated Humphrey on the arcane worlds of currency and commodity markets. Humphrey strengthened his political base in the heartland among farmers, processors, and cooperatives.

When Humphrey ran for president in 1968, Andreas became a key financial supporter and took on high-level tasks, such as feeling out David Rockefeller about becoming secretary of the treasury in a Democratic administration. The banker was noncommittal. Some supporters, including Robert Strauss, the former Democratic National Committee chairman, have insisted that Andreas would have had a place in the cabinet if Humphrey had won. Humphrey and Andreas spent election night in 1968 at Andreas' Minnesota home watching the vice president lose to Richard Nixon. After the election, Humphrey re-entered the Senate and became a reliable backer of positions favorable to ADM.

Thomas Dewey, the former Republican presidential candidate and governor of New York, arranged an invitation for Andreas to attend Nixon's inaugural. Dewey and Andreas had been close for years. In fact Andreas had introduced Dewey to Harry Truman during the 1948 presidential contest. A proponent of consensus building regarding food, farm, and export issues, Andreas had a penchant for backing political opponents financially—a custom called "slopping both hogs" in the Midwest—and even for getting them to relax and socialize together. Because the friction between Republican and Democratic Farm-Labor parties was sharper and more ideological (along capitalist/socialist lines) than the partisan rivalries in most states, it surprised Minnesotans that Andreas entertained Humphrey and Republicans simultaneously.

The habit of putting political opposites together became most pronounced at the Andreas complex of penthouses and apartments in the Sea View Hotel, a resort in Bal Harbor, Florida. Humphrey and Dewey visited frequently and, according to Andreas, became great friends. Bob Dole, then Republican Senate minority leader, and Democratic House Speaker Tip O'Neill bought units, as did Robert Strauss and television commentator David Brinkley, whose Sunday political show ADM sponsored.

During the early fifties, the relationship between Dewey and Andreas, the Cargill vice president, ripened over golf, fishing, and the high protein content of soybeans about which both were passionate. Dewey bought soybeans to bake in the bread of the New York prison system. After Dewey left government in 1954, he became a corporate lawyer known for extensive international contacts. Andreas installed him as principal spokesman and special counsel to the National Soybean Processors Association and put him in charge of handling the Andreas children's trust funds. The pair traveled the world, and Andreas made use of Dewey's entrée in foreign capitals, especially those in the hands of conservatives who would not have been as friendly to Humphrey. Most notably Dewey introduced Andreas to Francisco Franco, the Spanish dictator, which resulted in an end to Spain's complete dependence on local olive oil and the importation of American soybean oil for cooking. In 1971 Dewey collapsed after a round of golf in Florida with Andreas, who found him dead in his room at the Sea View Hotel. Andreas transported the body to New York on the ADM plane and became one of the pall bearers. He also donated 3,500 shares of ADM stock—then valued at $101,500—in Dewey's honor to a fund drive headed by Governor Nelson Rockefeller to refurbish the Capital Hill Club, the Republicans' posh preserve in Washington, DC, and thereby gained membership.

In 1972, *Parade* listed Andreas among the thirty most powerful Americans. During the 1972 election year, Andreas' circle overtly donated about $400,000 to the presidential campaigns of Humphrey and Nixon. These donors included Dwayne, Lowell, Paul Thatcher (the family money manager), National City Bank of Minneapolis, (a unit of ADM) and Michael Andreas, twenty-three, who appeared on the political radar screen with an $11,000 gift for Nixon but nothing for his godfather Hubert Humphrey.

Dwayne Andreas also became linked with Watergate, the web of related scandals that surfaced on June 17, 1972 with the botched break-in of the Democratic National Committee's headquarters. The White House quickly denied any knowledge of the crime that President Nixon termed a "third rate burglary" and "bizarre." The seven suspects carried new hundred dollar bills, electronic equipment, and had shadowy backgrounds. One of the burglars, Bernard Barker, fifty-five, a Cuban-born American citizen, had fought against Batista during the island's revolution, then broke with Castro, fled to Florida, joined the Bay of Pigs invasion, and had worked with the CIA for eleven years.

The first tie between Watergate and the White House arose from records of Barker cashing two large checks totaling $114,000 through his Florida bank account shortly before the break-in. One, for $89,000, came from a Mexican bank. The other, a Florida cashier's check for $25,000, bore the signature of Kenneth H. Dahlberg, chairman of the Minnesota Committee to Re-Elect the President.

When Dahlberg revealed that the money had come from a Nixon supporter whom he refused to name, the scandal began to boil with questions of who actually financed Watergate. The Justice Department under Attorney General Richard Kleindienst, a Nixon loyalist, declined to pursue the matter. The FBI, under the caretaker leadership of L. Patrick Gray, obeyed a White House request not to get involved because tracking the Dahlberg check supposedly would compromise CIA secrets. However, the Florida state attorney subpoenaed Dahlberg to a deposition where he testified that the $25,000 came from Dwayne Andreas. The Nixon campaign then explained that due to Andreas' close relationship to Senator Humphrey, it had attempted to preserve his anonymity in order to spare him embarrassment.

Dahlberg also appeared at the first Watergate trial, a brief affair in Florida before the 1972 election. The state attorney accused Barker of misusing a notary seal to cash Dahlberg's check and convicted him. The trial, a historical footnote, resulted in the first Watergate sentence, sixty days, which the judge suspended.

The Andreas money shocked many who knew of the closeness between the ADM chief and Humphrey. The Nixon campaign played down the implication of disloyalty. Republican Finance Committee chairman Maurice Stans argued that "Andreas believed that either man [Humphrey or Nixon] would have made a good president for the country."

The larger questions involved legality. Congress recently had enacted the first major federal election reform law in forty-six years. It ordered campaigns to report the names of donors making large contributions after April 7, 1972. Kenneth Dahlberg had dated the check April 10, 1972. The Nixon campaign received it the following day. In August 1972, the General Accounting Office (GAO), an independent arm of Congress, referred matters to the Justice Department for possible criminal prosecution. One pertained to the use of campaign money for the expenses of G. Gordon Liddy, leader of the campaign's lawbreaking "plumbers." The others involved the Andreas money that had been received after April 7 but had not been reported. Moreover, the $25,000 had been blended into an unregulated, unreported "slush" fund of $350,000, whose contributors included Robert Vesco, the rogue financier then under investigation for securities violations, and Robert Allen, the president of Gulf Resources, a Texas energy company with an Environmental Protection Agency (EPA) problem.

As for Andreas, then as in 1995, his company found itself under investigation by the antitrust division of the Justice Department. At the time Andreas also sought a federal charter for a new bank to be built in a suburban Minnesota mall. His partner in this venture happened to be Kenneth Dahlberg, the Republican fund-raiser who had solicited his $25,000. Evidently, on February 9, 1972 (well before the end of Humphrey's candidacy), Andreas promised Dahlberg $25,000 for Nixon at his bank's board meeting, held at the Sea View Hotel. On March 15, 1972, Andreas stashed $25,000 in cash in a hotel safe deposit box in Dahlberg's name.

As the new campaign law's deadline approached, the Republicans became eager to collect as many large contributions as they could without having to report them. On April 7, Dahlberg appeared at the Sea View, but the vault was closed. Andreas passed him the cash on a golf course two days later. Dahlberg felt uneasy about traveling with a box of bills, so he converted the cash to a cashier's check the next day and gave it to Maurice Stans on April 11, 1972. The Dahlberg check next went to G. Gordon Liddy, who had Barker re-cash it in Florida, and the proceeds wound up with the Watergate burglars.

The Republican campaign took the position that neither it nor Andreas had done anything illegal because the money had been *pledged* well before the April 7, 1972 deadline. The Justice Department declined to prosecute. Justice's antitrust investigation of ADM also went into limbo. However, the government granted the bank charter to Andreas and Dahlberg within eighty-six days, which critics regarded as unusually quick especially considering that the shopping mall would not be built for two more years. Nixon's controller of the currency, William B. Camp, defended the quick approval by noting that fifty applications out of a total of 424 during the past five years had been granted in less than a hundred days. The explanation failed to please House Banking Committee Chairman Wright Patman, who found the rapid processing of the Andreas-Dahlberg project inappropriate since two other groups were competing for the same charter at the mall. Moreover, the Andreas charter was granted two days before a hearing was scheduled on one of the rival group's applications. The hearing never occurred, and the competitors' charter applications were automatically dropped.

The other Nixon supporters, whose contributions had gone into the slush fund, also received favorable attention. The EPA backed off Robert Allen's environmental problem. Vesco was treated so well that Stans and former Attorney General John Mitchell were indicted for conspiring to obstruct justice and making false statements to a grand jury. Vesco, who became a fugitive living in Costa Rica and Cuba, never faced trial.

As the Watergate crisis simmered before the 1972 election, the Republicans created strategies to contain it. One involved Dwayne Andreas. After the June break-in, Lawrence O'Brien, the chairman of the DNC, and others filed a lawsuit against the Committee to Re-elect the President, popularly known as CREEP, chaired by John Mitchell. The White House wanted the case stopped to prevent it from uncovering and disgorging damaging information. John Erlichman, the president's domestic advisor, induced the IRS to investigate O'Brien. The audit produced evidence that O'Brien had a six-figure income in excess of his salary from the DNC. As John Dean, the White House counsel, wrote in his 1976 memoir of the period, *Blind Ambition*, Mitchell then decided on a plan to call Andreas "to tell him to pass the word to Mr. O'Brien that we might find a way to end the nuisance of his tax problem if we can find some way to end the nuisance of his lawsuit. I think he'll realize that this might be a very satisfactory solution to a tough problem for everyone."

A few days later, according to Dean, Mitchell revealed, "I called Andreas and he told me that O'Brien is interested in working something out, but can't do anything. He says the lawsuit is beyond his own control, because he's got so many co-plaintiffs in with him, the Democratic co-chairman and so forth. He can't make a move by himself so that's out." As it happened, a federal judge feared that the litigation could prejudice the rights of Watergate criminal defendants, including Liddy, to a fair trial and halted the O'Brien suit. As an aside, evidence exists that Mitchell did not completely trust Dwayne Andreas, due to his association with Humphrey. The attorney general had considered bugging Andreas' hotel suite even before the break-in of O'Brien's office.

The O'Brien-Andreas connection came up again during Senate hearings the following year when John Erlichman testified that O'Brien had been on Dwayne Andreas' "payroll" and was under Andreas' pressure to make a compromise settlement. Erlichman also testified that O'Brien's successor as the Democratic National Committee chairman, Robert Strauss, also wanted to settle. O'Brien denied the story. Strauss did not. As it happens, the suit was eventually settled quietly.

In 1972, the White House used its clout to prevent Andreas from being investigated by the House Banking and Currency Committee whose chairman, Wright Patman, seventy-nine, a Texas populist, was one of only six white congressmen on the infamous Nixon enemies list. The Patman committee aimed to investigate whether the transfers of the Dahlberg and Mexican money caused criminal banking violations. It questioned whether the bank charter in Minnesota was awarded unlawfully as "a quid pro quo" for the political contribution. Patman sought to hold televised hearings and asked his committee to approve subpoena power to pull in Andreas, Dahlberg, John Dean, John Mitchell, and others.

The still intact White House put on a full-court press to prevent the Patman hearings. It won unanimous support from the committee's Republicans and from five southern Democrats, as well as the vote of New York Democrat Frank Brasco, whose grand jury investigation for bribery the Justice Department suspended (Brasco would be convicted in 1974). The hearings, which would have occurred before the 1972 election and could have affected it, were voted down 20-15. Before Nixon resigned in 1974, the quid pro quo for the charter was considered by the House of Representatives among the particulars on which to impeach the president.

Ironically, when Dwayne Andreas finally was indicted by Watergate Special Prosecutor Archibald Cox in 1973, the allegation had nothing to do with the $25,000 cash contribution or the bank charter. Cox's charges, filed in Minneapolis federal court, claimed that Andreas had consented to four separate illegal $25,000 contributions to the 1968 Humphrey-Muskie campaign through a company known at the time as First Interoceanic Corporation that Andreas controlled. Then as now, campaign contributions by corporations violated federal electoral law. The charges in Minneapolis each carried a potential one-year sentence and a $1,000 fine and were the only ones lodged against 1968 campaign transactions.

Seldom accessible to the press, the mysterious Andreas could not be reached for comment, but Humphrey immediately issued a strong statement on behalf of his "long-time close personal friend and supporter. I know through many years of being associated with him that he would not knowingly violate any law. He is a highly respected member of our community and a man held in high esteem by his associates in business, and civic life." Because the allegations involving Andreas dealt with the Democratic campaign, they enhanced the reputation for even-handedness of Special Prosecutor Archibald Cox. However, Cox personally did not get to see the Minnesota matter through to completion. Due to his dogged efforts to assemble Watergate evidence even if it led to the president, Cox lost his job on October 20, 1973 in the infamous "Saturday Night Massacre."

The Justice Department continued to handle the case against Andreas, but the effort seemed to lack fire. On one occasion, the trial was postponed because the defendant was in Europe. Nor did Andreas show up for the eventual proceedings in July 1974, where, for reasons that remain unclear, the government neither pressed for his presence nor demanded a jury trial. Andreas' lawyer, the eminent Edward Bennett Williams, perhaps the country's ablest advocate of accused politicians, argued that the disputed funds actually constituted loans from the corporation to Andreas, whom the Minnesota judge then acquitted without a word of witness testimony. Of all those caught in the web of the Watergate legal system, only two of those who stood trial—former Texas governor John Connolly and Andreas— emerged unscathed, unsentenced, and unfined. Both secured acquittals with Edward Bennett Williams, whose Washington firm, Williams & Connolly, often would counsel ADM in the future.

The Watergate era buffed Andreas' reputation for having nine lives, liquidity, influence, and a taste for secrecy. In 1974, a Senate Watergate report also raised concerns about $362,000 in ADM stock donated to Humphrey's 1972 primary campaigns. No charges resulted. The Senate committee could not get to the bottom of the dense maneuvers.

The committee revealed that Humphrey's blind trust acquired 2,500 ADM shares in 1969 that landed in Humphrey's campaign in 1972. The Senate could not detect where the stock came from or how much if anything it cost the trust. Through a spokesman, the Humphrey "family" consistently denied that Andreas gave them gifts of ADM stock.

Andreas' role in Watergate came up again in 1996, when a deposition transcript from President Nixon's secretary, the late Rosemary Woods, was released. In it she recalled that during a 1972 visit to the White House, Andreas left an envelope containing $100,000 in cash. The cash spent a year in the White House. Then Nixon, under siege from investigators, gave Andreas back the money.

In the fall of 1997, the scholar Stanley Kutler published transcripts of 201 hours of previously unreleased White House tapes. The dialogues of July 25 and August 1, 1972, between Nixon and his chief of staff H. R. Haldeman dealt with the boxed cash, then about $300,000, including Andreas' $100,000. But, as Haldeman put it on July 25, 1972, "We can get all we want." The purpose of the money according to the aide on August 1, 1972 was "to make sure there's no discontent in the ranks," of those who had been arrested. Nixon was equally clear. "That's what the money is for. . . . They have to be paid."

Did Andreas bring the president hush money intended to help keep Nixon in power and prevent the Watergate story from coming out? Regardless, Andreas' hand-off of $100,000 to the president, or any public servant, flies in the face of a one person/one vote democracy.

After Watergate, Andreas' money figured in another scandal. In 1978 Hubert Humphrey died, and President Carter appointed the Minnesota senator's long-time chief aide David Gartner to one of five seats on the Commodity Futures Trading Commission (CFTC). When it came out that the Andreas family recently had given Gartner's children ADM stock worth $72,000, a furor erupted.

Created by Congress in 1975, the CFTC, as an independent agency, succeeded the Commodity Exchange Authority (CEA), a unit of the Department of Agriculture. Unlike the Securities Exchange Commission (SEC) that had played an aggressive watchdog role since its Depression-era birth, the CEA "was seen as the handmaiden of the exchanges," in the words of agribusiness historian Wayne Broehl. One such exchange would be the Chicago Board of Trade, whose frenetic grain pits, wild speculation, client-skimming, and market-cornering made the stock and bond markets seem pure by comparison.

Like other major processors, ADM used the CFTC-regulated futures markets heavily, which allowed the company to lock in the prices of grains and other crops. President Carter, who did not know Gartner personally, had appointed him on the recommendation of Vice President Walter Mondale, another former Minnesota senator.

Quick to come to his own defense, Gartner revealed that the Carter administration had been aware of the ADM stock before making the nomination. The *New York Times* editorialized against the Andreas-Gartner connection as "too close for public comfort" and in favor of Gartner's resignation, which Carter requested. But the president lacked the power to fire Gartner because of the CFTC's independent regulatory status.

Gartner refused to acknowledge any conflict of interest insisting that "the CFTC has no more effect on the price of soybeans or soybean futures than the SEC does on the price of GM stock." Nevertheless he agreed to sell the ADM stock and to stay out of all matters involving the company. He and his allies also maintained that most of the commission's work involved general rule-making, not affecting processors so much as traders. But a big part of ADM's operation and bottom line involved making constant trades to achieve favorable prices on raw commodities that the company bought, as well as on certain exchange-traded finished products, such as the soy oil it sold.

As it happened, Michael Andreas owned a seat on the Chicago Board of Trade, which he bought from his father in 1970, and Dwayne Andreas had acquired sizable interests in a handful of commodity trading firms in Illinois and Iowa. The scandal continued to swirl amid revelations that the Minneapolis National City Bank, for which Andreas had secured a charter during Watergate, had lent money to Gartner without demanding collateral. Following the loans and stock gifts, Gartner, while still Humphrey's aide, wrote a letter over the senator's signature to the Department of Agriculture arguing in favor of the high sugar tariffs, a position in step with ADM's interests. Again questions arose about a quid pro quo, but Gartner had a ready answer. His goal had not been to benefit ADM but Minnesota sugar beet farmers. Gartner served out the balance of his term under a cloud. Dwayne Andreas maintained that when the ADM stock went to Gartner's family, "I never dreamed he'd have that kind of job."

Initially high hopes existed for the new CFTC. But in the early years, the understaffed body hardly rippled the surface of the complex industry. Responding to criticism, its jovial first chairman William Balsey would say he had less police at his disposal than Rockville, Maryland had. In particular, the CFTC came in for criticism for not dealing with a new structural problem that arose in the 1980s when large grain companies, including ADM and Cargill, began opening divisions that traded for the public. ADM Investor Services bought ten seats at the Chicago Board of Trade. Representing the public, at least theoretically, could lead to conflicts of interest especially if the deals done by the trading subsidiaries were made with an eye to benefiting the parent company rather than the private client. Wayne Broehl has also pointed out a potential conflict if the subsidiary traded in opposition to the parent's objectives.

In 1988 the Board of Trade, through its Business Conduct Committee, began investigating allegations that the ADM traders had manipulated the price of soy oil. The panel asked to meet with Mick Andreas, who refused on the advice of lawyers, though he volunteered to speak with the CFTC in Washington. No evidence indicates that the weak federal agency took him up on the offer or otherwise confronted him about the allegations. The Chicago Board however responded by fining Mick Andreas $25,000. The young man gloated over it, "I was kind of proud. It was the largest fine up to then ever."

What happened next greatly added to ADM's reputation for power, vengeance, and influence with the government. For two years ADM trained FBI agents on its trading floor in Decatur in the labyrinthine practices, jargon, signals, customs, calculations, and other intricacies of the commodities business. Two of the agents assumed false identities, worked for a time at ADM Investor Services, then quit and struck out on their own. Each purchased a half million dollar seat on the Chicago Board of Trade, a lavish apartment, and the trappings of a high-rolling lifestyle, including a new Mercedes Benz and a Rolex. In an ironic preview of Whitacre's espionage, they used microphones embedded in jewelry and fountain pens to record mischief, including boasting by fellow traders of overcharging clients, recording false times of deals (prices can change by the minute), and not giving clients their full shares of proceeds. The sting operation known as Operation Sourmash netted forty-six indictments for racketeering and related charges. When asked if ADM's training of FBI agents amounted to a payback for the board's treatment of his son, Dwayne Andreas responded wryly, "All [the FBI] did was to ask us to plant a couple guys in our company. What kind of a citizen wouldn't do that?"

Before the Decatur raid, ADM also had cemented its ties to political leaders of all stripes. From 1980 through 1995, ADM and Andreas family interests gave almost four million dollars to Democrats and Republicans with the balance tipping slightly towards the latter.

During the 1996 presidential election, ADM gave $295,000 in soft money to Democratic party committees and $405,000 to Republican party committees. However, this didn't tell the whole story. In 1994, a $100,000 ADM check supported a Clinton presidential dinner. In 1992, ADM wrote a check for $400,000 for a Bush dinner. Dwayne Andreas and his wife gave $10,000 to Clinton's transition team after the 1992 election and $70,000 to Newt Gingrich's Political Action Committee (GOPAC), which mobilized for the 1994 midterm election. Both Illinois senators and numerous other legislators, especially from the farm belt, benefitted from ADM's largesse. In addition, ADM has its own PAC that supports key politicians.

But ADM did not simply support politicians, it celebrated and nurtured them long after their service. Andreas built a statue to Reagan in Decatur, organized Democratic House Speaker Tip O'Neill's retirement dinner, donated $1 million to the Nixon library, bought Jimmy Carter's floundering peanut farm for $1.5 million, and gave another million to Habitat for Humanity when Carter became associated with the nonprofit home builder. Loyalist Robert Strauss won legal work and a seat on the ADM board seat after his government service. Andreas friend David Brinkley got a position flacking for ADM after his retirement. (Ironically, the first ad that Brinkley made was so vague about whether it was conveying news or selling a product that ABC-TV banned it.)

Probably no legislator had toed the ADM line with more fealty than Bob Dole. In addition to hefty campaign financial support, Dole and his wife Elizabeth bought a Sea View condominium from Andreas at a below market price. The Doles and Andreases gave an annual party at the Sea View. Andreas also gave Dole's foundation $300,000 and contributed $1 million to the Red Cross when Elizabeth Dole became the president. Bob Dole also notoriously campaigned on the ADM jet, paying the price of a first-class ticket. If he had won the presidency, Sea View would have become the "Winter White House," much as Bebe Rebozo's Key Biscayne villa became Nixon's getaway.

ADM treats politicians well because of its businesses. A persistent political concern of ADM involves sugar, which at first seems unimportant for a company that processes grain. Price protection in the form of tariffs keeps foreign sugar out of US markets and doubles domestic prices. Among the most criticized programs in Washington, sugar support deprives the treasury of about $1.5 billion per year and costs consumers approximately $3 billion per year or $60 for a family of four. Granulated sugar remains a household staple for cooking, baking, and sweetening. The anticompetitive overcharge is most burdensome for those who have limited budgets for food, including the poor and people on fixed incomes. Thus, it resembles a regressive sales tax and enrages consumer advocates. Environmentalists fault the tariff for promoting sugar cane cultivation in South Florida that disrupts the delicate Everglades ecosystem with runoff from fertilizers. Major sugar producers favor the program not only because it insures high prices, but also because 40 percent of the treasury's loss goes to the largest 1 percent of cane plantations and annually hands at least $1 million to each of the thirty-three largest US sugar farmers.

Why does such a skewed law exist, and how can it survive? The principal answer derives from corn, the nation's number one cash crop. ADM uses enzymes to distill a sweetener from corn starch called high fructose corn syrup (HFCS). Producing it costs substantially more than refining cane sugar. But with sugar price supports, high fructose costs about thirty percent less than sugar. The corn sweetener largely has replaced sugar in the soft drink industry.

As the leading and low-cost maker of HFCS, ADM has grabbed a dominant share of the soft drink market. The company likes to pretend that HCFC's quality rather than protectionism accounts for its success. Dwayne Andreas tells a colorful story about causing Pepsi to drop sugar by describing to its chairman how rats thrive in the holds of sugar freighters and urinate in the product, turning it yellow.

But the real bottom line is still the price of sugar and how the bipartisan farm bloc labors to preserve the supports. ADM plays big roles in their efforts, sometimes lobbying through trade groups such as the American Sugar Association, which printed false newspaper ads claiming that Americans pay less for refined sugar than do Brazilians and Russians. The *Washington Post* exposed the ads as frauds when it showed that the American prices were based on pounds, while the other countries' figures were computed in kilograms, making claims about cheaper sugar for Americans blatantly false. Moreover, each dollar of profit ADM achieves from HFCS costs the taxpayers ten. In keeping with its tendency to hedge and to be poised if the political pendulum swings, ADM owns 8 percent of Tate & Lyle, a British sugar refiner. But Tate & Lyle owns A.E. Staley, the second-leading US high fructose maker, which like ADM is based in Decatur. Cozily interlocked to the point of incestuousness and propped up by government, agribusiness understandably lacks a reputation for letting markets run free either in this country or abroad.

ADM's interests generally coincide with those of other American agribusinesses, but not always. For instance, as a processor, it favors cheap soybeans and other raw materials and dislikes certain domestic strategies that elevate prices, such as paying farmers not to grow crops. On other issues when ADM is in sync with the great body of American agriculture, the company lobbies through trade associations that it helps to finance. When possible, ADM prefers to let farmers hog the television cameras and handle the legislative arm-twisting. However, when the issues are sufficiently important to ADM, its contributions and personal ties to political leaders often carry the day.

As in the Food for Peace effort, ADM took the lead in the Department of Agriculture's Export Enhancement Program, a system of advancing credits to foreign buyers that lowers the prices of farm products that they purchase. Between 1985 and 1995, the program resulted in additional earnings of about $130 million to ADM. In 1995, Andreas testified to the Senate in favor of continuing the credits, on behalf of a group called the Coalition to Promote US Agricultural Exports, and warned that without the enhancement American grain would rot in silos, and could not compete abroad since foreign governments shore up local farmers with subsidies. "Let me tell you," insisted Andreas, "when it comes to agriculture there is no such thing as a free market."

Until the fall of Communism, ADM continued to champion subsidized trade with the Soviets during the remainder of the Cold War. Andreas and his family liked dealing with the Russians who reliably paid their bills. Washington and Moscow made it possible for Andreas to go to Russia at will.

Indeed the ADM jet became one of only two aircraft permitted to penetrate Soviet airspace without an escort. The other belonged to Armand Hammer, the president of Occidental Petroleum, whose ties to the Soviets dated back to Lenin. Received with warmth in the Kremlin, the senior Andreas was hosted by red leaders at banquets and boar hunts.

In 1984, he became chairman of the US-USSR Trade and Economic Council, a business group that favored giving more export credits to the Soviets. Robert Strauss, appointed ambassador to Moscow by President Bush, also dependably vocalized the logic that if we failed to flood the Soviet Union with food, it would became unstable, hard liners would rise, and peace would fail. The wisdom of giving Soviets credits began to show cracks in the early 1970s. During the Nixon round of détente, the Kremlin bought so much subsidized wheat that it cornered the market, and the US bushel price jumped 300 percent. The Oil Producing and Exporting Countries (OPEC) took note and used the artificial inflation in wheat prices to justify hiking up world oil prices fourfold.

Andreas' devotion to the lucrative trade with Moscow sometimes led to fawning in the face of Soviet aggression. For example, he objected to the grain embargo imposed in 1980 by Washington against the Soviets after they invaded Afghanistan. "We shot ourselves in the foot," Andreas argued. "It didn't hurt the Soviets, who took their business to other countries and the Common Market." Three years later, East-West relations soured again when the Soviets shot down Korean Airlines flight 007, killing all passengers aboard and causing Washington to temporarily recall the US ambassador. The tragedy took place shortly before an agribusiness exposition in Moscow involving over a hundred companies. Slated to head the American group, Andreas decided not to cancel his trip and urged his peers to participate rather than "let this fair go down the tube. . . . The Russians are not just another grain buyer. They've bought billions of dollars worth over the years and have never defaulted. You get your impressions of people like them from what you experience not from what you dream."

At the fair Andreas gave the plenary address praising the United States and Soviet Union for exercising restraint and "maturity" in the wake of the tragedy by not resorting to hostilities. "Trade," he concluded with a flourish, "is a tool for peace. It can thaw the ice in relations between states. It can bring the citizens of those states together in harmony and partnership." The performance caused fellow grain king Walter Klein, the CEO of Bunge, a vast privately held enterprise based in Argentina, to say, "it was evident to all present that Dwayne had taken charge. That day he *was* the US ambassador." The *Wall Street Journal* labeled Andreas "Moscow's Favorite Businessman."

Andreas predicted the rise of Gorbachev a year before the little-known agriculture minister achieved the top rung in Soviet politics. Their mutual farm backgrounds created warm personal ties and a springboard for trade that earned ADM $250 million per year. Particularly concerned with the protein needs of his people, Gorbachev let ADM ply them with textured vegetable protein and soy burgers.

Even as perestroika failed to produce predicted gains and Gorbachev's power slipped, Andreas remained his biggest booster calling the Soviet leader the "messiah of reform" and predicting his long stable rule. Pat Buchanan ridiculed Andreas for replacing Armand Hammer as the Soviets' "trained poodle." But no one could call Andreas stupid about politics, whether in Washington or Moscow. In keeping with his well-honed ability to hedge and cultivate both sides, the ADM leader also gave Boris Yeltsin the royal treatment, installing him in a cabana at the Sea View during an American visit and driving him to a Russian Orthodox church service in Andreas' stretch Rolls Royce limousine.

But no ADM political effort, foreign or domestic, created as much controversy as ethanol. Since the Civil War, rural Americans have dreamed of fermenting farm surplus and marketing it as fuel. Like other early auto builders, Henry Ford championed the idea, and his 1908 Model T could burn ethanol, gasoline, or any combination of the two. Expense, however, long stood in the way of developing a viable ethanol industry. The distilled product can cost more than twice as much as wholesale gasoline. For more than half a century, the nonfossil fuel dropped from view.

During the 1970s America gagged on surging prices and artificial shortages of gasoline enforced by OPEC. President Carter called energy independence the "moral equivalent of war." Dwayne Andreas convinced him to throw the government's weight behind gasohol, a nine-to-one blend of gasoline to alcohol, touted as being cleaner than normal fuel since the added ethanol raises oxygen content (octane) and decreases carbon monoxide fumes, a key cause of air pollution and the greenhouse effect. An array of lobbies supported by ADM, including the National Corn Growers Association (NCGA), the Renewable Fuels Association (RFA), and National Oil Seed Producers Association (NOPA) made the case to Congress that the fledgling industry should be nurtured.

From both sides of the aisle, farm bloc legislators led by Bob Dole of Kansas, who described himself as the "Senator from ethanol," pushed through major subsidies for the fuel, a corn by-product. The largest loop hole involved a 5.4 cent per gallon exemption for gasohol from the federal fuel excise tax, that resulted in a whopping 54 cent per gallon subsidy for bulk ethanol producers because of the nine-to-one ratio. Congress also mandated the Department of Agriculture to issue loan guarantees for the ethanol distillers. Ethanol subsidies deprive the treasury of about $770 million per year. Each dollar of ADM profit from ethanol costs taxpayers thirty dollars.

ADM committed itself massively to ethanol, winning 70 percent of the US market by 1990. Its ethanol division grew to at least seven times the size of any competitor. Moreover, its levels of efficiency surpassed the rest of the industry. Able to produce either ethanol or HFCS, ADM "wet mills" never needed to be banked and rarely slowed down. The versatility enabled ADM to hit seasonal peaks by producing large amounts of HFCS during hot weather when the demand for soft drinks was high and floods of ethanol in winter when greenhouse inversions caused the EPA to order the use of fuel additives in such cities as Las Vegas and Phoenix. The more ethanol, according to ADM, the better for America. The company predicted that at least half of motor fuel would contain the additive, and that foreign dependence would be snapped. But at critical points, ADM used political influence to preserve its near monopoly rather than expand the supply. For instance in 1980, President Carter's campaign chairman, Robert Strauss, called the White House and successfully made the case for slapping a high tariff on Brazilian ethanol. After Carter lost the election, Strauss joined the ADM board of directors.

The following year, Andreas asked the Department of Energy to cancel loan guarantees to ADM's smaller rival producers. During President Reagan's Caribbean Basin Initiative (CBI), an attempt to spur development through duty-free trade, ADM lobbied successfully for tough limits on imports of ethanol from the region.

How could a propped-up fuel like gasohol survive? As financial columnist Jane Bryant Quinn put it, "the recipe for successful politics shows similar proportions: nine parts of regional pandering overlaid with one part of national purpose." In order to keep the ethanol flowing, Dwayne Andreas often played the jingo card. "This is the Midwest versus the Middle East. It's corn farmers versus the oil companies."

The emotional appeal coupled with campaign support caused politicians to engage in bizarre behavior. Receiving campaign contributions from Andreas in October 1980 as well as ADM's promise to build a new ethanol plant in key campaign state Iowa, Carter, who earlier had supported gasoline additives on questionable evidence, now implemented the ethanol import tariff. His order overruled the treasury department, which found the trade barrier unnecessary to protect jobs. After Carter left office, ADM reneged on the promise to build a new plant. In the desperate days before Reagan's victory, Carter's team approved a range of loans to the ethanol industry, some with little or no review. Much of the money flew to farm states supposedly on the fence.

Later, a Reagan administration inspector general found irregularities in the approval process and rescinded the loans. But after this forgotten bump, the Reagan era became a heyday for ethanol.

Andreas probably had his warmest presidential relationship with Reagan, who came from Dixon, an Illinois farming town north of Decatur. The two leaders liked to reminisce about their common backgrounds. Reagan also admired the ADM Sunday morning commercials, which endeared the president to Andreas, who personally had approved the ads. In 1984, Andreas convinced Reagan to campaign in Decatur, and he became the first president to stop there since Truman in 1948. Afterwards, Andreas commissioned a larger-than-life statue of Reagan for ADM's plaza on a granite mound engraved with the president's words:

> From corn and soybean processing that produce food products to feed the hungry world to your pioneer work in ethanol that increases demand for farm products, you create new jobs and lead to greater energy security for our country.

During Reagan's second term, the industry won an outright gratuity from the administration. After a breakfast meeting between Secretary of Agriculture James Lyng and Andreas, the government announced a plan to give corn away, not to the armies of homeless then emerging in the wake of the termination of Democratic social welfare programs, but to the ethanol industry that had griped about high crop prices. Lyng and Andreas both insisted that they had not discussed the handout during the meal. Regardless, ADM got the largest share, about $29 million worth of free corn. When critics argued to Lyng that the corn should have been awarded to distressed producers rather than to the agribusiness giant, the secretary inveighed against "a means test," because "the government should treat people equally. The Constitution calls for that." President Bush also supported ethanol, a surprise to some given his oil background. In particular, he relaxed volatility requirements on the fuel that the EPA had sought to toughen.

The fuel increasingly drew disappointing reviews. Because gasohol was more volatile than gasoline, more of it boiled away at the pump. Gasohol threw off additional hydrocarbons and therefore created more smog. It also provided poorer fuel economy, about four to five less miles per gallon than gasoline. In 1986, the US Department of Agriculture called it "an inefficient use of the nation's resources." Five years later, a pivotal study by Cornell agronomist David Pimental proved that it actually took 72 percent *more* energy to produce a gallon of ethanol than a gallon ultimately would yield, due to the energy expended in growing, harvesting, transporting, and fermenting the corn. The 1977 Clean Air Act actually barred ethanol for a time because it increased nitrous oxide emissions. The elite National Academy of Sciences (NAS) found that ethanol "would not achieve significant air quality benefits and, in fact, would likely be detrimental." The Department of Energy saw no environmental benefit. The Congressional Budget Office pointed out that fast evaporation of ethanol in hot weather promoted ozone pollution. In 1997, the General Accounting Office confirmed gasohol's minimal environmental value, reported that its effect on energy independence was virtually nil as it reduced petroleum imports by only 1 percent, and concluded that the ethanol industry would collapse without subsidies. Moreover, since one out of five ears of corn went into gas tanks, the cost of feed increased by 22 to 40 cents per bushel raising the prices of poultry, pork, and meat. Since the tax exemption affected the Federal

Highway Trust, it has siphoned about $7 billion out of the nation's infrastructure of roads and bridges.

Ethanol became highly controversial during the Clinton administration, especially as eliminating unfunded mandates, balancing the budget, and welfare reform drove the administration and the Republican congress. In a noteworthy speech, Secretary of Labor Robert Reich challenged the lawmakers and think tanks of Washington to end "corporate welfare," the subsidies and tax loops worth about $75 billion to American business, about a third of the value of safety net social programs. The debate on eliminating the tax breaks for ethanol was led by House Ways and Means chairman William Archer, a Texas Republican, who never had benefited from ADM or Andreas money. He received no support from his normal political ally Newt Gingrich. The farm lobby branded Archer a puppet of petroleum interests. As for the oil companies, they favored an octane boosting methanol (wood alcohol) additive made from natural gas. The product called MTBE costs half as much as ethanol and is as clean.

When Senator Tom Harkin, a populist Democrat from Iowa, the number two ethanol producing state, had been sued for libel, an Andreas check for $10,000 arrived in his defense fund. Now on the floor of the Senate, Harkin swallowed 200 proof ethanol and dared its detractors to drink methanol, known to be lethal or at least blinding. There were no takers. There was no point. The issue was gasoline and how it could be extended. President Clinton, who waffled on corporate welfare, steadfastly supported ethanol and, in mid-1994, mandated its use in order "to create thousands of jobs for the future," and "protect our environment, our public health, and our farmers."

The mandate accomplished the impossible. It joined as plaintiffs in a lawsuit environmental groups such as the Sierra Club, who saw ethanol as worthless, with the American Petroleum Institute, the principal lobby for an industry that had resisted the additive for years and now favored MTBE. A federal court tossed out the mandate viewing it as unjustifiable social engineering to promote Midwestern agriculture, in violation of a law whose sole purpose was clean air. The court noted that the "use of ethanol might make air quality worse."

But the subsidies remained, and for the most part they poured into one company. "Ethanol" reported the conservative CATO Institute, a think tank with a libertarian bent "keeps ADM drunk on tax dollars." In sum, about 43 percent of ADM's profits came from subsidized products. In the 1990s it surfaced that ADM had become the number one recipient of corporate welfare. In 1997, Clinton and Gingrich forces managed to beat back a bipartisan attack on the 54-cent excise tax exemption. Even before, ADM must have perceived the growing dissatisfaction with its gravy train. Dwayne Andreas was aging, and no one else in the company had his feel for public officials. Ethanol and high fructose probably could not cling to federal protectionism forever. The Soviet Union had collapsed. Had fear that the political process would end ADM's subsidies caused the company to look increasingly for other ways to inflate profits, including price fixing?

THE RISE AND FALL
AND RISE OF ANTITRUST

*"[T]he competitive struggle without effective
antitrust enforcement is like a fight without a referee."*
—Thurman Arnold

In some ways the record fine paid by ADM in 1996 came as no surprise. ADM was not a stranger to antitrust allegations. In 1965, it and eleven other firms paid fines for fixing the prices of bakery flour. In 1976, ADM pleaded no contest when charged with the short-weighting and false grading of grain for export. Two years later, ADM and two other companies were convicted of conspiring to fix prices in the Food for Peace program. In 1982, the government began a case to force ADM to spin off some of its HFCS mills over an allegation of monopolization, but in 1991 a federal judge dismissed the charge. In 1994, ADM was named in an alleged conspiracy to rig prices, bids, and allocate markets in the liquid carbon dioxide business, which supplies soft drink bottlers and municipal water systems. ADM paid $80,000 to the state of Florida and $1.4 million to the victims of the scheme in order to extricate itself from the case.

Not just a stain on the corporation's already tarnished record, the 1996 fine also amounted to a milestone in the noble century-old experiment to keep markets fair. Long before business had to contend with social security, sexual harassment, civil rights, occupational safety, and environmental regulations, corporations had to be wary of Washington's concern over antitrust.

After the Civil War, the agrarian Jeffersonian civilization gave way to rapid industrialization, urbanization, and traumatic shifts in population and lifestyle. Our time has seen an equally wrenching change as the industrial age passes. Both periods boast revolutions in communications. The late nineteenth–early twentieth century saw railroads, cars, and telephones end the isolation of Americans once separated by great distances. Ours is an era of global communications and information exchange. Both times are challenged by huge and disturbing concentrations of wealth and economic power.

In the 1840s there were about twenty millionaires in the United States. At the end of the century, there were twenty in the US Senate and over 4,000 in the country. A popular magazine ran an article entitled "The Coming of the Billionaire," which caused a stir. How could anyone become so inconceivably wealthy? It was impossible, or was it? The same reaction would be created today if *Time* or *Newsweek* predicted that Bill Gates or another computer Croesus would become a trillionaire.

After the Civil War, bare-knuckle competition ruled the economy and was especially fierce among railroads with about one in five going into receivership. The railroads began to form "pools" to set prices and divide up markets in order to avoid the ruinous rivalry, and soon they were imitated by other industries. But the pools had flaws. They could not enforce discipline on independent and unruly companies that chose to undersell the herd. John D. Rockefeller, who favored lockstep control, was particularly unimpressed with pools, calling them "ropes of sand."

Still in his twenties, Rockefeller gained control of a refinery in Cleveland during the 1870s when oil was discovered in northwestern Pennsylvania, a hundred miles to the east. The discovery made the automobile age possible and probably did more than anything else to save whales, the prior major source of oil. Rockefeller understood that whoever controlled distribution controlled oil. He used a system of rebates with railroads to drive out the competition and developed a vast network of pipelines that he called "iron arteries." With income greater than that of most states, he bribed legislators and bought fields and refineries. Establishing the Standard Oil Company, after only seven years in business, he controlled over 10 percent of the oil industry in the United States.

Rockefeller's drive for monopoly was unquenchable. In the 1870s, he and his allies formed a pool known as the South Improvement Association that began an extortion racket against railroads referred to as "drawbacks." Basically, the association made clear that it would withdraw its freight unless a carrier kicked back to the Rockefeller interests not only a substantial part of its rate but also a portion of what its competitors had paid.

Public outcry caused the association to disband, but not before Rockefeller and his corporate *consigliere*, the lawyer Samuel C. T. Dodd, came up with a body blow to smash competition. Dodd invented the trust, a scheme that brought forty oil companies under tight control. Stockholders in the forty firms turned their shares over to a group of trustees headed by Rockefeller, who gave them dividends. As for the trustees, they won full voting control over the forty companies, which they could direct to fix prices and divide markets. The key weakness of the pool, that a dissident member could break away and undersell his coconspirators, was eliminated.

At the same time, a legal shift occurred. Most states long had had laws that prevented corporations from holding stock in other corporations. In the 1880s New Jersey, looking for new sources of income, began allowing companies incorporated in the state to hold shares of other companies, including those located out of state. Standard Oil swiftly incorporated in New Jersey as did other trusts. New Jersey fattened on registration fees, and other states copied the plan. Trusts soon dominated major industries including rubber, whiskey, sugar, steel, lumber, and trolley lines.

By the turn of the century, there were more than 300 of these behemoths, and they exercised a powerful hold on public imagination. Cartoons depicted them as spiders with all of economic life tangled in their webs, grinning octopi curling their arms around the homes, farms, and necks of common people, and obscenely bloated hogs.

Rockefeller, an avid gardener, defended snuffing smaller businesses. "The American beauty rose can be produced in all its glory only by sacrificing the early buds that grow up around it." The trusts became the central moral question in American politics between slavery and the dispute over whether to enter World War I. Both political parties included trust fighting in their national platforms in 1888.

Although the fear of trusts was general, the approach to them was not unified. A major dispute involved tariffs. Populists in the west and south favored protectionism as a way to bolster smaller, emerging American industries against hated European competition.

However, eastern reformers, including lawyer Louis D. Brandeis, America's first consumer advocate, favored free trade as an antidote to high prices set by monopolies. Testifying before Congress, Brandeis called protectionism the "mother of trusts." In addition to Brandeis, who later joined the Supreme Court, fighting trusts shaped a number of major political careers, including those of Wisconsin senator Robert LaFollette, and, of course, President Theodore Roosevelt. America's first generation of investigative journalists, the "muckrakers" Ida M. Tarbell, Lincoln Steffens, and Ray Stannard Baker closely followed the power plays of Rockefeller and other trust bosses, including J. Pierpont Morgan, the Wall Street banker, who raised the unheard of sum of $1.4 billion to combine numerous steel companies into United States Steel, then the world's largest corporation. The plight of the common man in a time of the economic gigantism gave rise to *The Jungle* by Upton Sinclair and *The Octopus* by Frank Norris, novels which angrily detailed the workings respectively of the beef-packing and railroad interests.

By 1890, it became clear to Congress that the country clamored for antitrust legislation. Some states already had antimonopoly statutes, but they proved ineffective in the face of trusts that operated regionally or nationally.

Floor leadership in the Senate fell to John Sherman, an Ohio Republican. Now largely forgotten except in regard to the law that bears his name, Sherman who sat in the Senate longer than anyone else in the nineteenth century (thirty-four years), also served as secretary of the treasury and state departments, and three times tried for the presidency.

The scion of an American political dynasty that began with Connecticut's Roger Sherman, a signer of the Declaration of Independence, Sherman fit within a small elite of sub-presidential figures including Henry Clay, Daniel Webster, and John C. Calhoun, who exercised claims on the country's conscience. Sherman's older brother was William Tecumseh Sherman, whose victories at Shiloh and Vicksburg and epochal slash-and-burn March to the Sea made him the most famous northern general after Grant. Ironically, General Sherman was personally soft on slavery. But his brother, a moderate, was its implacable foe. As a congressman in the 1850s, he opposed legislation that would have allowed newly admitted western states to foster slavery. Joining the Senate in 1861, he took the lead in efforts to finance the Civil War and Reconstruction.

After the war, he demonstrated considerable political courage. When Ohio rejected giving blacks the right to vote by 50,000 votes, Sherman voted in favor of the Fifteenth Amendment providing universal (male) suffrage. In addition, he favored an income tax and, on anti-imperialist grounds, opposed war with Spain as a shallow pretext to annex Cuba.

With silver hair, full beard, lean 6'2" frame, square jaw, and large furrowed brow, he looked the part of a senatorial patriarch. Not especially eloquent, he tended to lard speeches with census and economic data in keeping with his optimistic view that the American free enterprise system and way of life would yield unprecedented prosperity. Sherman's fiscal acumen and great personal wealth—mainly from land speculation—also made him acceptable to financial interests.

From the first, the idea of federal trust control raised thorny political questions. For one thing, it cut against states' rights. Plus, the legislation seemed to embrace an inherent contradiction: the intent of antitrust was to preserve the free market, but its effect involved regulating, controlling, and limiting entrepreneurs. Loathing for the monopolists, however, overcame such abstractions. To Sherman a trust equalled "a kingly prerogative inconsistent with our form of government. If we would not submit to an emperor, we should not submit to an autocrat of trade with power to prevent competition, and to fix the price of any commodity."

Signed into law by President Benjamin Harrison on July 2, 1890, the Sherman

Antitrust Act was refreshingly short and simply written given the complexity of the problem it addressed. In Section 1 it outlawed, "every contract, combination in the form of a trust or otherwise, or conspiracy, in restraint of trade or commerce among the several states, or with foreign nations." Section 2 provided punishment for "every person who shall monopolize, or attempt to monopolize, or combine or conspire with any other person or persons, to monopolize any part of the trade or commerce among the several states or with foreign states."

The first application of the act was a debacle. In 1893, Grover Cleveland filed a suit against the American Sugar Refining Company, which had paid off its competitors, grabbed control of 98 percent of sugar processing in the United States, and raised prices accordingly. In a supremely silly decision, the Supreme Court called manufacturing a local process that did not directly affect interstate commerce, and, therefore, forbade the federal government from breaking up the sugar trust, which continued to gouge customers. Neither the Cleveland nor McKinley administrations dared to use the Sherman Act again.

In 1901, Theodore Roosevelt became president following McKinley's assassination. Because of Roosevelt's patrician roots, big business initially viewed him as friendly. In 1902, relying on the Supreme Court's sugar trust ruling, Morgan and railroad magnates E.H. Harriman and James Hill formed a train trust in the Northwest that the new president believed was "possibly the first step toward controlling the entire railway system of the country." Roosevelt ordered the Justice Department to attack the trust. The suit surprised Morgan, who knew Roosevelt personally, and sent him a note offering, "If we have done anything wrong, send your man [the attorney general] to my man [Morgan's attorney], and they can fix it up." But Roosevelt, who previously revealed reformist leanings, feared that monopolies might be what Marx and the socialists had said they were, the last stage of capitalism. Roosevelt felt compelled to wield "the big stick" to fight the trusts.

When the Supreme Court handed down a five–four decision for the government, Roosevelt won the nickname "trust buster." The narrow victory probably was the high point of his first term. It spawned a host of new Sherman Act suits against trusts including Standard Oil, American Tobacco, and meat packers, such as Swift, for fixing prices in the Chicago stockyards. Swift fought hard for antitrust immunity, claiming its cows were bought and sold locally. Justice Oliver Wendell Holmes, Jr., a Roosevelt appointee, rejected the argument noting that cows were in the "stream of commerce."

With the Age of Reform in full swing, Congress passed new laws outlawing secret railroad price rebates, providing for slaughterhouse inspections, and assuring the purity of food and drugs. This was also the dawning era of megacorporations, and they conducted business in ways unimaginable to the founding fathers.

New questions arose about the power configurations in American life: Which was more powerful—Washington or Wall Street? Who was more powerful—Roosevelt or Morgan? In his second term, Roosevelt declared that no "free people will permanently tolerate the use of the vast power conferred by vast wealth . . . without lodging somewhere in government the still higher power of seeing that this power is used for and not against the interests of the people as a whole."

In truth, Roosevelt was no extremist. Unlike Brandeis and Ida Tarbell, the president did not see the huge combinations invariably as evil. He tried to stake out a middle ground, advocating tough prosecution for "bad trusts" such as Standard Oil, but not for "good trusts" such as International Harvester, the farm machinery maker that seemed not to gouge consumers. Also, Roosevelt had no desire to regulate firms to death. As he told the English historian George Trevelyan in 1905, "Somehow or other, we should have to work out methods of controlling the big corporations without paralyzing the energies of the business community."

Roosevelt also made a grave error and one that would be copied by ensuing administrations by allowing his personal relations with business leaders to color his policies. He especially despised the beef-packing trust, perhaps because it mocked the failure of his cattle ranch in the Dakota Badlands in the 1880s. Not only did the administration prosecute the trust, but Roosevelt invited Upton Sinclair to educate and assist federal inspectors.

But the pendulum swung the other way when Roosevelt dealt with Morgan and the equally formidable Judge Elbert H. Gary, the chairman of US Steel. When US Steel tried to absorb a Tennessee coal and iron company, Roosevelt agreed to meet with Morgan and Gary before the stock exchange opened on the morning of the purchase. The industrialists promised that the takeover target was in dire straits, and that they were making the acquisition for altruistic rather market-cornering reasons. Gary even volunteered to open US Steel's books to Roosevelt, who declined the offer and gave his word that the government would not file an antitrust suit. Later, during the administration of his protegé William Howard Taft, it became apparent that Morgan and Gary had deceived Roosevelt. When Taft prosecuted US Steel under the Sherman Act, Roosevelt broke with him and ran for president as the candidate of the Bull Moose Party, which gave Woodrow Wilson, a Democrat, the White House. Between them Roosevelt and Taft brought over seventy antitrust prosecutions.

Courts for the most part adopted Roosevelt's good trust/bad trust dichotomy. In 1911, the United States Supreme Court outlawed and disbanded the Standard Oil and American Tobacco trusts. In smashing the monopolies, the Supreme Court adopted a two-fold approach. Some antitrust violations it declared "per se" or automatic breaches of the law. These included price-fixing and carving up markets among competitors. Other practices had to be weighed in order to determine whether they were reasonable.

In upholding the breakup of Standard Oil into forty component companies, the Supreme Court found that the trust had resulted in an "unreasonable restraint of trade." By implication the court gave a green light to reasonable restraints of trade. In short, the court would allow market cornering if a company won its position through hard work, leading edge products, or other legitimate means.

The rift between Taft and Roosevelt created opportunities for the Democrats in 1912. Their opinion leader on trust and corporate issues, Louis Brandeis, advised candidate Woodrow Wilson, who took a Jeffersonian line and played on Main Street's loathing of conglomerate powers. Wilson pointedly refused to divide trusts into the good and bad or to become an apologist for their supposed efficiency. "Monopoly," he argued "always checks development, weighs down natural prosperity, and pulls down natural advance. The instinct of monopoly is against novelty."

The US Steel Corporation and Judge Gary stimulated a response as negative in Brandeis as it had been positive in Roosevelt. When Gary gave his wife a half-million-dollar string of pearls, Brandeis scored it as "the same sort of thing that brought on the French Revolution."

In a less personal vein, Brandeis maintained that "there are no natural monopolies." He studied trusts in leather, glue, newspapers, stationery, wood, cut flowers, paper bags, merchant shipping, and other industries. He saw price manipulations as the trusts' stock in trade. Early price cutting killed smaller rivals. Later, price fixing forced consumers to pay whatever the monopolist decreed. The eventual bloat made for laziness and inefficiency, what Brandeis called "the curse of bigness."

Favoring a tough legislative course, Brandeis was largely responsible for a bill introduced by Senator Robert LaFollette that branded any combination acquiring over 40 percent of the market as presumptively unlawful. He championed the Federal Trade Commission (FTC), which President Wilson signed into law in 1914. The FTC included five members appointed by the president, not more than three of whom could come from the same party. As a nontrial avenue to stop trust formation, the specialized group could hold hearings and issue "cease and desist orders" that could be upheld or challenged in circuit courts.

In 1914, Wilson also endorsed the Clayton Act, which sharpened the teeth of the Sherman Act by forbidding industries to discriminate in prices among buyers of the same commodities. The Clayton Act likewise banned giving special reductions to customers who agreed not to deal in the goods of a competitor. But the new law also set up sacred cows exempted from antitrust prosecution. Perhaps not surprisingly, these included the former victims of the big trusts, from farmers, who were permitted to establish price-setting cooperatives, to labor unions, who could form virtual monopolies at industrial work sites. The government also designed a loophole for national emergencies. In 1933, at the height of the Depression, Franklin D. Roosevelt suspended antitrust enforcement.

In the late 1930s the clamor for renewed attention to antitrust revived. Influential figures, including Interior Secretary Harold Ickes and German refuge writer Franz Neumann, took the position that antitrust enforcement would help prevent massive industrial concentrations that could become fascist as they had in the Third Reich.

In 1938, FDR announced his determination to rekindle antitrust and placed Yale Law professor Thurman Arnold in charge. Among the most influential American lawyers of the century, he served as the mayor of his hometown, Laramie, Wyoming, and as dean of the law school at West Virginia University before joining the faculty at Yale in 1931. During the thirties, Yale Law School became an oasis of liberalism and social philosophy in contrast to Harvard and other stodgy bastions that continued to focus on producing elite mandarins. Yale had attracted William O. Douglas, the prominent civil libertarian and future Supreme Court justice from Columbia Law School. Educational reformer Robert Maynard Hutchens taught evidence and rose to the deanship at Yale law school at twenty-eight before leaving to become the radicalizing president of the University of Chicago. Also at Yale, Harold Laski from the London School of Economics imparted his views on the modern state. At the center of it all was Arnold, an irrepressible, charismatic, pipe-smoking poet, who became Douglas' mentor. Arnold foresaw that law was changing, that soon lawyers would be as prominent or notorious as their clients, and that issues would be tried in the court of public opinion as well as in real courts. Thus, he stressed understanding media and how to manipulate it.

At Yale, Arnold designed a point system for law professors. The number of points awarded was based on the prestige of the publication in which one's name appeared with five points for a mention in the *New Haven Register*, ten for the *New York Times*, twenty-five for a national news magazine, and 100 for inclusion in a *Times* editorial. In keeping with the social rebellion at Yale, Arnold declined to turn out the typical law review articles and ponderous case books. Instead, he authored brilliant, iconoclastic, and extremely popular volumes on the modern capitalist system including *The Symbols of Government, The Folklore of Capitalism,* and *The Bottleneck of Business.*

Arnold's overarching theme was reality. The old language of the progressives, including such terms as character, decency, shame, conscience, and even democracy, was ceremonial and largely meaningless to him. The motivating forces in society were organizations such as those built by Ford, Rockefeller, and political machines. Arnold regarded them and their accomplishments with grudging admiration. He also faulted antitrust enforcement. Outspent and outgunned by the big corporations, the government initiated only about ten cases per year. According to Arnold, these prosecutions were meant to show that the targeted companies were bad (a ludicrous concept to him).

He denounced Theodore Roosevelt as "the man with the big stick that never hurt anybody." There was some truth in the charge. The pieces of broken monopolies like Standard Oil and American Tobacco often did not compete, but functioned as oligopolies that divided markets and used parallel pricing. To Arnold, "the competitive struggle without effective antitrust enforcement is like a fight without a referee. In such a context the man who puts on brass knuckles will win. The situation will not be solved by hanging mottos of fair play on the floor posts of the ring."

Arnold, who favored a new theory of prosecution focusing on benefits to consumers, became the most active trustbuster in history. During his five-year reign, the antitrust division of the Justice Department swelled fivefold to 190 attorneys (Theodore Roosevelt had had five). True to form, Arnold pointed his guns at conspiratorial practices that jacked up prices in industries that affected average Americans such as food, clothing, and construction. In some years, his filings approached 100 cases. In five years, his department initiated 44 percent of the cases started by the government since the passage of the Sherman Act. His constant speaking, writing, and distinctive press releases on predatory practices aroused the ire of the business community. Staid Attorney General Francis Biddle restricted Arnold's case filing privileges. From then on the antitrust division had to win Biddle's agreement in order to prosecute. Biddle also forbade Arnold to write press releases, which became a centralized task under the attorney general's control.

Though prolific, Arnold and his department were not entirely successful. His pro-consumer case against union practices in the housing industry was defeated in the Supreme Court. His antimonopoly efforts against defense contractors like General Electric fizzled when war mobilization began. The department did achieve a lasting victory in 1940 in the Socony-Vacuum case. Arnold, who argued for the government, convinced the Supreme Court that major oil companies in the Midwest had conspired to raise gasoline prices. Writing for the majority, new Supreme Court justice and old Arnold friend William O. Douglas ruled that price-fixing agreements were "unlawful per se," and in themselves constituted restraints of trade. The consumer had won. Afterwards, the rule of reason would not be applied to collusive pricing or market allocation schemes.

By 1943, Arnold had grated on enough people in government and business that FDR removed him from the job with a promotion to a judgeship on the Federal Court of Appeals for the District of Columbia, then held to be the country's second most powerful court and a stepping stone to the Supreme Court. Ironically, Arnold's tenure at Justice is remembered for a good-and-evil morality case. Before

World War II, Exxon made a deal with the Germany's mammoth I.G. Farben. Exxon agreed to stay out of chemicals, and Farben pledged to stay out of oil. The two companies conducted patent exchanges that continued after the invasion of Europe. Exxon's collusion probably weakened the war effort because the company failed to pursue petrochemical processes for making artificial rubber. According to Arnold, who filed the case in 1941, what Farben and Exxon "were trying to do was look at the war as a transitory phenomenon and business as a permanent thing." Exxon eventually paid a fine of $50,000 and released the patents. However, its top management was publicly disgraced, and, after the war, President Truman pronounced the conduct treasonous.

Arnold, who found judging dull, resigned from the bench in 1948. With two of his Yale proteges, Abe Fortas and Paul Porter, he formed a law firm in Washington. Arnold, Porter, and Fortas rapidly grew into a formidable Beltway institution and model for the post-war legal community. For one thing, the firm broke the gentleman's agreement among major firms and hired Jews (Fortas, who was Jewish, would be named to the Supreme Court, but would resign in 1969 in a scandal over his acceptance of a stipend from a foundation). Also, the firm had major corporate clients but also fought for liberal causes.

America also embraced contradictions. In the post-war era, antitrust became a plank in the American civic creed, as trustbusting found its way into school books, and most big corporations published stern warnings against bid rigging and price fixing. During the American regency of Japan, General MacArthur injected antitrust and antiestablishment of religion clauses into the defeated nation's new constitution. In fact, American antitrust and antiestablishment feelings spring from the same Jeffersonian roots, but neither makes much sense in the Japanese cultural or historical context. Not surprisingly, the Japanese amended their antimonopoly law within a few years after occupation to permit most price-fixing and cartels. It kept the Japanese Fair Trade Commission (FTC) as a toothless tiger.

In post-war America, antitrust grew in both prestige and power with proponents in Congress like Senator Estes Kefauver. The fine for a basic Sherman Act violation rose from $5,000, where it had stood since 1890, to $50,000. The Eisenhower administration imposed a much needed revolving door rule to prevent Justice Department attorneys who left the antitrust division from servicing private clients under investigation or indictment by the division. Justice Hugo Black, an affable Alabaman and shrewd former New Dealer, led renewed support for antitrust on the Warren Court. He read the Sherman Act with an ardent literalness. Because the legislation itself contained no rule of reason, he understood the act to outlaw all contracts, combinations, and conspiracies of any kind in restraint of trade, plus all attempts to monopolize even a part of a market.

In 1957, Black and the Supreme Court forced DuPont to "shed" its substantial stake in General Motors. The *New York Herald Tribune* reported that "the whole American corporate structure is shaken" by the forced divestiture.

During the 1960s Justice Black's decisions stopped shoe, beer, bank, glass, and aluminum mergers. The court forced GM to spin off Euclid, a maker of heavy construction equipment. It ordered the Continental Can Company out of the glass business. It stopped Philadelphia National Bank, the second largest bank in its area, from marrying Girard, the third, resulting in a combined 36 percent market share, simply because it was "likely" to lessen competition. In a stunning Black opinion that today seems antique, the court blocked a merger between two Los Angeles food chains, although the combination would have had just 7.5 percent of the LA market. Targeting Black, *Fortune* editorialized against "antitrust in a coonskin cap."

In 1961, the government prosecuted General Electric, Westinghouse, Allis Chalmers, and Ingersoll-Rand for an elaborate price-fixing scheme that cost consumers about $3 billion, probably the biggest organized swindle in American history. The case produced evidence of high-level rival executives who met secretly to carve up markets. The sensational guilty pleas of managers who also were family men, community leaders, and church deacons led to front-page coverage and large fines, but the judge imposed jail terms amounting to a month or less.

The government continued to prosecute popular cases, especially in health. It successfully challenged drug cartel control of tetracycline and quinidine (for cardiac arrhythmia) bringing down the price of both. William Orrick, Lyndon Johnson's antitrust chief saw no reason to engage in complex rule of reason analysis. He told Congress that the "concentration of industrial power may lead to a police state. Can anyone doubt that the pre-war experiences of Germany, Japan, and Italy have provided the wisdom of the nation's concern over the concentration of economic power?"

In the late 1960s and 1970s, antitrust came under fire from intellectuals identified with the so-called Chicago School. Following World War II, the University of Chicago gathered an impressive array of economists who were critical of government intervention in the economy, including Nobel Prize winners F.A. Hayek, Milton Friedman, George Stigler, and James Buchanan.

The most prominent Chicago School jurist has been former judge Robert Bork author of *The Antitrust Paradox: A Policy at War with Itself*. Bork favors bigness so long as it does not harm "consumer welfare." He takes Justice Black to task for performing little economic analysis, terms Ralph Nader's antimerger attitude "nihilistic," and reserves special wrath for the late Justice Brandeis, whom Bork believes sentimentally favored bending antitrust to protect small businesses, even if the results "could favor values opposed to consumer welfare." Bork insists that conglomerate efficiency can improve the economy, but opposes price-fixing arrangements.

During the sixties and seventies, an influential strain of liberal economists led by John Kenneth Galbraith of Harvard and Lester Thurow of MIT also turned against antitrust law, including the ban against price fixing. Called statists or industrial policy advocates, they saw American corporations competing at a disadvantage in world markets against unregulated foreign companies including state-backed monopolies. They pointed to the Japanese economic miracle stewarded by that nation's Ministry of International Trade and Industry (MITI) as the favored form of future development involving joint planning between business and industry.

To Galbraith, who had participated in the federal Office of Price Administration that stabilized prices during World War II, "controlled prices are necessary for this planning. And the planning itself is inherent in the industrial system. It follows that the antitrust laws, in seeking to preserve the market, are an anachronism. . . ."

Like Bork and the Chicago School, statists welcome rather than fear huge corporations. They see no real difference between having twenty airlines or five, three car companies or two. They put a liberal spin on their views by insisting that the new monopolies will work closely with the government and big labor, be lobbied effectively by citizens groups, and become environmentally sensitive.

During the 1980s, huge mergers became common. The Reagan administration routinely filed briefs in the Supreme Court supporting anticompetitive activity among rivals, such as the joint venture between General Motors and Toyota, the world's two largest car companies. The trend continued into the 1990s with unchallenged mergers in the banking, brokerage, and accounting industries. The nineteen principal defense contractors became three. World Com swallowed MCI. Microsoft collaborated with Apple and bought Web TV and a cable company. Occasionally there would be an interesting exception as when court-appointed lawyers for indigent defendants in Washington, DC, agreed not to take cases unless the courts promised to raise their rates, and the Supreme Court found collusive combination in support of price elevation illegal.

Antitrust seemed all but dead. Academics in the field debated whether any combination would be too big for the Department of Justice to stomach. What if GM ate Ford, Microsoft married IBM, or Coke drank Pepsi. In the present climate would anything be too big to be legal?

At the same time the consolidation wave had begun to affect the quality of life. Many Americans now lived in communities with one newspaper. Health care consolidations occurring virtually overnight meant that patients suddenly had little or no choice between hospitals. Local banks, pharmacies, gas stations, and corporate headquarters often vanished.

Yet something else was and is going on. Its undercurrents first were felt during the Reagan administration. Reagan's top antitrust attorney, William Baxter, a committed Chicago Schooler, dropped the government's ten-year case against IBM, an epic pullout that the *Wall Street Journal* termed "a trustbuster equivalent of Vietnam." But Baxter also enforced the breakup of AT&T, including the splitting off of the ten regional Baby Bell telephone companies. As it turned out, Baxter made the right calls on both. By the eighties, IBM, a lumbering giant, already was getting clobbered in the market, rendering the lawsuit irrelevant. With technology mushrooming, that market was fluid and had few real barriers to entry.

AT&T, which the government had attacked unsuccessfully in 1913 and 1949, was another story. Its affiliates made it expensive and difficult for other long-distance companies to connect with local loops and for consumers to use equipment or phones made by anybody but Western Electric, an AT&T company. By now the much studied breakup has produced a gamut of positive gains, including that average long-distance prices for residential customers have fallen by more than 50 percent, and the range of equipment, services, and options such as voicemail, call waiting, and conferencing have expanded exponentially.

On the other hand, in an area where market entry was limited by the fixed resources of airports, the government did not get involved. Due to the wave of airline mergers in the 1980s, higher ticket prices have resulted for passengers. Washington drew object lessons from these industries. During the late eighties and nineties, funding and personnel cuts in antitrust enforcement implemented during the Reagan era began to be restored.

Current trustbusters found a world similar to a century ago in terms of the amalgamation of economic power. Then as now, there were a handful of major press lords, energy companies, steel makers, and railroads. But now a handful of fiber optics networks, chip makers, and software systems shaped communications. The tendency to fix prices, rig bids, and carve up markets remained just as real as in Sherman's time. Noting the parallels, Robert Pitofsky, the newly appointed activist chairman of the Federal Trade Commission (FTC) observed, "1990 is like 1890."

As in the early twentieth century, the government's antitrust policy remains inconsistent. One day the government will stop Microsoft from insisting that consumers use its internet browser. On another, it will allow the blending of Bell Atlantic with NYNEX. In truth most mergers go unchallenged. Bigness is not as much the target as is the arrogant, cheating conduct of bigness especially price fixing.

Congress gave a clear sign of the new bipartisan attitude on enforcement when it raised the maximum penalty on a single Sherman Act violation from a one-year misdemeanor to a three-year felony in 1990. The maximum corporate fine also climbed from one million to ten million dollars, per count. In the early 1990s, the government regularly started employing blue-collar law enforcement tools: FBI agents, informants, wiretaps, body wires, forensic lab work, grand jury subpoenas, and multiple charging—"throwing the book" at business defendants as if they were common criminals. Additional counts included mail and wire (telephone) fraud, tax evasion, and racketeering. The business press took note when some market splitting waste haulers also were charged with extortion for vandalizing the car of a competitor who refused to join the conspiracy, and when buyers who rigged bids at real estate auctions were booked for interstate transportation of stolen goods because they carried their profits from Washington, DC to Maryland.

An architect of these thrusts was Gary Spratling, deputy assistant attorney general, who presided over criminal antitrust enforcement including seven regional offices in Atlanta, Chicago, Cleveland, Dallas, New York, Philadelphia, and San Francisco. Spratling, a thirty-year veteran of the department, endured the lean years of the Reagan administration in the San Francisco office, which he headed after serving as a trial attorney. A broad-chested man with wavy dark hair, lively eyes and a full-mustache, Spratling, fifty-nine, became the most highly decorated antitrust attorney in Department of Justice history. Twice the recipient of a presidential citation, in 1997, he won the first attorney general's award "for contributions to a free economy" and became the only prosecutor to be named Antitrust Lawyer of the Year by the California Bar, the field's most prestigious private honor. Spratling called current antitrust a "revolution" and a "whole new ball game." It pleased him that the division and its prosecutions after a long lull have staked a claim to the national consciousness, popping up in headlines, at cocktail parties, and in executive offices. To a great extent, this resurgence flowed from the large fines, including the $100 million that ADM paid.

A lawyer with an MBA from Berkeley, Spratling understood the machinations of commerce, especially the fact that as big businesses increasingly cross borders, so will white-collar criminal conspiracies. The realization caused him and his colleagues in 1996 to approach the US Immigration and Naturalization Service (INS) about a longstanding problem. In the past, it was practically impossible to "flip" foreign companies and their managers implicated in intentional conspiracies by offering favorable plea agreements in exchange for their cooperation against other conspirators. Because the INS regarded antitrust felonies as crimes of "moral turpitude," warranting exclusion of the perpetrators, it might allow the foreigners to come into the United States for trials, but otherwise would stop them at borders.

As a practical matter, foreign conspirators had no incentive to cooperate at trial because they would still lose the highly prized ability to travel and do business in the United States. Following fractious bureaucratic negotiations, the antitrust division reached an accommodation with INS called the Memorandum of Understanding (MOU). Under it, the division can petition the INS to grant "preadjudication relief." In other words, the INS could consent to a guilty plea deal, including the defendant's continued right to travel domestically in exchange for testimony. To date, INS had granted all the preadjudication petitions.

As Spratling predicted, offshore entrepreneurs often rushed to plead guilty and inform against their colleagues with the certainty of no future hassles from customs agents and INS border patrols. "The foreign companies and their senior executives buy peace with us." He praised the MOU as a "critical tool for investigating and prosecuting international cartel activity." While building the lysine cases with ADM at the hub of the conspiracy, the Justice Department under the MOU won cooperation and secured guilty pleas against three Asian companies (one Korean and two Japanese). In prosecuting the citric acid cartel, "the promise of unencumbered travel into the United States was a major inducement" in gaining the plea and cooperation of Bayer subsidiary Haarman & Reimer, which paid a $50 million fine.

In a related trend, the antitrust division had begun participating in about thirty Mutual Legal Assistance Treaties (MLATS) with foreign law enforcement agencies. A shift in international circles from centralized economies to unfettered capitalism has resulted in a new emphasis in other countries on protecting their markets from cartels. The practical effects are considerable. Foreign governments and the United States now share data about criminal economic activity. Law enforcement agents also coordinate their activities. For example, to prevent Canadian conspirators from destroying information when their American counterparts receive search warrants, the FBI and Royal Canadian Mounted Police routinely conduct raids at the same time.

The international focus has transformed the division. From 1987 through 1990, the government failed to prosecute a single foreign defendant. In fiscal 1991 only 1 percent of defendants were foreign. Since then, federal grand juries have looked into cartels operating in twenty countries on four continents. When I spoke to Spratling, about 20 percent of the corporate defendants were based abroad. Spratling made clear that the government held no bias against foreigners but that "this is the nature of cartels today."

Spratling's biggest breakthrough came in 1991 when he discovered that a section of the federal crimes code could apply to antitrust. The statute allowed the government to set fines at up to twice the economic loss to the society or twice the gain to the violator, whichever was larger. "Every judge so far," said Spratling, "has agreed with us" that even the enlarged $10 million maximum fine in the Sherman Act would not limit a company's exposure. Suddenly fines climbed to twenty, thirty, and in ADM's case, even a hundred million dollars. "We went to huge fines so a corporation no longer can look at this as just a minor expense of doing business."

Because of the vast volumes of commerce involving the companies then under review by federal grand juries, Spratling correctly predicted that fines would exceed ADM's. The results have been impressive. In 1991 the division collected about $20 million in fines. By 1997 the figure had jumped tenfold to $205 million, and in 1998 it rose to $267 million. In 1999 Roche Holding and BASF respectively paid fines of $500 million and $225 million for setting quotas and prices in vitamin markets. The double-the-loss, double-the-gain provision also scared a lot of companies into cooperating and cutting deals.

Another new strategy for inducing cooperation utilized amnesty. In order to get it, a company must report an antitrust violation before the division detects it and then inform against other guilty firms. Qualified companies "pay zero dollars in fines." A similar opportunity exists for individual executives to avoid prosecution and fines by divulging evidence against violators in their own companies as well as against other conspirators.

When the division or the FBI discovers a crime against competition, the corporation still can get what Spratling calls "extra credit" for subsequent cooperation. The government's deal with ADM, which reduced its fine and gave executives assurances of no prosecution provided they cooperated against Wilson and Andreas, drew criticism for being unrealistic in its assumption that those on the payroll would act against Dwayne Andreas' son. "Look," insisted Spratling, "if Dwayne or anyone lies, he loses all his protection from prosecution." But the attorney grudgingly admitted that cooperation from ADM "is not the most forthcoming."

Another sticky issue related to the government's surgical charging of Michael Andreas and Terry Wilson with only a single Sherman Act count for lysine price-fixing. Spratling pointed out that both would serve "real time" if convicted, up to three years a piece, a far cry from the coddling of the electrical conspiracy case. Plus, the pair could fork over millions in fines. But the failure to force them to contend with ancillary charges of mail fraud, wire fraud, and racketeering seemed at odds with using blue-collar rather than white-glove tactics in dealing with economic crimes.

From a prosecutorial standpoint, surgical charging constituted an exquisitely ethical, pro due process position, that few defendants have the chance to enjoy. It also amounted to a gamble because the jury must say yes or no rather than split the difference by convicting but not on all charges or to a lesser offense. Johnnie Cochran's first brilliant move of the O.J. Simpson case occurred before he stepped into the courtroom, when he convinced Los Angeles District Attorney Gil Garcetti not to seek the death penalty. As a result, the jury could not consider compromising on a life sentence for the killings. Cochran made sure that reasonable doubt meant acquittal, rather than a partial victory. As defense attorneys know, surgical charging especially favored prominent people without criminal histories. Spratling was aware that the ADM jurors could shake their heads at the complexity of the economic arrangements presuming them to be business as usual and acquit.

His concerns also extended to whether the jurors would believe the foreign cooperating witnesses, who pled guilty to felonies, paid relatively small fines ($50,000.00

to $75,000.00) and retained their freedom to wheel and deal in the United States. He expected the defense to blast these informants "with their pass from incarceration while we're prosecuting the hometown guys, but this was the only way to get the foreign guys here. The challenge for the government team is to put all that in perspective. The evidence of the violations is massive. The executives are sitting in meetings. The video recordings show these people dividing up the world. Indeed, the quality of these tapes caused everybody else [besides Wilson and Andreas] to plead guilty."

The weight of Whitacre creased his brow. Of the mole/money launderer, Spratling sighed, "he had a highly refined ability to deceive. You can't tell what that guy's gonna do. He is most unpredictable. I hope to God, we never have a difficulty like this again. I assure you we had no concept of what he was up to." He paused then added, "I don't know what we can do structurally to keep this from happening again." Spratling expected Whitacre to take the Fifth Amendment at trial. Would the government bring up Whitacre's cooperation in the price-fixing investigation at his upcoming sentencing on numerous counts of embezzlement related offenses? Spratling was quick to point out that the jurisdiction over the matter belonged to the Justice Department's fraud section, which earlier had declined my request for an interview. "But yes," Spratling said, "I think cooperation will be raised." In this, he proved wrong.

It was the trial that worried him most. "Using an informant who defrauded a company of $9 million," he shook his head, "the jury could get mad." Another problem involved a Japanese defendant, who had agreed to appear, plead guilty, and testify for the government, but now refused to return to this country. Spratling "cannot comment on whether the [US] government made a request to the Japanese government to extradite him for that crime." Then he paused again. "The trial won't be a cakewalk for either side. If we lose, it's going to be because the jury did not like the government's case. If we win, it's because the jury understands the FBI agents were exercising every reasonable control that they had under the circumstances."

PART III THE TRIAL

SHAPING THE TABLE

"[T]he Court will not tolerate any implicit or explicit attempts to interject impermissible references to race or national origin during the trial."
—*Judge Blanche Manning*

A modern white-collar trial is really the tip of an iceberg. Beneath the surface and mainly invisible to the jurors, media, and others who come to court lies the mountain of documents, witness interviews, research, discovery fights, and preparation that constitutes the bulk of the work.

In the spring and summer of 1998, the four legal teams generated stacks of elegantly crafted, if acidic, briefs for the court. On the eve of trial, Judge Manning distilled these and found herself faced with a host of questions laced with complexities. In large measure, how she decided them would determine the complexion of the trial and whether it would be fair.

The Andreas team presented the court with a "Motion to Exclude Inauthentic Audio Tapes" made by Mark Whitacre. The defendants argued that the tapes could not be vouched for as accurate in court, since Whitacre could not be forced to testify as to their making and completeness. Therefore, the government would lack "clear and convincing evidence" that the tapes truly reflected the conspirator's conversations. Judge Manning rejected the argument. The modern trend is to admit a tape if any participant in or observer of the recorded conversation can swear to its accuracy. This is enough to pass the "rational juror test," since such a person hearing the material could find it reliable.

Andreas next challenged the tapes made of him and Whitacre meeting with representatives of Ajinomoto in Irvine, California, on October 25, 1993. The prosecution took the position that the tapes were critical and highly incriminating pieces of evidence. The defense said they should be excluded because they did not cover the entire session in Irvine, and therefore they failed to give the complete context.

In effect, unrecorded portions may have helped the defendant. Manning dismissed Andreas' argument "as self-serving conjecture."

Andreas and Wilson both moved to keep Mark Whitacre's statements on tapes and to the FBI from coming into the trial. The defendants relied on a leading Supreme Court case, *Bruton v. United States* (1968). *Bruton* bars courts from admitting confessions that incriminate a codefendant, unless the person who confessed is available to be cross-examined, which Whitacre was not. The government said *Bruton* did not apply, since Whitacre's statements weren't confessions. They were simply part of the context of the investigation. Generally, Manning agreed. But, she declined to give the government the wholesale right to submit to the jury all 103 of the contested statements, many of which were similar. The "repetitive nature of the evidence could unduly prejudice Andreas and Wilson." Instead, she would rule on each Whitacre statement as it arose during the trial.

If the court was going to admit the tapes, Andreas wanted them to be edited to eliminate "offensive language." His lawyers claimed the profanity had nothing to do with price-fixing and would prejudice the jury. The government argued that the foul-mouthed remarks reflected the defendant's callous intent to price fix. Manning did not believe the jurors would be shocked or swayed by words they often had heard before. She refused to censor the tapes.

Andreas tried to purge evidence of the earlier citric acid conspiracy from the current lysine price-fixing case. This was a very close call. As Manning noted "direct evidence of other crimes, wrongs or acts is admissible to prove motive, opportunity, intent, but *never* to show a propensity to conform with criminal behavior." A fundamental tenet of fair trials is that they don't convict people simply because they have been "bad" on other occasions. But as Manning explained, the citric scheme could be introduced at trial "if it is intricately connected with the lysine conspiracy, arose from the same transaction or series of transactions related to the lysine conspiracy, or if it is necessary to explain the context of the lysine conspiracy."

In order to reach her decision, Manning poured over transcripts of meetings involving Andreas, Wilson, and Whitacre. The jury, she found, could interpret the conversations "to suggest that the defendants sought to model the lysine conspiracy on the citric acid conspiracy."

Plus, the two conspiracies overlapped. The citric scam occurred between 1991 and 1995; lysine took place from 1992 to 1995. Both involved additives sold worldwide by ADM. As Manning noted, the citric issue "will undoubtedly prejudice Andreas," but the federal rules of evidence bar only "unfair prejudice." Andreas could not meet the test of showing that the issue "invokes horror or other emotional responses" that would cause the jury to decide the case on some other basis than the evidence. So, citric was in.

Again, the severance issue arose. The efforts of Andreas and Wilson to have their cases severed from Whitacre's were widely publicized. Less well-known and almost unreported was Andreas' attempt to gain a separate trial from Wilson's.

Wilson and Andreas wanted Whitacre out of their trial because they feared a two-front war. On one hand, they knew they would be attacked by the government. On the other, they suspected that Whitacre's defense would involve tarring them. Moreover, since Whitacre probably would not testify, they could not cross-examine him. They said this violated their rights under the confrontation clause of the Sixth Amendment.

Manning was unimpressed. "Defendants can choose their friends and enemies but rarely are permitted to choose their co-defendants." Nothing about the antagonism between them and Whitacre would "prevent the jury from making a reliable test about their guilt or innocence," which is the Supreme Court's litmus for severance.

Manning refused to buy the confrontation clause argument. The clause applies only to testimony against an accused, and Whitacre was not expected to testify. If he did take the stand, the defense teams could cross-examine him to a quick. So, there was no problem.

Andreas' motion to separate his case from Wilson's was based on two theories. First, his lawyers insisted that the citric acid evidence against Wilson could mistakenly be held against Andreas by a confused jury. Manning denied the motion as premised on a "misstatement of fact" because the government's citric evidence, if believed, implicated both defendants. Andreas' lawyers also strongly argued that a joint case with Wilson would lengthen and prejudice the trial against their client. Manning rejected multiple trials as an idea that "would beget delay without any objective benefits to the parties or the court."

Andreas and Wilson could not have expected to win their severance motions nor did they need to win them in order to win the trial. Now, however, they presented the last and only motion they absolutely needed to win.

In discussions with the court, Wilson and Whitacre's attorneys argued that evidence of the company's multimillion-dollar civil settlements of civil antitrust suits involving lysine, citric, and high fructose should not be presented to the jury. The government generally agreed. Civil settlements admit no liability, so they have no place in a criminal court where wrongdoing must be proven beyond a reasonable doubt.

But in 1996, ADM had pleaded guilty to criminal charges of fixing the prices of lysine and citric acid and paid heavy fines. The defense was eager to keep this information out of court. Manning recognized that if the evidence came in, the jury could convict the defendants "based on guilt by their association with ADM."

In short, the jurors would know that the corporation committed felonies. It like-wise would understand that the corporation acted through individuals, who included the defendants. They would be found guilty.

But the corporate guilty pleas also included provisions compelling the cooperation and testimony of ADM employees. The government insisted it needed to bring out the agreements to show the jury what motivated an ADM witness to testify against his colleagues. Generally, such matters relating to deals may be probed by either side, since they affect credibility. The law was on the side of the government but Manning, who took the motion "under advisement to be decided at trial," appeared to be leaning the other way. She ordered the government not to make any mention of the ADM corporate guilty plea during opening statements.

The prosecution also presented a raft of motions including one to "Preclude Evidence or Argument Regarding Alleged Government Misconduct in the Course of the Investigation." Specifically, the government wanted to prevent the defense from arguing that the FBI had deviated from its guidelines on taping and inform-ers. The government likewise objected to the Andreas–Wilson plan to show that the FBI failed to take key investigative steps while building the case, and that it knew Whitacre was unreliable due to the informant's polygraph failures and the inter-nal appraisal of the FBI's vaunted Behavioral Science Unit (BSU).

Now Manning rebuffed the government. The items it sought to quash were rel-evant to the credibility of Whitacre. Moreover, she would let the Andreas and Wilson teams explore the alleged "ulterior" motives of Whitacre to snag the presidency of ADM and of the FBI agents to advance their careers. She termed such base motives "the oldest reasons to shade testimony."

The federal attorneys argued against allowing the defense to present any evi-dence that the lysine collaboration was reasonable or economically justified. Judge Manning conceded that "price-fixing is a per se violation which imposes criminal liability if the defendants had specific intent to agree to conspire regardless of the conspiracy's actual effect on commerce." Nevertheless, she took the matter under advisement. She would wait until trial to see if the government could "produce evidence which proves that the defendants knowingly agreed" to conspire. In effect, the door still remained open to a reasonableness defense, probably the most dan-gerous one that the government could face in a price-fixing case.

The government also moved to bar the defense teams from raising the possible fines and prison terms their clients faced if convicted. Such references would stim-ulate sympathy for otherwise upstanding white-collar defendants. Manning men-tioned that such information would not be relevant to guilt or innocence. The defendants did not contest the motion, and the government probably believed it was out of the woods on the issue.

The prosecution voiced its fear that the accused would attempt jury nullification, the defense of arguing that the jury should disregard the law. Manning properly prohibited such a defense and directed the lawyers not to make "impassioned pleas expounding upon the defendants' virtues as employers and how potential convictions would affect their families."

Another area of passion and prejudice that concerned the government involved race. In particular, the prosecutors wanted to prevent a "yellow peril" anti-Asian approach. The defendants argued that they needed to be able at least to introduce issues reflecting the international nature of lysine competition. Manning agreed to allow "acknowledging a competitor's national original or race when they are used merely to identify the locations or individuals involved in this action." But she admonished the defense against "appealing to ethnic animosities" and made clear that "the court will not tolerate any implicit or explicit attempts to interject impermissible references to race or national origin during the trial." She promised that this ruling would be "strictly enforced."

The government also moved to prevent the accused from trying an entrapment defense. Manning noted that entrapment is the type of defense that places a burden on the defendants. They must show that "the government induced them to commit the crime, and they lacked predisposition to engage in the alleged crime." Manning reserved ruling on entrapment as "premature." She would have to see how the evidence developed at trial in order to make the call.

Lastly, the government moved to block a selective prosecution defense. The accused complained that they had to face trial and prison. But, others involved in the alleged lysine racket were able to cut deals for immunity. This disparity, claimed the defendants, constituted selective prosecution. "Well, it does," wrote Manning, "but not impermissible selective prosecution," based on discrimination or in retaliation for exercising a constitutional right. She explained that the government has prosecutorial discretion about whom to charge with a crime. It need not prosecute everyone. Therefore, she granted the motion to exclude any reference to selective prosecution. However, the inequality of treatment between those on trial and those given immunity soon would be apparent to the jurors. How they would respond was another question.

The trial began on July 9, 1998 in the middle of a broiling Chicago summer. The windowless courtroom seemed overly cool due to the cranked-up air conditioning that had the crowd rolling down sleeves.

Between the bar of the court and the judge's bench was a cramped array of technology: eight computer work stations, half as many giant television monitors, and digitalized Elmo machines that could instantly scan and broadcast a document without the need for transparencies and overheard projections.

Much of the crowd was from Decatur. From the beginning, ADM would charter buses to bring the friends and families of the accused, plus assorted well-wishers. They sat on the right side, facing the judge and away from the jury box, and mingled gregariously. In the first two rows sat the families of Mick Andreas and Terry Wilson, including their wives and strapping offspring. Dwayne Andreas, wearing a hearing aid and flashing a friendly grin, attended with his wife Inez and grown daughter Terry.

Mick Andreas looked as relaxed as he had during pre-trial motions. He joked with and greeted friends in his commanding basso profundo voice. His wife Sally chatted amiably about shopping in the Loop and her earlier trips to Chicago to see the Bulls.

Consistent with his role as a heart patient who had sought not to go to trial, Terry Wilson now seemed quiet and recessive. He had lost a good deal of weight and wore a sickly pallor that was striking in midsummer.

Mark Whitacre's appearance was even more remarkable. He was fit and trim, having lost about twenty pounds. His suit was two sizes too large, as was his collar which gaped. He was darkly tanned from the Carolina prison yard, and he had shaved his head. There was nothing in this lean scarecrow of the lumpy "type A" executive who had been sentenced for fraud only four months before.

The crowd seemed disappointed on the first day when it became clear that the court had to go through several rounds of business before reaching the opening statements and testimony. First, Judge Manning handled a bitter sideshow that had been lingering in the case. The defense had subpoenaed documents from Dickstein, Shapiro, Morin & Oshinsky, one of the plaintiff's law firms that sued ADM for civil antitrust violations. Specifically, Andreas and Wilson wanted the records of contacts between the Dickstein lawyer Ken Adams and shareholders' activist David Hoech. They accused Hoech of buying information from Whitacre while he still worked at ADM, which Hoech turned around and sold to ADM's competitors. The defense argued that the information "would reflect strongly on Mr. Whitacre's credibility."

The government responded firmly that "David Hoech is irrelevant to these proceedings. Mr. Whitacre's credibility is not relevant to any of the informant's taped statements." Rather, Whitacre's words would serve only as a context in which to place those of the conspirators.

Judge Manning listened patiently, then quashed subpoenas for the civil firm's records. "I guess," she offered matter-of-factly, "I fail to see how any of that could be relevant." In her view, either there was an agreement to fix prices or there was not. Whitacre's "motivation" hardly mattered. In rejecting the defense's position, she had served notice that the trial should stay focused and not meander through the various testy skirmishes that could absorb and bias the jury.

The Andreas and Wilson defense teams seemed unwilling to accept that Hoech and the civil class-action lawyers would not be targeted in the current trial. Kristina Anderson, Wilson's Chicago local counsel, rose to level a charge. A young well-tailored advocate who recently won a measure of notoriety by being named one of the "Real McBeals" by *Chicago Magazine*, Anderson accused the Dickstein firm of receiving at least two faxes from Hoech in May 1995, a month before the Decatur raid, following which Whitacre had been "outed" as a mole.

The implications of the lawyer's remarks were clear. She was accusing Hoech and Whitacre of being in collusion with greedy plaintiffs' lawyers during a highly secret government undercover mission. Moreover, the alleged monetary motives, interests, and biases of witnesses are usually fair game for cross-examination. But Richard Leveridge, a senior partner with Dickstein, swore to the court that his firm had not received any faxes from Hoech before the raid. Leveridge challenged Anderson to produce the records of the faxes. She never did. Predictably, Manning refused to reverse her ruling.

Then attorneys for the *New York Times*, *Wall Street Journal*, and *Chicago Tribune* intervened on First Amendment grounds to seek the copies of the transcripts of the tapes made by Whitacre. Manning earlier had ruled against sequestering the jury in a hotel. On the other hand, she remained concerned that they would be confronted with headlines and media reports, perhaps based on materials not even before them such as portions of tapes not introduced into evidence. That would deprive the defendants of their right to a fair trial. It outweighed the public's First Amendment right to read the transcript in her view. She denied the motion of the newspapers.

Then the Andreas team made a serious challenge to the prosecution. On July 1, 1998, the Tenth Circuit Court of Appeals sitting in Denver had sent shock waves through the law enforcement community in a decision called *United States v. Singleton*. In *Singleton*, the three-judge panel tossed out a conviction based on an informant's testimony. It ruled that the government could not grant leniency to a witness who had been involved in criminal activity in exchange for testimony.

Tenth Circuit law does not control the Northern District of Illinois, which is part of the Seventh Circuit. But Judge Manning could have found the Tenth Circuit decision "persuasive" and followed it, particularly if she felt it would be affirmed by the Supreme Court and become the law of the land.

The *Singleton* opinion also had populist appeal. The three-judge panel in Denver raged against prosecutors buying testimony with leniency. Adoption of *Singleton* by Manning would have resulted in suppression of the statements from ADM's coconspirators and gutted the government's case. Manning knew that there was "contrary authority" in the Seventh Circuit, and that widespread adoption of *Singleton* by the Supreme Court or federal courts would mark a sea change in criminal law. It therefore was unlikely to be upheld. She rejected the defense motion and moved on to jury selection, called voir dire.

Voir dire is a French term meaning to see and to say. Allowing the parties an opportunity to view the prospective jurors and to hear what they have to say is supposed to promote fairness and prevent people with biases from being chosen to sit in judgment. It seldom works that way. While jury selection may be the most important part of a case, and outweigh even compelling evidence—recall O.J. Simpson— it often is given short shrift in trials. In all but homicide cases, voir dire usually is conducted superficially by the judge or even by a clerk. Questions are asked en masse to the venire (panel of prospective jurors) to save court time. The result is that a herd mentality sets in among the candidates who answer as they think they should in front of a group or fail to volunteer responses at all. Jurors often are picked by lawyers without a clue as to their true biases or whether they would be appropriate for the case.

Ordinarily, voir dire takes a morning. Judge Manning devoted three days to the process. To her credit, she asked all the initial questions to the eighty panelists in the venire. These included whether they knew any of the lawyers, witnesses, or defendants, or held stock in, were employed by, or did business with ADM or any of the alleged coconspirator companies. Moreover, she not only allowed the lawyers to interrogate individuals, but permitted them to depart from the standard questions that often yielded predictable, unrevealing replies.

The judge probed attitudes towards the courts, the FBI, informants, wealthy defendants, price-fixing, trade associations, expert testimony, and video and audio taping without the permission of the subject. She asked if they could sit in judgment of other human beings when the penalty could be jail. The process was time consuming, but it seemed to weed out people who clearly could not have been impartial.

If any prospective juror showed the slightest unease about a question, Manning allowed the lawyers to interrogate him or her individually. This questioning occurred in hushed tones at a table in the front of the courtroom or back in the judge's chambers.

The judge gave each side nine peremptory challenges. These "strikes" allowed a lawyer to remove a juror for any reason. The lawyers also could move to eliminate a juror who seemed incapable of being fair. Such challenges "for cause" are rare since many people hide their slanted views. Perhaps due to the nature of the ADM case or the searching voir dire, prejudices percolated to the surface in Judge Manning's court.

The process dragged on. Jurors grumbled in the gallery while awaiting their inquisition in chambers. The Andreas and Wilson teams used their local Chicago lawyers extensively to help them pick the jury. In chambers late one afternoon,

Andreas' Chicago counsel Joseph Duffy said, "I had to step out in the courtroom for a moment. It looked like the movie *Twelve Angry Men*. Nobody in there looked happy." Jack Bray quipped that it was "more like *Eighty Angry Men*."

Judge Manning pressed on in typically deliberate fashion, making sure that each person revealed every iota of bias, whether gleaned from media accounts of the case or from life experiences. At one point, a young Japanese woman named Miwa came into chambers. It was a signal moment. She said that use of undercover snitches offended her personal ethics, but she would lay these aside and follow the court's instructions on the law. She also volunteered her strong aversion to capital punishment, which of course had no role in the case. Based on her views, Miwa fit the profile of an ideal defense juror. After she left the room, Reid Weingarten moved immediately to strike her for cause. "I think there was a disconnect at every turn with that prospective juror. I think she's warehousing a bunch of things that will make her unqualified to serve. I just had this rumbling discontent throughout the entire interrogation."

Manning denied the motion, but for once, played into the defense's hands and stated, "you certainly can exercise a peremptory if you so desire." In effect, she told the defendants that they could use their discretionary strikes to remove an Asian. The ruling probably was her single pretrial mistake. But it was a major one that would affect the tone of the trial.

Tuesday, July 14, 1998 was the final day of jury selection. As usual, before the venire was called into court, Manning asked the government and defense attorneys if they were ready to proceed. All but Bill Walker uttered the usual, "Yes, Your Honor."

On his feet, Whitacre's lawyer drawled, "I am ready to proceed, Your Honor, but Dr. Whitacre is not." Everyone in the courtroom knew that Whitacre was capable of surprises. But, Manning decided to take the bull by the horns. She did not pull the parties into chambers or ask for a sidebar. Instead, she directed Whitacre to "step forward and advise me as to what the problem is."

Whitacre approached the bench and asked to make a statement. Before his client could begin, Walker started speaking. "Dr. Whitacre wishes to be tried in absentia, that he be sent back immediately to his parent institution, and that he'd waive his right to be present for picking a jury and during the entire trial."

Reddening, Walker added that he disagreed with his client. The case was complex; he wanted Whitacre to sit beside him and help with tactical decisions and analysis of the evidence as it came in. The lawyer feared that he might be stopped from calling his client as a witness (if they made that choice) since the federal prison at Butner, North Carolina was 8-hundred miles away. If the defendant's decision to testify was made at the last moment, immediate travel arrangements might be impossible.

Among the most difficult decisions a court can make pertain to the rare situations when a client and his lawyer disagree. Manning, who still wanted to hear from Whitacre, warned him that he now would be making statements in open court. Since these could compromise his right to remain silent, she cautioned him not to touch on the issues in the case. He agreed, but began speaking so rapidly that she had to slow him down.

Beginning again, Whitacre insisted that "I can defend myself best by not being located here." He described life on the twenty-first floor of the Metropolitan Correctional Center (MCC), in Chicago. In North Carolina, he lived in a minimum security setting with convicted businessmen, lawyers, and politicians. The MCC was maximum security. It housed a number of violent actors including gang members from the Latin Kings and Garden Disciples who roamed freely. His floor had 108 inmates but only one guard.

Informants of any stripe including those who betrayed white-collar conspiracies were not popular. The gang members had begun asking if he were the same Mark Whitacre in the news. He denied it.

The reasons for Whitacre's changed appearance became clear. He did not look at all like the informant whose picture was flashed on TV and ran on the front page of the Chicago papers. But now his cover probably was blown. Four folders of documents from his lawyers had been stolen at the MCC. Others he had shredded rather than leaving them in his cell.

In Butner, he was left alone. He had a locked storage bin for his voluminous legal materials. Plus, the North Carolina prison had provided witness protection measures including a false identity. Telephone access, visiting arrangements, and food were also superior at Butner, as was sleep. Butner had an enforced "quiet time" at 10 PM. At the MCC, inmates carried on until about 4 AM. Then he had to get up at five for transfer to a court "holding tank" at six.

He called Butner his "home." "If you look at the legal definition of home, it is where you're going to spend the next several years, and actually right now my home would be in a minimum security prison in North Carolina and not here."

Whitacre worried aloud that he could not remain composed in the courtroom. "I think it's a disadvantage for me to be in front of the jury in this particular case. I feel very strongly emotionally attached to this case. I've worked for the FBI for many years on this case, and then to be indicted . . . has been a very strong emotional drain." He paused. "When certain things are said by certain witnesses," he thought his anger would become plain. "So, I'm requesting that I not be placed in front of the jurors."

He complained that no one close to him could attend court to give him moral support. All his immediate family members had been subpoenaed by the other defendants. As potential witnesses, they were sequestered and could not come into court until after they took the stand. Whitacre decried the situation as harassment and noted that Wilson's and Andreas' friends and families had not been put through the same indignity and thus could sit in the courtroom.

Whitacre felt he could help his attorney just as well from Butner. If he chose to testify, the logistics could be worked out. "I have very good contacts with the BOP [Federal Bureau of Prisons]. I know for a fact that they have at least one plane come here each week and sometimes two, and I feel that the chance of getting here within a day's notice and certainly within two days' notice would happen if I was called upon as a witness in this trial by my attorney."

Manning remained concerned about "whether you're knowingly, intelligently and voluntarily waiving your right to be present at trial." He rehashed his educational attainments including his new law degree from a correspondence school in California. Then she gently probed his mental status. At the BOP's Springfield medical facility, he said he had an "extensive evaluation" and received a "clean bill of health." While a "civilian psychiatrist actually had me diagnosed with a bipolar disorder and taking lithium," the prison doctors, "clearly said I was not bipolar." Presently, he was not under the care of a psychiatrist and taking no medication. As for his earlier suicide attempts, the prison medical staff feels "that the stress of this case is the reason why I reacted in certain ways that I did. . . . There's much evidence with many doctors that I do not have any type of manic depressive or bipolar disorder or any other mental disorder."

With Manning leaning Whitacre's way, Walker remonstrated, "I think it's vital that he's here assisting me in this case," which he considered one of the most complex in twenty years of trial work. Plus, he did not accept his client's view that it would be a snap to return to Chicago to testify. "He seems to think it's pretty easy, but I don't think that the marshals' service is a travel agency."

Judge Manning then asked the bottom-line question to Walker. "You've had a lot of contact with Dr. Whitacre: based on your observations, is it your opinion that he is competent to waive his presence?" The lawyer conceded, "He's competent to waive, your honor. But sometimes you can be competent and not make the right decisions." He seemed uneasy with the fact that Whitacre's private psychiatrist at the University of North Carolina had prescribed lithium, which the BOP evaluation countered. "I find in my twenty years that the federal system takes people off their medication very quickly."

Jim Griffin raised an important point. How would government witnesses identify Whitacre without being able to point to him in court? Whitacre's appearance had changed so much that pictures could not be used. Again over his lawyer's advice, Whitacre volunteered to "stipulate" to his identification by any witness.

The other defense attorneys seemed as nonplussed by the proposed absence of the mole. They expressed worries that the jury would think their clients more culpable because they were sitting in court. Manning rejected the argument saying that she could instruct the jury to draw no inferences from a defendant's presence or absence.

The she cautioned Whitacre again. "I don't think that it's the best idea for you to waive your presence. I think it's probably a really bad idea." But she recognized that it was the defendant's right to be tried in absentia and let him go. In so doing, she dealt a blow to the strategy of the other defendants. They undoubtedly would have preferred Whitacre to be present for his branding as a Judas entrapper, and saboteur, in the hopes that he would act out or at least visibly color in front of the jury.

The ADM defendants' lawyers seemed surprised. Weingarten rued, "it puts a bizarre piece into the trial." The defense would have to make do with finger pointing at an empty chair. Bray and Weingarten again called for a severance. But Lassar and Walker successfully objected to duplicating efforts. By allowing Whitacre to leave, Manning reluctantly had made another decision that would keep the trial on track and the jury from being distracted.

After excusing Whitacre, the judge completed voir dire. By the day's end, eighteen people had been chosen, enough for twelve jurors and six alternates. In her typically insightful fashion, she told the group that she would not reveal to them who were the alternates until the time of deliberations. This would keep all of them listening throughout the long weeks of testimony.

SPINNING

"[Y]ou know, the main thing is if we were trying to fix prices,
we ought to be fired for being so fucking incompetent."
—Terry Wilson

In a surprising move, the scholarly Jim Griffin, rather than Scott Lassar, the seasoned criminal prosecutor, gave the opening statement for the government. A slight, pale wiry man with a thatch of prematurely white hair and an elfin grin, Griffin headed the antitrust division's midwestern field office.

Because they want the jurors to regard the acts of defendants as serious and criminal, prosecutors seldom inject humor into a trial. But Griffin began on a light note. Obviously, this was not a gruesome or sexy crime. "There's not," he told the eighteen people in the box, "a price-fixing police television program."

Griffin was not a charismatic presence, but he was a true believer in the antitrust law. He conveyed his zeal to the jury by using real-world examples of how price and volume conspiracies among appliance makers would jack up the price of the refrigerators that average people would have to buy.

Then he moved to the arcane world of lysine. ADM entered the $600 million global market in 1992 and that same year began attending price-fixing meetings with competitors, as the jury would learn from video and audio tapes.

How did the government get the tapes? Griffin related the strange story of Whitacre's complaint of sabotage and extortion by an Ajinomoto engineer named Fujiwara, which led to a complaint by ADM to the CIA, "who made the determination to notify the FBI." That resulted in the involvement of the special agent Brian Shepard. At Griffin's request Shepard shyly stood up in the courtroom. Shepard initially began taping Whitacre's phones in order to catch the extortionist. In November 1992, ADM suddenly told the FBI to "go away. You're not investigating us anymore. . . . We don't want you talking to Whitacre. We don't want you talking to any of our executives. We don't want you with a recorder or monitor on Whitacre's phones." Griffin paused for effect. "Even though they were supposedly the victim of this extortion, they didn't want the investigation to go forward."

But the FBI stayed with the scent that led back to Whitacre. The expensive new plant under his control was not functioning well. He fabricated the sabotage story as an excuse. He also admitted to the price-fixing scheme, and though "reluctant," had agreed to cooperate with the FBI. To the bureau's consternation in August 1995, "it was discovered that back in 1991 and continuing all the way through the spring of 1995, Mark Whitacre was stealing money from ADM."

In essence, the government had made an extremely difficult strategic decision. Whitacre's $9 million embezzlement had nothing to do with the antitrust conspiracy. It had no relevance to the determination of guilt or innocence at the ongoing trial. But the government figured that the Andreas and Wilson lawyers would find a way to get it into evidence. Certainly they could use it to attack Whitacre if he took the stand. If not, perhaps they would try to spin the fraud against the FBI.

Straining to limit the damage, the prosecutors decided to bring up the informant's misconduct in their own case. It would be an embarrassment but at least not something that they had hidden. At the same time, Griffin distanced himself, the prosecution, the FBI, and, by inference, the jury from the mole who had served the government for two years. "Throughout this trial, not once, never will we ask you to rely on anything that Mark Whitacre says."

For almost an hour, Griffin emotionlessly outlined the evidence the jury would hear regarding conspiratorial meetings in Mexico City, Hawaii, Paris, Zurich, Tokyo, Sapporo, and elsewhere around the globe. Most of the deeds were captured on tape. Griffin promised that "you will hear from a government expert who will tell you that those tapes have not been altered."

Some of the government's case would come from live witnesses who had been coconspirators but received light or no punishment in exchange for "cooperation." Griffin did not say whether anyone from ADM would be testifying for the government. Nor did he allude to the ADM corporate guilty plea, which required the assistance from employees in return for limiting the government to prosecuting the three on trial. He did tell the jurors that the defense would attack prosecution witnesses including "the FBI agents who are sitting here, the FBI agents who collected a mountain of evidence against these defendants."

Griffin also explained that occasionally during the conspiracy some of the companies cheated each other on price and volume goals. The prosecutor maintained that episodes of competitive behavior, whether devious or not, did not let the ADM executives off the hook. The government would prove that they had made agreements to fix prices and limit volume. Under the Sherman Act, he explained to the jury, "the agreement is the crime."

By now it was lunchtime. Manning ordered a recess. After the jury left, the lawyers began to spar. Mark Hulkower, the feisty second chair on the Wilson team, strode to the podium. Hulkower, who often handled the disagreeable tangents to leave Reid Weingarten free to focus on the big picture, immediately moved for a mistrial. Hulkower charged Griffin with breaking two advocacy rules. First, he said the prosecutor, with his examples of refrigerators and other consumer goods, had placed the jurors "in the shoes of the victims." Second, Griffin had mentioned Wilson's role in another ADM price-fixing conspiracy, citric acid, that was not the subject of the trial. Hulkower inveighed that this had prejudiced and inflamed the jury.

Manning denied the mistrial, but heard another Hulkower motion to remove Brian Shepard from the courtroom until he took the stand because the "reliability and credibility of the case agent are at stake." Manning granted the motion and Shepard marched out. His FBI colleague Robert Herndon was allowed to remain.

Now it was Jack Bray's turn. He unveiled a chart he wanted to use during his opening statement. It showed that the price of lysine actually was higher before ADM entered the market in 1992 and then rose again after the raid in July 1995, when ADM's role as an alleged conspirator ceased. The defense hoped to seed the idea that ADM's activity was not anticompetitive; but that it positively affected the market and consumers by lowering prices.

Griffin argued that the prices before and after the conspiracy were irrelevant to whether an illegal agreement had been struck. He accused the defense of trying to circumvent the judge's ruling that this was a "per se" case by mounting a "reasonableness" defense. Unswayed, Manning overruled the objection and allowed Bray to use the contested chart. Bray's poster underscored that the defense's strategy would be audacious. The ADM defendants were not content to be seen as not guilty of any price-fixing violation. They also wanted ADM's foray into lysine to be viewed as a good thing.

When Bray rose to open, he faced the common problem of a jury sluggish after the noon meal. A consummate diplomat, he tweaked them by mentioning "I always get a little sleepy right after lunch." Almost immediately they started to pay close attention. Bray introduced his client as a hands-on boss with an open-door policy, a man whom everybody called Mick. Whitacre, he said, took advantage of Mick's trust and goodwill to tape him surreptitiously. From recordings the jury would learn that Mick was "a very friendly man, he's very easy to talk to." But Mick never once used the term "price-fixing" in any of the tapes. To Bray, the government's "inability to produce a tape like that after two and a half years . . . is itself reasonable doubt." Moreover, he previewed a taped conversation in which Mick mentioned that "we don't make [illegal] deals at ADM, you will hear that out of Mick Andreas' mouth." Bray was careful not to give the impression that his client would or would not testify. Rather, he played on the theme of treachery by Whitacre. It was Whitacre who used the damning terms about a price-fixing agreement, and Whitacre who was so vicious that he would get his trusted friends arrested in order to seize command at ADM and destroy the Andreas family, many of whom were in the gallery.

Back in 1992, Bray said, Mick was the executive vice president and assistant to the president, Jim Randall. At ADM, Mick specialized in trading commodities and developing "feed stocks," which in recent years came to include biotechnology products. Since Mick did not have a biotech background, he hired and came to rely on Mark Whitacre, "a very young man and a PhD from Cornell." In particular, ADM wanted Whitacre to lead it into the world lysine market, but this was a big gamble because of the "Asian cartel," which for decades had controlled the manufacture and trade of the amino acid.

> ADM had watched for several years while the big Ajinomoto Company of Japan, and the Kyowa Hakko Kogyo Company of Japan had simply dominated the world, together with their lesser competitors, and in the process of dominating the world market in lysine, they had carved up the market in the United States, carved it up in a completely illegal way, carved it up in a way that essentially cost people far more than lysine should cost.
>
> But they also saw something else. They saw that many United States companies, big companies, Merck, companies of that sort, had tried to dent that market, had tried to fight, in a sense, that Asian cartel, and had given up for probably a variety of reasons. But one of them had to be that they didn't think they had the staying power to deal with them knowing that this was a foreign cartel.
>
> But ADM finally made the decision. We're into biotechnology. This is a good product. It's a good product for everyone, not just America, but for the world. And ADM said, we think we can build a plant.

The facility was huge. It had the capacity to "produce enough lysine to satisfy the world market." Now Bray flashed his chart. In 1988 before the plant came on-line "the Asian cartel" had fixed the price of lysine at $3.00 per pound.

Once ADM entered the market the price plummeted. At the time of the raid in 1995 it was "in the area of 97, 98 cents a pound." ADM's activity saved consumers "something like $100 million in lysine prices."

Now Bray put the faintest note of indignation into his perfectly modulated voice. "What ADM did from the mind and perspective of Mick Andreas—as opposed to the completely different hidden agenda of Mark Whitacre—which I will get into in a moment—what ADM did in his mind is wage fierce competition against a criminal cartel from Asia, a war of economic self-defense. And this cartel did, what you might guess they did, turned full force on ADM. Began surveillance of ADM. Began looking for ways to challenge ADM in the market." The cartel, he revealed, even tried to steal the microorganism from ADM's plant that made its strain of lysine.

As promised, Bray returned to Whitacre, "who the evidence will show is prone to lie about virtually anything and is a man who lied most of his life. Some of the lies were inexplicable. For instance, Whitacre would present himself as an orphan who had been adopted, which was false. Under pressure where it would actually help him, he's willing to falsely accuse others," Bray insisted. In the bogus Fujiwara plot Whitacre had accused six ADM coworkers of collaborating with the extortionist, "and everyone of them was completely innocent."

The FBI quickly learned that Whitacre was a liar and, according to Bray, should not have done business with the biochemist. But, "they were salivating so much after an Andreas that they went right on and signed up Whitacre."

Now the lawyer levelled a more serious charge against the bureau regarding Whitacre's embezzlement and money laundering scheme. "He continued to steal money from ADM. He continued to do it right under the nose of the FBI," which either condoned the $10 million theft or looked away from it. Whitacre's greed demanded an elite lifestyle, including horses and a Ferrari. The FBI agents "were making their careers, putting an Andreas up on their wall."

Bray derided the other government witnesses whom he termed "cooperators." Mainly Japanese, they had enjoyed "years of predatory conduct on the American market, years of predatory conduct worldwide that went unchecked until ADM came in." Now instead of getting up to three years in prison, they would get their "reward"—immunity for "testifying against and perhaps seriously damaging their biggest competitor."

As Bray knew, a criminal defense lawyer may not gain sympathy from the jury by signalling that his client can go to prison if convicted. The potential penalty may not be mentioned except in a capital case, but Bray cleverly solved the problem by telling the jury the sentence that the "cooperators" had avoided. Jurors now knew that his client, a distinguished businessman, could spend three years on a federal penitentiary if they voted to convict. Their burden had become heavier. Bray had their full attention. Now he thanked them for it and drew smiles from the jurors "particularly since it was after lunch and not a one of you fell asleep."

Next it was Bill Walker's turn. A lone, sympathetic figure, he sat at a table far from the jury without his client, a team of lawyers, or a stack of lavishly produced exhibits. A beefy man with a large open face, he began speaking in a warm, downstate twang. He told the jury that his style was to be brief.

After twenty years of trying cases, Walker believed that midwestern juries appreciated lawyers who got to the point whether in openings, closings, or examining witnesses. He could not understand the logic of big-city lawyers who asked twenty questions, most of them repetitive or minutely different, when one would suffice. Nor could he fathom why ADM had gone to Washington to hire counsel when Illinois had plenty of able trial lawyers.

Walker well understood the scapegoating of his client. "What you've seen here so far is what I would classify as either a roasting of Dr. Whitacre or a butchering of him." He did not try to spin, minimize, or dispute the charges against Whitacre. "I believe you argue the case at the end and this is the opening statement." But, he pointed out that "it's interesting that Mr. Bray comes up and really puts down Dr. Whitacre, but ADM recruited him. I've never seen where a person goes to a company and says you got to hire me. They recruited him."

Moreover, Whitacre started the lysine operation "from scratch, from ground zero. Remember, he's the one who had the expertise. The evidence will show that. It wasn't done by Mr. Andreas or Mr. Wilson or anyone else."

He challenged the government's villainization of his client. "Everybody is here for one reason: Dr. Whitacre went to the FBI, and told them some suspicions he had, and from that we're in this trial."

Walker raised his client's strongest angle at the trial, which he knew from discussions in chambers that Judge Manning would reinforce in her instructions to the jury before it began to deliberate. "Dr. Whitacre was acting as a government agent from November 5, 1992, and the government knows he cannot be convicted of a crime from that date forward." So, the jury had a very narrow window in terms of looking at his misconduct. "Anything after that is irrelevant and immaterial" to Whitacre, though it could be used to convict the other ADM defendants.

Walker made a slow sweeping gesture towards the stacks of audio and video surveillance tapes on the government's table. "This is Dr. Whitacre's, not the FBI's work." The big man explained that the FBI could not have bugged anyone or broken the conspiracy without Whitacre. He urged the jurors to give his client "credit for bringing this out." Then he thanked them and went back to his lonely post.

During a break, Reid Weingarten jousted in chambers for the right to bring certain controversial "snippets" of testimony out in his opening dispute. The government argued that the disputed material was irrelevant and might never come into evidence. Manning listened and gave the green light to the defense.

After Manning invited him to proceed, Weingarten swaggered to the jury box with a distinctive rolling gait. Before he said a word, his body language conveyed comfort, confidence, and control. Weingarten knew he had a big problem. Unlike Mick Andreas' few and sometimes ambiguous taped statements, Terry Wilson's were numerous and incriminating. In order to defuse the issue, Weingarten immediately became personal with the jury.

> When I was a little boy, a girl named Janet Stillson lived up the street. When I would play with her, she treated me mercilessly. She said I was ugly. She said I was fat. She said I couldn't run fast. I was terribly upset by those remarks. I would go home, and I would talk to my big sister. My big sister today is a woman of great wisdom, and she had a lot of wisdom even back then. She'd say: Reid, does Janet let you play with her dog?
>
> Yeah.
>
> Does she let you play with her toys?
>
> Yeah.
>
> Does she share her cookies with you?
>
> Yeah.
>
> Then my sister would say: Judge a person not just by what they say, but by what they do.

Then he gave an example from adult life involving a Chicago White Sox game and two members of his defense team—Kristina Anderson and Monica Selter, who sat at the table with Terry Wilson.

> I wanted to see Frank Thomas the other night, so I bought a big bunch of tickets and invited all the members of my team to the game, including Kristina. Kristina was busy and didn't want to go to the game, but she didn't want to insult me. So I said: Kristina, do you want to go to the White Sox game?
>
> She said: Oh, of course. Great idea.
>
> If that conversation had been taped, you would have seen Kristina apparently agreeing with me that she wanted to see Frank Thomas with me that night. Well, what happened thereafter? Kristina said to Monica: I'm busy. The White Sox are bad this year. I don't want to see them.
>
> The best evidence of all, Kristina didn't show up that night at the game. Again, if you had seen the conversation between me and Kristina on tape, you would say there's an agreement. If you looked at what Kristina said privately with Monica or if you examined what she did, obviously Kristina never intended to agree to go to the game.
>
> Bottom line, you cannot accept these tapes at face value. The tapes are not the whole story. Reason number one, these competitors did not tell each other the truth. There were lies. There was bluffing. There was gaming. The reason for that in large measure is the history of this market carefully laid out both by the government and Mr. Bray.

In short, the foreign competitors and mostly the Japanese competitors had a stranglehold on the lysine market. I won't go through all the details. They had a cartel, and the price at one point shortly before ADM enters into the market was as much as $3 a pound. ADM enters the market, boom, the price plummets to 58 cents a pound. There is a panic in the cartel. There is hatred. There is fear, and there is distrust coming at ADM from this foreign cartel. The results are conversations between the competitors where, simply stated, they were lying to each other.

In sum, the tapes did not shed light on the "one issue in this case: Was there an illegal agreement between those [ADM] guys and the foreign competitors." Moreover, these tapes "are long, they're repetitive, and they're tedious."

In what may have been a mistake, he told the jury that the "most reliable evidence" on tape "occurs when the ADM guys are alone, and we call them locker-room conversations." Usually, these took place "before and after contacts with the competitors."

Even more than Bray, Weingarten tried to fan the flames against the Asians. "The Japanese competitors and Korean competitors hated, feared, and distrusted ADM. There is a document that you will see that indicates as much. It indicates that there were discussions and perhaps even an intention to bomb the ADM plant in Decatur." Of course, there was no real evidence of any terrorist plot. But Weingarten's image of a violent yellow peril had the jury sitting up straight. The allegation also made the *New York Times*.

Weingarten also cast conventional doubt on the evidence. The tapes were selective, and the FBI broke its own rules by not collecting evidence favorable to ADM. Plus, it failed to monitor Whitacre who was "the director, producer, and choreographer of this drama."

As for ADM, it did nothing wrong by meeting with competitors. It was gathering intelligence in order to survive in a "hostile amino acid world controlled by the Japanese . . . where no American company had ever succeeded." ADM had to gird itself for "predatory pricing by the Japanese [and] locking up of distributors with help from the Japanese government."

This was a ruthless arena. "The philosophy here is to hold the hand of your enemy so that you don't get stabbed in the back. They don't teach you this at Northwestern Business School, but this is the rough and terrible fact of life when you're a company trying to break into a cartel. Terry Wilson was like an intelligence operative in Mick Andreas' economic war of self-defense. At times he was gaining information, and at times, he was fooling the price-fixers into a false sense of security that ADM would even consider playing their game. You know what? It worked.

ADM, starting from a standstill, gained a significant foothold in the lysine market, a foothold they enjoy today."

Weingarten made sure that the jury would know his client, whether or not Wilson testified.

Terry is 60 years old. He's a family man. He's from Iowa. He's married. He's a corn man. This what he knows. He knows the corn business. From high school at the age of 17, he went into the Marines, and thereafter he soon found himself at ADM.

From the very bottom, he worked his way up to a position of significant responsibility. He is utterly loyal to ADM. He is proud of his association with the Andreas family. In the history of American agriculture, Dwayne Andreas is a giant, and Terry Wilson was and is proud of this association. Terry is a smart, tough, salty businessman with shrewd sense.

Weingarten revealed that Whitacre, the PhD, didn't like his client because of his lack of education. The Japanese detested Wilson because of his aggressive quest for market share for ADM. Eventually, the jury would see that the Japanese wanted Wilson removed from the negotiations in order to "have Whitacre participate alone" and do their bidding.

Weingarten went further than Bray in vilifying the FBI for allowing Whitacre to embezzle. "Emma, my chocolate lab, would have seen Whitacre was trying to rip off ADM. The FBI agents may testify that they didn't realize it but that's a line in the sand." Then, he confided in the jury. "You know Mark Whitacre busted two polygraphs." On the tapes, Whitacre "shoved words down people's throats." The FBI simply was eager to land a corporate "big fish" indictment rather than do the right thing and get rid of the mole. "You will see that the FBI in this case was nothing more than cheerleaders to Mark Whitacre." By the last meeting of the lysine cartel in Atlanta in 1995, shortly before the raid in Decatur, "no one is there from ADM but Mark Whitacre."

Weingarten dropped an intriguing tidbit. After the raid but before Whitacre was exposed as an informant, Whitacre and Wilson had dinner. Whitacre was wearing a wire and hoping to get more evidence from Wilson with "his defenses down" after several drinks. Then Weingarten added, "And I'll flat out tell you that Terry Wilson drinks too much, and he has a drinking problem." It was tactically questionable for Weingarten to disclose his client's vice. The lawyer had not screened the jurors for possible prejudice against alcoholics during voir dire. But, Weingarten wanted to place Wilson's final taped remark in the context of disinhibited candor. Terry says, "you know, the main thing is if we were trying to fix prices, we ought to be fired for being so fucking incompetent." Weingarten dismissed the prosecutor's evidence of previous price-fixing by Wilson in the citric acid market as a desperate ploy. "Two and half years of taping of Terry Wilson was not enough. . . . Citric acid is a completely different product involving completely different companies. These are European companies, completely different people."

Weingarten reminded the jury that a citric acid conspiracy was not on trial here, only lysine mattered. He poured passion into his finish.

> We busted up a cartel and brought the price of lysine down to a fraction of what it was. ADM's entry into the lysine market was the best thing that ever happened to the pigs and chickens of this country. Terry Wilson is a fighter, not a fixer. He honors ADM, and he honors the law of this land. The only agreement he ever reached with the competitors is that they didn't like each other.

After the openings, Manning called the lawyers back into chambers. The purpose was to reveal her own potential conflict of interest. "Yesterday I was advised by a former secretary, who happens to be a niece of mine—and she was my secretary in the appellate court for a number of years—that she is employed by a law firm that has some connection to this case. We didn't go into it. I didn't want to get into it." However, the names of Whitacre and Andreas had been brought up in the conversation by her niece. Judge Manning said that she was close to her niece, had in fact raised her, and still saw her often. The law firm where the woman worked had no role in the present trial. Manning assured those present that she and her niece would not discuss the matter again. It was a pregnant moment. Wilson's attorneys already had asked for a mistrial and could have renewed the motion on firmer grounds. Scott Lassar asked simply, "Judge, do you think you could be fair?" Manning replied, "Absolutely. Does anybody care to cross-examine me?"

Obviously questions would have bubbled up in a lawyer's brain. Who was the niece? Exactly what had she and the judge said? Could the niece be relied on not to rekindle the matter privately with her aunt? Why had the judge waited a day to reveal the discussion? But none were asked.

Bray and Weingarten each said they had "no problem" with the judge's disclosure and with her continuing to preside. Walker made conciliatory remarks. Since "there's a lot of money" involved in the web of related ADM litigation, "there's a lot of law firms involved." So, it was "natural" that a Chicago paralegal might end up in an office handling a piece of it.

He did want to know if the niece still lived with the judge. She said no, but volunteered that the woman had come to court during the last two days.

No one grilled Manning or moved for her recusal. It was a sign that each lawyer thought she was fair, and that each believed he was still in the hunt for a favorable verdict after the openings and early rulings.

10
MIMOTO

"We have an old saying at ADM. It's better to have them inside the tent pissin' out, than outside the tent pissin' in."
—Terry Wilson

Like many analysts of the criminal trial process, Alan Dershowitz has noted that the jury is most observant during the early witnesses and final argument. Since the prosecutor puts on its case first and argues last, Dershowitz believes that the structure of the trial favors the government. Naturally, the prosecution must be careful not to squander its strengths during these critical phases.

Scott Lassar took a risk when he decided to lead off with a Japanese business-man who had been involved in the conspiracy. Obviously, it would have been safer to start with an FBI agent or American executive, but Bray and Weingarten had attempted to stir the pot against the Asians. It made sense to deal with this animus early rather than letting it linger in the jurors' minds.

A tall squarely built man with a dark mat of precisely parted hair, Kanji Mimoto walked heavily to the well of the court. He took the oath, then slumped into the wooden chair. Invisible ropes tied him to the witness stand. Everything about him seemed to sag. He had a small pursed mouth and sometimes bit his lower lip. Before he spoke, a shade came over his face. He was the picture of shame.

Mimoto declined the court's offer of a translator. His English was functional, clipped and clear. At least initially, he probably enjoyed the advantage of witnesses who do not speak perfect English—jurors often think that they lack the ability to lie effectively.

Like most experienced prosecutors, Lassar got the witness' criminal conduct out of the way first. Mimoto admitted to pleading guilty to price-fixing. Lassar asked him to define the crime. "Price-fixing," he intoned solemnly, "means among the competitors to talk about the price and agree on the certain price, price to sell the products."

Mimoto then revealed his own misconduct. "I meet—I met with competitors of lysine, and I agreed on the sales price, and also we agreed on the allocation of the quantity, sales quantity."

The government's first exhibit was his plea agreement. It required him to pay a $75,000 fine and cooperate with the Justice Department. He swore that Ajinomoto did not give him the money for the fine. It came out of his own pocket. As for Ajinomoto, he reported that it too had pleaded guilty and paid a $10 million fine.

Now Weingarten was on his feet bristling to approach the bench. He griped about the testimony on the size of Ajinomoto's corporate fine as "having the potential for inflaming the jury."

Lassar shot back, "In his [Weingarten's] opening, he shows mugshots of all the Asians in Hawaii and talks about how lightly they got off. He certainly opened the door." Manning agreed and overruled the objection.

Cued by Lassar, Mimoto recounted the milestones of the price-fixing conspiracy. His credibility was critical to the government, especially in regard to the events before Whitacre began taping conversations in November 1992.

Judge Manning earlier had ruled that Mimoto's testimony about what others, including Andreas, Wilson, and Whitacre, had said on these occasions did not constitute hearsay. The Federal Rules of Evidence make these statements admissible in court. All that is necessary for a witness to testify about earlier statements and conversations is that the original speaker be a coconspirator who made the statement during and in furtherance of the offense. The rule is quite broad. Its goal is to bring as much of the criminal conversation before the jury as possible.

Mimoto had been with Ajinomoto for twenty-eight years. Initially, he sold amino acids, including lysine from Japan. Then he moved to Germany in 1976 to work for the company's 50 percent owned Eurolysine subsidiary. After a stint in France, he returned to Tokyo in the mid-1980s to become a section manager in the feed additives division. He reported to Hirokazu Ikeda, a general manager of the company's international department, who in turn reported to Kazatoshi Yamada, a managing partner. All were involved in the price-fixing conspiracy with ADM from 1992-1995.

This involvement finished his lysine days. Ajinomoto transferred him to Indonesia where its business was based on synthesizing monosodium glutamate (MSG), the pervasive flavoring molecule.

Predictably, Lassar drew an admission from Mimoto that price fixing of lysine had occurred long before ADM entered the market. The witness identified the traditional players. Ajinomoto was involved as were its European and American outlets, respectively Eurolysine and Heartland Lysine. The latter had its corporate headquarters in Chicago and operated a plant in Eddyville, Iowa. Another long-term conspirator was the large Japanese company Kyowa Hakko, which had a participating American subsidiary called Biokyowa based in St. Louis. A Korean company called Miwon, which later changed its name to Sewon, was a lesser producer. Its Sewon America branch was based in New Jersey. Another Korean producer called Cheil Foods joined the field at roughly the same time ADM did.

Lassar asked whether the pre-ADM plot also had fixed sales volumes for conspirators. This sparked a defense objection. Manning overruled it. Mimoto answered, "No."

It was an important point for the government. There are two ways for companies to rig a market. One is fixing prices. The other is by manipulating supply. By informing the jury that the earlier conspiracy had lacked the latter, the government had planted the idea that ADM's entry into the plot made matters worse.

In his resigned voice, Mimoto testified over the course of two weeks. Directed by Lassar, he laid out the conspiracy sometimes in numbing detail.

The first exploratory talks occurred in the spring of 1992. Wilson and Whitacre came to Tokyo to meet with Ajinomoto and Kyowa Hakko. The witness pointed to Wilson who was sitting under one of the huge TV monitors. Mimoto, of course, did not identify Whitacre, who remained out of court.

Mimoto had been present at a meeting on April 14, 1992. Wilson told those assembled that ADM wanted a trade association to which all lysine makers would provide sales figures. These could be audited. More important, he stated that each company should be assigned a percentage of the market.

The price of lysine then was under 80 cents per pound. Through what Wilson called "friendly competition," he said it should be raised first to $1.05 and then to $1.20. Wilson wanted the talks to continue but not in the United States, which he felt was too "dangerous" from a law enforcement standpoint.

The next major session occurred on June 23, 1992, in Mexico City. Wilson and Whitacre attended, as did representatives from Ajinomoto, Eurolysine, and Kyowa Hakko. The group, according to Mimoto, discussed the two other makers of lysine, the Korean companies, Cheil and Sewon, who were not present, and how to bring them into the fold. It was decided that Ajinomoto and Kyowa would update them on the Mexican talks.

At the meeting Whitacre said little. Wilson mentioned that no one at ADM was aware of the conference besides Mick Andreas. Wilson revealed how price-fixing producers of citric acid, including ADM, kept track of each other. Wilson told the lysine makers, "If we say we will sell [a set amount], we will do just that. We expect the same from you."

Ultimately according to Wilson, ADM wanted parity with Ajinomoto, the market leader. This would mean that each company would get a third of the market. But, Wilson was quick to point out that he did not have control over volume agreements. These had to be approved by "ADM management."

In Mexico, Wilson tried to build confidence in ADM. Mimoto recalled him saying, "We are not cowboys, we should be trusting and have competitive friendliness." At an easel, Wilson gave a demonstration about how much free-market conditions had hurt the lysine makers and benefitted the customers. Wilson wanted a price "no lower than $1.20 by the end of the year." The gathering agreed to raise US prices to $1.05 by October and to try to get Sewon and Cheil to cooperate.

Later in the summer of 1992, Mimoto came to Decatur to visit the ADM lysine plant at Mark Whitacre's invitation. Lassar asked, "In your experience is it unusual for competitors to visit each others plants?" Mimoto replied, "It is very unusual." But Ajinomoto felt that the trip was necessary because ADM was "claiming 115,000 tons of capacity which we couldn't believe," in the new plant. In fact, the facility was as formidable as ADM had boasted. Ajinomoto knew that Decatur could flood the market if the older producers failed to satisfy ADM with a big enough share.

Lassar also asked who had accompanied the witness to Decatur. Mimoto testified his supervisor at Ajinomoto, Mr. Ikeda, made the visit as did two "technical people." One was a Mr. Brehant, an employee of Eurolysine. The other was Mr. Fujiwara, from Ajinomoto's Tokyo headquarters. The latter name seemed to pique the jury's curiosity. They had heard of Fujiwara in connection with Whitacre's extortion scheme. Now they knew that such a person actually existed and had been inside the ADM plant.

Lassar asked why Fujiwara and Brehant had been present. Mimoto simply responded "as technical persons, they can better estimate the capacity of ADM." The prosecutor moved on to other steps in the conspiracy, which left questions dangling about what Fujiwara actually had done in Decatur.

The conspirators next met in October 1992 at the Hotel Pullman Windsor in Paris. Again Wilson and Whitacre represented ADM. Ajinomoto, Kyowa, and Eurolysine sent delegates. Finally, Cheil and Sewon also attended. All the makers of lysine in the world were present for the first time.

In order to disguise the purpose of the meeting, the group claimed to be a trade association and published an agenda. Lassar displayed the document to the jury. It listed topics such as animal rights and environmental concerns. "This is a fake agenda," said the witness, "a camouflage of the meeting."

"Why did you need a fake agenda for the meeting?"

"Because if we are asked why we are there, we can show this paper for this purpose." None of the subjects actually were mentioned at the session, which had a single topic according to Mimoto. "We discussed about the price of lysine." In fact, the producers agreed to set prices for each region in the world where the amino acid was marketed.

The group also agreed to meet on a quarterly basis to maintain their cartel, which did not always run smoothly. In the spring of 1993, the price actually dropped for two reasons, explained Mimoto. First, the conspirators did not always "keep their promise" to each other. Second, they did not yet have a sales allocation agreement, so there was still competition on volume.

Mimoto readily conceded that there was not always a high level of trust among the competitors, who perhaps kept their agreements "about 90 percent" of the time. Nevertheless, with constant reporting and checking of information "we could manage to keep the price with satisfaction."

The witness testified to attending numerous meetings of the cartel after Paris: Tokyo, May 14, 1993; Vancouver, June 21, 1993; Paris, October 5, 1993; Tokyo, December 8, 1993; Hawaii, March 10, 1994; Sapporo, August 27, 1994; Zurich, October 26, 1994; Atlanta, January 18, 1995; and Hong Kong, April 21, 1995.

During the conspiracy, Mimoto functioned as a facilitator and central clearinghouse of information, as well as a bridge to the Koreans, who often felt muscled by the bigger players in Japan and America.

He kept in regular telephone contact with Mark Whitacre. During these calls, he used the pseudonym "Mr. Tany." Wearing headphones, the jury heard many of the calls. The collaborators obviously seemed comfortable with each other. Whitacre had a pleasant, high-spirited midwestern radio voice. Mimoto often giggled. The calls had a certain sameness. The topics seldom ranged far from the nitty-gritty of market rigging, which customers received what prices, what volumes had been sold, and which coconspirators could be trusted. Perhaps if Whitacre had been available to the government, it would have used him as the historian of the crime. With Whitacre behind bars, Mimoto provided the particulars.

Following Paris, prices rose—especially in the United States and Europe—but not uniformly and not everywhere. In fact, without volume agreements, they sometimes fell. This led to friction. In order to keep the plan on track, Mimoto helped facilitate a series of high-level meetings.

For instance, in Tokyo in May 1993, the representatives of Ajinomoto and ADM debated about the size of the lysine market and ADM's actual sales. The Japanese insisted that ADM was inflating its share in order to get a larger-than-warranted "allocation" in the eventual volume agreement. From a surveillance tape made by Whitacre, the jurors heard the tough tobacco-cured voice of Terry Wilson educate the Japanese. Communications could be handled through an "official" trade association. He explained ADM's experience with a citric acid association whose members reported figures monthly. Plus, Swiss accountants annually audited the numbers. Wilson graciously nominated Ajinomoto's Mimoto to be the recipient of the monthly sales figures from all lysine producers.

Wilson described the successful volume agreement among citric acid producers. "We'd go strictly by percent and the market takes care of itself." Certainly, it had removed risk from the citric business where prices had climbed from $.58/lb. to $.82/lb.

In Vancouver on June 24, 1993, the conspirators continued to wrestle about volume. This meeting was not taped. But, Mimoto recalled that when Terry Wilson argued hard for a large ADM allocation, the other producers asked him to leave the room for an hour while they discussed and then declined ADM's volume proposal.

The group convened again in Paris on October 5, 1993 to set prices but still could not agree on volume. However, progress was made later in the fall.

A high-level meeting occurred in Irvine, California on October 25, 1993. Mimoto's two bosses from Ajinomoto, Ikeda and Yamada, were present as were Whitacre and Mick Andreas. Mimoto knew about the session but could not testify to it, since he wasn't there.

Whitacre sneaked a tape recorder into the next large group gathering. So the jury heard it on the tape. It was held in Tokyo on December 8, 1993. Wilson and Whitacre attended. So did Ajinomoto's Ikeda and Mimoto; Kyowa's Masaru Yamamoto and Seiji Hasumi, Eurolysine's Jacques Chaudret and Christian Sacchetti; and Sewon's H.K. Park and Jae-Moon Yun.

Now everyone was in the fold except Korea's Cheil Foods. ADM, Ajinomoto, Kyowa, and Sewon were within weeks of formalizing a volume agreement in which ADM got 67,000 tons; Ajinomoto (including Eurolysine) won 84,000 tons; and Kyowa got 46,000. Sewon would receive either 34,000 or 37,000 tons depending on if the Japanese producers agreed to an audit and what it showed. Wilson and Whitacre were taped touting Mimoto's role as hub. Each month the member companies would report their sales figures to the witness and he would distribute them to the group.

Wilson convinced the group that no one would be hurt by not competing on volume. Sticking to the allocated shares would work because of a system of guaranteed "buy-ins." If a lysine maker became aggressive and sold more than its share, then it would have to buy product from producers who sold less. In this way, the rigged fractions would be preserved. Nothing would be left to chance. Wilson explained how the brakes could be applied.

Wilson: Let's say ADM is really ahead after a reasonable reporting period. Three months in a row, we're runnin' well ahead of where we should be. You're gonna call up ADM and say hey bullshit. And we know we

> got to adjust. So, you should start seeing the next number
> start adjusting.
>
> *Ikeda:*   And uh feedback every month?
>
> *Wilson:*   Feedback every month.

He warned the gathering not to become lax about security when reporting numbers to each other and Mimoto. "We have to watch our telephones . . . it must be
very careful."

He schooled them again in the logic of holding an overt contrived "official
meeting." The bogus trade association would get a conference room, print an
agenda, and go through the motions of convening. One member of the conspiracy
would get a suite where the actual business of price-and-volume fixing would be
conducted.

> *Wilson:*   The only reason to have this association is to move the market to
> where it belongs. If that doesn't happen, then there's, there is no restric-
> tion on volume. It has to happen.
>
> *Sacchetti:*   Yeah, we should uh agree on one point, we have the choice
> between keeping the profit for us [or] transfer the profit to the customer.
>
> *Wilson:*   That's exactly right.
>
> *Mimoto:*   So everybody agrees.

There was no dissent to Wilson's plan, which included a reference to ADM's president Jim Randall being in the loop. Wilson spelled out the consequences if anyone broke ranks and started to compete. "If we get into a war again our volume
will not stay where it's at. It will go up. It's not a threat. It will happen."

Lassar wanted to make sure that the jury understood how the annual compensation or "buy-in" system worked. So, Mimoto explained it in court. "We had allocation for each company at the end of the year 1994. If some company exceeded
the allocated quantity and if some company is behind the allocated quantity, then
the exceeding company must buy lysine from the behind-schedule company."

The conspirators gathered in Honolulu on March 10, 1994, for the first session since
the group had started sending sales figures to Mimoto. FBI agents posing as wait-
ers and waitresses had smuggled tiny camcorders onto the premises. On July 28,
1998, the prosecutors switched on the court's oversized TV monitors and began
rolling the black-and-white tape.

The setting was a large low-ceilinged hotel suite, hung with vague watercolor
landscapes. Businessmen lounged in armchairs and sofas arranged in a *U.* Representatives of ADM, Ajinomoto, Kyowa, and Sewon attended the morning session.

The Americans and Japanese were dressed casually and seemed relaxed. The Koreans wore suits, chain-smoked, and looked stiff and lean.

At the flip chart, a younger Kanji Mimoto rapidly jotted numbers with a marker. He wore a double-breasted sport coat and a white shirt open to the chest. His jawline was firm and his eyes gleamed. He apologized for his handwriting and seemed pleased with the numbers, which showed that the conspirators were reporting sales volumes in line with their quotas.

The men began to discuss their remaining problem, Cheil Foods, the lone lysine producer that hadn't joined the cartel. But representatives of Cheil were on the island and had agreed to attend the afternoon session.

In the meantime, the gathering groused about Cheil. Eurolysine's Jacques Chaudret, a swarthy, balding Frenchman, spoke good English but periodically punctuated his points by saying "bon." He complained that Cheil was underselling the conspirators on his turf. "It's not a big total, but it's a real disturbing problem in Europe."

Terry Wilson comfortably sank into a deep couch. When he spoke, he gestured grandly at the ceiling with his big arms and hands. At first he feigned indifference about the maverick Koreans. "It is of no concern to me whether they report or don't report. We can go on by ourselves without them." But, soon he stated his true position, "As small as the market is, if you have a rogue elephant out there, he can destroy the market."

Chaudret chimed in. "That's what they're doing to the European market."

Mimoto added, "If Cheil is out of the group, it is very inconvenient."

"We have an old saying at ADM," growled Wilson. "It's better to have them inside the tent pissin' out than outside the tent pissin' in."

Some members of the group chuckled. Others struggled with the idiom. Mimoto wondered aloud, "outside piss?" Wilson explained curtly, "It's better that they be part of the group."

In the afternoon Cheil's J.M. Suh joined the gathering. A spindly, round-faced man with a Beatles haircut, he sweated nervously and asked a few questions.

Suh: So, everbody's checking every month?
Mimoto: Yeah.
Suh: What if system does not work?
Whitacre: I tell you what. It works in other products around the world.

Suh demanded 18,000 tons annually for Cheil "as our quota." The group, which had feared he would ask for at least twenty thousand, bargained him down to seventeen.

Mimoto: You are okay for that?
Suh: Yeah, I'm alright.

Mimoto: Okay then very good (laughs). Fantastic. So five companies agree
on the quantity for the first time.

The festive mood of the businessmen from three continents came through clearly
on the videotape. The group then engaged in consensus price-fixing for the second quarter of 1994. They divided the world into four regions: North America,
Latin America, Europe, and Asia. They went into country-by-country discussions
and set prices as necessary in dollars, deutsche marks, pounds sterling, pfennigs,
etc. for metric and nonmetric weights.

As a seasoned fixer, Terry Wilson was treated with great deference by the group,
despite his limited experience with lysine. He vehemently warned the other members about customers.

Goddamn buyers, they can be smarter than us if we let them be smarter. . . .
They are not your friend. They are not my friend. And we gotta have 'em. Thank
God we gotta have 'em, but they are not my friends. You're my friend. I wanna
be closer to you than I am to any customer 'cause you can make us money. At
least in this kind of a market, and all I wanna tell you again is let's put the prices
on the board. Let's all agree that's what we're gonna do and then walk outa
here and do it.

Wilson did not want to see the price and volume agreement fail. "You know if it
doesn't work, then we'll all be in the soup again, and everybody will do what they
have to do."

Then Wilson delivered a statement that has caused much controversy. "Okay
if we find somebody lyin', death or something like that. Something very bad would
happen, we would hire some mafia figure or something."

There was some nervous laughter. Was it a joke?

Then Wilson added, "Or Lorena Bobbitt."

Whitacre said, "She's in our department of downsizing." There was plenty of
laughter now. Chaudret offered that his company had "a plant in Italy, so we know
the mafia well."

Whitacre echoed, "We have a plant in the Ukraine so we know the mafia well."

Mimoto said, "Finger cut," an allusion to Yakuza henchmen.

Wilson and Whitacre stressed the importance of each company controlling its
own sales force. The sales reps had a tendency to become advocates of the customers and not stick to set prices. They told the group that the week before one
of ADM's best salesman, an eleven-year veteran, had given a customer the opportunity to buy lysine at $1.13/lb. when the fixed price was $1.16. So the salesman
was fired. "That's good," said Yamamoto, laughing.

"You get all this stuff from customers, and your salesmen are complaining," snorted Wilson, "but goddamn it, that's our job."

After Hawaii there were meetings in Paris and Sapporo to lock in prices and report volumes, build rapport, and cure rifts. Sewon became somewhat pesky again by demanding a bigger allocation for 1995 but generally stuck with the conspiracy.

On October 13, 1994, Wilson, Whitacre, and Mick Andreas took the corporate jet from Decatur to Chicago. They met Mimoto and Ajinomoto's managing director Kazutoshi Yamada for lunch at the Four Seasons Restaurant in the posh Ritz Carlton Hotel.

The jury got to hear some of the ADM executives' patter, which Whitacre furtively taped on the plane and during the ride from the airport. He and Wilson brought Andreas up to date on the conspiracy. The five companies dutifully were forking over figures to Mimoto. When ADM's sales fell behind the agreed-upon schedule, the other producers slowed down so that ADM could catch up and meet its tonnage quota. So, the plan was working. The trio also discussed Mimoto, whom Wilson called "a goddamn prick."

Whitacre agreed, "he has to be the leader, so we let him be it. We let him be the admin' guy and we sit and do business." Whitacre chuckled and added, "he's the quarterback." Wilson sneered, "he's the butler."

In the taxi, Andreas went into a high-spirited riff. He lampooned a speech he was slated to give soon on free trade that revealed his cynicism:

Good afternoon, everyone. Free trade. When the Chairman [Dwayne Andreas] asked me to speak about free trade, I couldn't help but recall a talk he gave recently to a sugar group in Sun Valley about the concept of free trade, and he answered with a question, what free trade? And that was a good question. Let me tell ya a little about the global environment we're really working in. Before I was even born, as it happens, my great-grandfather was a Mennonite farmer living in an area of Germany called Alsace-Lorraine, in the mid-nineteenth century Germany at the time. He was convinced by a well educated German economist named Debrook to enact free-trade in the farm sector of Alsace-Lorraine as an experiment. He learned that in college, I guess. It was called the great dynamics of economic efficiency. And the farm tract sector was made a free trade zone. Then, after a couple years, all the nations surrounding the area dumped their surplus crops in Alsace-Lorraine. It went broke and my great-grandfather, along with thousands of others were forced to leave, were forced to leave the farm. He ended up in Pennsylvania. His sons settled in Minnesota, where my father was born and here I am in Decatur. (Laughing). All thanks to free trade.

At times the discussion grew bawdy. Andreas planned to meet an old college flame, now twice divorced, in Chicago. Jokingly, he mused about what brand of condoms to buy.

The executives discussed which women in the office were available, their physical attributes, and what types of sex they were willing to have. There were plenty of these comments on the tapes. But Manning wisely kept them out of the trial to keep them from prejudicing the jury. Long afterwards they would leak out, to the consternation of ADM.

The lunch took place in a private room at the Four Seasons. The introductions started a bit stiffly. Mick Andreas tried a broad friendly midwestern greeting, "How are ya, Mister Yamada? Good to see ya." But the reserved Yamada politely began by introducing Mimoto. Mimoto, however, broke the ice by saying, "My name is Tany," an allusion to his code on price-fixing cells. Everyone laughed.

There was some chitchat about common acquaintances in agribusiness and banking. Mick dropped that his father was seventy-six and might retire, "He says it's just around the corner." The Japanese, of course, knew they were speaking to the crown prince.

Mick apologized for not coming to Japan. His time had been eaten up by ADM's acquisitions and construction during the past year, which cost a billion dollars. This triggered a discussion more or less about wealth, the wonders of the Ritz Carlton, and why Mick always stayed here, the best hotel in Zurich, and a mutual friend who had a castle in Scotland.

The men talked golf, and Mick snorted, "we have a saying in our company."

"Yes?" said Yamada.

"That the golfer's handicap is the number of days he works in a month."

Yamada ordered Chardonnay. Mick had a Bud. Then they got down to business. Mick complained about the low-ball pricing of the Chinese producers in citric acid. Then he disclosed ADM's plans to restrict its output of MSG "to about 50 percent of capacity." But now the Chinese were exporting cheap MSG, which caused Mick to fear that they would get into lysine and to wonder aloud, "what makes them so aggressive?"

Then he returned to the idea of meeting at Ajinomoto and offered to bring his father along. He suggested that ADM and Ajinomoto could form a joint venture in some business, perhaps a bottling plant—it didn't matter—in order to have a legitimate reason to meet. "It's a good excuse to get together and have something to talk about you know."

Yamada agreed, "Yeah right." Everyone laughed knowingly. Since both companies were publicly traded, Mick also probed swapping shares, "We could buy your stock, you can buy our stock and we'd both be richer."

The executives worried about Sewon, which had continued to show an independent streak. According to Whitacre the company was behaving "like another Chinese." Sewon's quest for more lysine volume could upset the conspiracy. Wilson said that even an extra "one thousand tons is too much." "Yeah, that's right," said Andreas. "You know, it'll destroy the whole goddamn market."

The men pondered the root of the problem. The company had been split in two because its chairman's two sons had been at odds. Now one company handled lysine and the other made MSG. "Yes, that's the unfortunate thing," said Whitacre. "The one that got the lysine side was not the brother we wanted."

Andreas asked whether it was possible for ADM to invest in the Korean lysine company. ADM, he added, sometimes invested in its competitors such as A.E. Staley, the other HFCS maker in Decatur. ADM had another godfatheresque saying. "It's important to keep your friends close and your competitors closer," said Andreas. But Yamada noted that Korea had a "very closed [stock] market" to foreigners. They agreed that Ajinomoto would continue trying to persuade Sewon to stay in line, which would be worth the effort since, as Whitacre pointed out, lysine currently was "a very good business . . . prices are up."

As the lunch concluded, Andreas wished his counterparts "good luck in all your business. We hope you make a lot of money. . . . And if you do, we will too."

The ADM trio grabbed a cab to take them back to Meigs Field, Chicago's airport for private planes. In the cab, the men snickered that Sewon hated Ajinomoto so Yamada would have his hands full. The jury also heard the ADM executives voice concerns about the security of their phones calls. Whitacre, of course, played along. According to Andreas, "You gotta be goddamn careful what you're talking about. He [Yamada] said the right thing though [with] too much volume the price is gonna go down."

The ADM executives however were not at all careful about what they talked about among themselves. On the way back to Decatur, the hijinks again included discussing women in the office.

The discussion was interesting on a number of levels. It showed the personal corruption of patriarchal power at ADM, where no female ever has penetrated the inner circle, a white male bastion, and where women were viewed as toys. Also, it underscored the effectiveness of Whitacre, with whom Wilson and Andreas felt completely comfortable. Conceivably, there was a part of the sex talk that Manning would have been justified in allowing the jury to hear. At one point, Mick Andreas began talking about the chairman of Ajinomoto, a Mr. Toba. Mick bragged that he had gotten Toba to come to Decatur.

Long time ago. He'd, he wouldn't, he didn't wanna come to Decatur. I said you
get to Decatur and I'll make sure you get laid. So I did, and he did, and then he
said, yeah, I'll come back to Decatur, anytime you want.

Since the remark arguably touched on the origins of the criminal relationship, Manning could have let it into court. But in an abundance of caution in keeping with
her goal of giving the defendants a fair trial, she kept it out.

After Chicago, the lysine association held another group meeting on January 18,
1995. All five companies and their subsidiaries sent representatives. But only
Whitacre attended for ADM. Mimoto explained that Atlanta was chosen as the
site because it was hosting "a poultry exposition. So, there was a very good reason for every lysine manufacturer to come to Atlanta. We can utilize this kind of
event as a good camouflage of our trip."

Again, the FBI masquerading as hotel staff had planted a camera, so the jury got
to watch the video tape. By now the conspirators were almost goofy with success.

Mimoto began the meeting by taking roll. Some of the participants drew big
laughs by pretending to be from ConAgra and Tyson, large lysine buyers who had
been cheated with cooked prices. Mimoto joked that they should save a place for
the FBI. When there was a knock at the suite's door, Mimoto said, "Yes, FTC?"
alluding to the other federal antitrust watchdog agency. In fact, the person was
Robert Herndon, an FBI agent masquerading as a banquet manager. The jury also
saw Herndon sitting at the prosecution table.

A couple of the people on the Atlanta tape seemed more somber. Jacques Chaudret of Eurolysine mentioned that "in Europe, they're cracking down" on price fixing.
Someone else suggested that they all should leave separately. The group assented,
although they rejected the notion of wearing dark glasses as over-the-top.

The business of the meeting included setting sales allocations for all of 1995
and fixing prices for the first quarter. The conspirators also reported on tonnages
for 1994. The last thing the jurors saw was Masaru Yamamoto of Kyowa Hakko
declaring his company's output of 47,554 tons while flipping through papers. Concluding, he lined up his sheaf by tapping its bottom smartly on the table, looked
Mimoto in the eye, and said, "right on target."

Lassar wound up the direct testimony by asking, "Mr. Mimoto, when did price
agreements and volume allocation agreements come to an end?"

"It was," said Mimoto, "on June 27, 1995." On that date, "the FBI invaded Heartland Lysine office with a search warrant," and also searched ADM. The witness

testified that "immediately" following the search of the Heartland subsidiary, he ordered the destruction of all conspiracy documents kept in Ajinomoto's main office in Tokyo.

The judge took a break. The direct examination, punctuated with tapes, had been effective. Everyone in the courtroom wondered how the defense would attack it. Reid Weingarten, Wilson's attorney, rose to cross-examine first. He quickly got to the point.

Mimoto was not a combative witness and Weingarten initially scored easily. Mimoto was forced to admit that Ajinomoto had dominated the lysine market with a 50 percent share until ADM came on line. Going back to 1970, there had been only Ajinomoto, Kyowa Hakko, and Miwon (predecessor to Sewon) producing lysine. Ajinomoto often met with its competitors, and the three had fixed prices since 1976.

Now Weingarten showed Mimoto a document prepared by Alain Crouy of Eurolysine, in 1992. It referred to the "old club." For the first time Mimoto was made to look shifty. He claimed not to have used the term and not to remember anyone else using it. But, he was boxed into defining it for the jury. "Old club means prior to the entrance of ADM and Cheil, all the existing lysine manufacturers."

Then Weingarten peppered him with questions about a letter dated June 28, 1992, from Hisao Shinohara, the president of Heartland Lysine, to Toba, the president of Ajinomoto. The government objected to the letter, but Manning received it. The jury then saw it in Japanese and translated into English. Mimoto admitted that Shinohara was on the Atlanta video tape that the jury recently had viewed.

Weingarten read the translation to the witness: "On every occasion, for example, when grain market prices started moving in a favorable direction for lysine in May, 'K' and us worked hard to hide the price in a collusive manner. Nevertheless with ADM's ambition, we could not even hold the price, resulting in a miserable outcome such as a drastic sales drop and exceeding inventory." Mimoto conceded that 'K' was Kyowa Hakko. He quibbled briefly about the term "collusive," as not a direct translation from the Japanese, but then backed down. The defense strategy —making ADM look like it was breaking up an Asian cartel rather than joining it and taking it over—was coming into sharp focus.

Weingarten pressed on to the next part of the Shinohara letter: "To compete with ADM, which has a different hair color with enough capital, will be a formidable one." Mimoto began to squirm. They were wading into racial waters.

Weingarten probed the meaning of "different hair color." Mimoto insisted it was not derogatory. It only meant "a different kind of company." Weingarten, of course, didn't buy it and asked questions about whether Mimoto had responded truthfully to Lassar's questions.

With Mimoto's credibility fading, Weingarten pressed him about the plea agreement. The witness was forced to admit his knowledge of the potential three years of imprisonment and fine of $350,000 or double the losses suffered by consumers, which could mount into the millions that would come with a price-fixing conviction. This was a clever way to teach the jurors the high stakes that Wilson and Andreas were facing. Plus, it made Mimoto's fine seem like a flea bite by comparison. Weingarten ticked off a list of the witness's colleagues in Ajinomoto, Eurolysine, and Heartland Lysine who had received immunity from prosecution and wouldn't pay a cent. As for Mimoto's fine, it covered only the conspiracy from 1992-95 but none of his previous decades of price-fixing activities. Nor was Mimoto prosecuted for obstruction of justice in connection with the shredding of documents at Ajinomoto following the June 1995 raid.

Weingarten asserted that the plea agreement carried "no order of restitution for the farmers who bought your lysine over the past twenty years." Weakly the witness said this was true.

The plea agreement called for Mimoto's "cooperation." But Mimoto had an unusual clause in his agreement in the event that he testified falsely. The feds would give him five days after a violation before seizing him. Weingarten drew a vivid picture for the jury. "And if, in fact, you don't testify truthfully, you can walk out of the courtroom, get on an airplane, stop for a couple days in Las Vegas, then go back to Tokyo, and the United States cannot lay a hand on you, is that true?"

Mimoto could not dispute the proposition except for stating that he would not go to Las Vegas because he "didn't care about such kind of town." In this regard, he undoubtedly was telling the truth. Price-fixing was intended to take the risk of out of business, so gambling probably wouldn't appeal to him. In addition, he professed to wish to continue to do business periodically in America, an option that would be foreclosed if his cooperation ceased.

Weingarten chided Mimoto for being put up at Chicago's pleasant Palmer House with all expenses paid by the government and free time for shopping and sightseeing. "This is almost like a paid vacation for you, isn't it?"

Mimoto flushed with pain. "Absolutely not. Do you imagine such an experience is a vacation?" The attorney accused him of speaking "tongue-in-cheek," and then it was time for lunch.

After the break, the tall, disheveled Weingarten continued his Doberman-like cross. Had not Ajinomoto rewarded the witness for his price-fixing role by promoting him to president of its Indonesian division? No, Mimoto insisted, it was a lateral move without a pay increase.

The FBI, Weingarten also pointed out, had not bothered to collect all of his telephone records during the 1992-95 period. This cast doubt on the government's case, since other calls might include information contrary to a conspiracy.

He jabbed at the witness for refusing to be interviewed by the Wilson defense lawyers. After all, Mimoto had cooperated fully with the government. So, he must be biased, scared, or both. No, said Mimoto. His own lawyer failed to convey the request from the Wilson team. He never knew about it.

Weingarten developed the theme of the witness's fear and loathing of ADM. The lawyer played up the fact that ADM had a huge plant, and that American farmers might be more inclined to deal with an American company. Tyson, the world's largest poultry manufacturer, suddenly switched its account to ADM from Ajinomoto, causing the Japanese company great concern. Weingarten got Mimoto to admit that he found ADM's pricing "predatory." He and his company feared that ADM would not limit its growth to lysine, but would expand into other amino acids pumped into feeds including tryptophan and methionine and affect Ajinomoto's markets.

Then Weingarten fired questions designed to make Mimoto look like an industrial spy during his Decatur visit:

Weingarten: And while you were touring the plant did you try to take something that didn't belong to you?

Mimoto: No.

Weingarten: What did you do?

Mimoto: Our company at the time was thinking and still thinking that ADM is using our patented strain for the permutation of lysine, but we didn't have good agents. According to the technical people of the company, to get the microorganisms for the permutation is very easy. They said to me if I touch the railing of the staircase, for example, in the factory, then I can collect the microorganism. So it is very easy to get some microorganism.

Weingarten: Were you wearing gloves?

Mimoto: Sorry?

Weingarten: Were you supposed to wear gloves when you did that?

Mimoto: No, I didn't wear gloves. Just I touched the railing of the staircase and I touched my handkerchief inside my pocket. So this handkerchief was analyzed after I came back to Tokyo.

Weingarten: Why didn't you simply say to ADM: We would like to examine your microorganisms?

Mimoto: I think it's not a good strategy to do so.

Weingarten: Now, is it corporate policy at Ajinomoto to visit other companies and try to steal their microorganisms?

The court sustained Lassar's objections, but Weingarten had made his point. Moreover, he was able to show that Ajinomoto's analysis of the strain was unable to find that it had been pirated by ADM.

Then Wilson upped the ante. "Do you ever recall a meeting with [lysine] competitors, not including ADM, where someone suggested that Asian competitors need to visit ADM's factory with a bomb."

"I don't remember," said Mimoto. "It must be a joke anyway."

Weingarten showed him a document written by a Heartland Lysine employee. A bomb was mentioned, probably as a joke. Weingarten let the matter dangle for a few extra seconds, then moved into trying to show that ADM and Ajinomoto were bitter rivals rather than cozy conspirators. On the television monitors, he placed a Heartland Lysine memo dated March 17, 1993, and made the witness agree with its assertions one by one. These included that "our lysine business is drowning," and that "we are at the forefront of competition with ADM." The memo, which was written almost a year after the two companies' alleged price collusion began, portrayed a rocky relationship.

Weingarten continued to read the memo from Mr. Uozumi at Heartland.

ADM has given precedence to price over good service and has made it clear that lysine is a commodity. ADM has not only intensified the competition among makers, but has also changed the clients' buying habits. In the past, people bought from us if the price was the same as the others. Now they may even take a second bid or even try to ask us a price 1.2 cent lower. There were bad mannered buyers who bid at a price at which they wanted to buy, trying to meet an offer that actually did not exist, so the way of buying became even more dirty.

Weingarten paused for effect. "Do you agree with that, Mr. Mimoto?"

"Yes," he sighed.

Moreover, the two companies lied to and cheated each other during their relationship. Mimoto was asked if Ajinomoto failed to report the amount of lysine sold for pet food and pharmaceuticals, as well as all the liquid lysine it produced. "Yes," said Mimoto, "but ADM did so."

In particular, Weingarten was eager to paint his client as an avid competitor. Mimoto claimed not to recall Wilson saying that ADM would not make deals. But, the witness conceded that he had made an effort to keep Wilson away from meetings.

Weingarten sought the inference that this was because Wilson favored competition. Mimoto, however, insisted that Wilson, in fact, had pushed too hard for collusion especially on quantity. But, the witness could not dispute that Wilson did not attend many of the price-fixing sessions. The lawyer ticked off a list of his absences. As for Whitacre, he was usually present. Moreover, Whitacre claimed repeatedly and as late as April 1995 that he would be the next president of ADM. Mimoto had heard these boasts.

On the morning of July 22, 1998, Judge Manning did not seat the jury. Instead, she called the lawyers back into chambers. "I have," she said, "another small fire to put out." Newspapers had been found in the jury room. Some had gaps where recent articles on ADM had been clipped out by court clerks. These were not of concern. But, a couple of the papers still contained the articles including a *Chicago Tribune* dated July 20, 1998, with a piece entitled "ADM Tapes Show Rivals Mistrust."

The lawyers examined the papers. Weingarten said, "What's lethal here is there's a reference to ADM's plea and the $100 million fine. Obviously, we think that would prejudice the jury. I think if a juror read this, we do have a mistrial."

Jim Griffin reminded the judge that she had not necessarily banned the information from the entire trial, just from the openings. She had not yet ruled that the corporate guilty plea would be kept out totally. But it certainly seemed that Manning was leaning towards blocking the evidence completely as too prejudicial. Jim Griffin argued, "Your Honor, even if they did read that [article], I don't think it's necessarily a mistrial. I think they can put it aside."

Manning decided to question jurors individually in chambers. The process took most of the rest of the morning. The jurors trudged in and swore not to have read anything about ADM either in the jury room or at home. The defense refrained from moving for a mistrial. Weingarten voiced satisfaction that "this will have a good effect on the future."

"Right," said Manning. "It probably helps to instill in them how serious we are about the prohibition against outside sources."

Back in court, Weingarten handed Mimoto a memo from Shinohara of Heartland Lysine that accused ADM of stealing its customers including Perdue and Tyson. When asked if he recalled this behavior, Mimoto conceded "vaguely, yes."

Weingarten concluded by embarrassing the witness. After establishing that Mimoto had 3,000 workers under his control in Indonesia, the lawyer asked, "Does Ajinomoto have a corporate policy about managers having criminal records?"

Lassar vociferously objected. "I think this is more Asian bashing by the defendants." Manning chewed thoughtfully on the issue, then allowed the question as material to "whether he's tailoring his testimony to conform to something his company might want him to do in light of the [corporate] plea agreement."

Weingarten re-posed the question. "There is no policy." said Mimoto. "So," snapped Weingarten, "Ajinomoto allows people to work when they have criminal records?"

"I think it's case by case," said Mimoto.

Late in the afternoon of July 22, 1998, Weingarten pulled from the witness that he had worked all his adult life for only one company, Ajinomoto. Weingarten sat down. Mimoto seemed very tired.

Bill Walker rose to cross-examine. Looking disorganized, he rooted through papers on his desk, creating a minute of uneasy dead air in the courtroom. Then he smiled and told the witness that he would be brief and not "using electronics or movies or anything like that."

Walker was not a hardball cross-examiner. He thought that the Eastern lawyers turned jurors off with laborious, microscopic interrogations. He preferred to get to the point. Walker began to review the documents destroyed at Ajinomoto after the July 1995 FBI raid. The only new data he elicited was that the shredding had been approved by the Ajinomoto legal department. For some reason, Mimoto had had his fill. After more than a week on the stand answering questions in English, Mimoto suddenly asked for permission to testify in Japanese with an interpreter. It was a stunning moment. The witness seemed beaten.

There was little else that Walker needed to do. He got Mimoto to agree with a government memo showing that the "volume of commerce" affected by Mimoto's activities in the price-fixing conspiracy was $122 million. Then Walker lobbed the witness a few questions about his guilty plea. The Justice Department had intervened with the US Immigration and Naturalization Service to allow Mimoto to enter the country despite commission of a felony.

Walker asked, "You like coming in and out of the United States, is that correct?"

The interpreter translated Mimoto's answer into English. "I used to like it, but because this happened, I have started not to like it very much anymore."

Walker tried to make a few points specifically on behalf of his client. Whitacre could be convicted only for price-fixing activity that occurred before November 5, 1992. Walker was partially successful in showing that the witness could not pin the mole to illegal acts before that date. Mimoto however insisted that Whitacre had confirmed a price increase with Ajinomoto in September 1992 by phone. Walker did not press him on it. The lawyer finally had the witness agree that the Department of Justice was the sole judge of whether he was cooperating in accordance with his plea agreement. Then Walker sat down. His questions had taken under an hour.

On Thursday, July 23, 1998, Jack Bray began to cross-examine Mimoto through an interpreter. Where Weingarten had been pugnacious, Mick Andreas' lawyer was icily smooth. Nevertheless, Bray's questions amounted to a punishing rehash for the witness.

In addition, Bray pointed out that when ADM misjudged the size of the lysine market, Ajinomoto intentionally did not correct the American company. The witness readily agreed with Bray that American trade associations commonly include industry rivals who exchange and publish information.

Bray portrayed Mimoto as the quarterback of the conspiracy. The lawyer deftly showed that the witness had spoken only once to Mick Andreas on October 13, 1994. As a sidelight, Bray elicited that Mimoto was ill that day with a "distracting" intestinal ailment, which could have affected his perception.

Bray tried to present the Four Seasons session as a mere lunch rather than a meeting of importance. Mimoto admitted that there had been no agenda and that he never even had alerted his boss, Ajinomoto chairman Toba, to the existence of the meeting despite the fact that Toba was in Chicago at the time and could have attended.

Bray referred to a portion of the Four Seasons transcript including Miwon's desire to increase its sales. The lawyer argued to the witness that this showed there really was no volume agreement. Mimoto did not agree, but he could not dispute that the word "agreement" did not exist in his conversation with Mick Andreas, and that Miwon (soon to be Sewon) had stopped reporting its figures. Mimoto conceded that this failure to report was "a problem."

Bray tried to reduce the impact of the ADM motto attributed to his client, "keep your friends close and your competitors closer." The lawyer insisted that Andreas "was equating the competitors with the enemies." Mimoto agreed. Then he concurred with the follow-up propositions that it was important—not illegal—to know "your competitors" in business.

Over a prosecution hearsay objection, Bray made Mimoto recall that Whitacre had told him that Mick Andreas had little contact with the lysine business. Then Mimoto admitted that the government had played surveillance tapes for him of conversations that occurred when he was not present. These included recordings of the cab rides and plane flights on October 13, 1992, when the ADM executives had been negative towards him and Ajinomoto. The inference was that this form of preparation was an underhanded way to shape him as a prosecution witness against ADM.

Bray also pounced on the nativist issues. He produced an Ajinomoto (here called Ajico) memo on communication to Mark Whitacre. It read, "We told him that the Japanese market is to Ajico what rice is to the Japanese people, and we definitely want you to get out."

Bray grew stern, "Is that what he was told?" The witness admitted it was. Bray insinuated that Ajinomoto (not ADM) desired no competition in the Japanese market in order to keep prices high. The lawyer tried a line of questions to prove that Ajinomoto's behavior followed the Japanese government's policy, but Manning disallowed most of it.

There was some brief redirect by the government. Lassar elicited that Mimoto did not believe Wilson when the defendant had said that ADM did not make deals. Mimoto saw it as posturing. Before the witness was excused, Bray and Weingarten told the judge during a whispered sidebar conference that they might need to call Mimoto back in the defense's case. Mimoto grew visibly angry, and his personal lawyer strode from the gallery to discuss the difficulty of his client returning from Jakarta, a twenty-hour flight. Nevertheless, the judge instructed Lassar to inform Mimoto that his and his company's plea agreements hinged on his continued cooperation.

Lassar did as he was told; the defense handed a subpoena to Mimoto's lawyer. "Can I resist?" asked the witness in apparent anguish. Manning said, "Well you can talk with your attorney."

Lassar quipped, "My hunch is that they've seen enough of Mr. Mimoto."

"We like Mr. Mimoto," smiled Weingarten.

Manning told the witness, "You're free to go back to Indonesia." At a minimum, the Andreas and Wilson lawyers had given notice that they were considering calling defense witnesses, rather than simply relying on cross-examination to create reasonable doubt.

11

IKEDA

"Out of chaos usually comes order."
—*Mick Andreas*

After two weeks, the jury had heard from exactly one witness. Now the judge declared a pre-arranged recess of a week. When court reconvened on Monday, August 3, 1998, a juror wanted out. She hadn't worked long enough to receive benefits at her new job and was desperate to go back to work. Both sides agreed to excuse her and an alternate took her place.

The prosecutors' next witness was Hirokazu Ikeda. A tiny wizened man in his sixties with gold rimmed glasses, Ikeda, who wore a hearing aid, looked older. Until his retirement in 1994, he had been Mimoto's boss and the rung on the corporate ladder between Mimoto and Yamada, the managing partner.

Ikeda, who dealt with ADM in English, chose to testify in Japanese with an interpreter. Jack Bray seemed distressed with the request and asked Manning to let him test the witness's ability to speak English.

Through the interpreter, Ikeda admitted that he was captured on audio and video tapes speaking English with ADM. He had prepared for trial by reviewing the transcripts of these tapes. But, he insisted that he had not spoken English since his retirement, and his ability had deteriorated. The judge allowed Ikeda to have an interpreter.

Ikeda's direct was conducted by Robin Mann, a dark-haired, middle-aged antitrust prosecutor. With a calm and empathic approach, she led Ikeda through the interpreted testimony. The slight Japanese man had worked for thirty-four years. Ajinomoto was his only employer. He admitted to participating in price fixing before and during ADM's time. Unlike Mimoto, he had not been charged with any crime. To him, his agreement with the US government meant, "I will not be prosecuted if I testify to the truth." If he lied, "I'll be charged with perjury."

At Mann's request, he pointed out Andreas and Wilson. He recounted that he and Yamada had met with both, as well as with Whitacre and ADM president James Randall in Decatur on April 30, 1993. Unbeknownst to him at the time, Mark Whitacre had recorded the meeting. Now Mann played the tape for the jury.

The meeting began with pleasant banter and the comparison of golf scores. The ADM hosts jokingly declined to offer artificially sweetened Diet Coke to the Japanese in favor of Coke Classic, which the Decatur executives called "coke high fructose corn syrup."

After a time, the two sides got down to explaining their businesses to each other. Mick Andreas tried to make the Japanese see ADM as the antithesis of Cargill, the country's largest privately held company. As Andreas put it, "we're a processing business that engages in world trade. They're a world trade company that participates in processing." Andreas also wanted Yamada and Ikeda to understand that ADM operated about forty businesses, all "very similar." On the other hand, he made plain that "I'm not an amino acid guy. I came up through the soybean crushing business."

Yamada raised the possibility of "a kind of association" for lysine producers. Andreas, who had been prepped on the idea, jumped on it. "Well, we have associations like that in almost all of our mature businesses, and we find that they are very helpful."

Andreas and Yamada discussed the low prices and excess capacity in the lysine market since ADM had entered it in 1991. Andreas held out a carrot, "Out of chaos usually comes order."

Yamada agreed that an association also would be in "the common interest for the other players." He asserted that even the Koreans would be interested.

The gruff Randall added, "We have a saying here in this company that penetrates the whole company. It's a saying that our competitors are our friends. Our customers are the enemy." Everyone laughed.

"That's very famous saying," said Yamada. "I know that, that Mr. Ikeda told me."

Andreas chimed in, "Keep your friends close and your enemies closer. That's another way of saying it."

Yamada had had long experience with the other lysine producers. So, Andreas asked him if they would turn over accurate figures to ADM, "or are we gonna run into people who would rather play poker?"

"Liar's poker," said Randall.

"To be frank," said Yamada, "it is not very easy to get the accurate figures." But Yamada offered that the managements of the other producers seemed receptive. He even suggested that lysine and MSG producers could be in the same group, an idea that did not take hold. Above all, he wanted the ADM brass including Andreas to come to a meeting of the lysine group in Tokyo as soon as possible. Randall said the Japan trip meant "getting laid and fixing markets."

At lunch the men got along well. ADM served and extolled its veggie burgers. "The world," grumbled Randall, "is full of health nuts." Ikeda got a laugh by asking for a Diet Coke.

After the Japanese left, Whitacre continued to tape his ADM conversation with Wilson and Andreas. Wilson congratulated Andreas. "I think you charmed the pants off them." He thought the meeting also went well because "Jim [Randall] didn't scare them." But the men understood that the situation was in an early posture, where the two lysine leaders would have to agree and then convince the lesser players:

Whitacre: Yeah. Well, one thing you made very clear, it don't matter what understanding we'd have between the two of us anyway, there's three other producers.
Andreas: That's right.
Whitacre: Two of 'em have an understanding means nothin'. Got to have all five.
Andreas: But I think they fully intend and I think, and, we even said too I told 'em, I'm sure they know that we have to agree first, or at least. . .
Whitacre: Yeah.
Andreas: Have some parameter of agreement before we go to the others.

The men discussed strategies for reaching a deal with Ajinomoto, even though there still seemed to be a lack of trust. Finally, Andreas offered, "well OK, I'm gonna talk to Dad about it and see what he thinks."

In addition, Mann introduced tapes of calls involving Ikeda, Whitacre, and Wilson in the summer and spring of 1993. The two companies agreed to maintain the price but did not yet have a volume agreement. Between calls, as Whitacre continued to tape, Wilson referred to Ikeda as "the mouse" or "that little son of a bitch."

The witness remained impassive on the stand. Mann asked him to authenticate the other exhibit, the government's central piece of evidence against Andreas—a video. He said he had reviewed the tape and found it accurate. Now it came up on the monitors.

Ikeda and Ajinomoto's managing partner, Kazutoshi Yamada, attended a meeting with Mick Andreas and Mark Whitacre on October 25, 1993 in Irvine, California. Terry Wilson was not present. He was in Belgium fixing the price of citric acid, a fact the jury would learn later. The first frames of the eighty-two minute video brought home that Ikeda had been transformed as utterly in the intervening five years as had Mimoto. On the tape, he could have easily been a man in his forties.

The FBI had shot the session, the only one in which Andreas appeared on camera, in an expensive but sterile suite that was virtually indistinguishable from the one in Hawaii. A breakfast table heaped with rolls, coffee, and big half globes of orange juice separated the pairs. Whitacre and Andreas sat shoulder to shoulder.

If Whitacre's extortion scam had bothered Andreas, the ADM vice chairman gave no inkling. Andreas had no clue that his colleague was informing on him. Rather, the two gave every appearance of enjoying a trusting, open friendship.

The Japanese duo gave off a different vibration—all business. Their relationship was more formal and frankly hierarchical. Ikeda, the complete company man, was eager to please his corporate chieftain. Quite tall for a Japanese, Yamada had a fringe of silvering hair, a high forehead, aquiline features, and sensitive eyes. He spoke softly and only when everyone else was silent. In fact, he preferred to let Ikeda do much of the talking while he, as leader, observed without revealing his feelings.

The Americans provided a stark contrast. Mick Andreas tossed his deep, authoritative voice around as he pleased. Whitacre, the aide, stayed more in the background. On the American side, the boss led the negotiations, though his understanding of the situation was based on its broad outlines, rather than on the details of which Whitacre had mastery.

Undercover FBI agents posing as waitresses with big teased hair filtered in and out. The Japanese seemed reserved when the women were around. Andreas was indifferent to them and did not moderate his voice when they served or cleared dishes.

As for Whitacre, he seemed to be playing a dangerous game. Periodically, he would open his briefcase to reveal and fidget with his tape recorder, making sure that the device was caught on camera. But none of the other men noticed it.

The tone of the meeting was low-key. Mick Andreas wanted Ajinomoto to know the matters under discussion were important enough to reach the top of ADM: "Myself, my father, and Mr. Randall all know all the time what's going on. Especially new business."

Andreas tried to be conciliatory. "Like you, we've suffered from the first half of our [lysine] plan," which he called "a painful experience" and "no fun." "At least," he added intriguingly, "we've kept everybody else out." He did not go into details but seemed to be telling the Japanese that ADM had kept the lysine club small and had successfully deterred other western companies from joining. He mentioned a few including Degussa, Whitacre's old employer.

Yamada asked an innocuous question: Why did ADM call itself the "supermarket to the world?" Andreas explained the phrase. "We provide food for people who sell food."

Then the men launched into a volume allocation discussion that involved not just their companies but also the other three lysine makers. Its premise was that with 14,000 tons of expected growth in 1994 in a world market of about 250,000 tons acceptable prices could be fixed. Andreas, who chain-smoked during the discussion and nervously pulled at his collar, announced that three other makers would get 2,000 tons each, leaving the rest for ADM and Ajinomoto.

Andreas: So we got fourteen thousand tons of growth.

Yamada: Yeah.

Andreas: In one year.

Yamada: Yeah.

Andreas: So the question is who gets that growth.

Yamada: Yeah.

Andreas: It doesn't matter whether we believe each other or not [as to the size of each producer's 1993 sales], that's how much growth there's gonna be. If it's, if the market's two thirty, it's gonna be thirteen thousand. If the market's two fifty, it's gonna be fourteen thousand. So it's, so it's one thousand tons difference. . . . Yeah. So now Kyowa . . . How much of that growth would they like to have compared to this?

Yamada: [referring to the total amount Kyowa wanted]: Forty-six [thousand tons].

Andreas: Forty-six.

Ikeda: Forty-six.

Andreas: So . . . Kyowa wants two . . .[Sewon] wants two.

Ikeda: Um hum.

Whitacre: CSA [Cheil] told us twenty at Paris, which . . . I know their plant's not even that big.

Ikeda: I think we gotta disregard because they say anything.

Andreas: Let's give them two. . . . I'll give 'em two. . . . Tell 'em they can't have any more than the other big guys there.

Ikeda: We have three.

Andreas: Well no you, we haven't decided what you've got yet. You're still at eighty-seven and we're still at sixty-eight. . . .[T]here's eight left. . . . So that's really the question isn't it? Regardless of what our, I mean if, you question whether we're gonna sell that much. We know that we're gonna sell that much. We question whether you're gonna sell that much and you know you're gonna sell that much. It doesn't really make any difference. What we've got is a growth of about fourteen thousand tons. . . . So the question is how do we share that growth. . . . [W]hat would we be willing to accept out of that fourteen thousand tons and what would you be willing to accept? Isn't that the question?

I would suggest we do the following. I'd suggest you tell the people that whatever they have in ninety-three, in nineteen ninety-three, which will be over in two months . . . that they can each have two thousand tons more in ninety-four and we get the rest between you and us.

Following additional discussions about a residual lack of trust, Whitacre piped up helpfully, "Do it like citric and submit the numbers."

Of the eight remaining kilotons (each worth over $2 million) Andreas awarded five to ADM and three to Ajinomoto. He levelled a threat against any company that refused to keep within its limit.

> There's another thing though you gotta keep in mind and these people have to keep in mind too. We have a lot more capacity than we're usin'.... And if in fact they don't agree and there becomes a free for all, and we start that again, our numbers are liable to be a lot larger than five thousand tons. . . . Because we'll grow at twenty thousand tons instead of five. So they have choices. Their choices are that we'll agree to only grow five if everything is good. . . . Or twenty . . .

Lastly, Andreas lectured the Japanese gently about pricing. He had reviewed some of the agreements that Ajinomoto sales reps had made with customers that locked in long-term prices and did not like what he saw. At ADM, he confided, pricing authority is "very centralized" at the highest level. The company had learned by experience that "over time our sales people became agents for the customers. . . . Consider how you can get better control and more centralized pricing authority." The tape concluded.

This time Bray cross-examined the witness first. Andreas' attorney repeatedly injected the term "Asian cartel" to describe the companies that dominated the lysine trade prior to ADM's entry. Asking questions through an interpreter, he made the witness admit that the group had met to fix prices, and that during the 1980s, Ajinomoto and Kyowa Hakko had carved up the US market by regions.

Then with aplomb, Bray pulled off an evidentiary coup. Almost invariably courts follow the rule that one party may not introduce evidence during the other party's side of the case. Although the prosecution had not rested, Bray wanted to submit a raft of documents from the Asian companies showing their greed, control of the market, and distaste for ADM.

Robin Mann lodged the traditional objections. During a lengthy sidebar, Bray and Weingarten raised the inconvenience of making the witness return during the defense case just to authenticate documents. Weingarten added strong rhetoric. The Japanese companies had turned over "two million documents, many of them highly exculpatory." So, the defense should be allowed to use a few specific items in a timely manner. Manning basically agreed.

The defendants were making a small sacrifice by presenting evidence on the government's side of the case. They probably would be giving up the opportunity to move for a dismissal (based on insufficient evidence) after the prosecution rested. But they knew that the government had a strong enough case to survive such a motion.

On the other hand, they had preserved the option of not putting on a formal defense with witnesses. If they chose, they could rest after the government's case, knowing that they had gotten some of their best evidence before the jury without subjecting their witnesses (especially their own clients) to cross-examination.

Bray began putting documents stamped *maruhi* up on the monitors. Ikeda said *maruhi* meant *confidential* in Japanese. The first, a November 1992 memo, stated that the "three previously existing companies" should "stick together" apparently against ADM. The document came from a meeting of the Asian companies to which ADM had not been invited. Bray posted another Ajinomoto document written after Cheil had become a lysine producer. It said "the four Asian companies should join together to deal with 'D.'" Ikeda conceded that 'D' was a code for ADM. Another *maruhi* document referred to a "strategy against competitors." The only competitor was "D."

Bray grilled Ikeda on whether he had visited ADM's representative in Tokyo, a Japanese national named Sughi Tani, in order to tell the Americans to stay out of the lysine market. Ikeda admitted the meeting with Tani. But, Ikeda said he did not "recall" arguing against ADM's entry into lysine.

Ironically, Mimoto's use of the pseudonym "Tany" now came into focus. Mimoto evidently chose the name of a Japanese ADM employee so that any outsider discovering the calls would think they were internal to ADM, rather than evidence of an illegal conspiracy between two companies.

Next, Bray brought out a memo from Ajinomoto's president Tadasu Toba dated December 7, 1992, to his employees. Bray said December 7 (anniversary of Pearl Harbor) with subtle emphasis. According to the government, the conspiracy with ADM was well under way at the time. But Toba called ADM's lysine effort "the hardest competition we have ever had." Bray asked Ikeda if he agreed.

This put the weary witness between a rock and a hard place. By agreeing with his CEO, Ikeda could undermine the prosecution's position. Ikeda, who seemed to be straining to preserve his plea agreement to assist the government, nevertheless, answered "yes" but offered that Toba's words were chosen simply "in order to get as much cooperation as possible from everyone" in the Japanese firm.

Bray flashed another 1992 Ajinomoto document that quoted Ikeda's immediate boss Yamada "encouraging people in the lysine business in Asia to stop the hurricane started by ADM." Then Bray asked Ikeda to explain a sheet written in Japanese by Kazuhiro Uozumi of Heartland Lysine in March 1993. Uozumi's words were "I think our lysine business is drowning." Another document was entitled "strategy anti-ADM." Ikeda had to agree that a portion of it said "fight at any cost whatever ADM price is. Kick ADM out of the market and direct them to other products." Ikeda tried to argue that this was simply a discussion point or option, not what Ajinomoto eventually did.

Bray accused Ajinomoto of trying to "steal" ADM's lysine microorganism. Ikeda said he learned after the fact of Mimoto's attempt. Bray asked, "Did you disapprove of what he did?"

"No," said the frail man, "not particularly."

Then Bray pummeled Ikeda with a 1994 letter to him and Mimoto from Christian Sacchetti, a Eurolysine executive. Writing in English, Sacchetti wanted to know "how do we hide" volumes of lysine sold by Ajinomoto, Eurolysine, and Heartland Lysine from ADM.

Robin Mann was on her feet objecting, "That was not his [Ikeda's] statement." Manning sustained the objection.

Bray torqued the question and asked it again. "What did you understand you were to do in response to the question 'how do we hide?'"

He got the answer he wanted from Ikeda, "My understanding is that we were only to report lysine that was used for feed." Continuing to probe about a "separate set of books," Bray forced Ikeda to admit that Ajinomoto did not disclose its sales of liquid, pharmaceutical, and pet food lysine to the five-company group.

Bray unearthed a January 1994 Ajinomoto memo about parking 3,500 tons of lysine out of view of the group's auditors. One sentence read, "Hide 1,000 tons in Thailand internal business." When asked if he had discussed hiding lysine in Thailand, Ikeda answered, "I don't remember concretely."

Bray put an internal Ajinomoto memo on the 1992 Mexico City session up on the screens. The Japanese firm intentionally understated the size of the market "in order to suppress ADM," in other words, to keep ADM's production low.

Bray pressed the witness on the trade associations. Ikeda had to admit that forming one in lysine was Yamada's idea. Also, he stated that there were legitimate reasons for competitors to meet and exchange information apart from price-fixing.

When questioned delicately about a May 14, 1993 meeting in Tokyo, Ikeda conceded that Wilson said that ADM did not make deals. The following month in Vancouver, according to Bray, Wilson said, "We want you to know that obviously we can't agree period." Had the statement been made? "Yes," breathed Ikeda, "that is true." Bray began to explore the most damaging part of the direct testimony, the video of the meeting with Andreas and Whitacre in Irvine, California. First, the lawyer established that the session lasted from 9 AM till noon, not simply the eighty-two minutes contained on the earlier video. Bray wanted to play the balance, but Mann successfully objected, saying that it could be played during the defense's case.

Bray tried to draw comfort for his client from the video. Ikeda admitted that his boss Yamada knew more about lysine than Andreas who was not "an amino acid guy" and had forty businesses to run.

Independent of the video, Ikeda said he had little recollection of the Irvine meeting in October 1993. Moreover, he had been exhausted from his late flight, and the meeting had occurred at what would have been 2 AM in Tokyo.

Bray suggested that after the portion of the meeting recorded by the video camera, Andreas showed hostility to Yamada, while Whitacre continued to audio tape. Ikeda did not dispute that Andreas had said, "I don't care what you people think, our figures are right, so . . . you just go ahead and do whatever you want."

At some point, Judge Manning became concerned about the accuracy of Ikeda's testimony. At sidebar, she turned to Bray, "I think you've got him to admit quite a bit [but] he really didn't understand the words or may have misinterpreted a lot of what's been said."

Without a struggle, Bray led Ikeda to agree to other propositions, including that Andreas had commented that the lysine market was big enough to provide ample opportunities for all producers to grow. Using transcripts and tape snippets, Bray made the witness acknowledge that a number of legitimate pieces of business were transacted in Irvine. The backbone had gone out of Ikeda. He seemed to shrink in his chair.

Bray went for the knockout. He tried to get Ikeda to recall a statement by Mick Andreas in Irvine after the videotape was turned off. Hadn't Mick adamantly stated there was "no deal"? Ikeda sat up a bit straighter. He swore he couldn't remember such words from the ADM leader. Bray wanted to refresh his recollection by playing a segment of audiotape made by Whitacre. Objecting vigorously, the prosecution beat a path to sidebar. At the bench, Lassar told the judge that the mole's tape contained the phrase "done deal" rather than "no deal."

The defense made a vigorous argument based on the "rule of completeness," a key evidentiary concept. The rule allows the defendant, with the court's permission, to introduce a piece of transcript during the prosecutor's case provided that it relates to another segment already introduced by the government. Before deciding the question, a judge usually asks for the position of the other side, which is what Manning did.

Finally, the scales fell from the government's eyes. It realized that the defendants were trying to build reasonable doubt without formally presenting evidence. Robin Mann refused to consent. She maintained that the tape snippet was irrelevant and not part of an earlier conversation played by the government and would therefore not complete it. Plus, she rejected Bray's interpretation of the contents. "I'm saying there's not a good faith basis for that." Fighting words.

Manning excused the jury. She wanted to hear the tape. She listened to it on the courtroom's audio system, then through head phones, then on a boom box, and finally with a special digital tape player that she borrowed from the government.

A car motor, probably the noise of a taxi pulling away, obscured Andreas' words. "Frankly," said Manning, "it's practically unintelligible." She couldn't hear the word "deal" at all.

Bray pointed out that his was still a logical construction. Besides, the court could hear the "long O" sound that goes with 'no' not 'done.'"

"It goes with a lot of things," Mann shot back. Manning decided not to let Bray play the tape to Ikeda. If Mick Andreas wanted the jury to believe he had said "no deal," he would have to testify and the tape could be played then.

Bray asked the witness a few more questions, mainly about Whitacre's treachery. Then he turned over the cross to Walker, who took three minutes to re-establish some dates of the conspiracy that bore on Whitacre's defense and sat down.

Weingarten stood and gave the witness a big toothy grin. "The good news," he told Ikeda, "is that I'm going to be shorter than Mr. Bray. The not-so-good news— I'm going to be a little longer than Mr. Walker." Several jurors smiled. Ikeda winced.

Wasting no time, Weingarten banged away at the witness, proving that Ikeda had pioneered price-fixing in the Japanese lysine trade. But Ikeda had not revealed this to the FBI when he cut his immunity deal in 1996.

Weingarten established that Ikeda was involved when his company and Kyowa Hakko had divided up the US market. The split gave Ajinomoto and Kyowa 50 percent. Weingarten became indignant, "And that resulted in American farmers paying more for lysine than they otherwise would absent that agreement—isn't that true?"

The old man became coy, "I can't at this time make a judgment on that."

Similarly, when Weingarten asked if the announcement of ADM's entry had caused the price per pound of lysine to plummet from $3.00 to $1.20, Ikeda professed not to recall.

Weingarten charged ahead. Despite his criminal activities, Ikeda never had been prosecuted in Japan or Europe. Plus, the witness's activities on behalf of Ajinomoto had not ceased with his retirement in 1994. Rather, he had stayed on as consultant until March of 1996, almost a year after the raid at the company's Heartland subsidiary. He conceded that Ajinomoto was paying all his expenses while he was in Chicago and covering the costs of his lawyer, whom it had picked.

Wilson's lawyer dissected internal Ajinomoto memos showing great fear of ADM because of its advantages. These included raw materials and the huge new plant. ADM also presented a "US company flag ship" with "decisions made in the US for the US" An Ajinomoto fax from the period said that the decision of Tyson to switch to ADM "concerns us gravely."

Weingarten showed another Ajinomoto document from early 1992. Didn't it refer to ADM as "the enemy"? Ikeda said a better translation from the Japanese would be "competitor."

But "competitor" helped the defense almost as much since the government was trying to prove collusion.

Weingarten directed the witness to a portion that read, "ADM's penetration to (sic) the market has fundamentally changed the supply and demand structure and ruined price determination mechanisms." Then the lawyer asked, "Price determination mechanisms meant price-fixing to Ajinomoto, did it not?"

"Not necessarily," came the soft reply.

Weingarten was unrelenting. He insisted that Ikeda had met with ADM's Tokyo representative, Sughi Tani, in order to try to bribe ADM to stay out of lysine. Ikeda said he recalled nothing like that.

Weingarten pressed the witness on whether during the meeting Ikeda had offered to buy soybean products from ADM, in order to make up for ADM's loses if it got out of lysine. At first Ikeda said he did not remember any discussions about buying soy. Then he changed his mind and said he did but that it was unrelated to the lysine issue.

Weingarten portrayed his client as a die-hard competitor hateful to the Japanese. The lawyer asked if Wilson always insisted that ADM "would be as big as Ajinomoto in lysine." The witness admitted that Wilson had said this "several times," but not every time they had met.

Weingarten asked if he "found Wilson to be an extremely aggressive business man?" Oddly, the interpreter piped up that Ikeda was having trouble accepting a translation of the word "aggressive" in Japanese. Of course, this made the witness look evasive. But Weingarten continued to push for the answer he wanted.

"Are you aware," the lawyer continued, "that there was a meeting in Seoul on August 27 [1992] with the Asian cartel wherein there was actual discussion about trying to keep Mr. Wilson from attending a meeting?"

"I don't remember exactly that," said the witness. Weingarten made him review a Japanese document about excluding Wilson. Now Ikeda conceded, "I remember that there was such a debate," and that "Mr. Wilson was a very tough negotiator."

Weingarten cleverly finished the afternoon session by questioning on another Japanese document that had been written by the witness. It predicted that ADM would try to be as big as Ajinomoto and then pass it in lysine sales.

Questions about whether the witness had wanted to control ADM's growth led to a discussion of the Japanese word *kensei*, which according to Ikeda is a "little different from control. It's closer to stop and that's what I intended to say." The lawyer pounced on the point, "And isn't it true, from the first day ADM had entered the market to the last day you worked at Ajinomoto your primary responsibility was to try to stop ADM."

"If you're referring to stopping ADM from taking our market share, yes, then that's correct."

Weingarten stopped for the day. He had given the jury something to sleep on.

On Thursday, August 6, Weingarten hit the ground running. He established that Ikeda was a member of the board of Heartland Lysine, then confronted him with a November 1992 document from Ajinomoto's North American branch. "Canadian sales" it read, "were a disaster. . . . ADM was extremely aggressive, and Biokyowa [Kyowa Hakko's American subsidiary] was selling a lot of material at old prices in the face of a price increase."

"Is that piece of information consistent or inconsistent with a price agreement between Ajinomoto and ADM?"

"I would say," said the witness, "it's possible from the passage that it's inconsistent."

The phrase "consistent or inconsistent with an agreement" became a mantra to Weingarten. He used it again and again to get Ikeda to admit that phrases in Ajinomoto's own documents were indeed inconsistent with such a conspiracy. Examples included ADM's repeated price discounts to Tyson and Ajinomoto, hiding of tonnage ADM sold to Purina from ADM volume reports, and the 1993 memo from Heartland complaining "that our lysine business is drowning."

Ikeda also had to concede that matters inconsistent with price-fixing came up at the April 1993 meeting at ADM. For instance, Ikeda recalled Mick Andreas stating, "My dad always says that the best cure for low prices is low prices."

Weingarten softened the impact of James Randall's slogan about the competitor being the friend and the customer being the enemy, which Ikeda recalled. From his years of experience, the witness admitted that sometimes customers cheated and played tricks. For example, they fibbed that they could get lower prices from other producers. "I have experienced that," said Ikeda, brightening slightly.

Weingarten continued to pump the witness based on Japanese documents, many not written by Ikeda. Lassar asked for a sidebar. He complained that letting the defense use such materials was improper and had "boomeranged on the government." Manning was unswayed. She would allow latitude on cross-examination.

Weingarten had the minutes of June 11, 1993 Ajinomoto management meeting on "lysine strategy." The lawyer focused on a paragraph reporting that "the lysine business is no longer structured to yield profits due to price competition resulting from the entry of ADM." The lawyer asked if this report "is utterly inconsistent with a fixed market?"

Ikeda began to quibble in Japanese with the interpreter. Finally, he conceded, "I believe they were saying that there was competition."

Then Weingarten turned to a government exhibit, the transcript of a phone call involving Wilson, Whitacre, and Ikeda following the meeting in Vancouver in late June 1993. At Vancouver the Asians had tried to limit ADM's production. On the phone Wilson had said, "We're calling to give you a response. Obviously, we can't agree." But the document was a mixed bag for the defense since Wilson also said, "We intend temporarily to maintain our current level of sales and production." Weingarten asserted that companies frequently state their "intentions as far as sales and production are concerned" and "it's perfectly legal to do so."

"I don't have an understanding of it being illegal," said Ikeda.

Weingarten displayed a Eurolysine document from August 1993 for the witness. It referred to price wars involving lysine in 1992 and 1993. Weingarten asked if Ikeda remembered two price wars. "I would guess from the passage that we just read that there probably was."

Weingarten was mindful that the document preceded the Irvine meeting in October 1993. He asked if there had been immediate disagreements among competitors after the meeting "as to what was or was not agreed to at Irvine?"

Ikeda said he had discussed the problems and "in the end came to an adjustment." But that adjustment, the lawyer insisted, had been reached with Whitacre, not with his client. Nor was it completely successful. Wilson put a document in front of the witness showing that in February 1994 ADM was underselling Ajinomoto in Australia by 35 cents per kilogram. Another document from March 1994 showed ADM offering cheaper lysine in Asia. Another from Eurolysine, also dated March 1, 1994, reflected the same complaint regarding Europe.

Weingarten completed his cross on a high note. "Isn't it fair to say that after Irvine, ADM was either underselling you or attempting to undersell you in Australia, Asia, and Europe at least?"

Ikeda answered, "They were attempting to undercut us, or the customers were attempting to mislead us."

Robin Mann had her work cut out for her as she rose to rehabilitate the witness. Redirect examination in a federal court is extremely limited. A lawyer is supposed to ask about only matters that came out on cross but were not raised on direct examination. Mann began by making the defense look unfair. She put an Ajinomoto document back on the monitors that Weingarten had used to show discord among the conspirators at Mexico City in 1992. Mann directed the witness to a passage that Weingarten had not pointed out. It reported that "we will aim for prices at the levels of $1.05 delivered for North America [and] Europe. . . . All of the companies are in basic agreement on the above."

Mann reminded the witness that "both Mr. Bray and Mr. Weingarten talked about an Asian cartel. Who was part of the cartel in 1993 and 1994?"

Ikeda answered, "It was Ajinomoto, Kyowa, Miwon, CSA [Cheil], and ADM." In other words, it was not exclusively Asian.

Mann revisited the phone conversation of June 29, 1993 that followed the Vancouver meeting. She directed the witness and the jury to a phrase in the transcript on which Weingarten fastened during cross. Terry Wilson had said to Ikeda, "obviously we can't agree." Mann wanted to know if Wilson was referring to price or volume. Ikeda clarified that it was only about volume.

Belatedly, the defense objected that the "question" called for speculation on what was in Mr. Wilson's mind. The judge overruled, and Mann forged ahead in the transcript of the post-Vancouver call.

She hit upon a portion where Ikeda said, "We try to maintain our price we agreed the other day," and Wilson replied, "yes." In other words, though volume questions may have remained after Vancouver, price had been fixed. Ikeda agreed.

On re-cross which is limited to matters arising on redirect, the defense asked questions implying that Ikeda was more cooperative with the government than with them. Also, they tried to re-interrogate on the threat or joke about bombing the ADM plant, about which Ikeda again swore he knew nothing. Since these questions were argumentative or previously asked, Manning sustained objections to most of them.

Then Bray did something unusual. He asked and received permission of the court to call Ikeda out of time, in other words as a defense witness during the prosecutor's case.

Bray used Ikeda to introduce another segment of videotape from the October 1993 meeting in Irvine. At an hour and twenty minutes, it was two minutes shorter than the piece presented by the government. It contained an extensive discussion between Andreas and Yamada about Orsan. The French company was divesting its half of Eurolysine. Ajinomoto owned the other half.

Now the two executives discussed which companies would be good buyers for Orsan's Eurolysine stock. Andreas and Yamada both insisted that the buyout of Orsan's shares be strictly legal from an antitrust standpoint. Both, in short, wanted to avoid what is called a horizontal merger among competitors.

The footage was of questionable relevance, although Manning allowed it in the spirit of giving the defendant his day in court. Bray hoped the jury would conclude that his client was a law-abiding entrepreneur rather than an antitrust conspirator. The government believed that the segment as easily could be read as showing that Andreas and Yamada did not want the divestiture and resulting merger to draw antitrust scrutiny, which could blow the cover on their cozy lysine deal. The tape concluded at the end of the day on Thursday, August 6, 1998. Mann wisely asked no questions. With a small smile, Ikeda left the witness stand and travelled back to Japan.

12

WHITE RATS

"We [ADM] are not cowboys. . . . [W]e have to stay friendly."
—*Terry Wilson*

On Monday, August 10, 1998, Robin Mann called the government's third witness, Alain Crouy, a lean French engineer with dark receding hair and a well-cut suit. He spoke with a slight accent and declined the interpreter on hand.

Crouy had been chairman of Eurolysine from 1990-1993. In a friendly, almost charming tone, he admitted to price-fixing and conspiring on volumes. He, too, had an immunity agreement. He explained that if he failed to testify truthfully, he would be prosecuted for perjury and antitrust crimes.

Crouy described the "co-management" of Eurolysine. Ajinomoto had to approve of decisions, but Crouy himself ran day-to-day operations and reported to the president of Orsan, Phillippe Rollier. Crouy was now CEO of a French company called LaFarge Aluminates, in which Orsan had a controlling interest.

Crouy corroborated what Ajinomoto witnesses already had said. The importance of his testimony lay in the unspoken message that price-fixing was not simply the work of demonic yellow people. Nice white Europeans did it, too, and so, by extension, did Americans.

His own participation in price-fixing started in Mexico City in 1992 where ADM, Kyowa, Ajinomoto, and Eurolysine "reached a tentative agreement" to "try to raise prices to $1.05 per pound by September-October and $1.20 by the end of the year." He took notes during the meeting in English, which were supplied to the jury. In the notes, he recorded Wilson giving tips to the group such as, "In citric acid independent auditors audit everybody every year in between reporting figures to ECAMA" (the European Citric Acid Manufacturing Association). Wilson also was negotiating for ADM's market share. Crouy wrote that Wilson "thinks he can probably sell 33 percent to management." Crouy testified that he learned that the upper management to whom Wilson referred who would address volume agreements were "Mr. Andreas and Mr. Randall." In negotiations, Wilson tried to be conciliatory saying of ADM "we are not cowboys. . . . [W]e have to stay friendly." After the meeting, Eurolysine followed the agreement and raised its prices.

Crouy testified that in April 1993, he and Phillipe Rollier met Wilson and Whitacre for dinner at a steakhouse near O'Hare Airport. The price of lysine had gone down because of some behind-the-back competition by the conspirators. Whitacre had taped the meeting, which was played for the jury.

Wilson drank heavily through the meal. He was angry about the lysine price but pleased with Eurolysine's observance of the price agreement. "The only place that it works is Europe. The only place that it worked, really worked . . ."

Amid clanking silverware and rattling ice cubes, the diners discussed why the conspiracy had not yet been perfected. As Crouy put it, "Nobody limited quantity, the [low] price made it difficult."

"We don't disagree with that," said Wilson, who expressed rage to Crouy over the delays and excuses of the others after Mexico:

> We went out and we said okay. Our price is gonna be [arrived] at in steps. That's what we agreed on. And we did it and we did it across the board without hesitation and you know what happened. That's when we found out, well, it takes time. So people sat in Mexico and told me what they were going to do and they did not do it. The reason they didn't do it as they explained to me is they need time. Now, they didn't tell me in Mexico they needed time. They told me later they needed time. . . .
>
> So okay, well alright. We'll take some time. Then [they] finally got to the point, well we don't always know what our salespeople do. Well, Alain, I don't listen to that bullshit. That is bullshit and I won't put up with it. Would you?

After ordering more wine, Crouy advocated the use of trade association meetings, which he called a "pretext" and a "shell" to get things back on track. "Good thing," said Wilson chomping steak. "Any reason to have to meet. We agree with that a hundred percent."

"So maybe," said Crouy, "we are running into a time, where uh, we have to uh, try to make a another price."

"Yeah," said Wilson.

"Because," added Crouy, "Miwon is essential to my health." (The French did not want price competition from the Koreans in Europe.)

After the plates were cleared, Wilson ordered decaf and another scotch. He demeaned Ajinomoto's management for its lackluster performance in implementing agreed-upon prices.

At the same time, he praised Jim Randall and Mick Andreas. "They take an active role." A lingering question about the government's handling of the case is why Randall never was indicted. Whitacre also described Andreas to everyone as having overall control of the volume issue. The mole expressed hope that Andreas would be able to work out the market shares soon.

Repeatedly, Wilson griped about "the culture" of the Japanese, which in his mind preferred patience over action.

Our choice is to do just exactly what we said we would do in Mexico . . . exactly. That's what we said we would do. That's what we wanna do from day one. And we tried to do it. Now you can believe that or not, but we tried to do it. And it didn't work. Be patient. Don't get excited. You're not patient enough. The culture. Okay, let's do the culture bit.

All the Goddamn things that are as insane as anything I've ever, well OK, culture. Let's do it. Let's be patient. We won't give up any business. We'll be competitive but let's watch what's goin' on. The market did start to move in the US. I'm the first to admit it. . . . I've never known anything so aggravating, OK. But I have to say that eventually it did start to move.

On the other hand, Wilson congratulated the French.

Crouy: Let's not forget that if, if the prices went up in Europe, it's because we talked in Mexico first.
Wilson: That's right.
Crouy: And then because we talked in Europe a lot after. I mean it didn't just . . .
Wilson: You made it happen.
Crouy: . . . go up like that.
Wilson: You made it happen.
Crouy: Yeah, well, I mean so . . .
Whitacre: Well managed. Well managed.
Wilson: In essence it's what we're tryin' to tell ya. It was well managed. It can be managed. It was well managed, and it happened. Unfortunately, that wasn't true everywhere.

As the evening wore on a tipsy expansiveness took hold. At one point Crouy returned from the men's room in high spirits, as if he had just seen one of the local wonders of the world, namely ice in the urinals. Elated, he boomed in French. "Il y a des glaçons dans la pissoire!"

The talk grew loose and at times incoherent. But, it did seem as if the men were exploring new areas for collusion including MSG, xanthum gum, and three amino acids: threonine, tryptophan, and methionine.

On the way back to Meigs airfield, Whitacre continued to tape. Wilson was pleased with the meeting except for the Frenchmen's loyalty to Ikeda. "They're, they're, they're just trying to defend that little cocksucker," he groaned boozily.

Whitacre also taped the next group meeting, which occurred in Tokyo on May 14, 1993. Crouy was there, so Mann played the tape for the jury. All the participants seemed friendly and cooperative. Mann asked Crouy about an exchange between Wilson and Mimoto where they cautioned the group that all reports of sales volumes to Mimoto would be kept highly confidential. What was the need for confidentiality in a legitimate trade association, especially if all the competitors were involved?

Crouy explained, "Because having quantity allocations is not legal, it has to be very confidential."

On the tape, Wilson also warned that "communication must be at an absolute minimum, and it must be contained. It cannot be at any other level than, in our case, either Mark or I. It just can't be."

Wilson told the gathering that the volume limitations they were discussing meant that they could not divide up the market by captive customers and refuse to sell to others. A "don't touch [each other's] customers policy" surely would arouse suspicion if certain buyers could not obtain lysine at all.

For two days, the defense crossed Crouy. The Frenchman's testimony had mainly implicated Wilson. The witness never had met Andreas. So one of Wilson's lawyers, Mark Hulkower, handled most of the questions. Hulkower hammered Crouy for a day and a half. For the most part, the poised Frenchman stood up well, but the feisty lawyer also scored several points.

Crouy was made to reveal that he had met with the government at least five times in preparation for his testimony, which included a practice cross-examination. He understood that keeping his immunity agreement would hinge solely on whether his testimony was to the "satisfaction of the United States."

Hulkower unearthed a government record prepared by Agent Brian Shepard of a meeting with Crouy in Brussels in January 1997. According to Shepard's notes, Crouy had claimed that no price agreement had been reached in Mexico City in 1992. This did not square with Crouy's testimony on direct. Hulkower milked the discrepancy. All Crouy could say was that he could not account for what Shepard had written. A neat point for the defense, it wedged the credibility of the witness against the word of the lead investigator.

Hulkower also showed that while with Eurolysine, Crouy had spoken repeatedly with Whitacre by phone, but the government had no tapes of the calls. That could point to selective taping or even destruction of evidence.

Wilson's lawyer ridiculed Crouy for his immunity calling it a "complete pass" and a "get-out-of-jail free card." Like previous witnesses, Crouy had ample time to flee the country if he failed to cooperate. All of his ex-cronies at Eurolysine were given the same laxity.

Hulkower drew a vivid picture of the heyday of Eurolysine in the late 1980s when the price was above $3.00. He contrasted this with the dark days during two price wars after ADM arrived on the scene. He showed the witness a Eurolysine document that grimly reported ADM's goal of taking over 50 percent of the lysine trade by 1995.

Hulkower fanned more anti-Japanese feeling. He gave the witness Ajinomoto documents showing that Tokyo had sent a Japanese man named Suda to "watch over the French" at Eurolysine, which the lawyer called "spying."

He focused the witness on many of ADM's early activities. These were consistent with trying to get data on market size, "that as a newcomer to the industry it would be hard for them to get normally." To prove that Eurolysine feared and distrusted ADM, Hulkower gave Crouy a memo in which his boss, Rollier, wrote, "We have to band together, all four of us against ADM." Crouy had to concede that the document was dated November 1992, which was after the Mexico City and Paris meetings.

To blunt the sting of the April 28, 1993 Chicago tape, Hulkower presented another FBI report of an interview with Crouy. In it, Brian Shepard said the Frenchman had characterized the dinner meeting as "general in material and involved each in attendance getting to know one another," which sounded fairly innocuous.

When Hulkower asked if Crouy had described the meal with Whitacre and Wilson in this way to Shepard, the witness blanked. Finally, Judge Manning snapped, "What's the answer? You have to answer."

Crouy said, "Well, I'm thinking," and finally, "I don't remember."

Bill Walker had very few questions for Crouy. But he did play with the fact that Crouy's notes of the Mexico session were copies. Crouy had destroyed the originals. Jack Bray's associate Kevin Dinan predictably took a few minutes to develop that Mick Andreas had not been at the Chicago dinner or in Tokyo a month later. Crouy had never met or spoken to Andreas. He did recall that in Tokyo, Wilson told the group that "Mick Andreas said 'we don't make deals.'" Robin Mann chose not to re-direct.

On the morning of August 12, the courtroom was edgy with rumors. It had leaked that the government's next witness would be an ADM employee. The individual would testify against Wilson and Andreas pursuant to the corporate guilty plea agreement. But, who was the insider?

One candidate was Mark Cheviron, ADM's director of security. A somewhat murky figure, Cheviron reportedly had made ADM's phones impossible to tap and had played a role in cutting off the FBI's investigation of the Fujiwara affair. It was known that he had appeared before the grand jury that had indicted the defendants.

However, it was not Cheviron's testimony that the opponents were debating at sidebar. Rather, the defense was seeking to make Manning reconsider an earlier decision she had made to allow Barrie Cox to testify. The Wilson and Andreas teams pleaded that Cox's proposed testimony, which related to fixing the price of citric acid had no place in the trial. One of Andreas' advocates, a seasoned Chicago criminal attorney named Joe Duffy, told the court that citric and lysine were not similar enough to constitute on admissible pattern of conduct. ADM, he argued, had entered the lysine trade through manufacturing. But the company had "bought the citric business; and when they bought it, they had existing customers, so they had 35 percent of the market."

Pushing the envelope, Duffy made a rather startling admission. "I think the case against Mr. Andreas is a very close case. I think he's entitled to a fair trial; and I think the only way he gets a fair trial here, Your Honor—and he's gotten a fair trial today because of you—is to not allow in collateral evidence that has nothing to do with lysine.

"Mr. Cox is not a co-conspirator in lysine. He's not a codefendant. We're talking about an entirely different industry. My fear is that the inference that will be drawn by this jury will never be cured by a limiting instruction; and it's going to be so prejudicial to Mr. Andreas that when the jury gets back there, they're not going to be able to keep it straight." In sum, they could convict on the basis of another crime rather than the one that had been charged.

Mark Hulkower added, "If the government drops citric acid in the middle of this, all of sudden we are fighting on a second complete front."

Not only was the government planning to present Cox, it was struggling to introduce the ADM corporate guilty plea. "The plea agreement," intoned Jim Griffin, "is offered solely as it affects the credibility of the ADM corporate representative Mr. Cox, and to rebut any inference that ADM was an aggressive price-cutter, which would not participate in a price-fixing conspiracy."

Manning was not moved by Griffin. The plea did not necessarily affect Cox's credibility. Plus, corporations plead guilty for a variety of reasons, "one of which is an economic decision. I think to allow the plea agreement of ADM would be unfairly prejudicial and outweighs the probative value." By now, the afternoon was over. The ruling on Cox would be tougher. She wanted "to do a little more reading" overnight and promised to rule the next morning.

When court reconvened, Manning was ready with her decision. She would not disturb her earlier ruling of July 8 allowing the government to present Cox. Moreover, she clarified that he could testify against both Wilson and Andreas.

Bray made a last ditch effort to keep Cox off the stand. A grand jury in San Francisco was investigating citric acid and could come down with indictments. Thus, many valuable records were impounded in San Francisco and remained unavailable to the defense. But, the prosecution insisted it had turned all of its materials on Cox over to the defense, which could not claim a lack of preparation. Again refusing to budge, Manning asked for the jury to be brought back into the courtroom.

Barrie Cox took the stand. In his midfifties, thin, and pale, Cox had light wavy brown hair and a small plain face. Cox never let his gaze stray to either of the defendants. Upon being sworn in, he bit his lower lip in apparent torment. It was the last piece of emotion he would show. He made no gestures. His hands remained in his lap. His speech was clear and soft.

Prompted by Griffin, Cox indicated that he lived in the United Kingdon, where he worked for ADM as president of the food additives division. In 1990, he had been based in New York as a vice president for marketing of chemicals at Pfizer, a large drug company now famous for Viagra. When Pfizer sold its citric acid plant to ADM, Cox came with the deal. He reported to Terry Wilson.

From 1991 to 1995, Cox, under Wilson's supervision, had been involved in a price-fixing and sales-volume conspiracy of citric acid on a "global" basis. Four other companies had been involved: Haarman & Reimer (a New Jersey-based subsidiary of the German-based Bayer AG); Hoffman LaRoche of Switzerland; Jungbunzlauer of Austria; and Cerestar (a Dutch subsidiary of the French agricultural giant Eridania-Beghin-Say SA). Together they accounted for about 65 to 75 percent of the world supply.

At meetings, mainly abroad, the companies agreed to a "quota system" to control volumes as well as price levels. For ADM, he and Wilson attended the sessions. There was never any doubt in his mind that the activity was illegal.

Cox recalled an incident in 1990, shortly before he joined ADM. He had lunch in Decatur with Wilson and Mick Andreas. Andreas asked if he could arrange meetings with the other citric manufacturers. Cox said he could.

Immediately after joining ADM, Wilson asked him to schedule meetings with Hoffman LaRoche, Jungbunzlauer, and Haarman & Reimer. Cox set up sessions with each firm in Europe. Wilson accompanied him. Their travel vouchers were admitted into evidence.

The citric companies all complained that prices were depressed. They agreed to raise them on a worldwide basis. A volume allocation for each company was set based on the average of its last three years of sales.

Cox explained how volume was controlled. "Basically, there would be a system of compensation that any company that sold in excess of the quota would buy the following year from any company that was by definition under its quota."

The group, which now also included Cerestar, set up a trade association, the

European Citric Acid Manufacturers Association (ECAMA) in order to hold seem-ingly legitimate meetings. Cox described ECAMA as "a combination of cover and conveniences." ECAMA had a fall meeting in Brussels and a spring session at a mem-ber company's site. Cox explained that there always was a meaningless official meet-ing followed by an "unofficial" meeting where the ongoing strategy of the conspiracy was developed. The official ECAMA meetings had an agenda. The unofficial meetings did not. Cox made notes at the latter but destroyed them after-wards. Wilson attended unofficial meetings through November 1994.

The group covertly reported sales figures each month to a secretary at Hoff-man LaRoche. Once the total was received she would feed back the numbers to the individual companies. Cox called in figures for ADM. He always conferred on the fixed price and allocation with Wilson.

The conspiracy did not work perfectly. On occasion, the companies, including ADM, cheated on the price. During the unofficial meetings, one frequent topic was "the fact that complete adherence to the agreement that had been made was not being honored by all members." Wilson was involved in these discussions.

The citric conspiracy ended in mid-1995. ADM transferred Cox to England in April 1996 with a raise and not much to do. It was the government's firm contention that Cox was moved out of the country to keep him away from the FBI and the grand juries investigating ADM, but this was not voiced to the jury.

Cox said the group internally did not refer to itself by its public name; ECAMA. It preferred to use "G-4" and later "G-5" after the French firm Cerestar was included. He recalled that he and Wilson had agreed upon Cerestar's share, which was about 5 percent. ADM's negotiated slice of the market was "26.3 [percent] or something like that."

Cox surprised many observers by stating that Pfizer earlier had fixed citric acid prices. But, he testified that he personally had not been involved with those efforts.

The G-5's biggest fear was China, which had begun producing large quantities of low-cost citric acid. In January 1995, "basically as an official ECAMA represen-tative," Cox travelled to China with Rolf Soiron, the CEO of Jungungzlauer who was serving as chair of the official group. The pair threatened the Chinese with antidumping litigation for exporting "excessive quantities of material and damag-ing the European market." Of course, ECAMA could not follow through with its threat because a suit would blow the cover off its conspiracy.

The government wanted Cox to testify to a joking remark he made to Whitacre after returning from China. "You know," Cox had told the mole, "what we ought to do is take a squadron of B-52s and bomb them." Hulkower knew what was com-ing and objected. Manning hauled the lawyers to sidebar. Jim Griffin took the posi-tion that the defense had been allowed to introduce the Japanese joke about bombing ADM's plant.

"I don't see any connection," said Manning.

"They're both ludicrous," said the prosecutor.

Manning was incredulous. "So, if one side offers something ludicrous, you're saying that the other side should?"

Losing ground, Griffin tried again, "I'm saying that we're offering this to show how ludicrous their argument is."

"That's far-fetched, counsel," replied Manning, who sustained the objection.

Griffin shifted to the behavior of Wilson at the height of the citric conspiracy in 1992 and 1993. He had told Cox, "If ever any of this goes wrong, you are on your own." Cox took this to mean that ADM would try to distance itself from him if the scam were exposed.

The prosecutor asked Cox if Wilson had claimed during the citric conspiracy that he was bluffing simply to get information from competitors. (This was Wilson's defense to the lysine charge.) Cox uttered a simple "no."

In September or October 1995, about two months after the raid at ADM and the outing of Whitacre as a spy, Wilson had met with Cox. Cox testified that Wilson had said "there was bad stuff on the tapes" that pertained to lysine. The defense objected, but Manning allowed the remark as relevant to "consciousness of guilt."

Griffin tendered the witness to the defense. The lawyers flocked to sidebar. Weingarten moved for a mistrial. "I believe they've dropped essentially a stink bomb in the middle of the lysine trial. We have 200 hours of tape and millions of documents in lysine. The jury has the enormous task of understanding what's going on in lysine, and now all of sudden we have to deal with Swiss, Austrian, and German competitors."

Surprisingly, Jack Bray joined the motion, though Cox had offered no testimony that he or Wilson had told Andreas anything about the citric plot. Manning asked what was "the harm" to his client?

"The harm," maintained the lawyer, "is enormous because of the hierarchical setting [at ADM] and the misuse being made of this evidence."

Manning denied the mistrial. Bray renewed his motion for a severance from Wilson and Whitacre. She quickly denied that, too. Now Bray wanted a "limiting" instruction that would prevent the jury from holding anything that Cox had said against Andreas. The government vehemently opposed the request. Citric was tied to Andreas through remarks made in his presence on the lysine surveillance tapes. Plus, Cox had supported the notion that the citric conspiracy was a model for ADM.

Manning took lunch to consider the issue. After recess she denied the motion because "where there is some evidence that indicates that other crimes or other acts are in furtherance of a conspiracy, such evidence is admissible." She said that her instructions to the jury at the end of the case would suffice. She was especially impressed by a reference to the citric acid conspiracy on the Irvine videotape.

The defense would not let go. Hulkower said he was "just shocked . . . the bell has rung." He saw an instruction at the end of the case as "far too late."

Bray objected to the use of "innuendos" rather than evidence against his client. Manning was firm, "Your vehement objection is noted for the record." She called the jury in. Hulkower got up to cross and perform damage control. First, he distanced the witness from lysine. Cox admitted he had nothing to do with the commodity.

Lysine and citric acid were unrelated products. "It's animal food versus people food, correct?" The witness agreed. Hulkower began to trash Whitacre because, during his period of undercover taping, "he had been embezzling money hand-over-fist from ADM." Cox said he had heard of the theft.

Moreover, the mole had told Cox a strange lie. According to the witness, Whitacre had fabricated a horrid childhood in which his parents both were killed when their car hit a deer, and he went into an orphanage at an early age. Later he was adopted by the wealthy family that owned the King's Island amusement park outside Cincinnati. It was all a bizarre fantasy.

"Do you know," Hulkower asked Cox, "whether . . . it had become public knowledge that Mr. Whitacre told his friend and gardener that once I get Mr. Wilson on tape, I can make these tapes say anything I want?"

Griffin instantly objected. The question lacked any foundation that such a conversation between Whitacre and gardener occurred, much less that it had become "public knowledge." If so, what relevance was there to "public knowledge." Plus, it called for hearsay.

"It really is totally inappropriate," Manning said of the question. But she seemed to know that she had been good to the government in her recent rulings on Cox, from which the defense was still smarting, so she bent. "Let's have this as the last such question." Hulkower asked it.

It was a minor mistake. The combative lawyer had asked the question without knowing the answer. Cox's response was that he did not know "whether it was common knowledge or public knowledge." Moreover, jurors would expect the defense to present the "gardener and friend" to see whether Whitacre actually had made the boast.

Frustrated, Hulkower targeted his opposing counsel. This was a departure. Bray and Weingarten, though maximum advocates, had been unsparingly gracious to their opponents in open court. This approach made sense because jurors want to decide weighty questions not ego battles. Now Hulkower chose to pick on Robin Mann, the sole woman on the government team.

Cox had been prepared for court by Mann. Hulkower pulled from him that she had asked Cox not to use a certain big word in court.

For some reason Hulkower did not pursue what the word was. The lawyer asked if Mann had indicated "why you shouldn't use that word in front of the jury." "Because," said Cox, "it was a word that might not be understood by the jury."

Hulkower pressed, "Because? Any reason?" In his typical flat way Cox replied, "She said because they might not be as educated as you are."

The lawyer paused to let the insult sink in. But the jury seemed unbruised. He continued to ask questions about whether prosecutors "cautioned you about using big words or anything like that," and got a toneless "no" from Cox.

Hulkower tried to show that unlike the elite lady lawyer, his client was down-to-earth, just like the jurors. This led to a surreal dialog with Cox.

Hulkower: And in the course of your dealings with Mr. Wilson did you have occasion to come to know his wife?

Cox: I have met his wife, yes.

Hulkower: Is that his wife Mary Jo Wilson in the blue dress in the first row back there?

Cox: That is Mary Jo, yes.

Hulkower: Sitting next to Sally Andreas?

Cox: Yes.

Hulkower: Do you know Mr. Wilson's four children?

Cox: I only knew one of his children.

Hulkower: Do you know either of his grandchildren?

Cox: No, I don't.

Griffin objected. Introducing the defendant's background usually is irrelevant except at sentencing. That's because our system is supposed to convict or acquit based on the evidence, not on whether the defendant's background is sympathetic. Moreover, Cox professed to know little about Wilson's life prior to joining ADM in 1990. But Manning let the lawyer toil on leading Cox heavily through the facts that Wilson was only a high-school graduate with a Marine background who had worked his way up at ADM, from what Hulkower called "a clerk accountant type position."

Still seeking jury rapport, Hulkower attempted humor in a discussion of the growth of the use of citric acid in laundry products during the early 1990s. "Is citric acid in detergent what gives it that lemony-fresh smell?" "No," Cox said, "citric acid has no odor."

Briefly Hulkower touched on Cox's first interview with the FBI in October 1996. Cox revealed that he told the FBI that he and a Cargill representative had had price and volume discussions about citric acid.

Hulkower asked, "And did you tell [the FBI] that you had discussions with an individual at Cargill about the bidding price for certain accounts?"

"That is correct," said Cox.

Cargill and ADM are the giants of American agriculture. But the highly secretive Cargill is the General Motors and ADM is the Ford. Cox's revelation would be intriguing to anyone who followed agribusiness or antitrust. Even an exploratory attempt at setting prices or volumes or rigging bids can be a violation. But what was the jury to make of the news? That Cargill was too big to be prosecuted? That the government's enforcement practice was not uniform? That all companies engaged in price-fixing, so it wasn't a big deal? Hulkower allowed the data to dangle. The relevance never was.

By now the judge was asking Hulkower if he was almost finished. The lawyer seemed to realize that his main goal of destroying Cox's credibility still lay ahead. Shifting gears Hulkower began digging into the structure of the citric conspiracy. There were two levels according to Cox. The conspirators called themselves masters and sherpas. Masters were the big-picture people who made decisions and set policy. Sherpas took orders and did the low-level detail work. Usually, Cox said, he was a sherpa, but sometimes he functioned as a master.

Probably Hulkower realized he had made a mistake by "opening the door." At any rate, he tried to slip unnoticed into another area. But the prosecution had not been hibernating.

Hulkower tried to finish on an emotional note. He asked Cox a series of questions regarding his client's "attitude towards Japanese competition." Griffin objected to each of them. Nerves frayed, Hulkower asked for a sidebar. "The government table is about a foot from the jury. It's about as close to the jury as it is from me. It may just be me and my questioning, but every time I've been up there for the last two days, they are saying things to each other like, 'outrageous,' and 'I can't believe it,' audibly. And I'm hearing it and I know the jury's hearing it as well."

"Outrageous," Griffin countered, "was said with my standing up and making an objection to the court because what you were doing was outrageous."

At sidebar, Griffin argued that Hulkower was making "an appeal of bias" against "Japanese business people." Wilson's attorney insisted that his line of questions was central to the defense of gathering information and bluffing to beat the "Japanese cartel." "All right," said Manning, "I will hesitantly overrule the objection." Hulkower picked up where he had left off. _

Hulkower: Mr. Cox, I'm guessing you don't remember the question?

Cox: Correct.

Hulkower: I had asked you whether you and Mr. Wilson had occasion to discuss his attitude towards Japanese competitors and Japanese business practices, and you indicated that he, like you, did not like the Japanese way of doing business.

And the next question I had asked, which I'll attempt to ask again, is what in particular did Mr. Wilson indicate to you he did not like about the Japanese way of doing business?

Cox: I think basically that it was very difficult to compete on sort of a level playing field with a Japanese—with a sort of Japanese, Inc. mentality.

Hulkower: And when you say the "Japanese Inc. mentality," what do you mean?

Cox: They would frequently work together to further Japan before effectively competing perhaps against themselves.

Hulkower: Japanese companies would work together to fight or beat American companies that were trying to break into a market?

Cox: Yes. It's sometimes very difficult to get into a Japanese market.

Hulkower: And there were specific examples of this that Mr. Wilson was aware of in his conversations with you?

Cox: I believe so, yes.

Hulkower: And Mr. Wilson expressed to you his belief that he viewed Japanese business practices as unfair, predatory, and that companies worked together to defeat American business?

Cox: That is a reasonable summary.

On this low note, Hulkower concluded his cross. Manning invited Bray and Walker to question the witness, but each quietly declined.

On re-direct Griffin established that G-5 sold about a half a billion dollars of citric acid per year and that the price was elevated by 30 percent during the conspiracy. He sought more clarification on "masters" and "sherpas," and then asked the question that Hulkower had omitted, "What was Mr. Wilson?"

"He was a master," said Cox.

Cox left the courtroom without looking to either side. Though weird and robotic, his testimony was virtually unimpeached. It had been devastating to Wilson. Unless the jury bonded over prejudice or the defense came up with a miracle witness—perhaps the defendant himself—Wilson probably would go down. He seemed to realize this. The remaining air went out of him. Sometimes he sat quietly with his wife in the first row rather than at the table with his lawyers. Frequently, in the midst of testimony, he would walk out of the courtroom, which is very unusual for the person on trial. There was a rumor that he had sneaked a bottle into the building, but no one saw him drink.

THE HANDLER

"It's not unusual to have someone who lies to the
FBI and we work with him. It happens every day."
—Brian Shepard

Near the end of the court day, Scott Lassar called Brian Shepard to the stand. Shepard looked calm and resigned as he took the oath. His face was still boyish, but his hair had grayed since the hearings of the previous fall. The rapport between the lead agent and attorney on the long, labrynthine case was evident. Lassar put Shepard at ease as he guided him through his biography. Born in nearby Kankakee, Shepard had started in 1972 as a document aide in the FBI's lab in Washington, DC. Accepted into a highly selective class for special agents, he graduated four years later. Then he was assigned to "foreign counterintelligence" in New York. Lassar asked what that meant. "I worked on spy cases against the Russians," Shepard said.

"Ok," said Lassar, "I won't ask you if you caught any." Several jurors laughed. Shepard smiled shyly.

In 1983, he requested a transfer back to Illinois where his wife also had roots. The FBI had a field office in Springfield. Shepard became the agent in its Decatur satellite.

Lassar directed his attention to November 4, 1992. Shepard and two FBI supervisors went to a meeting at Mick Andreas' home. Andreas' personal attorney Jim Shafter, who attended much of the trial, was also present.

Andreas explained the problem. ADM produced lysine. Its main competitors were Japanese companies; the largest was Ajinomoto. After Ajinomoto employees toured the ADM plant, Mark Whitacre received a threat by telephone. The caller, according to Andreas, told Whitacre that Ajinomoto had paid an ADM employee to compromise the lysine vats by injecting a virus. On the stand, Shepard recalled:

Mr. Andreas then said that Mr. Whitacre told him that this person who is second in command at Ajinomoto who had contacted Mr. Whitacre had told him for $6 million, which had been a negotiated price [between Whitacre and the caller], that he would identify the person who had injected the virus. And not only would he identify that person, but he would say—would point out where the contamination occurred, how it occurred, and also would provide the microorganisms that were necessary for production of lysine and the microorganism necessary for the production of monosodium glutamate, MSG, which were more disease resistant than their current microorganism.

Mr. Andreas then said that because of the allegation that Mr. Whitacre had told him about he immediately contacted his father and that his father had contacted an attorney in Europe who had contracts with sabotage specialists and that that sabotage specialist had contacted their [ADM] director of security.

At this point, Judge Manning stopped the testimony to read an unusual "stipulated" document containing information agreed upon by all defendants and the government. "All right ladies and gentlemen," she instructed, "you are to take the following facts as true:"

On September 25, 1997, a high-level executive of Archer Daniels Midland, ADM, not a defendant in this case, was interviewed by the FBI. He stated that in the fall of 1992, while living and working in Europe, he had a conversation with Dwayne Andreas alerting him that he would be receiving a telephone call from Michael D. Andreas about a problem in the United States that needed his attention.

Shortly after this call, the ADM executive stated he received a call from Michael D. Andreas. During the telephone conversation Andreas stated there were start-up problems with an ADM lysine plant in Decatur, Illinois. Michael Andreas told the executive that Mark Whitacre had told him the reason for the start-up problem was that a person in the plant was engaged in sabotage of the lysine production process and that the saboteur was working under the authority of the number two person in a large Japanese company, Ajinomoto Company, Inc.

According to the executive, Andreas told him further that Whitacre was told the identity of the saboteur would be revealed for $10 million and that for that money ADM would receive a new bug resistant to the contamination and which would be a stronger bug that would provide better yields.

According to the ADM executive, Andreas asked him to contact the Central Intelligence Agency, CIA, a nonlaw enforcement agency of the United States Government in Europe and report these allegations. The executive claimed it was common in Japanese culture for the Japanese government to be intertwined in Japanese business and, therefore, they thought the Japanese government might be involved in the extortion. Thus, according to the executive, Andreas was concerned that the relationship between the United States and Japan could be strained.

They were also concerned about ADM's legal position if ADM paid the extortionist without the agency's help. The executive also stated he knew the agency was not a law enforcement agency, and he does not recall any discussion with Michael D. Andreas about presenting this matter to law enforcement.

The ADM executive contacted the CIA, which determined on its own, that proper jurisdiction for this domestic matter belonged with the FBI and referred the extortion matter to the FBI.

The jury sat wide-eyed during the strange recitation, which raised numerous questions. Who was the high level executive? His identity never has been revealed, but it is possible that he was G. Allen Andreas, who before the trial had replaced James Randall as ADM's president. This Andreas, a lawyer, had headed ADM's European operations in 1992. Why the unnamed executive would have contacts with "sabotage specialists" and/or the CIA remained unanswered. So did the change in the ransom from $6 to $10 million.

Lassar returned Shepard to the story. After he left Mick Andreas, Shepard scheduled a meeting with Whitacre. Someone from ADM called twice to put off the interview, which finally occurred at Shepard's office.

Whitacre arrived with Mark Cheviron, the ADM director of security, who asked to be present. It was an unusual request. The FBI generally tries to interview individually in order to preserve confidentiality, but Shepard consented to the request. Whitacre's story matched Andreas', but Whitacre identified that caller as "Mr. Fujiwara."

Shepard next agreed to meet with Cheviron. The ADM director of security was eager to be kept up-to-date on the status of the FBI's investigation. Cheviron said that he had been embarrassed on an occasion during the Chicago Board of Trade sting in the 1980s, and he didn't want that to happen again. Shepard stated he would apprise Cheviron on the status of the investigation but that "there were certain things I could not reveal to him."

On the following evening, November 5, 1992, Shepard went to Whitacre's home. The FBI wanted to install a phone tap in order to record calls from Fujiwara.

Whitacre did not want to talk inside, so they sat in Shepard's car. Whitacre said that he had been "coached" by Mick Andreas and Cheviron to say that the Fujiwara calls were coming in only on the ADM extension in his home, called an OPX line.

Over the next four hours, Whitacre explained that on behalf of ADM he was involved in an international price-fixing conspiracy involving lysine. Meetings were taking place around the world. Japanese and Koreans were involved.

Whitacre aired other dirty laundry at ADM. According to Whitacre, Jim Randall, recently had hired a man to steal a valuable organism used to produce bacitracin, an antibiotic.

Whitacre said ADM wanted information about the Eddyville, Iowa plant of Heartland Lysine, a subsidiary of Ajinomoto. According to Whitacre, Randall told Cheviron to devise a plan using prostitutes.

In court Shepard revealed that "Mr. Randall told him [Whitacre] that Cheviron had arranged for some girls to befriend these [Heartland] employees and that he then asked Mr. Whitacre to compose a list of technical questions about Ajinomoto's production to give these girls so that they could obtain that information from these employees."

The day after the talk in the car, Shepard and four other agents met with Cheviron at the FBI field office in Springfield. In court Shepard recalled that "Mr. Cheviron testified that he had spoken to Mr. Dwayne Andreas [who] was concerned about the FBI investigating high-level executives at ADM and also was concerned that he didn't want the FBI looking in all their closets." Cheviron said he believed the extortion claim and wanted to make the payment in conjunction with the FBI. Cheviron again voiced his desire to be kept up-to-date about the FBI's investigation. This time John Stukey, head of the Springfield office, explained that not every fact they gathered could be revealed to ADM.

The same day Shepard re-interviewed Whitacre, who added a wrinkle to the extortion saga. His teenage daughter, a student at a military school in Indiana, had received a call from a man who sounded Asian. The caller told the girl that he no longer would cooperate with ADM. Whitacre informed Cheviron and Mick Andreas about the call and said he no longer wanted anything to do with solving the extortion mess.

The next day Shepard learned that Cheviron and Richard Reising, ADM's corporate counsel, called Whitacre, who told them that there had been no such call to his daughter.

Lassar interjected in amazement, "what the heck did you think was going on at that point?" "It was very confusing to me," Shepard shook his head. "It was very confusing."

On November 8, Shepard went back to Whitacre's house. He brought his supervisor, Dean Paisley. Whitacre gave them his expense reports from his price-fixing travels. He also outlined lysine's sudden shift from losses to profits at ADM.

The following day Shepard had a message on his answering machine from Cheviron complaining that the FBI was tapping two lines at Whitacre's home instead of one. As a result, ADM no longer would cooperate in the extortion investigation.

"Is it unusual in your experience," asked Lassar, "for the alleged victim of the crime to refuse to cooperate?"

The afternoon session was ending. Manning sustained Weingarten's strident objection, but the jury had a point to ponder overnight.

Shepard was back on the stand in the morning. Lassar asked what was the next step "after Cheviron told you on November 9 that ADM was no longer going to cooperate in the extortion investigation?" Shepard said he tried to confirm price-fixing. He met Whitacre, not at home, but at the Best Western Motel in Decatur. Whitacre signed a consent form for Shepard to surveil his calls. Whitacre dialed Mimoto at Ajinomoto's headquarters in Tokyo and Jhom Su Kim at Miwon in Korea without success. Finally, he reached Masaru Yamamoto of Kyowa Hakko in Tokyo.

The two discussed a lysine price of $1.05 per pound decided upon in Paris. Raising it higher would be difficult due to competition from soy meal. To Shepard, who recorded the conversation, it confirmed Whitacre's price-fixing claim. Lassar played the tape for the jury.

Ultimately, the investigation produced a large library of tapes for the FBI. Ironically, it almost ended on November 9, 1992, after the first recorded call when Whitacre suddenly refused to cooperate. Shepard testified that Whitacre "said he had learned that what he was doing [for ADM] was not illegal, and that I was hurting innocent people, such as himself and the Andreases and others." In fact, Whitacre would not make another tape for the FBI until five months later on March 12, 1993.

Meanwhile, Shepard kept pushing for answers about the extortion plot. On December 21, 1992, Whitacre submitted to a polygraph. After failing it, he confessed to fabricating the whole extortion story, including the parts about a mole in the plant, the viral sabotage, the shakedown by Fujiwara, and the approach to his daughter. Whitacre told Shepard and the polygrapher that he made up the lies to justify the malfunctioning lysine plant, which was his responsibility.

Lassar wondered why the FBI failed to alert ADM to lies. Shepard told the court that the bureau didn't want ADM to know that Whitacre was still furnishing information since the company remained the focus of an antitrust investigation.

Shepard also disclosed that a month after his November tirade, Whitacre fed the FBI a tantalizing piece of information: an ADM employee named Wayne Brasser had been fired for refusing to participate in citric acid price-fixing. The tip had checked out. Shepard knew that Whitacre could provide reliable information.

Whitacre posed the government with a huge dilemma. He possessed undeniable leads, but he had admitted to weaving fictional crimes. On December 29, 1992, the United States Attorney's Office in Springfield drafted a thirteen-point "court cooperation and testimony" agreement to provide Whitacre with "use immunity." This meant that the government pledged not to use any truthful information it received under the agreement against him. Whitacre promised "to act solely at the direction and under the supervision of the FBI." Whitacre had to keep his role secret. Compliance also meant not contacting the subjects of the government's investigation "without the prior knowledge and approval of the FBI."

The core prohibition read, "You agree that you will not engage in any criminal activity of any kind without the prior knowledge and approval of FBI agents and this office." In other words, law enforcement expected him to keep fixing prices but not to break any other laws.

Whitacre signed the agreement on January 3, 1993. In his own hand, he added another condition, "Furthermore, I agree to take a polygraph test at any time."

Lassar asked, "Did Mr. Whitacre violate this cooperation agreement with the government?"

His anger barely suppressed, Shepard replied, "Yes, by not telling us about his fraud activity." For embezzling ADM funds, Shepard related that Whitacre had been sentenced to nine years. His voice rising slightly, the agent swore that he never had suspected Whitacre of fraud during the thirty-three months that the mole had toiled on his watch.

Shepard recalled that Whitacre took a second polygraph test. On March 10, 1993, the operator asked Whitacre questions in two areas. Had Cheviron coached him on directing calls to the OPX line? He said yes. Was he more involved in price-fixing than he had let on to the FBI? He said no. Whitacre flunked both.

Before the test Whitacre had shown signs of resistance to the government. He made excuses not to talk, claiming when he did that ADM had been scared away from price-fixing by having the FBI around. Failing the second polygraph led to another confession. He and ADM in fact had been involved during the past five weeks in price-fixing. Plus, there would be a high-level meeting between Mick Andreas and Ajinomoto's Kazutoshi Yamada on April 30, 1993.

The FBI could have cancelled Whitacre's cooperation agreement and arrested him for lying to the agency (a felony) and other crimes. But, Whitacre presented unusual opportunities. He was a divisional president of a major American corporation. Shepard did some research. The FBI never had had a more highly placed operative in a business.

Whitacre again agreed to make tapes. Shepard gave him several recorders. One was a Nagra reel-to-reel machine. Built specifically for the FBI, it could be hidden in the false bottom of a briefcase but activated from outside, or it could be attached to Whitacre's body. The FBI used both methods. Whitacre wore it at the April 28, 1993 restaurant meeting with Wilson, Crouy, and Rollier. He used it again two days later at ADM headquarters when Yamada, Ikeda, Randall, and Andreas met.

Shepard testified that Whitacre had little control over the Nagra, which had no rewind button and no speaker for playback. However, the mole also was provided with a standard microcasette machine that on other occasions he could place in his suit coat or pants pocket. Whenever Shepard had advance notice of a meeting he set up the Nagra for Whitacre. The microcasette machine was used mainly for the frequent encounters at ADM when price-fixing would come up in office chatter.

Whitacre's tips also provided the FBI with advance notice of the major price-fixing sessions, allowing the bureau to arrange surveillance. For example, Shepard was at the Hotel Pullman Windsor in Paris during the October 5, 1993 lysine group session. But, the French government forbade the FBI from audio or video taping. Shepard could not enter the closed "unofficial" meeting, but he was at least able to see the participants in the hotel.

On native soil in Irvine, California, Shepard was not hamstrung. He planted a video camera to capture the conference among Andreas, Yamada, Ikeda, and Whitacre and operated it remotely from an adjacent room through microwaves. He watched the session as it transpired.

Lassar asked the agent what he witnessed. Weingarten objected calling such testimony improper since the tape already had been played. The judge disagreed, "Overruled—he observed it."

"I remember," said Shepard," that there was a discussion about a purchase of a business to begin with between Mr. Andreas and Mr. Yamada. Then after that, there was a discussion about the volume for lysine, and Mr. Andreas and Mr. Yamada agreed on a volume allocation that day."

In Shepard's opinion, the meeting was important for two reasons. First, he saw the ADM and Ajinomoto honchos cut the deal. Second, a big chunk of what Whitacre had been saying was confirmed. As a result, the FBI continued to let the mole make tapes.

Shepard approximated the total number of tapes at "120 to 130." Usually, Shepard got the tape back from Whitacre within two days of its making. But, sometimes it took longer because of the ADM manager's "very busy schedule" at work, which frequently included travel. The tape hand-offs were made in parking lots and hotels around Decatur. Shepard would listen to the evidence "as soon as I got back to the office." The tapes never seemed to have been edited, spliced, or otherwise rigged by Whitacre.

Lassar questioned whether Shepard ever thought when reviewing tapes that

Whitacre appeared "to be trying to get people to say things that weren't true." Shepard simply said "no." The tapes also confirmed what Whitacre was telling the FBI about the lysine trade at the time.

Lassar began anticipating cross-examination. He knew that one issue that had been important in pretrial proceedings was what the lawyers on both sides termed "nomenclature." Different types of investigations required different types of controls. Lassar asked Shepard if he had used Whitacre in an "undercover investigation." No, said the agent explaining that "undercover" meant "inserting" an agent into a criminal enterprise, such as a fencing ring.

Nor was Whitacre an "informant" within the FBI's definition. Informants are individuals whose identities are not released. Informants neither testify nor make tapes. They give tips. Lassar asked if Shepard could give an example. "Yes, someone calls up or talks to us about drug information who says Johnny is selling drugs to Joey on the street, and they have knowledge about that sale. They don't want to testify."

The bureau's stringent requirements on undercover and informant based operations would not apply. Whitacre simply was a "cooperating witness because he consensually recorded conversations for the FBI."

Since Whitacre did not have the training or experience of an FBI agent, he was not expected to perform at the high level of a bureau operative working undercover. Nor did the FBI have to make the "suitability determination" required for using an informant.

"Why not?" wondered Lassar.

"Because the proof is in the pudding, so to speak, with a cooperating witness because they are making recorded conversations with the subjects of an investigation."

Shepard readily admitted not to having previous antitrust experience. But, throughout the investigation, he had had supervision from Springfield and from headquarters in Washington, DC.

Yet, it was primarily his responsibility to run Whitacre. He told the mole to tape conversations of "a criminal nature" and "to record the entire conversation when he did it," but not to tape "conversations that were of legitimate ADM business."

"Why didn't you want him to record every conversation he had with Mr. Andreas and Mr. Wilson?" asked Lassar.

"Because," Shepard responded, "I didn't want him to invade their privacy. I was very concerned about that."

Shepard added that Whitacre was the bureau's best and perhaps only option in the investigation. Security was quite tight at ADM. It would not have been realistic to place an agent inside the building. He revealed that the bureau had tried to use a transmitter to relay Whitacre's conversations, "We attempted to get signals outside of ADM. It was not possible."

Lassar wanted to know if Whitacre was expected to tape every lysine conversation in its entirety. Shepard said that sometimes a conversation would begin when Whitacre had his coat, containing the cassette recorder, off. So, the opportunity would be missed. On other occasions, the tape would run out before the conversation was over. Obviously, Whitacre could not stop and reload in front of his cronies, so he would miss parts. At other times, a conversation would begin innocently, then veer into price-fixing. Unless Whitacre was wearing the recorder and able to activate it unobtrusively, he would lose the moment. Nevertheless, Whitacre had recorded a huge trove of tapes. Shepard never was suspicious that there weren't more.

However, the mole's work did not always please the FBI. Whitacre seemed too eager to get James Randall on tape uttering the now famous ADM maxim about the competitor being the friend and the customer being the enemy. Shepard testified that he told Whitacre, "You know if it's going to be said, it's going to be said. Don't worry about it. Don't be so anxious about it."

Whitacre also tended to "tell people little white lies for no reason." In court, Shepard gave the example of the mole informing Andreas that Mimoto had called the night before, which in fact was false. "I told him," said Shepard, "there was no reason to make up things like that."

Shepard also swore he never instructed Whitacre what to do as a price-fixer. "We wanted whatever normally would happen to happen and not to influence what the business part of that was going to be."

Lassar highlighted the fact that Whitacre's tape production had fallen after the December 1993 Tokyo meeting. Shepard explained that "by that time the conspiracy had been pretty much perfected and there was no reason to get tapes of Mr. Andreas and Mr. Wilson because Mr. Whitacre was then in charge of continuing the conspiracy, and collection on a routine basis of the contact with Mr. Andreas wasn't necessary."

Lassar asked one last question that was probably perplexing jurors. If the government had proof of the illegal conspiracy in 1993, why had it allowed the activity to go until June 1995? Shepard replied, "We were trying to collect evidence of price-fixing on other product lines."

Early on cross, Bray revisited the FBI's problem in Paris. The bureau had not conducted surveillance "I take it because French authorities would not give legal permission to do so?" Shepard assented. Andreas' lawyer then pointed out "that the

Japanese government had indicated that the FBI couldn't come over and tape a meeting, correct?" Shepard agreed. Yet Bray maintained the FBI had a tape of the meeting.

Shepard struggled to explain the seeming contradiction. There was a loophole. An FBI legal attaché had contacted the Japanese government, which according to Shepard, allowed that Whitacre "could make tapes as a businessman if he made the decision to do so." Shepard offered that it had been Whitacre's choice as a private corporate executive to make these recordings.

Bray found it bizarre that Whitacre, while in Tokyo, was both an independent businessman and an informant on a leash. The roles seemed at odds. He picked at the point mercilessly, but Shepard quietly stood his ground.

Changing tacks, Bray made Shepard admit to the mole's many flaws. Whitacre was difficult to control, prone to lie, and as the agent put it, "he was always energized, period. He was full of energy. If we suggested something to him, with his exuberance and enthusiasm he would keep talking about it and talking about it." It would be hard to refocus him.

Bray tried to paint Shepard as Whitacre's enabler in crimes. The first was the Fujiwara extortion. Hitting an ironic note Bray asked, "It never ever occurred to you that Mr. Whitacre himself was trying to steal the money, the ten million or six million as the case may be?"

"That's correct," came the answer.

"Never occurred to you?"

"No."

Bray pried into the agent's experience with extortion, including training at the Quantico academy and discussions inside the bureau. "Weren't there mentions made by some people in the FBI that the extortionist could be your guy himself?" meaning Whitacre.

Grudgingly Shepard allowed, "I think it was mentioned."

Artfully, Bray continued to push Shepard to contradict earlier testimony about not suspecting Whitacre before his confession of the Fujiwara fraud. Professing difficulty in reconstructing almost six-year-old events Shepard admitted, "It may have crossed my mind."

Bray shifted into the arguably benign conduct of "ADM having requested the assistance of the CIA on this very extortion." Moreover, Mick Andreas, on November 11, 1992, "welcomed you into his home" and described the lysine business, ADM's new plant, and its competitors. Shepard admitted as much. Bray hoped the jury would believe that no crook ever would solicit law enforcement attention.

In contrast Bray showed that Whitacre was evasive during the initial contact at his house. Whitacre had not even let Shepard come inside, preferring to talk in the car.

For hours Bray went over Whitacre's deceit during the Fujiwara affair. Perhaps the worst of it involved his giving Cheviron a list of ADM employees who were suspected of working with Ajinomoto in the alleged sabotage plot. Cheviron sent the list to Shepard on December 16, 1992, well after the FBI agent knew that Whitacre had fabricated the sting plot.

Bray asked if inclusion on the list would constitute "a very serious accusation concerning these people?" Shepard said, "yes," but never alerted ADM security that the named employees were in the clear. Nor did the FBI tell ADM that there was no saboteur causing the lysine plant shutdowns, each of which resulted in a $7 to $8 million loss.

Bray pressed, "And did you—anyone—you or anyone suggest going to ADM and saying, 'you can at least pursue other technical reasons for those breakdowns. You don't have to worry about Fujiwara being a saboteur. That story was phony. You can devote your resources and your money in other directions to try to find the solution?'"

Shepard said "no" because the "overriding concern" was protecting the identity of the mole. Disclosing what the FBI knew about Fujiwara would have revealed "the fact that we were still talking to Mr. Whitacre." It could have cost him his ADM job and listening post inside the company. The FBI's antitrust investigation would have died. However, Shepard said he did contact Cheviron to tell him that the FBI had no leads in the extortion investigation and was closing it down.

Bray tried to suggest that this too was a lie because the FBI knew that Whitacre had confessed to the "crime." Lassar objected that Bray was arguing with the witness. Manning sustained, but the line of questions did not end. Rather, Bray took to its logical conclusion that the FBI relished Whitacre's lie.

"Now in fact," said Bray, "the FBI was very excited at the prospect of using the predicament that Mr. Whitacre was in to get him to try to give up bigger name defendants. Isn't that correct?"

Shepard replied, "We knew we had an opportunity to obtain more evidence about that [price-fixing] crime."

Now Bray quoted from an FBI internal document. "The results of this [failed] polygraph may have initiated one of the most significant investigations in the history of the Springfield FBI Division." Shepard did not dispute the remark.

"Whoever wrote that," said Bray "was pretty excited about getting Mr. Whitacre to cooperate, correct?" Manning sustained an objection, but the point was made. Bray kept challenging the FBI's ethics:

Bray: Was the intent to continue to use [Whitacre] to pursue an investigation that the FBI concluded was bigger and better for the FBI than indicting Whitacre for what he had done, correct?

Shepard: We had made a determination to go forward with Mr. Whitacre, yes.

Bray: Notwithstanding all these lies?

Shepard: That's correct. . . . It's not unusual to have someone who lies to the FBI and we work with him. It happens every day.

Bray explored anti-Japanese sentiment. He tried to show that Whitacre had injected the theme into the case. At ADM headquarters, Whitacre had touted the novel *Rising Sun* by Michael Crichton as an accurate rendition of Japan's industrial espionage efforts against US businesses.

Under Bray's questioning, Shepard recalled a taped conversation where Whitacre told Andreas that the Japanese "knew a lot about us. . . . No doubt about it. They knew every move we make. It's amazing what they knew. It really is."

Bray also scored points off Shepard when he asked him, "Now Mr. Whitacre had complete pricing authority at ADM for lysine, did he not?"

Shepard admitted, "I believe he did." Then he seemed to realize his error and suggested that final approval came "from Mr. Andreas or someone else, Mr. Randall possibly." He became more emphatic. "He discussed what he was doing pricingwise with Mr. Andreas, I know that."

But Bray seemed to lose the jury when he embarked on the long dusty road of regulations pertaining to undercover agents, informants, and cooperating witnesses. In vain, the lawyer tried to make Shepard agree that an extensive written suitability investigation should have occurred with Whitacre. All Shepard had done was to check his arrest record, which had come up clean. Under suitability guidelines, any known prior criminal activity such as the bogus extortion plot could disqualify an informant. For the umpteenth time Shepard said Whitacre was a cooperating witness and not an informant. The lawyer and the witness went round and round. Jurors became glassy-eyed. Manning declared a recess. At sidebar, there was more dreary rambling until the end of the day about whether 1980 US attorney general or 1990 FBI guidelines applied. Lassar became exasperated, "We shouldn't be burdening this debate." Manning seemed to agree.

On Monday, August 17, 1998, Bray probed new areas. The FBI had called its Behavioral Science Unit (BSU) into the case. The famed unit, known for tracking serial killers and other sociopaths, sent an agent to Illinois. Shepard told the agent his concerns about Whitacre's suicide threats and periodic breaks in cooperation but received no specific guidance from the BSU.

Shepard also admitted that Whitacre had asked for financial guarantees in addition to immunity. Specifically, the mole wanted payment equal to ten years of his ADM salary, if he lost his job. The FBI turned him down flat.

But Whitacre wasn't planning on being unemployed. From time to time, he told Shepard of his expectation to become president of ADM. He did not think his role as a spy would spoil this ambition. To the contrary Shepard said, "he had a vision once it did become overt that he would be recognized as the knight in shining armor by the board of directors."

Bray then wondered about the name of the investigation. "Who was Harvest King? Was the King Dwayne Andreas or Mick Andreas?" Shepard said he had no one in mind. It was just "a code name."

After lunch Bray raised the subject of theft. Shepard swore he first heard about it when Whitacre, in August 1995, "admitted to embezzling $500,000."

Bray had Shepard describe the fraud. Strangely, there was no objection from Walker. Shepard explained Whitacre's use of phony invoices to grift funds that he hid in Swiss and Cayman banks.

Finally, Judge Manning called a sidebar to ask Walker if he was objecting or seeking any type of limiting instruction to protect his client. Walker declined to object. "If they want to keep rehashing it [and] beating the crap out of him. . . . There is no damage control on that."

Manning seemed unsatisfied, "Well, you are representing counsel."

"Right," said Walker.

"I just want to know," the judge added, "because there are no objections being made."

"Right."

"And, I guess," Manning continued, "I need to know exactly what your position is because I can envision problems down the road." Manning was saying that she could see an appeal if Whitacre were convicted, based on his own counsel not keeping out the evidence of a completely separate crime.

Walker remained firm. "The position is we are not hiding anything on it."

In fact, a Whitacre strategy had begun to emerge. Even if convicted of price-fixing, Whitacre would probably not do more time than the nine years he was serving. This was because his illegal price-fixing activity had stopped on November 4, 1992, when he started cooperating. His cooperation almost certainly would win him a concurrent sentence if convicted. However, if acquitted, he still would not serve a day less on his fraud sentence, a severe punishment that he considered the work of ADM. Despite the apparent cordial relations among his counsel and those of the other defendants, Whitacre had an abiding hatred for his old employer.

Being a magnet in the antitrust trial for testimony about extortion, fraud, lies, and erratic behavior probably would not hurt Whitacre or increase his penalty. However, targeting him could backfire against Andreas and Wilson. Their basic hurdle was simply to show that they did not make an illegal lysine deal. Pounding Whitacre and his FBI handler was a dangerous diversion and drain on their court time.

Back before the jury, Bray proved that Whitacre's confession to Shepard of embezzling $500,000 vastly undervalued the multimillion-dollar theft and was another lie. The attorney also showed that the mole had had prime opportunities to record his client, which resulted in relatively little taping. One example was the eleven hours of travel back from Irvine. Whitacre was with Andreas the whole way but turned in only thirty-one minutes of tape. The defense's point was that Andreas could have made all manner of exculpatory statements but the evidence had been discarded or never recorded.

Walker's cross-examination of Shepard took less than one hour and broke little new ground. Walker was able to fix Whitacre's first suicide threat as occurring on November 18, 1992, less than two weeks after he had begun cooperating.

He tried to present his client as sympathetic. The FBI could not have gotten the audiotapes without Whitacre. Shepard admitted that videotaping would not have been possible without advance intelligence from Whitacre.

Walker elicited that Whitacre was a good deal more cooperative than the governments of France, Japan, and surprisingly Canada. In fact, Canada forbade the FBI from taping, though Shepard revealed that the Royal Canadian Mounted Police made its own video of the conspirators entering and leaving the Vancouver meeting in June 1993.

The image emerging from the testimony was that the mole was highly stressed by keeping up with the demands of functioning underground for the FBI and above ground at his job. Walker brought out that after signing his cooperation agreement in January 1993, Whitacre could not discuss his spying with a doctor or lawyer. To do so would breach the secrecy clause and leave him open to prosecution.

The FBI had a vested interest in keeping Whitacre away from a lawyer. While Shepard knew he could not legally bar Whitacre from seeking counsel, "I also knew that if he had, in fact, talked to an attorney, any attorney worth his salt, when [Whitacre] told him about what had been going on, [the attorney] would say: Are you stupid to keep talking to the government?"

In addition to the fear of indictment, Whitacre also was motivated by the bond with Shepard that developed over two and a half years and by being what Walker called a "part of the team." The jury could hear the closeness in a snippet of audiotape when Shepard dealt with his mole warmly. "That's super, Mark, super," Shepard responded to Whitacre's report of having taped Wilson.

At sidebar, Walker previewed questions he wanted to raise about Whitacre becoming seriously depressed in 1993 and 1994 without the ability to see a doctor. Also Walker had prepared questions designed to elicit that Shepard had instructed the mole to plant documents on certain ADM executives' desks before the June 27, 1995 raid.

Lassar protested that Whitacre was trying to win a jury nullification verdict. Walker responded sharply that he did not believe in nullification, the doctrine that provides that jurors can disregard the judge and the law when they reach a decision. But, Manning sustained the objection because the alleged breakdowns and evidence planting occurred beyond the November 4, 1992 cooperation date, after which Whitacre's conduct could not be judged or punished.

Aiming to erase any speck of sympathy for Whitacre, Reid Weingarten began cross-examining Shepard. The first question was, "Did you know during the investigation that Mark Whitacre had falsely disavowed his parents?" But, the agent knew nothing about the mole's "orphan" tale.

Weingarten turned to Whitacre's lies in the investigation, exhaustively detailing the Fujiwara affair and the pair of failed polygraphs. "And the net of that is that you never knew when he was telling the truth and when he was lying, fair?"

"That's fair," said Shepard.

"Ok. Have you ever heard of a situation where a CW [cooperating witness] lies, he flunks a poly, he confesses, his confession is a lie, he flunks another polygraph, he lies some more, and the FBI sends him out in the world with a tape recorder? Have you ever heard of anything even remotely close to that scenario in your twenty years in the FBI?"

Shepard said "no."

Weingarten pinned the agent for an admission that each lie that Whitacre told to the bureau was a felony, carrying a jail sentence of up to five years. But, the FBI neither had charged Whitacre nor rescinded the cooperation agreement.

"And isn't it also true," said the lawyer, "that you would not have put up with Mark Whitacre for a nanosecond had it not been for the lure of the big case involving an Andreas?"

"I can't answer that," Shepard said softly.

The lawyer placed the FBI 302 form of November 16, 1992 before the witness and began reading aloud, "Whitacre advised that the FBI was destroying his family and stated that Whitacre's treatment by the FBI was unfair in that Whitacre was honest, told everything he knows but that the FBI is going to hurt Whitacre and Mick Andreas and other innocent people." Shepard admitted that Whitacre had made the statements, but only because the mole had doubts about going forward.

Weingarten challenged Shepard with another 302 from two days later. "Source stated," the lawyer read, "that the reason he did not furnish information requested by writer was because if source attempted to record any conversation with source's superiors, it would only implicate the writer." The witness conceded Whitacre was the "source." Shepard was the "writer" and the memo was an accurate record of the interview.

Weingarten read another 302 from November 24, 1992. "Whitacre advised that Wilson told Ikeda that it would be a legal association." He stressed "legal" and continued, "Whitacre said that Wilson then told Ikeda that ADM would never do anything illegal, and Whitacre said that Wilson repeated that claim several more times during the meeting."

Shepard conceded that at times Whitacre had made exculpatory statements about Wilson and Andreas. Then Weingarten checked off the familiar litany of the mole's lies, forcing the agent to acknowledge each one.

Weingarten pushed his luck by adding ADM's use of hookers at Heartland Lysine and its stealing of a bacitracin microorganism to the list. Shepard would not concede that these were lies. On the contrary, the FBI had investigated these matters. "In my opinion," swore Shepard, "they are true." The agent said that tapes of Randall and Cheviron corroborated their roles in these affairs. Also, the FBI had interviewed some prostitutes and recovered "a list of questions that were composed to ask those [Heartland] employees."

The answer seemed to stop Weingarten in his tracks. To recover, he asked whether Cheviron or Randall had been indicted. Shepard said no. Weingarten wisely did not ask why. To do so would have opened the door to a discussion of how ADM had negotiated in its corporate guilty plea for no one besides Mick Andreas and Wilson to be charged in exchange for a $100 million fine and cooperation from other employees in the investigations.

Weingarten moved back into safe territory—Whitacre's greed. "Did he ask for a bounty? Did he want a piece of the action of any money's recovered?"

"Yes," Shepard said. This time Weingarten continued to dig for an explanation and it backfired.

Shepard recalled, "On one occasion he talked about [it]. I think he said he thought ten products were being price fixed. Then he had a figure for the amount of commerce that was affected, that if each of these companies got fined, it would be that much money." Whitacre wanted an unspecified percentage of each fine.

The damage was done. Weingarten inadvertently had elicited that price-fixing pervaded ADM product lines, not simply lysine. To bounce back, he returned to Whitacre's personal corruption:

> *Weingarten:* So he was eager to line his pockets based upon his work for
> you, correct?

Shepard: Yes.

Weingarten: And this is all while he's stealing $10 million from ADM.

Shepard: Yes.

Weingarten: What was his salary at ADM?

Shepard: I think he said that it was when I first met him maybe 250 to 275,000.

Weingarten: So his salary was at least a quarter of a million dollars, he was stealing $10 million, and he wanted more on top of that.

Shepard: Yes, but he never got anything from the government.

The agent went on to modify the answer slightly. The FBI had given Whitacre $270 to pay for a suit coat altered to accommodate wiring and placement of the Nagra tape recorder. Shepard could not help but interject that this was for "over two and a half years" of work.

For a moment, Weingarten went back to the $10 million embezzlement, feigning horror that Shepard had not discovered it "on your watch." Then the lawyer moved into the alleged conspiracy. Competition, he bruited, was inconsistent with price-fixing. At times, "There was fierce competition in the market place, correct?"

Shepard replied sharply, "During the times that the agreement wasn't in place, there was."

Weingarten forced Shepard to agree that there were legal factors that affected the price of lysine including a flood, seasonal demand that peaked in the summer, and pressure from rival products, including soy meal and fish meal. But Shepard insisted these issues were not pivotal in the investigation. The conduct of ADM and its competitors was. "The fact that they were agreeing to set prices and set volumes was of paramount importance to me. That's the heart of our violation."

Cynically, Weingarten shot back, "Thank you for sharing that with me."

Weingarten tried to point out the absurdity of an FBI policy that made recording obligations more stringent when an agent was placed in an undercover role than when a cooperating witness was used. Shepard could do little but shrug and say that that was the system he worked under.

The laxity in the cooperating witness rules included no requirement of immediate tape collection. Using a chart, Weingarten noted fifteen times when Whitacre held a completed tape for more than three days. In 1994, there were occasions when he kept tapes for twelve, thirteen, fourteen, sixteen, and in one case twenty-eight days. The longer Whitacre held the evidence, Weingarten said, "the greater possibility of mischief; is that true?"

Shepard said, "certainly." He also conceded that the FBI under some circumstances allowed operatives to mislead sources in order to get information. But, Shepard felt that the only lies Whitacre had told subjects were "nonsubstantive."

Weingarten tried to cast doubt on the completeness of the FBI's other data collection methods. Whitacre was supposed to tape all calls with competitors. But, the FBI did not seek his phone records in order to determine whether he had.

"Are you saying as you sit here today that you don't know that Whitacre's [telephone] toll records reflected dozens of calls that weren't recorded?" the lawyer asked. In fact, the defense had discovered about eighty such international calls. Shepard said he had learned during the pretrial motion phase of the case about these calls. But, many of them were quite short. It was unclear that Whitacre actually had made contact with a conspirator, and if so, that the contact was substantive. Shepard said he did not seize or subpoena the records for the phones in question because they both belonged to ADM. One was Whitacre's office phone; the other was his business cell phone.

Weingarten also showed that Whitacre's recording habits occasionally became bizarre. Once Whitacre taped Shepard without the agent's permission. On another occasion, he turned in a tape of an extraneous discussion with his daughter. Twice he turned in tapes on which he had recorded himself going to the bathroom. On the several occasions when he provided Shepard with price-fixing tapes, Whitacre recorded himself bragging about the material. "He exaggerated all the time," Shepard told the court.

Weingarten played a snippet of the tape on which Whitacre recorded Shepard. Whitacre was exuberant, saying "you're really gonna love this one." The mole described some conduct of the Koreans and discussions with Terry Wilson. Shepard sounded especially enthused. Also, the agent wanted Whitacre to get Andreas and Wilson to use the word "agreement." Then Shepard asked on the tape, "Did Wilson have a few nips before they came in?"

"And it seems," Weingarten snarled, "that some of the exuberance rubbed off on you."

Shepard replied calmly "a lot of this was handling," which he explained involved his gut feelings. Problems pertaining to handling faced every special agent who ran spies and snitches. Basically, the agent had to use judgment to strengthen the bond with the informer so that the ticklish operation would succeed.

As for the remark about Wilson drinking, Shepard said, "it was a little joke." The agent disagreed with Weingarten's characterization of it as revealing an effort "to take advantage of Terry Wilson's vulnerability" to alcohol.

Weingarten successfully proved price wars in lysine in 1992 and 1993. Further, the price was dropping in "absolutely fierce competition" in 1995 as the government planned its raid. Shepard said he did not pay close attention to price changes, especially at the end.

Following the raid, the agent induced Whitacre to have dinner with Wilson at Wilson's club. Weingarten asked, "And it was Wilson's practice while at the club to consume alcoholic beverages, is that true?"

"I am sure he did," said Shepard.

Weingarten established that what Wilson said on tape on the occasion was, "You know, the main thing, if we were trying to fix prices, we ought to be fired for being so fucking incompetent."

Weingarten looked at the agent and then to the jury. "And that's certainly not the confession you were hoping for, is it?"

The agent replied, "We never thought he would confess anything."

The court let Bray ask some follow-up questions pertaining to the raid on June 27, 1995. At 5:20 PM on that evening, Shepard and FBI agent Robert Herndon showed up at Mick Andreas' house.

In court, Shepard agreed that they had told Andreas that an antitrust investigation had been afoot for a long time. Then they played one of the audio tapes that Whitacre had made—Shepard could not remember which one—for Andreas.

Shepard recalled Andreas' response, which was that he understood the antitrust laws and had not broken them. Andreas maintained that the recorded material did not sound like a violation. The executive also expressed his view that there was nothing wrong with competitors talking together about business.

At this point, the court dialogue between Bray and Shepard shifted to a more surprising aspect of the 1995 confrontation—an overture by the FBI to let Andreas become a cooperating witness.

Bray: And you at that time asked him to assist the FBI in its continuing investigation regarding ADM's competitors, did you not?

Shepard: Yes.

Bray: And you told him you would suggest he do this in order to keep his company from being singled out?

Shepard: Yes.

Bray: And that he would have one chance, and it was right here and now, to agree to assist and cooperate in the investigation?

Shepard: Yes.

Bray: You also told him that if he talked to anyone, if he told his father or told an attorney, that opportunity would evaporate?

Shepard: We told him that it had to be confidential.

Bray: And at no time did he interrupt the interview while you were conducting it for the purpose of asking to have an attorney there, did he?

Shepard: I think he mentioned it, and we didn't say he couldn't have one.

Bray: But he continued with the interview?

Shepard: Yes, he did.

Bray: And he did say, did he not, that after the interview was over, the first call he would have to make would be to his father?

Shepard: Yes.

Bray: And in the course of the discussion, he told you that he would cooperate with you, but he would not wear a recording device on anyone, is that correct?

Shepard: Yes.

Bray: And, in fact, he said the would never be a spy and would never wear recording equipment?

Shepard: That's correct.

Bray: But he told you, did he not, that he was a law-abiding citizen and always tried to cooperate with law enforcement?

Shepard: Yes.

Bray: And he said that he would, despite the restriction he imposed, cooperate with you to the best of his ability, correct?

Shepard: Yes.

Bray: But that he would have to consult with his father and his attorney before doing so. He said that?

Shepard: Yes.

Bray: And he told you at the end of the interview that he was planning to immediately contact his father and the company attorneys, correct?

Shepard: Yes.

Bray: And that he cordially escorted you out of the house at the end of the interview?

Shepard: Yes.

Bray: You were finished with the interview at that point?

Shepard: Yes.

Bray had no further questions. Lassar asked for a sidebar. The US attorney urged the court to give him the opportunity to raise the corporate guilty plea. He felt that the jury would conclude that Randall and Cheviron were innocent of stealing the microorganism for bacitracin because the government did not prosecute them.

Lassar told the judge that "in return for pleading guilty to fixing prices in lysine [and] citric acid, they are promised that they will not be prosecuted for the theft of technology, that's the bacitracin, and Mr. Randall and Mr. Cheviron both come under the plea agreement." Plainly, Lassar was worried. Without the explanation of the plea, the jury could believe that the allegations against Randall and Cheviron were baseless, and by extension so were those against the defendants on trial.

Bray argued that nothing in the testimony "opens the door" to introducing the plea agreements. The defense had been careful never to say "anything that connotes a complete innocence," regarding Cheviron and Randall, "or anything inconsistent with these guilty pleas as to ADM, the total corporation." The judge indicated that she would read the transcript over night and rule in the morning.

At the start of court on Wednesday, August 19, 1998, Manning made clear that she was sticking with her earlier decision not to admit the corporate plea into evidence. Similarly, she kept out the tape between Whitacre and Wayne Brasser, which the government argued would show that ADM had fired Brasser for refusing to fix prices. She also would keep out all evidence tying Terry Wilson to fixing prices in sodium gluconate and lactic acid. Nor would the government be permitted to dig deeper into the bacitracin theft or the use of prostitutes. Manning was giving a clear message that the defendants before her would be tried on lysine alone.

Nevertheless Lassar seemed upbeat. Early in re-direct he asked, "did Mr. Andreas or Mr. Cheviron tell you that Whitacre had lied to them about his daughter [being called by an Asian]?"

Shepard said no. The answer supported an inference that ADM would tolerate lies by Whitacre because he was a cog in the lucrative conspiracy to fix prices. It would neither fire him nor report him to the FBI.

On cross-examination it had come out that ADM had stopped cooperating with the extortion investigation, then offered to start again. But the company wanted new ground rules. Cheviron said that ADM would cooperate only if the FBI did not talk to Whitacre. Plus, only Cheviron was supposed to have contact with the alleged extortionist. The new terms, said Shepard "made me believe some of the things [Whitacre] was telling me about his coaching and the lack of cooperation by ADM."

Lassar and Shepard also rebutted the notion that the FBI was so eager to nab an Andreas that it deviated from its guidelines. Shepard ticked off a host of targets from the coconspirator companies and swore that the investigation would have continued even if Andreas had not been a subject.

Lassar probed the agent about the personal cost of the case. Old friends in Decatur stopped talking to him and his wife after the raid. His eyes brimmed with tears. For a moment he held the bridge of his nose between thumb and forefinger. The jury saw the burden of the case on the agent.

"Why did you pursue the investigation?" asked Lassar.

"Because," replied Shepard, "the violation was there."

The defense had brought out that on November 24, 1992, Whitacre had told

Shepard that Wilson had spoken about using a lysine association legally. Shepard pointed out that Whitacre was not cooperating with the FBI when he made the statement and mainly stayed out of the government fold from mid-November 1992 through mid-March 1993. Then he provided information steadily until shortly after the raid.

The defense's thrust was that Whitacre was so slimy that the government never should have continued to use him. Lassar asked why it did. The gist of the answer was that the FBI found the taped evidence of price- and volume-fixing credible.

Shepard was particularly impressed with tapes that Whitacre made while debriefing Andreas following price-fixing meetings that the ADM vice chairman did not attend, including those in Vancouver and Paris. The agent was aware of the accuracy of Whitacre's reports to Andreas of the illegal doings and of Andreas' willingness to go forward. He testified that his spying on Andreas' behavior at Irvine also left him with no doubt of the executive's criminal role.

Shepard also said that in two-and-a-half years he never saw Wilson have anything to do with lysine that did not involve price-fixing. This was "something that confirmed what Mark Whitacre had told me, that Terry Wilson had been assigned to work with him by Mick Andreas in order to instruct him how to compose the scheme, to put together the people to get it done, and that was borne out."

On cross by the defense, Shepard had admitted that Whitacre had exaggerated in descriptions of what was on the tapes. Lassar asked if this had significance. Shepard said, "The tapes were the key to the investigation, not what he said about them."

Lassar asked why Shepard had not tracked the prices of lysine. "Because," he said, "it was immaterial to me." He was focused on the "elements of the crime," which he described simply as "an agreement or understanding among competitors reached on prices and/or volumes or both to violate the Sherman Act."

In a voice dripping with sarcasm, Lassar began to flay the defense's stance that ADM had been victimized by and tried to smash an oriental cabal. The prosecutor asked Shepard if Andreas had complained about price-fixing by Japanese when they first met on November 4, 1992. The answer was no.

Lassar continued, "And before the meeting in Irvine, did [Andreas] call you up and say, 'Brian, our major competitor is going to be talking about price fixing and you can arrest him on American soil?'"

Bray objected, "It's pure argument." But Manning overruled.

Shepard answered, "No, he didn't."

Lassar moved ahead in time to Shepard's interview with Andreas on June 27, 1995. Again, Andreas did not complain about Asians' fixing prices. On the contrary, Andreas told the FBI that the price could not be controlled because of variables like the weather.

Lassar then asked about the meeting with Wilson on the same summer night in 1995 at the Decatur Country Club. Shepard said Wilson seemed sober and claimed to be innocent of any wrongdoing. When questioned that night, he said he had never heard of using an association as a screen for price-fixing. He insisted he knew nothing about buy-ins to correct sales imbalances and audits to check allocations. He told Shepard and his partner Herndon that neither he nor anyone else from ADM had traded sales or production figures with competitors. Of course, the jurors already had seen and heard the tapes from 1993 and 1994 and could draw their own conclusions about Wilson's evasiveness in 1995.

The judge allowed Bray to re-cross Shepard again. He focused on the agent's report of the June 27, 1995 meeting with Mick Andreas. Shepard had noted that Andreas had said that price fixing was impossible because of uncontrollable factors. But, the agent did not use the word "lysine" in his report.

Shepard tried to explain that in the "context" of the discussion with Andreas, lysine was the only commodity that made sense.

But, Bray cut him off, "In the context of arguing this case to the jury, you are doing essentially what Mr. Whitacre did to you. You're exaggerating, correct?" Shepard shook his head.

Bray changed the subject to Whitacre's supposed admission to Cheviron regarding his lie about his daughter. "And isn't it true, that you don't know what explanation Whitacre gave privately to ADM about that." Shepard conceded the point.

But, Bray went a step too far in pressing the Fujiwara scandal. He read from a letter that Cheviron sent to the FBI in December, 1992. "Some of our production engineers feel that our [lysine] loss problems were due to not using a clinically sterile atmosphere and that no intentional contamination was responsible for our losses." Bray's point was to distance Randall from the scandal. But, the larger meaning of the letter, which would be exploited by the government, was that Cheviron and ADM knew early that there had been no sabotage, hence Whitacre was lying about the extortion in order to scam the company out of millions. Yet, ADM did not fire Whitacre, why? Because he was central to a much more lucrative price-fixing racket? Because he could blow the whistle on it? Again, the jurors would draw their own conclusions.

During his second recross, Weingarten put a new spin on the issue of whether Shepard had violated FBI recording policy. Bray reminded the witness that his retired FBI supervisor John Stukey had taken the stand in 1997 at the pretrial hearing. In his testimony, Stukey called Operation Harvest King an "undercover operation," necessitating recording all conversations.

On re-re-direct examination Lassar fielded the point.

Lassar: Mr. Stuky, was he retired when he testified?
Shepard: Yes he was.
Lassar: Does he know what he's talking about?
Shepard: I have my doubts about that.

Lassar also indicated that as the agent in charge, Stukey would have had to get approval from Washington for a formal undercover operation but never did.

Weingarten was on his feet to make the last point. Stukey had twenty-five to thirty years with the bureau and risen to a high level of responsibility.

"Are you saying today that Mr. Stukey didn't know what he was talking about?"

"I'll let his testimony stand, " said Shepard wearily. "I'm not going to make any judgments about it."

After two-and-a-half years, Brian Shepard's role in the case concluded. Lassar asked the judge to lift the sequestration order so that he could stay in court to see if his work panned out. Hulkower objected. But Shepard's testimony was over, so the judge allowed him to sit at the government's table after he stepped down.

The judge gave the jury a recess, and they filed out. Weingarten moved for a mistrial claiming that Lassar's redirect "was extraordinarily prejudicial." The government had introduced "an enormous amount of material about Agent Shepard's personal view of the guilt of my client."

Lassar countered that Wilson had opened the door by attacking the integrity of the investigation. Manning denied the motion, which Andreas did not join.

Hulkower also spoke for Wilson, whose chest pain was severe. He was lying down in a small room in the federal building. His wife was with him. He was "resistant" to going to the hospital. Hulkower asked that Wilson be permitted to remain outside the courtroom for the next two government witnesses who were largely technical.

Manning preferred to do what she had done with Whitacre. She wanted to hear Wilson waive his own Sixth Amendment right to be present. She offered to go to him. Weingarten demurred, "I frankly think he would have a heart attack if you walked in there."

Manning backed off. She agreed to let the defendant proceed at least briefly in absentia. Amazingly, no one called a doctor or paramedic for Wilson.

THE WINDUP

"[T]he big problem is to remember what lies I've told. Always you have to do that.
He [Dwayne Andreas] said that he said you really should write it down."
—*Terry Wilson*

The next witness was Allison Ebel, a scholarly Justice Department paralegal. She had reviewed ADM average sales of dry lysine per month from January 1992 through June 27, 1995. Then she prepared a large graph with an orange price curve and milestones for the dates of the meetings of the lysine productions. At the time of Mexico City meeting, which Ebel said was the first session of the conspiracy, the price was 63 cents per pound. From Irvine on October 25, 1993 through Atlanta on January 18, 1995, the price enjoyed a long plateau at approximately $1.20 per pound.

Under Hulkower's cross-examination, the paralegal admitted that she did not include liquid lysine, which typically was priced lower, since the conspiracy had concentrated on the dry form. The defense attorney elicited that she also had not considered the 3 percent rebates that ADM sometimes gave to customers. Regardless, the jury was left to stare at a year and half of high stable prices shaped like an impregnable mesa outlined in orange.

The government next presented Bruce Koenig, an acoustical expert retired from the FBI after twenty-five years. Koenig had testified in nearly 300 cases. His subjects ranged from wire taps of the mob, to recorded gunshots, to the tapes recovered from black boxes in airplane crashes. He had degrees in physics and forensic science, was widely published, and belonged to the elite societies in his field. Not surprisingly, the defense passed on the opportunity to cross-examine him on his credentials.

With approachable language, he explained the composition, recording, and erasure of magnetic tape. His work on the project was intricate and elegant. Each tape he handled received five separate examinations totalling fifty hours of work. In particular, he focused on background sounds, such as the buzz of neon lights and the whir of air conditioning. Significantly, there were no discontinuities in these, so he ruled out splices or physical additions to the tapes.

In addition, the sound patterns were set up on high-definition computer terminals to determine if the wave forms gave matching "signatures." They did. He concluded that the tapes were authentic originals that had not been rigged, edited, or artificially tampered with. He also said he had checked the work of the defense tape expert. This was a subtle challenge to the Andreas and Wilson teams to present their acoustical guru. For these services, which had begun in February 1996, Koenig charged $170,000.

On cross the defense showed that some of the tapes were not continuous recordings and included stops and pauses. Two tapes had been erased and then recorded over. The expert indicated that these events were common with such tapes and could be innocent.

But the defense's main point was that Koenig, at the prosecutor's direction, had examined only about 40 of the 239 surveillance tapes made by Whitacre. The expert could not vouch for the authenticity of almost 80 percent of the recorded evidence. Neither Koenig nor the government revealed why they had used such a low percentage and what went into the choice of the tapes sampled for analysis. The testimony also did not clear up whether Whitacre had erased or stopped taping when exculpatory discussions had started or whether he had erased and taped over them. Obviously, the study did not settle whether the remaining tapes had been tampered with or if they pointed to innocence. In short, the testimony created as many questions as it answered. It was hard to imagine that the government had gotten its $170,000 worth.

After Koenig the prosecution called another FBI agent, Robert Herndon. He had been sitting at the government table since the beginning of the trial. Lanky and raw boned, he stood well over six feet. A certified public accountant in his thirties, he had smooth features and soft brown eyes that made him look like an undergraduate.

Herndon had been in the FBI for twelve years, but only seven when he arrived in Springfield and was assigned as the junior agent on the Harvest King investigation. Prior to Springfield he did stints for the bureau in New Orleans, where he worked on savings-and-loan fraud and public corruption, including the takedown of a federal judge. He transferred to counterintelligence in Washington, DC where he spent three years in a round-the-clock undercover position that required a fabricated identity.

Assistant US attorney James Mutchnick, who was doing the questioning, asked how living underground had affected the witness and his family. Manning instantly sustained an objection. However, Mutchnick was able to elicit that Herndon's trial duties had separated him from his family since July 1. The fact had no relevance, but it entered the record. Attempting to evoke sympathy for a young well-educated witness with an important job was a questionable and dangerous trial strategy, especially since the jurors' lives also had been interrupted. The defense took note and in time would respond.

After arriving in Springfield in 1993, Herndon became "division auditor" due to his accounting background and "assistant undercover coordinator." In that role, his function was "to obtain alias and false ID for agents who may need it, for instance, a false driver's license or false credit card."

Familiar with undercover operations, Herndon tried to lay to rest the defense's contention that Harvest King was one that would entail recording all conversations and other strict formalities. Under Mutchnick's questioning Herndon explained that undercover meant secretly inserting an FBI agent or a police officer into a criminal environment or setting up a "fiscal circumstance." The latter was a business, typically "a sting-front type of office." In Herndon's view, Whitacre properly had been classified as a cooperating witness. From a practical standpoint it also would have been ludicrous to make him record all the "watercooler" conversations at ADM.

Herndon clarified that when Harvest King began it was focused on the dealings of five companies, the lysine producers. At ADM there were only five individuals targeted: Andreas, Wilson, Cox, Randall, and another employee whom he declined to name. The FBI was not interested in information on additional companies and people, which was another reason not to record all of Whitacre's communications.

Herndon revealed a few more of the day-to-day details of dealing with Whitacre. In order to meet with the mole, Herndon would call his voice mail at ADM and use a pager to leave beeping noises as a signal. When they met, the agent would retrieve recordings, supply Whitacre with fresh tapes and batteries, and test them. On some occasions, the FBI agent would fit Whitacre with the body Nagra for anticipated lengthy sessions since its reel-to-reel format could produce almost three hours of continuous recording. Herndon swore that none of the tapes he recovered struck him as tampered with or edited.

Herndon had served as an evidence collector and cataloguer for the FBI. Mutchnick asked him to identify a batch of ADM travel expense reports from the lysine trade. Some seemed less than truthful. For instance when Wilson travelled to Mexico City for the original conspiracy conference in June 1992, he listed his purpose as visiting "starch plants." When he went to Tokyo the following year, he wrote that "meeting with companies interested in China joint ventures" was his reason for travel.

Part of the agent's job involved surveilling Andreas and Wilson domestically and abroad. Herndon had come to know their voices and identified them when a series of short recordings were played for the jury. These were termed "locker-room" or "internal" tapes since they included speakers only from ADM. For the most part the conversations involved Whitacre previewing or reporting a lysine price-fixing session to Andreas, Wilson, or occasionally to Randall, and gave their responses.

On April 15, 1993, Whitacre met with Mick Andreas at ADM, before the mole went to Chicago to meet with Masaru Yamamoto of Kyowa Hakko. On the tape Yamamoto is referred to as the "little Jap" because his company produced less lysine than did Ajinomoto. The government played the tape to show that Andreas was interested in price-fixing and market control, but disappointed with Kyowa's inability to adhere to high prices.

> *Whitacre:* Well, today's the big day.
>
> *Andreas:* Today's the little day.
>
> *Whitacre:* The little, yeah, the little day. The little Jap.
>
> *Andreas:* Yeah, you're just goin' up there to listen, aren't ya?
>
> *Whitacre:* Yeah, that's what Terry and I just talked about, too. That we should just listen what he has to say and . . .
>
> *Andreas:* Who's going' just you and . . .
>
> *Whitacre:* Just me . . .
>
> *Andreas:* Terry Wilson?
>
> *Whitacre:* Just me and he alone, too.
>
> *Andreas:* Yeah, I think you should go up and listen and tell him how terrible it is that they never got the price up.
>
> *Whitacre:* Yeah.
>
> *Andreas:* How disorganized they are, or how disappointed we are and . . .
>
> *Whitacre:* Yeah.
>
> *Andreas:* And you know our plan is super good. Everything is fine except those guys who fucked up the market so that nobody could . . .
>
> *Whitacre:* Yeah.
>
> *Andreas:* Play.
>
> *Whitacre:* Yeah.
>
> *Andreas:* You told 'em the story about the left fielder.
>
> *Whitacre:* (Sighs)
>
> *Andreas:* Know that story?
>
> *Whitacre:* No.
>
> *Andreas:* Well the left fielder starts missin' every ball. It hit him in the head, it hit him in the shoulder. Finally the manager gets so mad he goes out [and says] get your ass off the field I'm gonna play left field, give me your mitt, give me your hat. He gets out there and first ball that's hit to him hits him right between the eyes, knocks him down. He gets up. He's

furious. He goes back to the dugout and he says see you dumb son-of-a-bitch you fucked up left field so bad nobody can play. (Laughs).

With FBI agents on the line in the morning, Whitacre called ADM from Chicago. The jury heard Whitacre report the view of Yamamoto that ADM and Ajinomoto, as the two lysine leaders, had to solve problems between them first in order for the plan to raise prices to work. An interesting sidelight of the conversation was that Claudia Madding, Dwayne Andreas' personal assistant, was present for a portion of the call with Mick. Without revealing details, Herndon testified that he had interviewed Madding.

The tactical genius of ADM often came through in the locker-room tapes. ADM liked to frighten the Asian companies with its huge production capacity that could knock the bottom out of lysine prices. ADM also knew that MSG was Ajinomoto's number one product. During a May 4, 1993 tape, Wilson laughed about how ADM got Ajinomoto to cede lysine market share by threatening to overproduce MSG, or as Wilson put it "to fuck the whole market up" with that product. In another taped discussion at ADM headquarters on May 20, 1993, the jury heard Andreas hold forth on how calls about price with the lysine competitors had to come straight into headquarters and could not be handled by ADM's sales reps.

At ADM it was appropriate to lie to and bluff with competitors to force them to keep prices up. But, as Wilson reflected on May 28, 1993, "the big problem is to remember what lies I've told. Always you have to do that. He [Dwayne Andreas] said you really should write it down."

The internal tapes were especially valuable when they followed meetings abroad where governments forbade taping. For instance the jury heard a June 28, 1993 recording of Mark Whitacre reporting at ADM on the Vancouver session of three days earlier. Mick Andreas was avid to hear the price and volume positions of the competitors. Andreas told Whitacre that "the thing to do" was for ADM and the competitors now to announce satisfaction with their allocations. Also, they talked about getting the market price up a nickel and schooling the competitors against giving "guaranteed prices" that thwarted across-the-board price jumps. Oddly the defense did not object to a later portion of the tape being admitted in which Wilson speculated that Barry Cox's recent hospitalization for chest pain was the result of a "guilty conscience."

The internal tapes were interesting because they recorded then ADM president James Randall's participation in price and volume discussions. Plus, they amply presented Mick Andreas' decision-making role. In a December 1993 discussion on the upcoming Tokyo meeting Wilson became emphatic with Whitacre, "Just go over there and play it like Mick wants us to play it."

Herndon likewise testified that his analysis of the tapes gave him confidence that Andreas was Wilson and Whitacre's boss in the conspiracy. Andreas was aware of his role. He allowed Whitacre to make lysine calls to competitors from inside ADM because the phones could not be tapped. The lines fed into a computerized scrambler. "Cheviron," said Andreas "is very good." Nevertheless, Andreas counseled discretion on the phone. "You just have to know what not to say."

Herndon believed Whitacre had less of a chance to alter recorded material than the defense thought. For lengthy tapes with competitors, Whitacre wore the body Nagra or used the one built into his briefcase. Also on occasion he was equipped with a new bureau device called an FBIRD (for FBI Research and Development), which recorded directly onto a microchip that could not be altered.

Herndon introduced about twenty recordings. He also cleaned up the mystery of why Wilson was not at the Irvine meeting in October, 1993. Wilson's ADM travel vouchers noted his presence in Brugge, Belgium, for the annual meeting of the European Citric Acid Manufacturers' Association (ECAMA), the price-fixing cartel for that commodity.

The last lysine meeting that Herndon saw was in Atlanta in early 1995. He observed it through remote video equipment. The camera was mounted a lamp in the suite where the competitors met. It was the same lamp that the FBI had used for all previous meetings, including Irvine and Hawaii. The agents had some concern that the participants would recognize the lamp, but they never did. After Atlanta, Herndon said "we were collecting evidence in other areas, and we were preparing to go overt or public with the case."

As a final question, Mutchnick asked why Mark Whitacre was used for over two years as a cooperating witness. Herndon responded simply, "Because he was in the position to provide us with the evidence that we obtained."

The government seemed pleased with Herndon's testimony and told the judge that it planned to call only one more witness, Masaru Yamamoto of Kyowa Hakko. The rapidly approaching conclusion of the prosecution's case caught the Andreas and Wilson teams offguard. Both asked for additional days off the following week to prepare their defenses.

Wilson, through his attorney Hulkower, renewed his motion for a mistrial. This time the basis was that Herndon had made "deliberate and calculated references to other products" in his explanation of why the Harvest King investigation continued after Atlanta. Manning reviewed the record and found Herndon's statements inoffensive, and more importantly not objected to by Wilson's lawyers, so she denied the motion.

It was late Thursday afternoon and as usual the court broke for three days. Over the long weekend, Herndon enjoyed the distinct and highly unusual advantage of

receiving the transcript of his direct testimony before submitting to cross-examination. It resulted in some uneasy moments for him. Herndon told Mutchnick that
his testimony had been mistaken one point: The agent had not been separated from
his family since July 1, just since July 31. Mutchnick relayed the information to Reid
Weingarten, who would cross-examine first.

Court resumed on Monday, August 24, 1998 with Herndon on the stand. Weingarten punished the witness for making a false statement under oath. The lawyer
implied that Herndon now had changed his testimony to avoid being caught in
a lie that would have been easy to prove since the witness's wife actually sat in
court early in the trial. The normally self-assured agent said of his lapse, "I just
blanked out."

Weingarten also accused Mutchnick of trying "to elicit sympathy" for your witness with "scripted questions" about the toll on his personal life in the bureau. An
objection was sustained, but Herndon continued to seem ill at ease.

Weingarten harped on Whitacre's intermittent taping versus the nonstop
recording that the defense insisted was required and less vulnerable to altering. Herndon agreed that the FBI had the ability to "handwire a building" for round-the-clock
taping when it obtained a court-ordered wire tap but did not seek one in this case.
Interestingly Herndon revealed for the first time that FBI agents once entered ADM
after dark, but he did not elaborate.

Weingarten threw Herndon's analysis of Wilson's travel records back in the
agent's face. How had he happened to miss Whitacre's three trips to the Cayman
Islands to deposit ADM's embezzled funds? Apparently the FBI never even checked
Whitacre's passport. Weingarten pushed the point. The defense wanted the jury
to infer that the FBI let Whitacre steal. Weingarten accused Herndon of not being
"interested" in finding out if Whitacre committed frauds "on your watch."

Herndon was taken aback. His speech became labored. "Well no," he said, "I was
extremely interested to find out. If I knew about it, I would have put a stop to it."

Weingarten maintained that the FBI also made no effort to check Whitacre's
domestic bank accounts or overseas calls. The attorney related that 70 percent of
Whitacre's calls to Japan went untaped and led to no FBI reports. The defense
was concentrating on the theme that lysine was Whitacre's personal conspiracy,
not ADM's.

Herndon testified that the FBI never had logged the microcasettes passed out
to Whitacre to see if they were the same ones he returned. Now Herndon had to
admit that it would have been a good idea. Without such a system, he could not
swear that the cooperating witness had not kept or destroyed recorded evidence.
Weingarten continued to challenge the witness, "Now, you never gave him an
instruction not to alter or destroy tapes?"

"Not a specific instruction like that," Herndon replied softly.

The lawyer began picking phrases from the "internal tapes" and made the witness explain them in front of the jury. Weingarten showed the agent the March 18, 1993 transcript. Herndon agreed that Andreas had said, "When they [the Japanese] come to me, I'm just gonna say, first of all we don't make deals." Plus, Herndon had to admit that "[t]hose type of phrases are expressed elsewhere, yes."

Weingarten read a portion of the April 28, 1993 tape transcript. Whitacre asked Wilson, "[t]here wasn't any understanding or agreement with anybody—was there?" Wilson responded, "No."

Herndon fought back gamely. "I think they're talking about the volume agreement not the price agreement."

Weingarten read an exchange to the witness from the transcript of an ADM "locker-room" tape on October 13, 1994. Andreas, Whitacre, and Wilson were joking about how much Ajinomoto and ADM were lying to each other. The defense's point was that the companies were playing hardball rather than conspiring.

Weingarten: Do you see on page 196 where Mick Andreas says, "I should've said, you know, the only trouble with you [Ajinomoto] guys keeping the numbers is that you fucking lie." Whitacre chuckles. Wilson says, "The difference between you and us is we know when we're lying."
Do you see that?

Herndon: Yes.

Weingarten: And do you see the conversation continuing and Andreas going; "You big fucking liar." Then Whitacre going, "Hey, Mick, you know the numbers we're turning in are a little different too, don't you?"
Do you see that?

Herndon: Yes.

Weingarten: Is it fair to summarize that there are many occasions in the course of the tapes that you played or that the government played last Thursday where the lack of truthfulness in the information being given and received is referred to?

Herndon: Yes.

Weingarten: Are there references made by one or more of the participants in these conversations to occasions wherein ADM is taking business from the competitors?

Herndon: Yes.

Dwayne Andreas at eighty before his resignation in 1998.

Dwayne Andreas (Center) gesturing to Mikhail Gorbechev (right) and Raisa Gorbachev.

Mark Whitacre arrives at federal court in Urbana, Illinois, to be sentenced for fraud, March 4, 1998.

Terry Wilson arrives at federal court for his trial in Chicago.

THE
LAWYERS

Reid Weingarten, Terry Wilson's lead trial counsel.

Jack Bray headed Mick Andreas' defense team.

United States Attorney Scott Lassar prosecuted Whitacre, Wilson, and Andreas.

Courtesy of Carol Renaud

Judge Blanche Manning and attorney Bill Walker listen to Mark Whitacre by speaker phone during his sentencing on July 9, 1999.

Mark Whitacre in federal prison on July 30, 1999.

David and Carol Hoech shook the foundations of ADM with their Shareholders'
Watch Letters.

OCT-25-93 10:44:25 A

FBI surveillance of Mick Andreas in Irvine.

Mark Whitacre adjusts the tape recorder in his briefcase during the Irvine meeting.

IRVINE MEETING   10/25/93

Andreas - ADM

Ikeda - Ajinomoto

Whitacre - ADM

Yamada - Ajinomoto

In Irvine, Ajinomoto and ADM, the world's two largest lysine producers, faced off and came to an understanding.

Kanji Mimoto of Ajinomoto collected and distributed the information that the price-fixers shared. In correspondence he used the code name "Mr. Tany."

Masaru Yamamoto in Hawaii.

An aerial view of part of ADM's ever-expanding agricultural processing complex in Decatur, Illinois, the largest in the world.

G. Allen Andreas replaced his uncle, Dwayne Andreas, as chairman and CEO of ADM a month before Mick Andreas was sentenced.

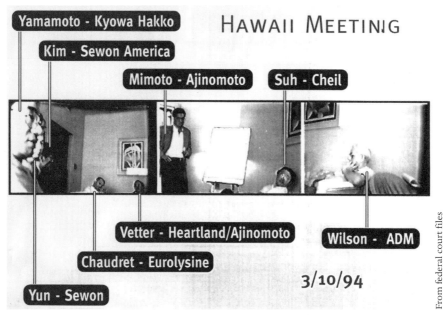

HAWAII MEETING

Yamamoto - Kyowa Hakko
Kim - Sewon America
Mimoto - Ajinomoto
Suh - Cheil
Vetter - Heartland/Ajinomoto
Wilson - ADM
Chaudret - Eurolysine
Yun - Sewon

3/10/94

In Hawaii all the world's makers of lysine finally were included in the conspiracy.

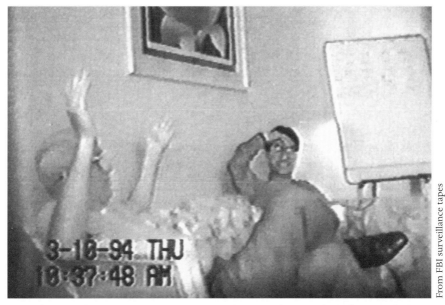

3-10-94 THU
10:37:48 AM

Terry Wilson tells the conspirators in Hawaii that, "It's better to have them inside the tent pissin' out, then outside the tent pissin' in." Kanji Mimoto is on the right.

Terry Wilson in Hawaii coached the conspirators on price-fixing methods.

Kanji Mimoto jokes about setting a place for the FBI in Atlanta.

TIMELINE OF MEETINGS AND PRICES

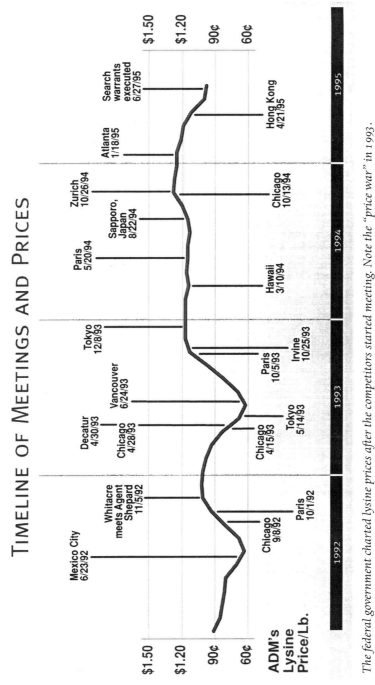

ADM's Lysine Price/Lb.

1992 · 1993 · 1994 · 1995

Mexico City 6/23/92
Whitacre meets Agent Shepard 11/5/92
Decatur 4/30/93
Chicago 4/28/93
Vancouver 6/24/93
Tokyo 12/8/93
Paris 5/20/94
Sapporo, Japan 8/22/94
Zurich 10/26/94
Atlanta 1/18/95
Search warrants executed 6/27/95

Paris 10/1/92
Chicago 9/8/92
Tokyo 5/14/93
Chicago 4/15/93
Paris 10/5/93
Irvine 10/25/93
Hawaii 3/10/94
Chicago 10/13/94
Hong Kong 4/21/95

$1.50
$1.20
90¢
60¢

The federal government charted lysine prices after the competitors started meeting. Note the "price war" in 1993.

From federal court files

PROGRAM

<u>October 1st, 1992</u>

AMINO ACIDS MEETING

9.00 a.m.   Meeting in the lobby
Hotel Pullman Windsor
Chairman : Mr K. MIMOTO

9.15 a.m.   Welcome and opening of the meeting

9.30 a.m.

1 -   Common Agricultural Policy and amino acid usage development

2 -   Main issues facing the amino acid industry :

■ Regulatory changes,

■ Environmental constraints and opportunities

■ Animal rights

■ Others

3 -   Representation of amino acid manufacturers in national and international organizations : ex. FEFANA, NFIA, etc.

4 -   Interest of setting an International Amino Acid Producers Association

5 -   Amino acid biotechnology and public perception, communication policy.

6 -   Miscellaneous

1.00 p.m.   Lunch

3.00 p.m.   Adjourn.

The phony "official agenda" of a lysine producers meeting in Paris. The real agenda was price-fixing.

_____3/11/93_____
(Date)

_____Decatur, Ill_____
(Location)

I, _____MARK E. WHITACRE_____,
(Name)

_____RR 1 Box 112, MOWEAQUA, ILL._____,
(Address)

hereby authorize _____BRIAN D. SHEPARD_____ and

_____JOE A. WEATHERALL_____, Special Agents of the

Federal Bureau of Investigation, United States Department of Justice, to place a

☒ Body Recorder   on my person for the purpose of recording any conversations
☐ Transmitter

with _____TERRY WILSON, JIM RANDALL, MICHAEL ANDREAS_____
(Name of Subject(s))

which I may have on or about _____3/12/93_____.
(Date)

I have given this written permission to the above-named Special

Agents voluntarily and without threats or promises of any kind.

_____Mark E. Whitacre_____
(Signature)

Witnesses:

_____SA Brian D. Shepard, FBI_____

An FBI authorization to send Whitacre into ADM wearing a wire.

THIS IS A 1 PART FORM — PLEASE TYPE — IF HANDWRITTEN PRESS HARD TO MAKE SURE ALL COPIES ARE LEGIBLE.

Remit BUSINESS FORMS CORP – DECATUR, ILL. – (217) 424-2444

ADM
ARCHER DANIELS MIDLAND COMPANY

AUTHORIZATION FOR EXPENDITU
(INSTRUCTIONS ON REVERSE SIDE)

AIR ☐ WATER ☐   AFE NO. _____

☐ CAPITAL AFE
☒ EXPENSE AFE
☐ LEASE AFE
☐ CAPITAL TRANSMITTAL   SEE SPECIAL NOTE BELOW

EST COMPL DATE __1/94__
AFE CLOSED DATE _____
PLACED IN SERVICE DATE _____

DIVISION __BioProducts Division__   CODE __138__   LOCATION _____   CODE __049__

CHARGE TO _____   DEPARTMENT _____   GENERAL ACCOUNT – RESP – DEPARTMENT CODE
(PLEASE TYPE CODING – MAKE SURE ALL CODING IS LEGIBL

TITLE: __Regulatory Approvals: lab tests, toxicity tests; animal regulatory trials; body retention tests.__

DESCRIPTION:
Even though bacitracin, tryptophan and threonine are feed additives, they are looked at as pharmaceuticals by the FDA (Food & Drug Administration) and other country governments. This is due to the fact that bacitracin is an antibiotic and that tryptophan and threonine are produced by genetic engineered organisms, and that the animals that consume them go into the food chain.

We estimate costs and completion times to be:

	U S A		All Europe-Countries		All Far East Countries		S. & Central America including Mexico*	
	$	Compl.	$	Compl.	$	Compl.	$	Compl.
Zn & Bacitracin MD	1,500,000	1/94	424,400	2/92	500,000	4/92	500,000-700,000	8/92
Tryptophan	1,000,000	6/93	271,000	2/92	500,000	4/92	400,000-600,000	8/92
Threonine	1,000,000	6/93	300,000	12/92	500,000	4/92	400,000-600,000	12/92

*Mexico is complete

ADMS 000229

NOTE: PROPERTY CONTROL SHOULD BE NOTIFIED BY APPROPRIATE FORM OF THE STATUS OF THE EQUIPMENT THAT IS BEING REPLACED.

		TOTAL EXPENDITURE FOREIGN FUNDS $	TOTAL EXPENDITURE U.S. FUNDS $

ESTIMATE PREPARED BY _____   DATE _____

EXPENDITURE REQUESTED BY _Mark E. Whitacre_   DATE _3/7/92_

ENGINEERING REVIEW _Mark E. Whitacre_   DATE _3/7/92_

CONTROLLER REVIEW _____   DATE _____

TREASURER REVIEW _____   DATE _____

EXECUTIVE APPROVAL

DIVISION MANAGER _Mark E. Whitacre_   DATE _3/11/92_

VICE PRES., PRODUCTION ENGINEERING _____   DATE _____

PRESIDENT OR CHAIRMAN _____   DATE _____

EXECUTIVE COMMITTEE _____   DATE _____

ADM's audit controls allowed $1.5 million to be transferred to a Swiss bank account in Hong Kong despite the fact that this authorization for expenditure (AFE) bore no necessary signatures except Whitacre's. The account was controlled by Ronald Ferrari.

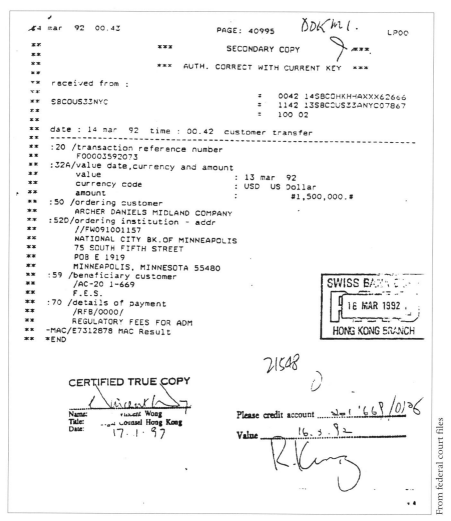

In 1995 Ferrari claimed not to know that the $1.5 million that entered his Swiss account came from ADM. But, his account statement said that it did.

March 14, 1992

PAYMENT AUTHORIZED: [stamp, handwritten]

Dear Mr. King,

As per my phone instructions please wire from my account

no. 201'669/ the following amount:

160,000 U.S. dollars to -

Mr. Reinhard Richter
Post Oak Bank
2200 Post Oak Blvd.
Houston, Texas
77056-4706 U.S.A.

Account no. 4000113

ABA no. 113001446

Phone no. 713-966-2268

Best Regards,

[SWISS B... 19 MAR 1992 HONG KONG BRANCH stamp]

SIGNATURE(S) VERIFIED BY:

April 10, 1992

PAYMENT AUTHORIZED [stamp, handwritten]

Dear Mr. King,

Please transfer US$ 1,140,000

from my account No.201'669 to:

Swiss Bank Corporation, New York for the
account of Swiss Bank & Trust Corp. Ltd,
Grand Cayman No. 101-WA-359-025-000 in favour
of ACC. No. 41327

Under Telex Advise to:
SWISS BANK & TRUST CORPORATION LIMITED
GRAND CAYMAN, B.W.I.

Please put the remaining funds of my account
into 1-year fixed interest instruments.

Also within 90-100 days I am expecting to receive
payment for 2 other projects. I will want
these funds also to go into longer maturing
instruments.

I will notify you by fax before they arrive.

Best Regards,

[SWISS BANK CORP. 14 APR 1992 HONG KONG BRANCH stamp]

Ferrari told his Swiss banker to wire part of the money to Reinhard Richter's account in Houston, and part to Whitacre's Swiss account in the Cayman Islands.

Weingarten plucked a phrase from the internal tape of December 1, 1993. Wilson stated, "It's just we're gonna sell what we want to sell anyway." Herndon acknowledged the accuracy of the remark, and the interrogation continued:

> *Weingarten:* It's also true throughout the tapes that were played before the jury on Thursday that there are numerous references to antipathy or lack of good feeling between some of the ADM participants and some of the competitors, is that fair?
>
> *Herndon:* Yeah, these guys did not like each other in my opinion.

The jury would have food for thought. Could individuals fix prices and allocate sales volumes while cheating and lying to each other?

Before concluding, Weingarten wanted to test Herndon's knowledge of Whitacre's 1996 allegations that he destroyed tapes at Brian Shepard's direction. The proposed line of questions involved hearing a charge that had been recanted by the mole and an issue that arose after the lysine conspiracy. Manning did not need to hear an objection before barring it as "just totally unfair."

Bill Walker was typically terse. He merely established that by the time Herndon joined Harvest King, Whitacre already was a cooperating witness. Therefore, the agent knew nothing that could legally be held against his client.

Bray's associate Kevin Dinan had little to add. But he did elicit Herndon's view that Whitacre was capable of fabricating evidence "because his statement to us about the extortion was a lie." Also, the mole "was a very energetic person. It's almost like he was on a sugar high all the time."

In addition, for the first time it came out that Whitacre had recorded his own false statements on a few tapes. "But, then he says on tape that it's made up," recalled Herndon.

Inadvertently, the lawyer stimulated sympathy for Whitacre. Herndon recalled Whitacre saying, "Isn't there another way of doing this? Do you have to keep on using me? Can't you find someone else to do the taping?" Such statements cut against the defense's axiom that Whitacre was on a quest to destroy Andreas in order to succeed him.

Unlike Shepard, who had been burned by Whitacre in a lawsuit and tried to seem reserved about him in court, Herndon readily admitted to commending the mole during the investigation. When the lawyer curtly attacked the agent for it, the tactic backfired because it gave Herndon a chance to explain his reasons for the praise. "Well, the information and the stress he was under in doing it, it's a combination. It's very stressful to be wearing a tape recorder and taping conversations.

So part of the 'good job' [praise] was just reinforcement there. The other part was sometimes there were meetings that were very powerful. Like Makaha, [Hawaii] I remember telling him, you know, 'good job.'"

Dinan mustered indignant disbelief, "You encouraged him, didn't you?"

"Yes. Again, it was twofold. It was wearing the equipment, letting the others talk, and then the fact that the evidence to me seemed to be pretty powerful."

The defense called for a sidebar and asked Manning "to take judicial notice" of the forty-page statement of facts from the Urbana federal court supporting Whitacre's guilty plea in 1997. If she granted their motion, the judge would read the concatenation of dummy companies, theft, wire transfers, and money laundering to the jury and instruct them that it was true.

The defense believed the document impeached the credibility of the Harvest King investigators. "Obviously," urged Weingarten, "it's been our theory from the first time we appeared in court that the FBI turned a blind eye to Mr. Whitacre's malfeasance."

The judge took a passing interest in Whitacre's plea negotiations. She learned from Walker that the 108-month sentence resulted when the Justice Department's fraud section became angry with Whitacre for failing to provide evidence against fellow accused embezzler, Sidney Hulse. As a result, Whitacre lost the initially offered deal of eighty-four months. From Mutchnick, Manning heard that relations between Department of Justice's fraud and antitrust divisions over ADM cases were chilly.

Manning returned to the judicial notice question. Her case and the fraud case in Urbana were "apples and oranges." The lengthy narrative against Whitacre could prejudice his right to a fair trial. Of course, Andreas and Wilson were hoping that the sleaze would rub off on the entire government's case causing the jurors to hold their noses and acquit. Manning refused to take judicial notice.

Dinan had a fallback position. He asked for permission to probe Herndon about the "particular thefts that took place while [Whitacre] was the cooperating witness with the government." She allowed it.

With the jury in the box, Dinan asked if Herndon knew that between April and November 1993, Whitacre stole approximately $220,000. Herndon said he now was aware Whitacre had embezzled but not the exact amount. Dinan pressed the same questions about thefts of $1.5 million in January 1994, $2.5 million in May 1994, and $3.75 million in February 1995. Each time he received the same answer.

Dinan switched back to lysine and pressed Herndon on whether he knew that the price passed $1.50 per pound in 1996. The agent had no awareness of the post-conspiracy rise besides what he had heard in court.

Mutchnick asked if the FBI could have used other conspirator witnesses besides Whitacre. Herndon replied that the FBI is "always considering flipping other people." But there was no one else. "As far as lysine, he was the guy. He was the person in the position to provide the evidence."

After the witness stepped down, Manning excused the jurors. The lawyers began sparring about the remainder of the trial. The prosecutors seemed uncertain and nervous about what type of case the defense would put on. Scott Lassar complained that he had not yet received any statements of defense witnesses.

Weingarten and Bray revealed that tactical decisions still were being made about the defense, and that they would provide witness statements in ample time for the government to prepare for cross-examination. Lassar was particularly miffed about not receiving the report and work papers of James Reames, the tape expert who had appeared for the defense at the suppression hearing the previous November. "When are we going to get those? After the witness testifies?"

Kristina Anderson shot back, "We got three boxes from the government the day that Mr. Koenig testified," including the government expert's report and assorted documents. She had to admit that Koenig's main notebook of findings was delivered to the defense the week before he took the stand.

The judge had little interest in tit-for-tat lawyers' games. She ordered the defense to identify its expert's document by the following Monday.

The trial resumed on Tuesday, August 25, 1999. But one of the jurors, an elderly man was sick and hadn't come to court. The judge could have dismissed him and proceeded with an alternate. But, she was sensitive to the fact that the missing juror already had made a six-week commitment to the case and probably would want to see it through. Many judges today are at least as concerned with their crammed dockets and the finite resource of court time as they are with being fair to all the people involved in a trial. But Manning, who was extraordinary in many ways, canceled court and told the parties and jurors to come back the next morning.

The following day began promisingly enough. Chicago has a reputation for beastly summers, but this morning's weather was perfect: sunny, seventies, not too humid, and a light breeze off the lake. Everyone arrived in the court on an upbeat note, everyone except the prior day's missing juror.

The court staff could not reach the man by phone. He could have been hospitalized, ducking, dying, or perhaps on his way to court. When he failed to arrive by ten, the judge asked for the lawyers' views. Lassar noting that the juror had dozed on occasion, suggested that he be cut. The defense wanted him to serve if possible, perhaps thinking that he would not be a master of the facts and could be reached with an appeal to antisnitch, antigovernment emotions. Manning refused to waste more court time and purged the juror.

Before going to back into court, Walker announced that there was a problem. His client now was in North Carolina. Because of recent articles in the *New York Times* and other papers, he had received new threats and been placed on a twenty-three-hour lockdown security range that permitted only one phone call per week. This wasn't the problem. Now Whitacre—against Walker's advice—had voiced a desire to take the stand. The problem was that it often took the Bureau of Prisons travel wing popularly known as "Con Air" weeks to process a request to transport a witness, notwithstanding Whitacre's earlier statement to the court that he was confident he could be rushed back to Chicago.

"Well, I'm sure with the good offices of the government," said Manning, "that the bureaucracy can be cracked."

"I wouldn't count on it, Judge, to be very frank," said Lassar. "They run the prisons the way they want to run the prisons." He was smiling ironically, and Manning asked why. "Have you read *The Trial* by Franz Kafka? It's about the bureaucracy."

"I realize," said Manning, "that it's pretty clear that the Bureau of Prisons operates the way they operate and even a court order doesn't mean they'll do what's in the order."

Recognizing that Walker's worry was real, Manning began making calls and putting the blocks in order for an expedited transfer, which she learned would take two to three days and be extremely expensive. But, the first step, she realized, would require setting up a conference call with Whitacre in custody to hear his choice.

The courtroom was not as shining as the day. Closing it the previous morning somehow had prevented it from being cleaned. Usually gleaming, it still bore yesterday's detritus: scratch paper, styrofoam cups, a couple of newspapers, and crumpled cellophane from vending machine cakes.

Jim Griffin called Masaru Yamamoto to the stand. The witness had a friendly fleshy face with full lips, a broad nose, and thick black eyebrows. Unlike Mimoto and Ikeda, he had not been transformed by the intervening years but looked much the same as he had in the surveillance tapes.

Still working for Kyowa Hakko after thirty-one years, Yamamoto had come from his home in Yokohama to testify. Like Mimoto he had pleaded guilty to one count of violating the Sherman Act. He had received a fine of $50,000 in exchange for his testimony. Like Ajinomoto, Kyowa Hakko had admitted guilt and paid $10 million to the United States and pledged its cooperation.

The witness declined an interpreter. He had no difficulty understanding questions, but his English was thickly accented and grammatically unpolished. When asked if he understood the consequences of testifying falsely, Yamamoto blurted,

"If I tell a lie, all agreement cancelled, and it's affect many peoples, even Kyowa Hakko peoples too."

Yamamoto's first job for Kyowa had been in accounting. When he joined the firm's export department in 1971, his involvement with lysine began. The company moved him to New York in 1978 and St. Louis in 1983. The same year he helped build the Biokyowa lysine plant with a 5,000-ton capacity in Cape Girardeau, Missouri. Before returning to Japan in 1989 he had expanded output to 15,000 tons. Until 1996, he had held the title of general manager of the biodivision of Kyowa. "My job," he said, "was control the sales of lysine in the worldwide." In 1996, after the scandal, he was transferred to the company's food division, which removed him from the lysine trade.

Griffin zeroed in on 1992-95, the period of the conspiracy. His boss, said the witness, was Mr. Akita, the senior managing director at Kyowa. Yamamoto identified the three companies involved in price fixing before the period as Kyowa, Ajinomoto, and Miwon. From 1992-95, ADM and Cheil joined the conspiracy, and Miwon changed its name to Sewon.

Griffin had Yamamoto describe the June 1992 meeting at the Hotel Niko in Mexico City. He represented Kyowa. Ajinomoto and ADM (Wilson and Whitacre) were also present. "Main subjects were to discuss about current price, market situation, and also volume and also some target price."

The two Japanese companies first proposed 40,000 tons to ADM as its market share. Wilson, who did most of the talking for ADM, objected to it. "He said they want one third of the market." After lunch Kyowa and Ajinomoto offered 48,000 tons to ADM. "Also, this number was defected" (sic) by Wilson. The "target price" discussion was more successful. All three companies complained about the market price of lysine. At the chalkboard, Yamamoto said, "Mr. Wilson wrote down how much the industry are losing in moneys by lower price." His calculations came to over $100 million.

Following the meeting, he and Whitacre talked price by phone. He kept notes of the calls in Japanese interspersed with English. The government put enlargements of the pages as well as translations up on the monitors. By phone on July 2, 1992 at 11:00 AM, Tokyo time, Yamamoto and Whitacre agreed that their companies would raise the price to 80 cents per pound.

On August 10, 1992, he and Whitacre spoke again. They agreed to raise the price to 95 cents on August 17, in the United States Griffin displayed another blown-up notebook page and translation. Following the discussion, Yamamoto called Mimoto of Ajinomoto, and Jhom Su Kim of Miwon. Both also agreed to the price.

More discussions led to a jump to $1.05 by September. But this time Yamamoto also informed Cheil. He described the meeting of the lysine companies that occurred that fall in Paris. It resulted in industrywide price setting.

At the end of 1992, the companies agreed to go to $1.20. But they could not hold the price because "we didn't have volume allocation. So each companies (sic) cannot control the supply. So, the supplies are more than demand at that time."

The group discussed the volume problem in Vancouver in June 1993. Again, Yamamoto had full notes, which were projected with translations for the jury.

In Vancouver, Wilson was at the board again, listing in columns the total tonnages for 1992, the expected total for 1993, and the predicted market size for 1994. Yamamoto had copied these figures in his notes. At this meeting Ajinomoto proposed market volume limitations for each company, but ADM and Kyowa rejected them. Yet, a collective price rise was accomplished in several quick jumps during the summer of 1993 in part because grain prices were climbing.

In October 1993, the group tried again but still failed to resolve volume. However, Ajinomoto told Yamamoto that Yamada of Ajinomoto and Mick Andreas would be meeting to settle the question later that month.

On November 10, 1993, he and an aide from Kyowa dined with Ikeda and Mimoto at a Tokyo restaurant. The pair from Ajinomoto related the volumes set at Irvine for 1994 based on a 245,000 ton market, with 67,000 for ADM, 84,000 for Ajinomoto, 46,000 for Kyowa, 34,000 for Miwon, and 14,000 for Cheil. If the market grew larger than anticipated, then the tonnage would be adjusted by an amount agreed upon later which was called "alpha" for ADM and "beta" for the other companies. Over dinner, Kyowa agreed to its share. The government had seized his notes from the meal, and they were screened in court.

His next jottings came from a December 8, 1993 gathering at the Palace Hotel in Tokyo. All the companies except Cheil attended. Wilson and Whitacre represented ADM. Wilson successfully proposed market percentages, both globally and regionally. Yamamoto wrote them in his notebook. Griffin projected them for the jury. In Tokyo, Yamamoto recalled that Wilson proposed that the producers report monthly sales figures to Mimoto. Wilson also mentored on the buy-in system. Griffin had Yamamoto explain it. "The end of that year, if one company sell more than this target and one company sell less, the company who sold more should buy from the company who sold less." Everyone present concurred. In addition, prices for the first quarter of 1994 were set. Wilson agreed to them for ADM.

During this testimony, Wilson sat patiently and alone at the foot of his defense table not writing notes or otherwise interacting with his lawyers. Andreas, on the other hand, sat next to Bray and vigorously engaged him.

Yamamoto also attended the March 10, 1994 session in Hawaii. He recalled it as the first meeting following the funneling of figures to Mimoto and the first attended by Cheil. Griffin showed him a large photomontage of the participants, whom he identified including Korean executives from Cheil.

Before the meeting, Cheil "accepted the minimum of 14,000 tons, but still they want more quantities. In Hawaii, the other companies proposed 17,000 which Cheil accepted." The new numerical breakdown appeared in the witness's notes. In Hawaii the group had its price powwow for the coming quarter. "We decided to maintain the dollar twenty," said Yamamoto.

With the direct almost concluded, Manning let the jury break for lunch. When she retook the bench in the afternoon, Griffin stopped her before she brought the jury in. He asked her to block Hulkower from cross-examining on a "highly prejudicial and totally inappropriate" document.

The problem was a Kyowa Hakko memo in Japanese (the defense also had produced a translation) sent to Yamamoto 1991. The writer, a Kyowa official based in the United States named M. Inoue, decried ADM's patriotic campaign to launch lysine. In particular, he lashed at an ADM ad that read, "There is a new world order in lysine. Soon over half of the world's lysine will be available in three colors: Red, white, and blue."

The writer rued that "ADM has just started a timely patriotic advertisement before the anniversary of Pearl Harbor. It's not businesslike, it's not ethical, and it's trouble for us. Don't we have any countermeasures besides crying ourselves to sleep? I think retaliatory advertisements would be counterproductive, but I'm very upset about it."

The government's position was that the memo was irrelevant to any eventual agreement between ADM and the others to set prices. Moreover, it could inflame the jurors.

Manning asked what was the purpose of the document. Combative as ever, Hulkower explained, "To show when ADM hit the ground in the lysine business, they hit the ground aggressively, hard, designed to take business away, and that created a climate and an atmosphere of open hostility and mistrust."

Manning, who had tried with mixed success to keep race out of the trial, wanted to see the context in which the document would come up. She told Hulhower to call for a sidebar before using it.

Once the jury came back, Griffin handed Yamamoto an envelope with handwriting on the outside and a Nippon postmark. Its return address was simply "Mr. Tany." There was no street number or city. Inside was a typed grid sheet containing 1994 sales results by month for the five companies worldwide and for four key regions: North America, Latin America, Europe and Asia/Oceania. Griffin asked if liquid lysine was included. By agreement it was not, Yamamoto explained, because it was a small market of 3-4,000 tons annually, all of which was bought by two or three companies.

Yamamoto said he had reported Kyowa's dry lysine numbers to Mimoto and assured they were accurate. Then he received the overall conspiracy statistics in the "Tany" envelope.

Yamamoto testified to being present at the meeting in Atlanta in January 1995 during the poultry conference. The lysine group was pleased because there was only a "very small difference between what was allocated and what was sold." He recalled the participants leaving the hotel room stealthily "because there are many customers, peoples walking around. We thought it better to leave separately. This will not cause any suspicion that five companies meeting together."

Yamamoto conspired with the group until June 27, 1995. "On that date," he recalled, "Biokyowa received a subpoena."

Hulkower thumped Yamamoto on cross for his "sweet deal." The lawyer brought out that the witness could have spent years in jail without parole if he had not chosen to plead guilty and testify. It amounted to another indirect plea for sympathy for the jeopardized defendants. Hulkower tried to show the witness's bias when he forced Yamamoto to admit to meeting six or seven times with the government while refusing to speak with Wilson's defense team before the trial.

In the early rounds, Yamamoto also scored a few points. Hulkower attempted to prove that Yamamoto was comfortably ensconced as "senior executive with the company." The lawyer was caught off-guard when the witness said, " I was demotion (sic)," referring to his job change after the scandal. Yamamoto gave the defense's theory a knock when he stated that the price of lysine had started to fall in 1989 before ADM signaled its entry into the market.

Hulkower hammered the witness about events in 1990-91 when ADM's huge dreaded plant came on stream. Buyers, distributors, and even Biokyowa employees jumped to the American company. Hulkower approached the bench with his request to use the controversial December 4, 1991 memo. Griffin remained adamant in his objection.

Manning had given the matter a lot of thought. "My major problem is really with the Japanese portion that alludes to Pearl Harbor," which she called, "very inflammatory." She ordered the defense teams to collect the binders of documents that they had distributed to the jurors and remove the references to the December 7 attack. After the housekeeping, Hulkower grilled the witness on every other aspect of the Japanese memo and the ADM "new world order" ad, which worried the memo writer.

The lawyer repeatedly asked Yamamoto to explain the meaning of the phrase "Don't we have any other countermeasures besides crying ourselves to sleep?"

Yamamoto was visibly upset. "He said crying, and we said yes, we just cry about these advertisements. We are Japanese."

Hulkower pushed, "I'm not sure what that means, though."

The witness was at sea. He began to scan the unredacted Japanese portion of the document. "Japanese means if American people say Pearl Harbor, we did Pearl Harbor, so no way we have to stand for it."

Griffin objected, but the damage was done. Manning looked at Hulkower. "Counsel, you've explored this enough. Why don't you go on to something else?"

Hulkower pressed the witness on whether his company had paid his fine. The witness said he paid it. The attorney argued that Kyowa could reimburse him after his testimony. Yamamoto disagreed, claiming that the plea agreement prevented that. Hulkower pulled out the plea agreement to show that it did not specify any rule on reimbursement.

> *Hulkower:* While we're on the subject, your expenses in flying from Japan, are you paying those?
> *Yamamoto:* No.
> *Hulkower:* Who is?
> *Yamamoto:* Company pay.
> *Hulkower:* And your living expenses in the United States?
> *Yamamoto:* Company pay.

Then Hulkower moved to the subject of David Hoech, the ADM shareholder's activist. Yamamoto admitted that between 1992 and 1995 Kyowa had paid Hoech's firm Global Consultants $175,000 to obtain information on ADM and other corporations. "We want public information," he said. "Not seeking secret." A moment later, the witness reconsidered. "Nonpublic [information] is included."

Some of the material that Hoech submitted to Yamamoto was routine financial information available in newspaper press releases. But, some of it also came from Mark Whitacre. For instance, in one 1992 memo Hoech wrote, "Whitacre told me they are going to be producing 17 million pounds of lysine per month by June and they are ready to have a price war on lysine. . . . His cost will be about 50 cents per pound."

Hulkower tried to force the witness to agree that the consultant had pried highly confidential cost of production data from Whitacre. Yamamoto replied that Whitacre earlier had told him the same thing, but he did not believe Whitacre at the time. Apparently, Hoech provided confirmation. The issue was important for Kyowa whose cost was 80 cents. ADM could survive at 60 cents in a price war. Kyowa could not. Hulkower argued that Hoech was bribing Whitacre with the Kyowa consulting money to spill ADM information. Yamamoto vehemently disputed the assertion, as did the government which said there was no evidence that Hoech had paid Whitacre anything.

Hulkower presented the witness with other Hoech memos indicating ADM's price goals at different times. Invariably, Yamamoto said that Whitacre gave him the same data and that Hoech's information on ADM usually was unnecessary. "I can talk to Mark Whitacre if I want to know," said the witness. Yamamoto described Hoech as a "monitor" who provided information that could be of interest to the Japanese firm on a host of companies.

"Now in addition to having a spy get this information," Hulkower snapped, "you also tried to figure out a way to sue ADM, did you not?" Yamamoto admitted that with the price of lysine crashing soon after ADM's leap into the market, Kyowa and Ajinomoto considered antidumping litigation. But, the idea went nowhere. "We just talk but nothing," said the witness.

Hulkower quizzed the witness on situations when the price-fixing supposedly was in effect, but ADM was underselling Kyowa. Yamamoto remained unfazed, "You are picking up some report, but the total tendency of the market price is going up."

Hulkower led the witness through the price war of 1992 then focused on 1993.

Hulkower: The price went down for six months, and for part of that six
    months it was even below your cost of production.
Yamamoto: Yes.
Hulkower: You were losing millions.
Yamamoto: Yes.
Hulkower: Ajinomoto was losing many millions.
Yamamoto: Yes.
Hulkower: ADM was suffering.
Yamamoto: Yes.

The witness was quick to point out that the first and second price wars were different because the second led to peace on volume.

At the first competition, we didn't know what's the intention of ADM, and we wondered how to do. Then we had the meetings, Hawaii, Mexico, Paris, and then we know ADM want to talk, want to organize association, want to increase the price. So, however, in volume allocation, we didn't agree. Meanwhile, we talk about pricing, and we increase the price, and then we started to talk about allocations.

In '93, in short time, very quickly prices go down. Then that time, we decided to have Vancouver meeting. So we know this time we can talk with ADM about the price-fixing and volume allocations. So the first price down and second price down is different.

Hulkhower tried to rattle the witness with documents. The first was a Sewon memo of a meeting of the Asian lysine companies in February 1993. Yamamoto professed no familiarity with the exhibit, which was in Korean (with an English translation by the government). "This made by Korean peoples."

Nevertheless, Hulkower pressured him about the reference that someone "needs to visit ADM's factory with bomb." Hulkower did not mention that this portion of text included the words "nonsense talk" and "joke."

Griffin objected vociferously and everyone gathered at sidebar. Manning was exasperated since she had ruled earlier on the issue. She chastised Hulkower, "The substance of the document should not be uttered in court other than in general." Hulkower could inquire only as to the witness's memory of the dinner.

With the jury back, Hulkower hounded Yamamoto about the memo. Again, the semifluent witness unwittingly did the barrister's bidding.

Hulkower: Read that paragraph to yourself, if you would, please.

Yamamoto: Yes, I read it.

Hulkower: Does that refresh your recollection as to the topics that were discussed during dinner?

Yamamoto: No, I don't.

Hulkower: Does it refresh your recollection at all as to any of the topics that were discussed during dinner?

Yamamoto: It's dinnertime, so I don't remember. This says "bomb," so I don't remember.

Hulkower: I'm sorry?

Mr. Griffin: Objection, Your Honor.

But it was too late. Manning announced the lunch recess, and the jurors filed out, some probably wondering about terrorism.

In the afternoon, Hulkower handed the witness his own company's documents. Some showed that even after the 1993 price war, ADM was picking off Biokyowa's major accounts including Supersweet and Wayne Poultry, which a Japanese memo lamented once was "BK's impregnable fortress." In addition, ADM sometimes cut prices in the United States, Australia, Mexico, and Canada without agreement.

Yamamoto remained confident in the conspiracy and its option of buy-ins. "In Tokyo meeting, we confirmed the shares and allocated the volumes. As long as we could sell that volume, we accuse (sic) other people's lower price, but it's not much concern for us. We could sell what we allocated."

Nor did he worry about losing business to ADM. "We lose, but the same time we gain the same amount from other customers." He recalled that the conspirators had agreed not to assign customers permanently at ADM's urging. To do so would be too obvious.

Andreas attorney James Phelan had only two questions for the witness. Yamamoto quickly conceded that he and Andreas never had spoken about lysine.

Then Phelan asked, "Mr. Yamamoto: Isn't price-fixing fairly common in Japan?"

The witness started his reply, "In some industry . . ."

Griffin was on his feet. "Objection, Your Honor, objection."

At sidebar, Andreas' lawyer argued "very simply, Your Honor, it's been part of our theory of the case that ADM took on—Mr. Andreas and Mr. Wilson took on— an Asian cartel. Mr. Yamamoto has testified for two days about his efforts to keep the price up in cooperation with Kyowa Hakko and Ajinomoto, and it seems like a fairly common business practice in Japan."

The judge was emphatic, "So far as I'm concerned, it's totally irrelevant."

Griffin tried to turn the tables. "We've had one more lengthy interrogation of a witness through document after document about ADM, ADM being competitive, not fixing prices, not following or not entering into a volume allocation agreement, and that's gone on all day today and part of yesterday. It just seems that we should be allowed to show that ADM has admitted that they fixed prices [and] entered a volume allocation agreement during this period."

Hulkower pleaded with the court that introducing ADM's corporate guilty plea "would be absolutely devastating. Nothing more prejudicial."

Since the corporate guilty plea covered behavior from June 1992 through June 1995, and Whitacre's "pass" extended only from November 1992, Walker joined the chorus. "It would crush my client. Devastating is not the word for it. It would be the end of the day for me."

Hulkower reminded the court that there were many reasons for a corporation to plead guilty including "economic considerations and shareholder considerations and the like."

"The fact of the matter," said Griffin," is that under oath [ADM] sent a corporate representative into this court to swear that in fact they had done this, and it's on the record."

The prosecutor continued. "It wasn't a nolo," a reference to a plea of nolo contendere that occurs when a defendant does not admit but does not contest the proof of guilt. "It was a guilty plea. And the corporate representative was asked: Did you do it? Did you do what's charged? Did you do the factual basis as stated in the plea agreement? And under oath he says yes.

"Yes, there were economic reasons for them to enter the plea agreement. They got a good deal in citric acid. They were facing hundreds of millions of dollars in fines there, and they paid a $30 million fine."

Manning feared depriving the accused of a fair trial. "I'm not convinced that the door has been opened, and I believe that it would just be tantamount to the court directing a verdict against the defendants, so I'm not going to allow it."

Yamamoto returned to the stand. Griffin asked a few more questions.

Griffin:　And when you had the volume allocation agreement for 1994—
Yamamoto:　Yes.
Griffin:　—did you in fact sell your volume?
Yamamoto:　We sold our volume.
Griffin:　The volume that had been allocated to you?
Yamamoto:　Yes.
Griffin:　And did Ajinomoto sell the volume that had been allocated to it?
Yamamoto:　Yes, they sold.
Griffin:　And did Cheil sell the volume that had been allocated to them?
Yamamoto:　Yes, they sold.
Griffin:　And did Sewon or Miwon sell the volume that had been allocated to it?
Yamamoto:　Miwon sold.
Griffin:　And did ADM sell the volume that had been allocated to it?
Yamamoto:　Yes, very close to the numbers.
Griffin:　So some customers were taken from you—
Yamamoto:　Yes.
Griffin:　—and you got some customers back—
Yamamoto:　Yes.
Griffin:　—throughout that period?
Yamamoto:　Yes.
Griffin:　And it all worked out—
Yamamoto:　Yes.

Hulkower had planted the idea that ADM actually was doing 20 percent more lysine business than it was telling Kyowa about. Yamamoto could not believe it. He trusted the figures submitted to and distributed by Mimoto.

Griffin asked finally, "During the period 1992 through 1994 how much did the price of lysine increase?" Yamamoto replied, "The lowest price was 65 cents and then we increased to one dollar ten, one dollar fifteen. So 70 percent or 60 percent jump."

The court took Friday off. Yamamoto flew back to Japan. Terry Wilson was sick with chest pains and cardiac arrhythmia. The defendant was in the hospital on Monday morning, August 31, 1998, when court reconvened. Reid Weingarten said that his client wanted to be in court when the jury was present. Lassar suggested sending the jury home, and Manning agreed. Weingarten reported that Wilson, who had a history of heart problems, hoped to be in court the next day.

"It may not," said Manning sympathetically, "be a question of what he wants to do."

"No, I understand," said Weingarten. "He has twenty years of experience, and I think he knows his body. I think he believes—I mean, he was terrified and thought he was going to go into the big one, but I don't think he thinks that way now."

The lawyers and judge spent the next few hours submitting, challenging, or trimming reams of proposed exhibits, most of which would be handled by the jury during deliberations. Where agreement could not be reached, "records custodians" took the stand to vouch for documents. In this way, pricing material from Sewon and Heartland Lysine was introduced. Usually, such tedious testimony occurs before the jurors. But, the attorneys agreed to spare them the agony because of Wilson's absence.

The defense also had some controversial witnesses on deck for the next day that the government was trying to exclude. So, Manning had to rule. The first was Barbara Holman, a feed buyer from Tyson's Foods, the world's leading poultry producer. Holman had been purchasing lysine for about twenty years. Hulkower said she could testify to her market experience before and after ADM's entry. The gist was that ADM's reps were hungry for Tyson's business. Competitive bidding and prices fell due to ADM.

Hulkower knew the cross-examination of Holman could cause the case to explode. The government would want to bring out ADM's guilty plea. Plus, Tyson had been part of a civil class action involving fixing lysine prices that ADM and other companies settled for $45 million. Hulkower derided the civil case. "Every time the antitrust division announces an investigation of anyone, there is a recognized group within the bar that on the first newspaper article files a series of class actions." Plus, it was an "opt-out" class meaning that Tyson and the other plaintiffs were stuck in it unless they took legal steps to get out.

But, Tyson had decided to stay in the class, and its share was not small. It received $2 million.

Hulkower's solution was to ask Manning to permit Holman's testimony but keep out the guilty plea and class-action settlement. Otherwise, "there's a huge sword hanging over our heads."

Manning would let Holman testify and not allow the civil settlement to come into evidence. Money was paid in the suit but without any admission of fault by ADM or the other producers. But, Manning ruled that Holman's testimony would trigger admission of the guilty plea because "there would be no appropriate reason to bar the government from showing what ADM actually did," by its own admission. The defense decided to forego calling the Tyson buyer.

Then ironically, the Andreas team proposed an FBI witness, Ellen Varounis. She had been assigned to the bureau's Office of Professional Responsibility, which investigates charges of misconduct in government. In 1997, she had interviewed Mark Whitacre and his wife Ginger when he charged that Brian Shepard told him to destroy tapes helpful to the defense.

"He was exonerated, right?" Manning asked about Shepard. In fact, there had been no explicit finding. Evidently, the investigation ceased when Whitacre recanted the charges.

Lassar scoffed at the evidence. "Well, this might break the all-time record for the most unreliable hearsay that was ever introduced in an American courtroom. First of all, it comes from Mr. Whitacre. Secondly, he's retracted it. Thirdly, it has nothing to do with any of the evidence in this case. What his allegation was: Mr. Shepard told me to destroy tapes regarding citric acid and fructose. It's not even lysine."

The defendants had another theory of admissibility. Since Whitacre was confessing misconduct to Varounis the remark was reliable as a "statement against penal interest and should be repeated in her testimony."

But Lassar was quick to note that Whitacre never claimed that he did anything wrong with the tapes. He had not said he destroyed them, only that Shepard told him to, which was recanted. "Indeed," said Lassar, "he comes up with this allegation after he knows he's going to be indicted, and he strikes out and sues the agent and makes up this wacky allegation which he retracted, and it's wildly prejudicial to the government to have it introduced in this case."

"Yes, I find that it is," said Manning. "It would be totally improper." In addition, it was hearsay. So, Varounis also went home.

The next morning before court opened the lawyers gathered in the judge's chambers for a speaker phone call to the federal prison at Butner, North Carolina. A correctional counselor named Jeremiah Robinson put Mark Whitacre on the line.

The judge allowed Walker to question his client. Whitacre stated that "after very careful consideration . . . I will waive my right to come back to testify, and therefore, I will not come back to Chicago for this case."

The defense also planned to call Rusty Williams, Whitacre's gardener, who had testified at the 1998 pretrial hearing. On the stand, according to Hulkower, he would report the mole's boast that "once we get these people—and that's including Terrance Wilson—on tape, we can make them say anything." The defense lawyer continued, "Whether he's speaking of splicing, whether he's speaking of manipulating, it's not altogether clear. What is clear is that he's talking about misconduct in one form or another, and that would fall within an exception to the hearsay rule."

Objecting strenuously, Robin Mann said the statement was just as objectionable as the one from Varounis. Plus, Williams was a shady figure whose story kept changing in interviews with the government.

Bill Walker never had met Williams personally but the gardener disturbed him. "I believe he's fabricated evidence. There's a running battle between Mr. Williams and Dr. Whitacre. He was his gardener, and he got paid lots of money." Repeatedly, Williams's lawyer called Walker eager for him to take possession of a "mysterious key." But William's lawyer would not say what it unlocked. Walker refused to accept the key that his client claimed never to have had. It was an odd and somewhat menacing scenario. Finally, Walker referred the matter to the FBI and Williams's lawyer stopped calling him. But Walker remained nervous about Williams. "To be honest with you, I think ADM has a lot to do with what this guy [Williams] says and doesn't say."

The judge was curious. "You say you believe ADM has something to do with Mr. Williams?"

Walker reminded Manning that Whitacre had lived in Dwayne Andreas' old home. The lawyer noted that the reason Whitacre had taken Shepard outside to talk on November 4, 1992 was because Whitacre believed the interior was bugged. As for Williams, his services ran with the land. "I know that every time that Mr. Williams or his attorney contacted me, it seemed that ADM was involved one way or another." The lawyer called the gardener "probably the most unreliable, most questionable, as-the-wind-changes" witness in the case. The judge kept Williams off the stand for the same reasons she blocked Agent Varounis: hearsay and lack of relevance.

In addition, the defense wanted to call a paralegal at Steptoe & Johnson, Weingarten's firm. She had analyzed Whitacre's phone records as well as ADM credit card receipts that would show multiple trips to the Cayman Islands and Switzerland. The phone records seemed like fair game to the prosecutors, but they and Walker railed against the bills from the Cayman Islands and Switzerland. Of course, the defense wanted to show that the cooperating witness was embarking on money-laundering junkets under his FBI handlers' noses.

Invoking his background as a federal prosecutor, Jack Bray argued the relevance of the evidence. "This is at least a suspicious circumstance, the number of trips he took to those two places that the agents indicated are essentially well-known to law enforcement officials as red flag venues. They're typical places for money laundering and embezzlement, and that at least goes to show the laxity of the supervision by the agents, [and] it lacks supervision in that they never even asked him what this was all about." In short, Bray was calling into question the credibility of the FBI agents and whether they ran the investigation in good faith.

The government countered that it would be unfair to allow the jury to draw an adverse inference from hotel bills. The Caymans were equally a vacation site. In addition, ADM had substantial holdings there, so legitimate business could be done. Walker added that the money laundering, to which Whitacre had confessed, involved wire transfers, not physically carrying cash in suitcases "like a drug dealer."

Manning wanted to see when the offshore trips occurred. The records showed one in 1991, one in 1992, three in 1993, and one in 1995. She agreed to let in the documents. To some extent, they could be viewed as "impeaching." Also, they tied to some evidence of travel that already had been introduced.

The defense now requested that Manning strike a line from a Sewon memo of a meeting with the Japanese lysine producers about the operation of the conspiracy. It read, "The Japanese understood that it was President Andreas' decision." Andreas was not at the meeting. To Manning, the phrase amounted to an untestable opinion rather than evidence. She ordered it removed so the jury would not see it.

On Wednesday, September 2, 1998, the jury returned for the last day of testimony. It was dry as dust. The government presented its final witness, Thomas Tomlinson, an accounting manager and records custodian at ADM in order to introduce financial, sales, and shipping documents. Tomlinson previously had furnished materials to grand juries investigating antitrust violations and Whitacre's fraud.

On cross-examination, the defense focused on the fraud. It brought out the dates and amounts of Whitacre's thefts. In addition, Hulkower questioned the witness on sales of both dry and liquid lysine. The witness presented a chart on the topic. When liquid lysine was included, ADM exceeded its allocated tonnages in the conspiracy by 10 percent in 1994 and by 40 percent percent during the first quarter of 1995. The defense strategy was to have the jury find that ADM was not playing ball with the other producers. In other words, its involvement in the conspiracy was a ruse.

On re-direct, the government established that the "reporting" in the conspiracy had included only dry lysine. Further, the summing of sales of dry and liquid was not traditional at ADM. Having the totals on the charts was an idea Hulkower conveyed to Tomlinson during pretrial preparation. The government objected to the charts and asked the court to strike them. Manning refused because the government had failed to object in time; plus, the information in the charts could be weighed by the jury.

Emboldened, the defense made an eleventh-hour attempt to have Manning reverse her earlier decision not to admit the statement of facts from Whitacre's guilty plea to fraud. But nothing new had occurred to make her change her mind, and she refused. The government rested.

The defense announced it would present only one witness, the paralegal at Steptoe & Johnson. The defendants would not testify. They would not call James Reams (their tape expert) an economic expert, retired FBI agents, Stukey and Paisley, or anyone from Whitacre's circle, including his parents and David Hoech. The judge was surprised. The decision stunned Bill Walker, who knew that Jack Bray had been preparing Mick Andreas for weeks to testify.

In essence, the ADM defendants believed they had reasonable doubt. To put on witnesses who could be singed on cross could ruin their chances for not guilty verdicts. They chose to bank on powerful closings.

The judge excused the jurors again and took the defendants pro forma motions for "judgment of acquittal." No one, including the lawyers, expected them to be granted. There was more than enough evidence to get to the jury. The real questions were how the jury would weigh it after it had been argued, attacked, shaped, and spun.

The judge quickly denied the motions to ditch the case, and the defense called its first and only witness. She was Akua Coppock, a poised young legal assistant. Coppock had spent the prior twenty months at Steptoe & Johnson analyzing the records of Mark Whitacre's cell phone, home phone, and credit card calls, and matching them up with similar records for Wilson and with the FBI 302 memoranda in the case. Among other things she found that out of fifty-five calls from Whitacre to Wilson, totalling almost four hours, fifty-four were neither reported nor mentioned to the FBI.

She also examined Whitacre's calls to numbers at Ajinomoto and Kyowa. Of 120 calls, eighty-seven, totalling eleven hours and twelve minutes, were neither recorded nor mentioned by the FBI. Some of the calls that left no evidentiary trail were lengthy. For instance, on January 24, 1994, there was a twenty-three-minute call from Whitacre to Kyowa. On April 12, 1994, there was a forty-four-minute call to Ajinomoto. Then Coppock presented the documents from Whitacre's jaunts to the Caymans and Zurich, and his bank transaction records.

Hulkower asked questions aimed at showing that Wilson was out-of-the-loop of price-fixing. For instance, prior to the Hawaii meeting of March 9 and 10, 1994, there had been no call to Wilson since February 3, 1994. After the meeting there was no call to him until fifty-four days later on May 4, 1994. Similarly for the Sapporo meeting of August 22, 1994, there was no call from forty days before the session (which Wilson did not attend) until twenty days after it. The last call before the January 9, 1994 Atlanta meeting was on December 8, 1999. There was no sub-sequent call to Wilson until June 5, 1995—137 days later.

Coppock produced elegantly rendered charts of all the calls. On cross, Robin Mann pointed out that over forty of the calls to competitors were quite short and perhaps had not gotten beyond a receptionist or voice mail. Therefore, they did not require taping or a 302 form. In addition, the forty-four-minute call from Japan did in fact appear in an FBI memo. Only forty of the untaped calls were over four minutes long. Plus, Coppock had no way of monitoring the face-to-face conversations between Wilson and Whitacre at ADM and elsewhere. Such communications probably reduced the need for telephone calls between the managers.

THE PITCH

"I wonder what they could be concerned about in ADM's closets,
what they wouldn't want the FBI looking for."
—Scott Lassar

One of the major choices a judge faces is when to instruct or "charge" the jury. Most judges charge after closing arguments by the lawyers, so that the last thing that the jury hears is the law it should follow. A small but growing slice of the judiciary charges before the closings in the belief that what they have to say should not be accorded undue emphasis in the total gestalt of the trial. Manning chose to charge before the lawyers' arguments.

Judicial instructions often are convoluted and hard to follow even in trials of crimes as easily grasped as rape and murder. Antitrust law is famously abstract, and it is not within the average juror's experience. But, Manning gave a charge that was clear as a bell. Remarkably, after almost two months of trial, she did it within a half an hour.

Manning outlined the basics: Each defendant was entitled to be judged individually and to be acquitted unless the government proved guilt beyond a reasonable doubt. Above all, each had "an absolute right not to testify. The fact that a defendant did not testify," she declared, "should not be considered by you in any way in arriving at your verdict."

Manning gravitated to specific instructions, touching on the evidence that they had heard. First, it was "lawful" for Whitacre to record conversations, meetings, and phone calls at the direction of the FBI. But, she forbade the jurors from considering "anything Mr. Whitacre said as evidence against the other defendants."

The judge explained that each defendant was charged with violating one count of Section 1 of the Sherman Act that outlaws every "contract, combination, or conspiracy in restraint of trade." Agreements to fix prices or allocate sales are *"per se* illegal without inquiry about the precise harm they have caused or the business excuse for their use."

She dealt with the thorny issue of bad faith, cheating, and competition among alleged conspirators. She told the jury that such evidence was "admitted to assist in deciding whether they actually entered into an agreement to fix prices. If the conspiracy charged in the indictment is proved, it is no defense that the conspirators actually competed with each other in some manner, or that they may not have lived up to their agreement."

She explained that price followership was not illegal. A company could copy another's prices as long as it was acting independently rather than by agreement.

Contacts, calls, and meetings among competitors were not in themselves illegal unless they were part of an effort to accomplish an illegal purpose. Attempts were enough to break the law. "A conspiracy may be established even if its purpose was not accomplished." But, an antitrust conspiracy could not occur within just one company. It had to involve "two or more persons" from different firms.

In order to find a conspiracy the jury did not need to see a contract. Rather, all the acts and words and circumstances were relevant. A conspirator had to be "a willing participant." An accused had to act knowingly and voluntarily in order to be convicted. But guilt could be proven even if a person did not participate throughout the conspiracy or interact with all its members.

She defined price-fixing and sales allocation. If the government proved either or both against a coconspirator, then he was guilty.

Presence at a criminal discussion, or "mere association" with another conspirator, could not convict a defendant. Even if a person acted in such a way as to further "some purpose of the conspiracy," he could not be convicted unless he had actual knowledge of the scheme.

In order to violate federal law, a conspiracy had to cover products in interstate commerce. The government had to prove that lysine crossed state lines.

She barred the jury from weighing whether other people should have been charged. But she instructed them to be vigilant about the immunity deals that the government handed such witnesses as Cox, Crouy, and Ikeda. "You may," said Manning, "give their testimony such weight as you feel it deserves, keeping in mind that it must be considered with caution and great care."

Likewise, the guilty pleas of Mimoto and Yamamoto that resulted in fines but no jail time warranted the jury's attention as affecting witness credibility. Plus, the pleas could not be considered in any way as evidence against defendants on trial. Similarly, she precluded the jury from pondering the matter or amount of potential punishment "as exclusively the responsibility of the judge."

Unlike many judges, she did not go over the evidence. That was the jury's province. Finally she empowered them. "You are the sole and exclusive judges of the facts."

In a federal criminal trial the government closes first. The defense follows. Then the prosecution has the right to give a rebuttal argument, which it almost always exercises.

Well known for closings in high-profile Chicago cases, Scott Lassar rose to address the jurors. Immediately, he tried to relax them. "The good news is that I'm only going to talk for a few minutes. The bad news is that they will be Hulkower minutes." The reference to the defense attorney's sometimes endless cross-examinations of government's witnesses drew laughter. In fact, the closing would take up most of the day.

With the jury loose, Lassar hit a populist note. "No matter who you are, the rich and powerful, the small and meek, everyone has their fate decided in criminal cases by folks like you."

The prosecutor rekindled the appliance analogy in Griffin's opening. Rival "salesmen agreeing to charge the same price for a refrigerator, that's price-fixing. It cheats the customers because the customer doesn't get to price shop. They don't get the lowest price because the appliance stores charge the same price."

Lassar threw volume allocation into the mix. With each store agreeing to sell only ten units, a salesman would feel secure. "I don't have to compete because I know under the allocation I'm going to sell my ten. I don't have to worry about the guy across the street because he's agreed that he's only going to sell ten also. So, he's not going to undercut me and take away my sales. So, the sales allocation scheme helps the price-fixing scheme, and the two often go together in the lysine conspiracy."

Lassar echoed a theme in Manning's charge:

As the Judge told us, the agreement is the crime. If you say, let's all charge the same price or you say let's allocate the sales volume, that is the complete crime. It doesn't matter why you did that. It doesn't matter what your motive is. Whether you had the best motive in the world, it doesn't matter. If you agreed to do those things, you are guilty.

It doesn't even matter if you said let's charge the same price and if you went out and changed your mind later. It doesn't matter. It doesn't matter if you actually charged the price that you agreed to charge. It doesn't matter if you cheated your customers. It doesn't matter if you made money. The agreement is the crime.

Now, let me make some general comments about the evidence before we discuss it in more detail. I think that you're going to see—and you probably suspect this already—that the case that has been presented here by the government is one of the most compelling and powerful that has ever been presented in an American courtroom.

During a closing, the lawyers on the other side usually try to appear calm and self-assured. But suddenly the defense teams were scribbling furiously. They knew that a prosecutor must never present his personal beliefs to a jury, and that such a move can cause a mistrial or reverse a conviction.

> Why do I make a statement like that? Well, the most powerful evidence you could ever have would be a videotape of the defendant committing the crime. You can't get better evidence than that. You've got it as to Defendant Andreas and Defendant Wilson.
>
> The next best would be an audio tape of the defendant committing the crime. You've got that as to Defendants Andreas and Wilson. You even have audio tape of the defendants discussing the crime, discussing their strategy in committing the crime. You've got that, too.
>
> In addition to that, you've got four coconspirators who testified from the witness stand and said: I committed the crime with the defendants.
>
> In addition to that, you've got their notes, detailed notes that the co-conspirators took, very detailed of every meeting that they had when they met with the defendants, again showing that they also conspired to fix prices and allocate the sales volume of lysine.
>
> In addition to that, you have the evidence about the price-fixing in citric acid, showing the intent of the defendants in lysine because of their knowledge of what happened in price-fixing in citric acid beforehand. In addition to that, the defendants both lied when they were interviewed and confronted by the FBI on June 27th, 1995.

In openings and closings, lawyers talk about the facts, but they do it differently in each phase. In openings, they outline the meat-and-potato evidence that everyone, including their rivals, knows will loom large in the trial. In the closing, they disclose and sell the inferences, nuances, and spins of the testimony and exhibits.

In addition, there is a kind of fact that a lawyer will bring out lightly during trial and neither dwell on nor hammer. All that is important is that the jury hears it. Then in argument the attorney will reiterate the fact, expose its significance, and point it towards a verdict.

A seasoned advocate, Lassar did all of these things. A true believer in his case on a number of occasions, he skated near the edge of prosecutorial misconduct.

Lassar wanted the meaning of the citric acid conspiracy to sink in with the jurors. "We learned it from Barrie Cox . . . and Mr. Cox dropped a bomb on the defendants in this case because he is one of them. He still works for ADM. He's still in charge of citric acid. There was absolutely no attack they could even attempt on Barrie Cox. They couldn't suggest that he was lying. They had to take what he said."

Lassar reminded the jury that Cox called citric a money-making scheme, not a way to learn market information or to cheat competitors. Plus, it was audited. ADM had a set market share (the same as in lysine). Cox, a sherpa, went over prices with his master Terry Wilson. "So, Mr. Wilson was in this up to his eyeballs."

Lassar recalled Cox's testimony that before he even went to work at ADM, Mick Andreas asked if he could set up a meeting with his competitors. "I wonder," mused Lassar, "what [Andreas] had in mind there?" The prosecutor revisited the times on the tapes when Andreas referred to the citric cartel in discussing how to run the lysine group.

In April 1996, the Englishman had won a raise and a London transfer from ADM. "Could it be that they hoped that the disaster that befell them wouldn't occur, that Mr. Cox would not return to the United States and take the witness stand and tell you folks that ADM was price-fixing citric acid before they started price-fixing in lysine?"

Lassar reminded the jury that Mark Whitacre had "absolutely nothing" to do with citric acid. The citric scheme was the root of the lysine racket, not the mole.

With so few producers, lysine was "a very easy market to fix. ADM could not have cared less about the impact on buyers. . . . There's a saying at ADM that penetrates the company and that saying is: The customer is the enemy, and the competitor is our friend. What kind of company is this that that should be their corporate slogan? The customer is the enemy."

Before choosing to enter the lysine business, ADM knew the trade's history as a den of price-fixing. Perhaps for most companies such a soiled past would have scared them away. But not ADM. "That was an attraction to them."

Lassar focused on taped statements that the ADM sales force was to be kept in the dark about lysine pricing. "The salesman could go off to another company and turn in the top people at ADM and report that there's price-fixing. So, the salesmen couldn't be trusted."

During deliberations, the jurors would have the audiotapes and videotapes as well as the means to play them. The prosecutor suggested they listen to a June 28, 1993 recording of Andreas and paraphrased what they would hear. "The Japanese don't have laws against it. They don't mind telling their salesman. We have laws against it. We cannot tell our salesmen."

The prosecutor asserted that this "case has an arsenal of smoking guns." He ticked some off: not telling the sales force; holding meetings that were "100 percent criminal" outside of the United States; falsifying business reasons for travel;

and Wilson's chalk talk to competitors in Mexico City, whom he showed that competition was costing them over $100 million per year.

Lassar began to give his own chalk talk. On a chart he placed the initials of the defendants, MA, TW, and MW at the heads of columns. Then he awarded points for their price-fixing activities.

Wilson and Whitacre both won two points for participating in Mexico City. Andreas got a point for being their boss and knowing about the meeting. "Now, if nothing else had occurred in the conspiracy and it didn't go on till June of 1995, all three defendants would already be guilty beyond a reasonable doubt for knowingly participating in the conspiracy to fix prices and allocate sales volumes."

He noted that after Mexico City, Whitacre became the go-between to the Japanese. For a meeting with Ajinomoto in Chicago followed by a series of calls, the prosecutor awarded him five points. The scorekeeping bored and befuddled the jury. When Lassar realized it, he departed from the stilted script in favor of a direct gut-level approach.

He blasted the fake agenda at the Paris 1992 meeting with its cynical inclusion of animal rights and environmental concerns. He ripped into Andreas for his taped criticism of the Japanese for not being able to control their sales reps and the resultant failure to keep prices up to agreed levels.

He dug deeply into the Fujiwara affair. Contrived by Whitacre, the sham shakedown by a Japanese saboteur itself warranted a book according to the prosecutor.

> Now, how could Mr. Whitacre ever hope to get away with such a crazy scheme, and why did he put the thing in here about that Mr. Fujiwara supposedly was going to give him the organism? Well, Mr. Whitacre was counting on two things. He was counting on, one, that Mr. Andreas, his boss, would never dare to call in the FBI or the police because of all the things that were going on at ADM and, number two, he thought that Mr. Andreas would be interested in buying some stolen technology from somebody, and he was right on both counts.

Lassar hastened to add that Whitacre would have realized he was in a lawless culture. He knew that ADM fixed prices in citric and lysine. Lassar reminded the jurors of a brief passage from Mimoto's testimony that ADM had stolen Ajinomoto's technology to make threonine, another amino acid, and indeed that Ajinomoto had sued ADM over the theft and won. Plus, Whitacre had learned that ADM "security" paid someone $50,000 to steal a bacitracin "bug" and used prostitutes to gather other information.

All the illegality at work would have emboldened Whitacre. Lassar reconstructed the absent defendant's thought process. "Nobody around here is going to call the police if I make up this [Fujiwara] allegation." Lassar paused, "And he's right."

The prosecutor raised the weird stipulation read by the judge. The unnamed "high-level ADM executive" in it had said that Michael Andreas decided *not* to call law enforcement in favor of a spy agency.

> One of the reasons Mr. Andreas wanted to bring in the CIA was that [he was] concerned about ADM's legal position if ADM paid the extortionist without the agency's help. You see, Mr. Andreas thought: If he's got stolen technology, we might want to buy that. But what if the FBI finds out? Well, we'll say we were dealing with the CIA on this. It's none of your business.
>
> So he was interested in buying that stolen technology, but he was not interested in calling the police. The judge's statement of facts also said: The ADM executive contacted the CIA which determined on its own that proper jurisdiction for this domestic matter belonged to the FBI and referred the extortionist matter to the FBI.
>
> So don't be confused about this. Mr. Andreas never called the police about this extortion allegation. He never in a million years would have called the police. It was the CIA that determined on their own to refer the matter to the FBI, and that's how Brian Shepard got into this investigation.

Regardless, ADM soon gathered that the Fujiwara sting was a hoax. Whitacre admitted that he lied about the mysterious threat from an "Asian-sounding" caller to his daughter. At about the same time, James Randall knew that the lysine problem was just a sterilization glitch, not sabotage.

Lassar became emphatic. Generally, employees who lie and steal are fired or prosecuted:

> *Question:* Why didn't Mr. Andreas fire Mr. Whitacre? He's either an embezzler or a nut making up these stories. Something is really wrong. Why didn't Mr. Andreas fire him? There's only one reason. He couldn't, because Mr. Whitacre was right in the middle of the price-fixing scheme in lysine. He was the go-between with the Japanese and Koreans fixing prices at that time during the fall of 1992. If he fired Whitacre, Whitacre could have blown the whistle on him. He could not fire Whitacre.

Again and again, Lassar painted the picture of a strange company. He mulled the shadowy behavior of Mark Cheviron. From the first Cheviron fought to know everything the FBI did, while placing limits on the bureau's investigation:

I wonder what they could be concerned about in ADM's closets, what they wouldn't want the FBI looking for. Then a few days later, when they find that Mr. Shepard is monitoring both of Mr. Whitacre's phone lines, they stop cooperating. Even though they're supposedly the victim of this sabotage allegation, they tell the FBI: Take a hike. We're not cooperating anymore. You're looking around too much.

A few weeks later, they say: Okay. Now we'll cooperate, but you can't talk to Mr. Whitacre.

Well, of course, that's nonsense. If you're investigating a sabotage allegation and Mr. Whitacre is the go-between with the saboteur, it's ridiculous to say you can't talk to Mr. Whitacre. But ADM doesn't want the FBI talking to Mr. Whitacre, doesn't want them nosing around because there's a lot of illegal activities going on there, and one of those activities is what the defendants are charged with in this case, price-fixing and sales allocation in lysine.

Lassar tackled the defense's image of Whitacre as a zealous snitch, eager to cooperate with the FBI in order to knock out his rivals at ADM and seize power. "Exactly the opposite is true." Within days after his evening in the car with Shepard, Whitacre refused to cooperate, made up excuses, threatened suicide, and even claimed that ADM had gone straight. He knew informing was "going to ruin his career." Only after he had flunked a second polygraph did the troubled executive allow the FBI to use him again.

The prosecution ridiculed the idea that Andreas had been entrapped by Whitacre. He quoted and played tape excerpts of Andreas giving orders to the mole and Wilson. For instance, on April 13, 1993, Andreas instructed Whitacre on dealing with Ajinomoto, "Say to them we did this once before, that we're willing to cut back our plant but not until the price comes through. We're not gonna do something for nothing, not gonna take less volume for the same price." In other words, ADM would put the brakes on the big plant but not until the Japanese showed they would enforce the inflated prices. Switching gears, Lassar returned to his score sheet and gave Andreas a point for conspiracy.

Lassar highlighted the furtive nature of the conspirators. Wilson and Whitacre disguised expense reports. Andreas warned Whitacre to be careful on the phone. He told Yamada that ADM price decisions had to be centralized and taken out of the hands of the sales force who "have a general tendency to want to be very competitive."

Andreas could not be satisfied with a deal just with Ajinomoto. On tape with Yamada, he voiced the necessity of bringing all five producers into the circle.

As for Wilson, Lassar called him an "expert price-fixer." His only role was to convey his illicit citric acid experience, including auditing, a shell association, and buy-ins, to the lysine group.

At lunch, the defense moved yet again for a mistrial. Weingarten complained that calling Wilson an "expert price-fixer" amounted to the introduction of "propensity." It is unfair to convict someone of a crime due to a background in another.

To Manning this was old wine in a new bottle. The government's evidence that Wilson actually used his citric background to pattern lysine was relevant. She was more troubled by the prosecutor's pronouncements on the strength of the evidence in comparison to other cases that were not in evidence. She chastised Lassar. The remark "at the very least no doubt was improper," but not to the extent of creating a mistrial. She also found his scorekeeping misleading and directed him to stop it once and for all.

After lunch Lassar went through foreign price-fixing meetings and the updates that followed them by Whitacre and Wilson to Andreas. As for ADM's periodic push for the same market share as Ajinomoto, Lassar branded it a negotiating position from which Andreas eventually cut an illegal deal at Irvine.

The prosecutor reminded the jurors of a point they might have missed on tape. Andreas expressed a desire to meet with "Yamada alone [because] Ikeda might put a wire under his jacket." To Lassar, Andreas was scared of being taped in criminal activity. Ironically, the executive guessed incorrectly who would record him.

Lassar had the jury recall that in the same conversation, Andreas gave Whitacre a raise from $250,000 to $300,000. The prosecution deemed it a reward for the mole's work as a go-between.

Lassar portrayed Wilson as an ADM loyalist whose sole chore was to fix the market. At the Tokyo meeting in December 1993, Wilson "reminds us of what the motive is for the crime." He asked the jury to listen during deliberations to Wilson's taped statement of how another price war could create devastation. A 30-cent drop would cost $112 million. A 60-cent drop would cost $224 million.

Lassar now took to calling Weingarten's client "coach Wilson." To undermine the defense stance that Wilson had been "lured" to Hawaii, seen price-fixing, and pretended to go along with it, Lassar played a video from the 1994 meeting. "He's persuading," said Lassar, "the other people. Let's put those prices on the board and go out and charge them and make this work." If Wilson had been pretending, "he's the world's greatest actor."

After Hawaii, Andreas and Wilson largely vanished from the lysine scene because "the scheme is working." Andreas, an extremely important person at ADM, had numerous other product lines and deals to absorb him. "He has overseen the fixing of the lysine markets. He's out of it. Mr. Wilson was only in lysine to fix the market. He has done so in Hawaii, and he is out of it."

Wilson did show up on a tape of July 13, 1994, to warn Whitacre not to keep the lysine group's sales chart in his office to prevent it from being seen by employees and visitors. Lassar encouraged the jury to listen to the tape. "I think he said I can tell pretty fucking quick what this is. It's got the whole conspiracy here."

Building to a crescendo, the prosecutor challenged the jury to recall what Andreas and Wilson said to the FBI on the night of the Decatur raid. He believed their statements were impossible to square with their recorded remarks:

There's one more event to talk about, and that event occurred on June 27, 1995, when the investigation became public and the scheme ended. Remember search warrants were executed that day, and the FBI interviewed Mr. Wilson and Mr. Andreas. And independently Mr. Wilson and Mr. Andreas had the same response to being interviewed. They lied and lied and lied. They weren't going to tell the truth about what happened to the FBI. Instead, they lied.

Mr. Wilson was asked, Have you ever heard of this idea of using a sales association as a cover for price-fixing? Never heard of such an idea. How about the idea of compensation with sales allocation of somebody buying-in at the end of the year? Never even heard of such an idea. Mr. Andreas said, I don't even make the decisions in my company. My father makes the decisions. Is that what it looked like to you on tape? He made plenty of decisions, didn't he? At least he did in the lysine price-fixing scheme.

Mr. Wilson was asked, Ever hear of the idea of audits to ensure that a volume allocation is working? Mr. Wilson: Never heard of such an idea. And Mr. Wilson also said, We don't even exchange sales or production figures with competitors. He lied.

Mr. Andreas said, You guys don't understand our business. You can't have price-fixing in our business. You can't control it. Too many factors. Can't have it. Hoping to blow smoke at them.

Neither Mr. Wilson nor Mr. Andreas knew how much trouble they were in, and they thought they could just lie and get away with it. Further evidence, of course, that they are guilty.

When the defense attorneys address you, they're going to come up with all kinds of different defenses all over the place. But when you're hearing all those defenses, ask yourselves why didn't we hear those defenses from Mr. Wilson and Mr. Andreas on June 27, 1995? That was their opportunity if they had a defense. They were confronted. That was their opportunity to give all these defenses. You're not going to hear those lies from the attorneys because the attorneys have an advantage over their clients. The attorneys have heard all the evidence the government has. They know before trial about all the tapes and all the witnesses, and so they have constructed new defenses for your benefit that they're going to argue to you, not the ones that their clients came up with, and that's evidence to you that the defenses you're going to hear are not true because if they were true, you would have heard them given to the FBI by Mr. Wilson and Mr. Andreas in June of 1995.

Lassar left the jury to fathom the social significance of the offense and their role in assessing it.

Ladies and gentlemen, the crime that you have heard about here is not the type of crime of need where someone robs a bank because they're needy. This was a crime of greed, a crime by an extremely large corporation that wanted to make ever more money at the expense of their customers.

By your verdict here you will tell the defendants that they are not above the law and that the customer is not the enemy.

Lassar's performance infuriated the defense, which collectively called for a mistrial. Bray railed against "the most unusual and emphatic comment on the defendants' failure to testify, I have ever heard." Weingarten deplored the notions that Wilson "had an obligation" to put forward his defenses in a twelve-minute interview with the FBI, that he should be faulted for not testifying at trial, "and that anything I say in closing argument tomorrow therefore is a lie is truly outrageous."

Manning looked at Lassar, "I am a little concerned about what you said."

Lassar replied, "If they had testified, I would have made the same comment: That they lied."

"Judge," added Joseph Duffy, Andreas' Chicago lawyer, "this is the worst I've ever seen by a prosecution crossing the line." Lassar "goes and he says to them, where's the defense? [But] they don't have an obligation to put on a defense. That's another constitutional violation."

Robin Mann fought to keep the case in court. "Your Honor, there's nothing wrong with getting into the false exculpatories given by defendants."

Manning wanted to read a copy of Lassar's closing before ruling on it. But a transcript would not be ready instantly. In the meantime, she asked Bray to give his summation. Before he did, she chastened Lassar in front of the jury for an earlier transgression:

Ladies and gentlemen, before we continue on with the closing arguments, I would just like to advise you that during the course of Mr. Lassar's closing argu-

ment he made reference to the strength of the evidence in this case as compared to other cases. Such references to other cases are totally irrelevant. So I
would instruct you that you should absolutely disregard any statements or references comparing this case to any other case, and you should decide this case
solely on the evidence presented in this case without regard to any comparison
to any other case.

Lassar sat poker-faced through the rebuke. But like everyone else in the courtroom,
he wondered how much it had reduced the impact of his summation.

The prosecutor's problem energized the defense. Bray immediately seized upon
it in his argument.

Now, the government started off the argument telling you that, whoa, we've
got the biggest, best evidence. This is the most overwhelming case in history.
Well, you hear that all the time. There are a lot of the most overwhelming cases
in history because prosecutors say that all the time. I have been doing this for
thirty-seven years. I can't remember when I ever didn't hear that the case against
my client was the biggest, most overwhelming—

Lassar objected and was sustained but too late. Bray was on a roll. The case was
not about Ajinomoto, ADM, or any corporation. It was about the "the liberty of
each of three human beings." The only question was whether his client was guilty
as charged beyond a reasonable doubt.

Andreas' conduct, he insisted, could not be criminal. It occurred in a "difficult
gray area" of international commerce "between legitimate business discussion, legitimate business competition, and legitimate exchange of information."

The government's case was horribly overstated. It involved no "terrible criminal wrongdoing." The term "threat" had been bandied about loosely by the prosecution. But, what really was it? "I've got a big plant. Not exactly a terrible threat."

The chief government witnesses—Mimoto, Yamamoto, Ikeda, and Crouy were
"people who have not been brought to account." Two received "fines and are gone."

How could it be an "overwhelming case" asked Bray? The government mole
was "a trusted insider" with "unlimited access" to Mick Andreas. "You sat here for
two months. You heard the tapes. You saw the posters. The only time you heard
the words price-fixing attributed to Mr. Andreas, to his ears or to his mouth, came
from Mr. Lassar. He made them up."

Bray was banking on a literalness defense. Andreas had never used the words
"price-fixing." Moreover, "Mr. Whitacre never in two-and-a-half years of taping
ever dared put those words up there."

The government, maintained Bray, would not have risked allowing its agent to be so explicit. If it had, Andreas would have kicked him out of the office, and the investigation would have disintegrated.

As for the mole, he was in a panic about his career:

> And panic focuses people. He saw in his panic on November 4, 1992, that he had an opportunity to turn over the skull, the neck, the head, of a great prize to the FBI, to give them the promise of worldwide headlines. In fact, he saw the opportunity and tried to turn over two skulls: Dwayne Andreas and Mick Andreas. And he promised them both on November 5, 1992, to Agent Shepard. And from the moment on, Agent Shepard had stars in his eyes.

The tapes mainly froze "a lot of talk about lysine. I am sick of hearing about lysine for two months. I imagine you are."

There was nothing wrong with learning about competitors' capacities, volumes, and markets. Forming trade associations is "done in every industry that is a worldwide commodity."

How could jurors get a fair look into the mind of Mick Andreas through the likes of Mr. Ikeda? When he met with Andreas, he spoke English. When he came to court and faced cross-examination, he hid behind an interpreter.

Many of the tapes were ambiguous and disjointed. One was not. It was a 1993 audio segment that the government did not play. After Ikeda and Yamada had left the Irvine meeting, Andreas sat down with Whitacre and said, "At ADM we don't made deals." Bray played the tape. Andreas' pronouncement sounded genuine, not tongue-in-check. Bray argued that Andreas' earlier remarks in conversation with the Japanese amounted to "legal bluffing, even legal disinformation to a company against whom they were waging competition. Legal, and that's all we are here for."

Bray refreshed the jury on the judge's instruction about criminal responsibility. Just because someone is an officer of a corporation does not make him guilty of the crimes of an employee. Mick Andreas "certainly is not criminally responsible for anything Mark Whitacre did operating for two and a half years at the behest of the FBI fixing prices." The evidence proved that Whitacre had had phone calls with the Japanese "all the time geographically fixing prices, leaving nothing to the imagination. Where, you might ask the array of FBI agents and prosecutors, is the tape, even one, of Mr. Whitacre coming back from one of those many, many telephone conversations with Mr. Mimoto and Mr. Yamamoto and saying to Mr. Andreas, I just got off the phone with Mr. Mimoto. We fixed the price."

Bray urged the jurors to listen to the tapes carefully during deliberations. In two and a half years, "a span just short of the presidency of John F. Kennedy," they would not discover even "one feeble transcript" of Mick Andreas actually fixing a price or volume illegally.

The jury was obligated to "strip away the adjectives and adverbs and hype," that resulted from the government agents adopting Whitacre's scam. Even they knew "he would grossly exaggerate things. They were duped."

Bray found the government's explanation for having no tapes between Andreas and Whitacre during the last year and a half of the so-called conspiracy ludicrous. Sure Andreas was busy. But, the new lysine venture was a major capital project. Whitacre was practically next door to Andreas in the corporate suite. It made no sense that Whitacre would not report on the status of such a significant project to his boss, unless Andreas actually was not involved.

Again and again Bray blasted the government for "not having the courage to put together the tape" that would clearly show whether Mick Andreas had real knowledge of price-fixing. Instead, the government left the case in "this grayest of gray areas," in "a cloud of doubt."

A by-product of not having a direct confrontation about illegal conduct with Andreas, and no recording of him over a year and a half, was that it left to Whitacre "a honey pot from which he could embezzle." It also made it easy for the mole "in a business sense to assassinate Michael Andreas, his one competitor to become the next president of ADM after the president, Jim Randall, who was getting up in years, retired." The sonorous Bray had the jury's attention.

As for the "locker-room" recordings, "those tapes show nothing but talk about volume, talk about how to get information, talk about who has what in this market, talk about how ADM can get accepted essentially in this market and stop being the outsider treated as a renegade by the other competitors, how it can deal with an Asian cartel who has tried to exclude it from the market and who has tried to beat it down at every turn."

By no means did these tapes constitute an illegal agreement. He repeated the court's injunction that a business could not conspire with itself.

The jury could conclude only that Andreas believed he was behaving legally. In the tape following the October 25, 1993 Irvine session, Andreas gave Whitacre "the lecture of his life" about ADM not making deals.

Another doubt arose from his client's behavior during the Fujiwara affair:

Mick Andreas was the one who asked the government to investigate Ajinomoto. Common sense, ladies and gentlemen. Mick Andreas in the exercise of your judgment is entitled to the full benefit of your lifetime of experience and common sense. And this is a big one. Ask yourselves would Mick Andreas, would anyone ask the government to come in, sit down and tell them go investigate Ajinomoto, with whom we've been having meetings, if in fact he was involved in a criminal conspiracy with them or if in fact he knew or believed or even suspected that Mark Whitacre was involved in a criminal conspiracy with Ajinomoto?

Bray faulted the investigation for blinding itself to the realities of price and competition in the trade. "Another reason that Mick Andreas is innocent is that in pursuing this whole case, the FBI intentionally closed its eyes to the real world of the lysine market. The agents testified to you that all we wanted to hear is what they said on tapes. To us, the words are the crime. It became to them a word crime."

He suggested that in relying on mere words, the government recognized the lameness of its case and tried to prejudice the jury with irrelevant profanity. The FBI ignored the ample evidence that the lysine producers lied and cheated each other on price and volume, evidence of bare-knuckle competition.

Bray implored the jurors to gauge the "actual impact" of ADM attempting to break into the market. The price of lysine fell from $3.00 a pound in the summer of 1988 down at times to below a dollar. He said that this cost the Asian cartel $100 million and saved consumers an equal amount.

In banking on words rather than deeds, the government was trying to sell tapes that were "unreliable in many, many ways." The content was based on Whitacre's discretion about when to record and what to preserve. The government's expert had found "bulk erasures."

To his detriment, Andreas had relied on Whitacre. Bray referred the jury to the first tape involving his client. On March 18, 1993, Whitacre assured his boss regarding the Mexico City meeting. "I mean there was for sure never an agreement, never." In the same tape, Andreas told Whitacre that when the Japanese "come to me, I'm just gonna say look, first of all, we don't make deals." Andreas added he would inform the competition that "we watch the laws very carefully."

Bray argued Andreas' awareness of "Japan, Inc." He knew that Japanese companies had "government support" and did not respect the rules "that American companies abide by. But he's telling [Whitacre] we're going to play it straight. I know where the line is and we're not going to cross it." Unfortunately, Andreas did not know "he was up against a hidden agenda of a tenacious individual who was out to get him."

The Japanese understood Andreas' law-abiding position at the time. The jury had heard Wilson inform them that Andreas would not make deals. But, the trial testimony of Japanese witnesses amounted to "mouthing the government's lingo much like puppets," because of their "sweetheart deals."

Bray milked the irony that the "Asian cartel" virtually had escaped punishment. It had "dominated the lysine market, controlled it for years and years [and] divided up the United States." Now it had used the US government to smash its American competition.

ADM naturally "was completely unwelcome" in the cartel. Bray reminded the jury of the Asians' opinions of ADM. "Their internal documents say things like: We have to stop the hurricane of ADM. We have to suppress ADM. We have to make ADM suffer from a bitter experience.

"These are documents that say they have to kick ADM out of the market. They talk about Japan. The witnesses describe Japan itself as a sanctuary market. It was particularly important to Ajinomoto that ADM not be able to sell at all in Japan."

ADM's goal in dealing with the Japanese simply "was to get the survival level of information." But their rivals wanted ADM "to wallow in ignorance, wallow in misinformation," and be the victim of "industrial espionage" when "they tried to steal ADM's lysine bug."

Bray played his Fujiwara card. It was the FBI who knew that the story was totally false and never alerted ADM even though its innocent employees had been implicated in sabotage. That led back to Whitacre. What kind of person would falsely accuse coworkers, claim to be adopted, and fake a threat to his daughter?

"He's lied to everyone involved in this case, and in the course of doing his embezzlement, he committed acts of dishonesty that are scarcely imaginable. He forged. He extorted. He embezzled. He created false companies, false invoices, false transactions, using Swiss and Cayman Islands bank accounts to steal from his own company."

The FBI stuck with Whitacre despite his failed polygraph, fabrications, wild "sugar high" energy, and penchant for exaggeration. "That exaggeration," said Bray boldly, "could cost a man his freedom."

Lassar was on his feet objecting. Sentencing was a matter for the court. Manning sustained and told the jurors to disregard the reference to punishment. But now it was in their laps.

Bray viewed Lassar's slant on ADM's choice of the CIA over the FBI as dubious. Contacting the intelligence agency made sense since it "was common in Japanese culture for the Japanese government to be intertwined in Japanese businesses and, therefore, [ADM] thought that the Japanese government might be involved in the extortion. That's why the CIA was picked." When the CIA brought in the FBI, "[t]hat was fine with Mr. Andreas, [who] welcomed the FBI, as you've heard, into his home." Moreover, Andreas was frank with the bureau about the meetings and plant tours with competitors.

Unfortunately, Brian Shepard "became buddies" with Whitacre, "the highest ranking corporate insider ever flipped by the FBI." Bray ridiculed the idea that the agents did not figure out that the mole also was the extortionist in the Fujiwara scam. "They saw history here. They saw their names in lights. They saw career advancement. They saw excitement. They saw no longer sitting at a desk all alone in Decatur."

So eager were they to bag "one of the most famous names in American business" that they threw out their own rules on undercover operations. He scoffed at the government's quibble that Harvest King was not formally undercover. Then he read from FBI policy:

> Consensual recordings can only be used successfully in the context of scrupulous adherence to clear policies regarding what conversations are to be recorded.
>
> Unrecorded conversations will be questioned, and a substantial number of them cause the integrity of the investigation to be challenged. A policy of recording as many conversations as is possible should, therefore, be pursued.
>
> Informants and cooperating private individuals should be instructed to record all telephone conversations with the suspects, regardless of whether it is anticipated the conversation will be pertinent. Face-to-face meetings should always be recorded unless the supervising agents determine it would be inadvisable for reasons of safety, security, or technical limitations.

Yet, the government allowed numerous conversations to go unrecorded. Bray's anger mounted. "Well, these rules don't apply to Whitacre. What rules do? Well, there are no rules." The FBI became lawless. It "abandoned taping controls," and "encouraged circumvention of Japanese law" when recording in Tokyo.

He switched to the law-breaking Japanese the government cultivated as witnesses. They had avoided three-year sentences and "multimillion dollar fines." It was another backhanded reference to penalties but drew no objection. Even if they stopped cooperating or lied on the stand, they still had five days to get out of the country. "So, their greatest penalty is that they have to pack quickly."

Bray reprised the judge's instructions. It was legal for a company at times to match its competitors prices as long as it acted through "independent judgment." At worst, this is what ADM did vigorously and his client's judgment always was independent. In a December 1, 1993 tape that had been played to the jury, Andreas reviewed the Irvine meeting and growled, "We'll do what the hell we want." To Bray, his client's words were those of "an innocent person," who also says "we abide by the law. I'm not above the law." He wanted a verdict that would spank rogue law enforcement:

> There may be an issue here whether the FBI is above the law or above their own rule book, whether it's more important that what happens here is that this is either the end of the FBI throwing away its rule book—there's been enough of

that—or if not the end of it, perhaps it could be the beginning of the end of it. At least it could be the beginning of the end of their sweeping a trash heap of failed polygraphs and other things like that under the rug and ignoring a complete massive embezzlement while they see stars in their eyes and go after someone else.

He thanked them, urged them to invoke the presumption of innocence since the "future of a man and his family is at stake," and asked them to cling to the actual evidence, not "the rhetoric of the government." He finished right before lunch. It had been a stunningly good closing that played upon themes of displeasure with the government, foreign competition, and snitches. It hit the evidentiary holes. The language was strong but not strident. It had been smoothly but not slickly presented. Mick Andreas strode out of the courtroom beaming.

Bill Walker's quick speech was sandwiched between Bray's and Weingarten's. The big man promised not to point fingers and to stick to showing defects in the government's case. "So what you're looking at is whether or not there was an agreement to fix prices before November 4, 1992." After that Whitacre was law enforcement's agent. "The government is telling him what to do, controlling him."

His client did not want the jury's pity, sympathy, or praise. "We don't want anybody saying: You did a good job, and you made all these tapes." By the same token, whatever they had heard about fraud or embezzlement could not taint their verdict as the judge had instructed.

Walker urged a simple factual test of the evidence arising between June and the November 1992 cutoff. He asked the jury to remember that Mimoto and Yamamoto had testified that no price-fixing agreement had been reached in Mexico City in mid-1992. Ikeda had testified there was a "tentative" agreement. However, an FBI 1997 interview form quoted Ikeda saying, "I do not recall whether there was a price agreement or not reached in Mexico City." The evidence could not clear the law's high hurdle of proof beyond a reasonable doubt. He saw no reason to deal with Whitacre's price and volume pronouncements. Since all of the government's tapes were made after November 4, 1992, "they added nothing whatsoever to Dr. Whitacre's guilt or innocence."

In July 1992, Whitacre had made some phone calls about raising lysine to 80 cents a pound. But these "followed" Miwon's lead. Miwon had not even been at Mexico City. So, the statement amounted to legal "price coordination," not criminal agreement.

Whitacre met with Mimoto and Ikeda on September 8, 1992. In court, Mimoto was asked directly if price-fixing had occurred at the meeting, and his answer was "no, it didn't."

Walker also had to cope with the Paris October 1992 session with the phony agenda. The lawyer read back the testimony of Alain Crouy. Crouy said "I think" and "I believe" there was price-fixing in Paris. But, in a January 1997 interview with the FBI in Brussels, he took the opposite view. In court, Crouy claimed not to remember making the Brussels statement. All of which, according to Walker, amounted to reasonable doubt.

Walker gestured to the government. "This table is excellent, an excellent set of lawyers and assistants and FBI agents." If there had been firm evidence against Whitacre, they would have unearthed it and presented it, "but there's no proof there."

During the break, Manning made clear that she wanted the jury to decide the case and would not grant a mistrial. She remained deeply concerned that Lassar's remarks ran afoul of the Fifth Amendment's guarantee of the right to remain silent. She was especially disappointed since he was not simply an assistant US attorney, but "*the* US Attorney." After the jurors filtered back she asked them to "pay close attention" and delivered a stinging "curative instruction."

Mr. Lassar told you that if the defendants had a defense they should have revealed it at the time they were confronted by the FBI. The defendants have absolutely no obligation to tell the FBI anything. And Mr. Lassar's suggestion to the contrary must be ignored.

Defendants are presumed to be innocent and are under absolutely no obligation to come forward with any evidence or witnesses. This is because defendants are not required to prove their innocence. The burden at all times is on the prosecution to prove each of the defendants guilty beyond a reasonable doubt. And any suggestion by the prosecutor to the contrary is inappropriate and should be ignored.

Finally, in his closing Mr. Lassar made reference to the fact that lawyers will construct defenses. This statement is inappropriate. You are instructed that you should absolutely disregard any such statement by Mr. Lassar concerning the other counsel in this case. Defense counsel, in my view, have acted properly throughout these proceedings, and any argument to the contrary by Mr. Lassar must be ignored.

Weingarten faced the jury after the judge had toasted him and roasted the government. It was not a bad position for a defense attorney to be in, and he immediately made the most of the opportunity to preach from high ground

Beyond any doubt, ADM, including Terry Wilson, busted up a long-standing Asian cartel in lysine. *Beyond any doubt* when ADM entered the market the price plummeted, and during the life of this alleged conspiracy never again got back to where it was before ADM arrived on the scene.

Beyond any doubt during this alleged conspiracy there were two long price wars. And as the FBI raided ADM, a third price war had started. *Beyond any doubt* at the end of the alleged conspiracy, when the trustbusters were celebrating their great work, what happened to the price? Did it drop because now there was free competition in the marketplace? No. As you've heard, when this alleged conspiracy ended the price war continued for a period of time. And when the conspiracy was over, the price rose to levels not seen before and before ADM had arrived.

And finally, *beyond any doubt* we introduced document after document after document after document from the competitors, from the period of 1990 through and including this alleged conspiracy, that showed ADM undercutting the competitors, ADM stealing customers and fierce competition in the marketplace.

This is a fixed market? Remarkably the government never challenges any of this evidence, any of the things I just said. Remarkably the FBI never looked at the marketplace. You would think if the United States of America is charging a price-fixing conspiracy, there might have been a bit of interest in what was going on between the buyers and sellers. But the FBI never looked.

Weingarten used an anecdote about his son to make a point. They had gone to an amusement park and put on virtual reality helmets for an experience called "Parallel Universe." The vivid computer images seemed real, just like the government's case, but were not. The prosecutor had used words on tape to construct a vision "that is not accurate, not fair, not complete." Above all, it did not match the world of deeds in a backstabbing business.

We said in our opening statement, judge us by what we did, not just by what we said. Look at our actions, not just our words. We readily acknowledged two months ago that we uttered words that were designed to cause the Asian and French competitors to believe at certain points that we are playing. We *owned* those tapes.

He blamed Whitacre—"liar, thief, bounty-hunter," and the FBI. The FBI "created an environment whereby he [Whitacre] could turn in only the evidence he thought would please them." The prosecutor's point that it could convict each without the mole's work drew his wrath.

The government says wait, wait, wait. It's not just the tapes. We have the co-conspirators. Another parallel universe was the notion that the government brought the Japanese conspirators to heel. They punished them and they put pressure on them to tell the truth. This is one of the greatest fictions of this trial.

The cartel's witnesses—Mimoto, Ikeda, and Crouy—could not be trusted because of their crimes, easy deals with the government, and association with a company that obstructed justice. "The second Ajinomoto realized the cops were onto them, they destroyed their documents. Can you imagine if that had gone on at ADM what the consequences would have been?"

Weingarten spent the next half hour flagging documents that reflected "the Japanese attitude towards competition." In a June 1992 letter, an official at Heartland Lysine wrote, "Unfortunately the lysine business has turned into a dog fight of price competition sunk in a bog that I can barely call a business anymore." This led the lawyer to editorialize:

> From the perspective of Ajinomoto, when there's price competition it's a dog fight that has sunk into a bog and it's scarcely a business. It's a business to the Japanese when it's controlled.

He was equally unsparing with the Koreans. On the monitors, he placed the summary of a meeting among Japanese and Korean producers written by a Miwon executive:

> "When your company, Eurolysine, started the lysine production, that is, from 1975 until present time, we have cooperated by restricting/inhibiting to five to ten percent level, five percent in the beginning, less than ten percent during the last ten years, of the European demand. Such cooperation that has been extended between the two companies for at least seventeen years is, I think, a true cooperation."

The more Weingarten read the angrier he became, hoping the jurors would have the same reaction. "So what the Koreans are saying, hey look, how can you complain about us? We have been fixing volume with you for seventeen years. Interesting, the next paragraph: 'The reason why the lysine industry is facing difficulties is because of, guess who, ADM.'"

The fact that ADM built "this monster plant" had the Asian cartel "terrified." Plus, ADM was turning lysine into a "commodity." Pitched previously as a "specialty product," it had fetched high prices. Moreover, sales reps had ensnarled buyers in longstanding relationships in which the producers had control.

The cartel became desperate once ADM began "meddling with customers." Ajinomoto even sent Mimoto to the Decatur plant "to steal a microorganism." This was extreme behavior to be sure, but it made sense to the Japanese giant given the expected loss of business. Weingarten displayed another Ajinomoto memo, "We estimate that ADM this year will 'cost' the lysine industry worldwide more than a hundred million dollars."

The lawyer played the race card. He put up the Ajinomoto document that described ADM as a company with a "different hair color."

> Now, I examined Mr. Mimoto about this document. Mr. Mimoto assured me that when the Japanese refer in Japanese language to people of a different hair color, no offense intended, and I'll accept that, but what it surely signals is that we have two worlds colliding. We have a Japanese language, a Japanese history, a Japanese economy, and a Japanese culture all in this industry profoundly different from ADM.

Weingarten anticipated the questions that would come up during deliberations. Why would his client meet with such hostile forces? "ADM was hungry for information from the opening bell." He reminded the jury of an old expression: "Know thine enemy." Plus, "ADM wanted to lull the competitors," to keep them from engaging in lawsuits, and "predatory pricing," and to give them a "false sense of security" that their customers were safe from ADM.

A consistent theme ran through the "foreign documents." ADM cannot be trusted. "They say ADM has said one thing and they do another. Now, this is not what they teach at the Chicago Business School. But this is the school of hard knocks. This is how it works in the marketplace." In essence, the attorney was advancing an extraordinary defense, probably unprecedented in American justice—the defendants were liars, so acquit them.

He took the government to task for not including liquid lysine in its "score card" of production quotas. With liquid, the figures were "way above what [ADM] represented to the Japanese their numbers would be." The objective of ADM, as made clear by Terry Wilson, was to be as big as Ajinomoto in market share. "On this point, he's inflexible."

A price-fixing conspiracy required at least two different companies. But, even the Japanese did not cross the line by making a pact with ADM. He pulled a 1992 document relied on by the government in which Ikeda wrote "if discussions go smoothly we will aim for prices at levels of a dollar five." He asked the jury to examine the language closely. "I told my son, if he does well this year, we will aim to go to the NBA finals. Do I have an agreement to take him to the NBA finals? Of course not. These are contingencies. If the discussions go smoothly, we will aim. There's no agreement there."

Price leadership and price followship were completely legal without a clear agreement. If the owner of a gas station on one corner sees that the station across the street can draw customers with prices a few cents higher, he would be a fool not to raise his.

Weingarten next recalled Brian Shepard's testimony that the mole "had pricing authority for ADM." The lawyer said there "was not a hint of evidence that Terry Wilson or Mick Andreas knew what Mark Whitacre was saying on the phone to Mr. Yamamoto."

Then he showed a Korean memo regarding constant fluctuation in world lysine demand. "The Koreans have it exactly right. You can't fix this market so easily because of economics and environmental factors."

Weingarten used document after document to make his points. He seemed married to the paper. The jury grew weary at times with the plodding approach.

He tried to rouse them with Fujiwara, but they had heard a lot about it already. He sneered at the FBI's position that it did not know that Whitacre was the scammer.

> I submit to you, any rookie cop in the world would come to the conclusion at that time what was going on here was a rip-off. But the FBI has testified in this case that that's not what's going on. They had fifty years experience around Whitacre and it never occurred to them that Whitacre was endeavoring to rip off ADM. You conclude whether or not that testimony is truthful. And I respectfully submit that you conclude that it's not. You have to ask yourself, why would FBI agents take the stand and try to blow that one by you?

Weingarten dwelled on the failed polygraphs, the FBI agents' toleration of Whitacre's misdeeds—"they smelled a big case. They smelled the roses," hence the flouting of bureau rules, and the mole's motives.

> We know about Mark Whitacre's greed. We know about his desire to get a bounty. That's not insignificant. On top of everything else. On top of his ADM salary, on top of the fact that he is ripping off ADM for millions, he wanted a cut in any money that was brought in by his cooperation. His greed knew no bounds. They knew he had a history of making false allegations.

When Weingarten focused on his client, he tried to turn Wilson's profanity to his advantage. "The theme song in this case from Terry Wilson as it pertains to the Japanese, and you've heard it over and over again, is F 'em. And I'm not thrilled with it. I'm not happy with it. I don't say it with a smile. It's gross, crude language. It's utterly inconsistent with a conspiracy."

Wilson's advocacy of lying also was a boon. Weingarten flashed a tape transcript on the screens. Lying was good "as long as you know you're lying." It was a way to stay "a step ahead of everybody else," especially Ikeda.

Late in the afternoon, Weingarten seemed to tire. He lapsed into the vernacular twice saying that the competitors "were pissed at ADM" for failing to make good on Whitacre's commitments. In his efforts to review the many meetings and tapes without reprising, Bray became rambling and disjointed at times.

Occasionally, he hit the mark as when he embroidered on the 1993 Heartland memo decrying that "our lysine business is drowning." He reviewed a 1993 tape in which Andreas and Wilson discussed driving some of the competitors, probably the Koreans, out of the market altogether.

He dealt with a Wilson remark to Mick Andreas. His client told Andreas that the way to handle the Japanese was to convey that "we watch legally what we do very very carefully—it's okay to make our intentions known. I'd stay away from saying we don't want to make deals." The statement, according to Weingarten, pointed to his client's innocence.

> Of course, the government is going to argue Wilson is saying, oh, we do make deals. That's not what he's saying at all. What he's saying is the Japanese make deals. And if we're gonna deal effectively with them, if we're gonna get our information, if we're able to pull their pants down, if we're going to prevent them from retaliating, we got to play them. So don't say we don't make deals. Simply say we make our intentions known and we follow the law. Be more subtle.

Weingarten also reminded the jury of Wilson's repetition of Dwayne Andreas' maxim: "There's no cure for low prices like low prices." But his continued jumping from date to date and document to document dazed the jurors.

Terry Wilson actually left the courtroom for a few minutes, late in his lawyer's argument. At one point, Weingarten asked for a sidebar, an extraordinary move during a summation. Jurors hate these whispered huddles. Why would the lawyer call for one at this critical stage?

"Judge," said Weingarten, "I've lost the jurors. Two jurors are essentially sleeping." The defense had argued for nine hours. Now he was about to enter the "most important part of the client's case." It would take time. Manning declared a recess until the following morning.

Court resumed early on Thursday, September 10, with the jurors refreshed. But Weingarten continued in the same ponderous vein, insisting, "it's all on the line for Terry Wilson." He declined to summarize the evidence. He plodded through more exhibits that stressed his client's toughness, environmental factors that affected lysine price, and above all more treachery among competitors.

He seemed more effective when showing the absence of evidence. For instance, he nailed the prosecution for failing to call any Korean competitors as Jim Griffin promised in his opening. To Weingarten, the testimony would have shown that the Koreans, like ADM, were not playing ball with the Japanese price-fixers but had "complete distrust" for the conspirators and were waging "fierce competition in the market place."

He argued that the absence of liquid lysine from the government's quantity figures belied any sales limitations on ADM's part. In fact, the company was selling far more than a 100 percent of its allocation. Weingarten asked, "What's the difference between dry and liquid to a pig?"

The liquid lysine issue tied nicely with Weingarten's attack on the Hawaii video of his client. The lawyer put a twist on Lassar's image of Wilson as a football coach saying "we're gonna trust each other. If I get my 67,000 [tons], I'll be happy." To the lawyer, the salient issue was that counting liquid ADM sold 75,000 tons. So, there was no volume agreement, and the coach act was pure deception.

Weingarten scoffed at the government's justification for the decline in tapes, especially locker-room tapes involving his client, after the Hawaii meeting in March, 1994. "Now, as far as the FBI was concerned, after Hawaii everything was done. You know, in theory, the agreement was reached in Irvine and was perfected in Hawaii."

To Weingarten, the period until the raid was a time of many moves in the lysine trade. He refused to accept that the recording had tapered off. "I believe the evidence supports the conclusion that it is extremely likely that Whitacre made a load of tapes in '94 and '95 and that they just didn't have the stuff that he believed they [the FBI] wanted. As a result, we will never have them either."

He presented a raft of documents to show that Hawaii did not quell competition. To the contrary, within days of the meeting, Kyowa complained that ADM had reduced prices everywhere but in Europe. In June 1994, Decatur offered discounts to big users. In July 1994, Koreans were upset by ADM's low truckload prices, and according to Weingarten, "were in a state of panic." Another 1994 Korean memo claimed that ADM was ignoring "the discussion system," that the Japanese had imposed on lysine for seventeen years.

In 1995, Kyowa raged against ADM's "stealth and provocation" in snatching customers. Heartland Lysine found ADM's preeminence in North American "assured," thanks to aggressive price-cutting. Ajinomoto saw "competition getting fierce." On April 25, 1995, a Heartland executive in Hong Kong advocated a "warship strategy" against ADM. "Is this," asked Weingarten, "a fixed market?"

Of course, Wilson's lawyer also had explaining to do. One problem was his client's post-raid interview with the FBI at the Decatur Country Club. The judge already had reduced the impact of Wilson's comments, but the lawyer still felt that he had to deal with them.

Weingarten pointed out that the FBI report noted that Wilson had "acted confused," which raised the inference of intoxication. "So Wilson has a twelve-minute conversation with the FBI in his club probably with a drink in his hand when he wants to talk to a lawyer, and the conclusion is for two or three questions that he's a liar and he should be considered a price-fixer as a result of that?"

The more meaningful conversation occurred later that evening when the FBI "wired up Mark Whitacre to go to Terry Wilson and try to get incriminating evidence for purposes of their case." Weingarten reminded the jurors that they had heard the tape of Wilson saying words to the effect that "you know the main thing is if we're trying to fix prices, we ought to be fired for being so f-ing incompetent." The lawyer asked, "Are those the words of someone with a guilty conscience. I submit to you they are not."

Barrie Cox, the Englishman on ADM's payroll who testified for the government, raised another thorn. Cox had testified to being in the thick of citric acid price-fixing with Wilson but had produced no supporting evidence. To Weingarten, "truly, the bare uncorroborated word of one person with no documents, tapes, or notes does not make a conspiracy in citric acid." Moreover, "if the government has problems with Terry Wilson in citric, they should charge him."

Weingarten repeated the court's limiting instruction on citric evidence. It could be used to show intent and context but not that "Mr. Wilson was more likely to engage" in the lysine conspiracy. "It would be wrong," urged Weingarten, "for you to convict Terry Wilson in this case because Barrie Cox says there may be anti-competitive activity in another product."

The government also had made much issue of fake travel vouchers. Weingarten spun it this way.

> But the point of all this was Terry Wilson wanted discretion. No, he didn't want his business all over ADM that he was meeting with the competitors. He obviously knew that this was an unorthodox mission to meet with, engage, and deceive the competitors. He didn't want everybody to know what was going on.
>
> Now, whether or not he visited a starch factory in Mexico may or may not be a lie, and I don't think it's appropriate to say it's a lie unless there's proof that he didn't. He certainly met with the competitors. He didn't put it on his voucher, but this is a matter of discretion. He wasn't defrauding his employer by taking trips that were not authorized. He wanted to be discreet. He did not want his business all over ADM or anywhere else because it could be misunderstood and misused, but that does not make him a price-fixer.

Winding to a close, he explained reasonable doubt as "a doubt that would cause a person to pause, to stop in a matter of significant importance." A single reasonable doubt required acquittal.

Weingarten began setting up free-standing billboards, each containing a "reasonable doubt" around the courtroom. There were twelve of them. The doubts were not new. Basically, they were sound bites, synopses of evidence that already had been argued.

In order to guarantee that the doubts would be remembered in the jury room, he assigned one to a juror. "I'm going to ask each juror to take back with you one piece. Hopefully, when you deliberate you can recall these specific points."

The approach was novel and somewhat dangerous. Some jurisdictions do not even allow individual references to jurors. It easily could backfire if a juror resented the task or believed his assigned doubt was worthless. On the other hand, if a juror took his doubt to heart and fought for it, that could be enough. All Wilson needed was a single standing doubt to go free.

The doubt assigned to the first juror was a document that showed the Japanese lysine producers lied to, competed with, and cheated each other. It called into question whether ADM was entering into an existing conspiracy or a shark pond.

Juror number two was asked to recall the 1993 Heartland Lysine plea to its parent Ajinomoto that "our business is drowning" because of ADM's full bore entry into lysine.

The third doubt was a blown-up piece of dialogue between Mick Andreas and Terry Wilson. Andreas wondered if ADM could be satisfied with the same market share as Ajinomoto over the next five years. Wilson said, "no." Weingarten added, "sometimes one word speaks volumes." The message that he wanted juror three to carry was that Wilson was a mighty warrior questing for primacy in international trade.

The fourth doubt was Wilson's remark repeating Dwayne Andreas' maxim about the necessity to remember lies in business, even to write them down. The inference was that lysine was a street fight with no rules.

The fifth doubt arose from a Japanese memo of June 11, 1993, which Weingarten reminded the jury was a year after the so-called conspiracy started. The billboard read: "The lysine business is no longer structured to yield profits due to price competition resulting from the entry of ADM." Weingarten gestured towards the government's table. "It is a reasonable doubt that this group has not proven to you the grand jury's indictment."

Blown-up testimony from Mimoto appeared on billboard number six. Mimoto wanted Wilson not to attend the group's meetings.

On number seven, Weingarten had mounted transcribed locker-room talk following Irvine. Wilson had said, "We're going to sell what we want to sell." Weingarten simply added, "Reasonable Doubt."

Number eight was Whitacre's second failed polygraph. Yet, the FBI still gave him "a free hand to do his magic."

Number nine showed an "absence of locker-room conversations" following the major meeting in Hawaii and afterwards. To Weingarten the void reflected a "concerted effort by Whitacre not to turn in any more exculpatory information." The lawyer maintained that that information should "have persuaded you that there was never an agreement reached involving Terry Wilson."

On the tenth sign were three Ajinomoto memos griping that ADM said it would do one thing and then did another in the market.

Number eleven highlighted similar Biokyowa documents showing that ADM was stealing its "key clients."

For number twelve, Weingarten had saved Wilson's raid-night remarks to Whitacre, who was trying to trap him. The lawyer termed these "crude words from this salty ex-marine, but not the words of a price-fixer."

Weingarten told the jury they had left "Mark Whitacre's parallel universe created by his handiwork with the FBI and found a marketplace that is healthy and competitive. . . . The right thing, the fair thing is to find Terry Wilson not guilty."

To no one's surprise, Scott Lassar exercised his option to present a rebuttal argument. "A young attorney," he began, "went to an older attorney and said, I have a trial coming up. What should I do? The law is against me. The younger attorney said, well, my clients are on videotape committing a crime, and the older attorney said, well, talk for a long, long time, and don't spend a lot of it talking about those videotapes."

In the hour that Lassar spoke, he told the jury again and again not to rely on the selective self-serving views of the evidence offered by the lawyers. Rather, "you can get yourselves some popcorn," and view and listen to the tapes "as many times as you want." He conveyed absolute confidence that the recordings incriminated Wilson and Andreas beyond any reasonable doubt.

The two defendants, he added, also had inconsistent defenses. "Mr. Andreas says I didn't make any agreements with anybody. We just made our intentions known and I wanted to get some market information. . . . I go around telling everyone ADM doesn't make deals." Wilson's defense was that if "I am agreeing to fix prices and allocate sales volume, then I had my fingers crossed and I didn't really mean it."

Lassar said neither made sense. If Andreas was just making legal intentions known, why conceal them and lie to the FBI. If Wilson simply wanted to pretend, why did he engage in locker-room discussions about whether competitors were sticking to price and volume agreements. He reread a couple of salient transcript sections and asked the jury to listen to the full recordings.

Bray had argued that the FBI targeted his client because the agents had "stars in their eyes." But the tapes, said Lassar, gave Shepard and Herndon "powerful information." If "they didn't pursue the investigation they wouldn't have had stars in their eyes, they would have had rocks in their heads."

The cheating among companies should not distract the jury because the producers were "all criminals." Lassar asked the jurors to note that the Japanese complaining about ADM's conduct invariably were not the high-level figures who had been at the price- and quantity-fixing sessions.

He derided the defense point that Wilson and Andreas never used or were confronted with the word "price-fixing." The test was awareness of the scheme not word choice. "They don't use the official legal term but that doesn't mean they don't know what's going on."

He raised the defense point that "you can't trust the tapes because Whitacre made them. Oκ," said Lassar, "No, you can't trust Mr. Whitacre's word. That's why there are tapes. That's why God invented tapes, so you can listen to the tapes."

Having drawn some smiles, Lassar reminded the jurors of the opinion of Bruce Koenig. According to the government's expert, the Whitacre tapes showed no signs of being altered or edited. Listening again would prove to the jury that "you're getting the whole conversations. . . . Because we have tapes, we don't have to believe anything Mr. Whitacre says. That's why the FBI gave him a tape recorder."

Koenig's testimony that two tapes had been erased and recorded over should not disturb them. "Now, does that mean that Whitacre erased them or did he just pick up tapes from the steno pool that had been erased? Mr. Whitacre made a quarter of a million dollars a year and embezzled millions more. I think he could afford to buy some new tapes if he wanted to throw some away. That doesn't mean anything."

He picked up Weingarten's point that the government had failed to call Korean witnesses. "Another diversion, where are the Koreans? Well, I guess we didn't have enough witnesses, the trial wasn't long enough. Second, the Koreans are here. Their documents are here. They had extensive notes. You can read about any meeting you want and you will see the Koreans' view of those meetings. The Koreans are here."

For the last time, he revisited the FBI guidelines issue. "That was another diversion and a waste of your time. That is nothing to do with the guilt or innocence of the defendants." The government's decision not to use undercover guidelines was "reviewed all the way up to Louie Freeh, the director of the FBI." It still made sense since there was no undercover agent involved.

The decision to keep using Whitacre also had proven correct. Nor had the mole been coddled:

And what is the outcome of using Mark Whitacre? Well, they uncovered a worldwide conspiracy to allocate sales volume and fix prices in citric acid, a worldwide conspiracy to allocate sales volume and fix prices in lysine, fines of 20 million dollars from the Japanese companies, guilty pleas of four companies, guilty pleas of three individuals.

And what did they have to give up to Mark Whitacre? Because he made all those tapes, did he get away scott-free for his cooperation? No. He's being prosecuted in this case for price-fixing and he's serving a nine-year sentence for his embezzlements.

Again, not to use the mole and his evidence "would mean the FBI agents had rocks in their heads." Whitacre's handler was still at the government table and Lassar looked towards him.

Did Brian Shepard have stars in his eyes? This wasn't easy for him. Remember, this was his hometown, the place that he had decided come to and spend the rest of his career with the FBI when he moved there from New York. This was the hometown of ADM, a big company.

He knew he wasn't going to be popular going after that company. He knew what might happen to him is what happened. People wouldn't talk to him. Old friends wouldn't speak to him. But he went after them because there was a violation and it was proven on tape. But the friends that wouldn't talk to him didn't know. . . .

Bray objected to an appeal for sympathy, Manning sustained, and Lassar wrapped up. "You people know that some of the people at ADM engaged in a serious crime, that is, conspiracy to fix prices and to allocate sales volume, and I'm sure that you will do your duty with regard to those allegations."

Shortly before 3 PM on Thursday, September 10, 1998, Judge Manning gave the case to the jury. She allowed the four alternates to leave, but she barred them from speaking to anyone about the trial until after the verdict. The decision deprived the lawyers and press of a preview of which way the jury would go, but it made sense. Manning felt that the deliberations would be lengthy. If one of the twelve became too ill to deliberate, she knew that the defendants would not consent to a verdict by eleven, and she could be forced to grant a mistrial. In order to prevent such a mammoth waste of time and effort, she kept the alternates on ready status. If one of the twelve became unable to serve, she intended to insert an alternate into the deliberations. As it happened, none of the alternates were needed.

Before deliberation began, Manning sent the jurors to a brief computer boot camp. The documents, recordings, and transcripts in the case were so voluminous that they defied convenient storage and cataloging. Instead, the government and defense by agreement each put a computer in the jury room with a selection of compact discs (CDs). Technicians from each side explained how to load and search the CDs so that jurors could find the exhibits, audios, or videos they wanted. In addition, they were taught to search the documents for particular words and phrases.

Not surprisingly, some of the jurors already could perform these functions. But Manning did not want the technologically adept to dominate the discussion, so she had them all trained, which took about an hour. It was only a generation ago that conscientious judges took steps to insure that literate jurors did not get the upper hand over nonreaders during deliberations.

Now the jury was on its own, and for the parties the waiting process began. Every day Bill Walker paced the halls of the courthouse. The other defendants set up catered meals for their teams in a spare office. The government lawyers went off to other courtrooms and cases. Reid Weingarten flew to Washington to represent former secretary of agriculture Mike Espy in a high-profile fraud trial in which he later was acquitted.

As the days wore on and the jury did not return with a quick verdict, speculation spread among the press that perhaps there would be a hung jury or a mixed verdict with at least one of the defendants going free. On Tuesday, September 15, the jury began sending notes to the judge. The first involved sound problems with the equipment. Some of the audio tapes could be heard only through a headset and there was only one. She sent back a technician.

The next day shortly before noon, they had a question about evidence.

Judge Manning,

The ADM jurors would like to know if we can use defendant number 1's exhibits as circumstantial evidence against defendant number 2.

The judge called all the attorneys back into court. She wanted their views on how to answer it.

On some levels the question was opaque. In the alphabetical indictment, defendants number 1 and 2 had been Andreas and Whitacre. But the two lead defendants in the trial had been Andreas and Wilson. On the other hand, the use of number 1 and number 2 might not refer to anyone in particular, but simply be a way to seek a general rule about the use of circumstantial evidence. The question showed intelligence, as well as the fact that at least someone on the jury did not want to violate a defendant's right to a fair trial.

The deliberators use of the term "ADM jurors" to describe themselves also was very interesting. It could be a simple shorthand. One, it could reflect a conscious or unconscious decision to view the defendant's conduct as identical with that of the corporation which the government had painted so darkly. Regardless, the defense did not object to the question and proposed that the judge simply refer the jurors back to her original instructions, of which they had a copy.

The prosecution also did not object to the question that at least seemed to suggest that the jury saw the value of the government's circumstantial evidence. But, Lassar wanted the judge to answer the question with a single word, "yes." Manning, however, agreed with the defendants. She sent the jurors a note directing them back to her charge.

Twenty-four hours later, the court received word of a verdict. As people filtered back into the courtroom, the prosecution and defense teams made friendly small talk. Walker continued to pace. Once the jurors were in the box, everyone in the gallery sat stock-still. Manning asked for the verdict from the jury, reviewed it, and read it carefully into the record. "We, the jury, find the defendant Michael D. Andreas guilty as charged in the indictment. We, the jury, find the defendant Mark E. Whitacre guilty as charged in the indictment. We, the jury, find the defendant Terrance S. Wilson guilty as charged in the indictment."

The room remained silent. Manning ordered her clerk to poll the jurors. One by one they rose to swear agreement with the verdict. She thanked them for their "conscientious devotion to duty" and excused them. Shepard and Lassar embraced.

She continued bail for Andreas and Wilson. Neither could meet her gaze. Wilson focused on the floor and Andreas stared at the ceiling as she instructed them to report to the federal probation office to begin cooperating with the process of preparing a presentence investigation report that would be provided to her before sentencing. She left the bench.

Andreas was hugged by his wife; they left the courtroom holding hands. Jack Bray promised an appeal. "We've been fighting this case for three years, and we're going to continue to fight it. We're not through." Mark Hulkower complained that the tapes "were the work of a master manipulator."

Standing alone, Bill Walker commented on his absent client. "Lassar wouldn't have any notches on his belt if it weren't for him. Dr. Whitacre thinks he's a great American hero. Not one person has said to this day, 'thank you.' I'm not saying he didn't do something bad—but all bad?"

The jury seemed eager to leave the courthouse and avoid the press. But, some members have spoken at least fleetingly of their experience and a picture has emerged of the deliberations.

As with many juries that serve over long periods, its members developed a strong rapport. Racial and gender divisions gave way to camaraderie. They reached their decisions by consensus and without taking preliminary votes. The length of their deliberations resulted from their meticulousness. Repeatedly, they watched the videos, listened to the audios, and read the documents.

They convicted Wilson first. He was "upfront in everything," said Fritz Dujour, a recently retired civil engineer for the city of Chicago. "The situation was so clear. The tapes were so incriminating." Next, they found Andreas guilty. The videos of Irvine and Hawaii sank him. Without these tapes, he probably would have been freed. There was some sympathy for the former ADM vice chairman because, as Dujour put it, he had been "railroaded" by Whitacre. "But the government has to use the means available to it. As long as you have a squealer, you have to use him."

Whitacre presented the greatest problem because the evidence against him had been limited by the court. "We thought he was crazy," offered Dujour, "to be taping and wiretapping against ADM when he had that kind of position and salary."

Linda Heflebower, an articulate printing executive, said, "the man's manic depressive and so manipulative." She offered that the mole's conviction also was a way to send a "statement back to the government" that they did not approve "of the way they did things."

To some extent, the jury bought into the defense's anti-FBI rage. "This little hick two-man office was trying to go for the gold," said Heflebower, who had trouble with the failure of the FBI "dummos" to discover Whitacre's "defrauding of the company."

At the same time there was sympathy for Shepard, especially when he wept in court. "He lived in Decatur," said Dujour. "When people found out about his role, the town turned on him."

The defense also made headway with its attacks on the Asian coconspirators. "ADM," said Dujour, "was tricked by the Japanese. I don't know how they can get away with all this. Mimoto only got fined $75,000. Then he goes to Indonesia to become a president of the company."

The engineer added, "It would have been nice to hear from the defendants." But, he professed that the jury took Judge Manning's instruction to heart and did not hold the failure to testify against them.

The anger about the government, the snitch, and the Asians also did not distract them. "Price-fixing is a serious matter," said Dujour. "It goes on all the time. But, the evidence came before us. We had the problem."

PART IV THE COVER-UP

16
THE HIT

"Life in prison has been better than life at ADM."
—Mark Whitacre

The ADM annual stockholders' meeting began at 8:30 in the morning on October 22, 1998, in the auditorium of the James R. Randall Research Center. There were about 1,000 people in attendance, mostly retirees and their spouses. Security was tight. There were bodybuilders straining the seams of their sport coats everywhere, listening to earpieces, and talking into their sleeves.

The meeting was convened by Dwayne Andreas, who looked like he had lost years instead of having gained them. He was eighty but could have passed for sixty with his rich tan and alert gaze. He conducted the session standing up and ran through the mundane matters with a light touch, occasionally injecting a small bit of humor into the proceedings.

He was ably assisted by G. Allen Andreas, the president and CEO, fifty-five, who had intelligent eyes and a wry professorial face. He smoothly delivered the obligatory address about the "new and unique set of challenges" facing agribusiness, ranging from global surpluses to El Niño, while stressing nutraceuticals, glossing over declining profits, and never mentioning the convictions.

The only fly in the ointment was Martin Glotzer, seventy-two, a stocky, good-natured investor and shareholders' rights advocate from Chicago, who owned 110 shares. Given the microphone, Glotzer asked how much the corporation had spent so far on legal defense and got a vague, probably low, answer of about $40 million. Then Glotzer reminded the gathering of the historical precedent of the huge criminal antitrust case in the early 1960s against General Electric, which rebounded to become a greater corporation. Referring to ADM's misfortunes, Glotzer said in a conciliatory vein, "This too shall pass."

By now Dwayne Andreas, who was still the master of his domain, had set a tone of tolerant condescension with a bored, stiff, frozen smile. Once Glotzer got to the meat of his speech, which was a proposal on the ballot for "cumulative" voting, almost no one was listening. Cumulative voting allows shareholders to multiply their votes by the number of directors. Since many shareholders fail to vote, activists can amplify their power and elect "minority directors." Born in the Midwest over a century ago, the reform was the brainchild of Joseph Medill, the crusading publisher of the *Chicago Tribune*. Some midwestern companies have adopted forms of it, including such giants as Ameritech and Commonwealth Edison. ADM, whose board likes to nominate its own directors, wanted no part of cumulative voting, which it claimed would give voice to "special interests" rather "than to the best interests of the stockholders as a whole." Nevertheless, the proposal won a respectable 28.88 percent of the votes cast, up 4.4 percent from the prior referendum of 1996, probably due to strong institutional investor support.

Andreas took a few questions from the floor about ADM internationally and entertained suggestions for boosting the stock value. The leader blamed the present low price on temporary world agricultural conditions. Then the meeting was over. Given the possibilities, such as a reprise of the local dissent 1995, it had been a breeze. Nobody knew that it was Dwayne Andreas' last session at the controls.

Judge Manning cancelled the January sentencing date and rescheduled punishment for February 26, 1999. On January 25, 1999, Dwayne Andreas resigned as ADM's chairman. He retained a board seat, a vote, and the title of chairman emeritus. He would continue to advise the new chairman, his nephew G. Allen Andreas.

During Andreas' twenty-eight year reign, the company had grown from 2,948 employees and 40 processing plants to 23,000 people worldwide and 274 plants. Effusive praise came from Andreas allies Andrew Young and Robert Strauss. The latter told a Chicago reporter that Dwayne was "one of the greatest men who ever lived." Andreas proponents insisted that the transition meant real change was afoot at ADM. Leading corporate governance reformer Nell Minow viewed the shift at the top of ADM to another Andreas family member as "cosmetic."

No explanations and not many details emerged from the reportedly emotional three-hour board meeting where the resignation was accepted. But few commentators doubted the connection to the disastrous criminal trial and upcoming sentencing of Mick Andreas. It seemed as if Dwayne was sending a message: No need to clobber the son in order to beat the father who already had toppled himself.

The February sentencing date came and went without a hearing. The new delay was caused by sparring over whether the court could impose an "alternative fine." The standard statutory maximum was $350,000. But the antitrust laws permitted judges to impose an amount of up to twice the gain to the perpetrators or twice the loss to the market. Under this theory the government was seeking at least $25 million apiece from Andreas and Wilson.

Their attorneys objected to such fines. Also, they accused the government of stonewalling their requests for information about the size of the market from ADM's coconspirators. The coconspirators' views on size could have been at odds with those of the Justice Department. That would make it harder for the prosecution to prove the amount of the alternative fine. The defense said that the information it received from the government regarding the coconspirators was woefully incomplete.

The prosecution replied that it had complied adequately, and to the extent permitted by law, given that the coconspirators were in other countries. On June 2, 1999, Manning issued a withering opinion.

> The government's response was, in this court's opinion, so incredible that it bordered on being ludicrous. It claimed that the lysine producers could not be compelled since the court's compulsory process power did not extend overseas. That argument was wholly deceptive since it ignored the fact that the government could force the lysine producers to turn over the documents under the terms of their existing cooperation agreement. When that opinion was discussed with the court during a recent status hearing, the government claimed that the extraterritorial enforcement of cooperation agreements was an unsettled question of law. Perhaps it is. But the court believes that if the circumstances were different and the lysine producers were withholding documents beneficial to the prosecution, the government would have boldly traveled into that uncharted territory and, in the worst scenario, simply revoked the agreements and indicted the lysine producers. The government played hard ball with Mark Whitacre and presumably could have done the same here.

The judge ruled that the prosecutor made documents available to the defendants in a manner that was "unsatisfactory." She scolded the government for forgetting that "a defendant has a due process right to be sentenced on the basis of accurate information" and refused to impose alternative fines. The most each defendant could get hit with was $350,000.

The government was furious. Prosecutors insisted that they had more than met the standard and threatened to appeal. Like so much else in this case, many of the pertinent documents were sealed, so it remains hard to assess each side's claim.

Sentencing finally occurred on July 9, 1999, a year to the day after the trial had started. Judge Manning spent the morning on mundane motions and scheduling issues. All the while, a crowd milled outside in the hall. Marshals barred the doors to the courtroom.

Shortly after noon, Manning took a recess and let the crowd enter. They filled every row. The press, which included the Chicago and Decatur media as well as the *New York Times, Wall Street Journal,* and networks with their pastel sketchers, packed into the jury box.

The wives, children, and well-wishers of Mick Andreas and Terry Wilson took their familiar places in the gallery behind the counsel tables that were ringed with the full rosters of defense lawyers. Dwayne and Inez Andreas did not appear for their son's sentencing.

No family was present for Whitacre. His lawyer, Bill Walker, felt confident that Manning would give his client no additional prison time. David and Carole Hoech sat in the rear of the gallery on the government side. Reporters, whom Hoech had fed extensive information, pretended to not know him. He glowered at the ADM people, who turned away.

As usual Whitacre did not appear. He preferred to avoid the Metropolitan Correction Center (MCC). The Wilson and Andreas defense teams had objected to Whitacre not coming to court, but Manning let him stay in custody in South Carolina. She decided to sentence him by telephone.

Several days before the sentencing, the judge indicated that she wanted to handle the call in chambers rather than in open court. But this unusual idea drew the ire of the government and the *Chicago Tribune,* which engaged a lawyer to fight it. Manning relented, and a speaker phone was hooked up in the courtroom.

The judge announced that she would decide Whitacre's punishment first. A case manager at the South Carolina prison camp took the call and put Whitacre on the line. Walker stood at ease in front of the bench.

Manning asked the lawyer and the government if they had any objections to the presentence investigation (PSI) report written by the US Probation Office. Following the trial, Jim Griffin had been promoted to chief of criminal enforcement for the antitrust division and moved to Washington. Back in Chicago for the sentencing, he answered for the government. In soft tones, he announced that the probation department had undercalculated the "volume of commerce" attributable to Whitacre during his pre-informant days before November 1992. The amount had to be upped from $14.9 million to $18.7 million. Walker did not demur.

What followed was a technical discussion on the arcane world of the federal sentencing guidelines. Emotionlessly, Manning explained Whitacre's "adjusted offense level." Because of the modification of the volume of commerce, he received five points instead of four. His base offense level for committing the antitrust felony was ten. She added three points because she adopted the probation department's finding that he was a "manager or supervisor" of the conspiracy. She gave "no credit for acceptance of responsibility." His overall score was eighteen. Again, neither Whitacre's lawyer nor the government objected.

Manning continued that Whitacre's "criminal history was two," since he had a prior conviction. Eighteen points in "history category two" guided her to a permissible "range of imprisonment" from twenty-seven to thirty-three months.

On the length of punishment, she had little discretion under the guidelines, only six months. But, she actually had tremendous leeway in dealing with the informant because she could make the penalty concurrent, which would not add to Whitacre's time inside, or consecutive, which would mean that it would start after the fraud sentence imposed in 1998 by Judge Baker in Urbana. Also, she had total discretion over the size of the fine, if any.

For a few minutes, Walker made a pitch for the "minimum guideline sentence" to run concurrently with credit for the sixteen months already served in the federal prison system. "Everything that's happened here has come from Dr. Whitacre. Without him there would have been no tapes and no prosecution." He asked Manning for "understanding and compassion." He reminded her that the probation department had concluded that Whitacre's age, future possibilities, and heavy interest and tax burdens would make any further fine uncollectible. Griffin added that the government had no objection to the concurrent penalty proposed by Walker and to no fine.

Whitacre's disembodied voice was clear, even, and, for him, unhurried. He reminded the judge that he had been the "sole informant for three years. The Department of Justice would have had no case without me. I risked my life and career. I received no emotional support or infrastructure from the FBI." While confined, he had kept his family together by moving it near the prison, maintained a spotless record, even received a furlough—"twenty hours of freedom"—and earned two more advanced degrees. "I was both young and stupid to play the risky and unethical corporate games of the ADM elite. Life in prison has been better than life at ADM." He finished intriguingly by offering that he was cooperating with another United States attorney's office in a new investigation against ADM.

If Walker had been brief, Manning was more so. Yes, a fine was uncollectible, so she would not impose one. "In mitigation, you did cooperate. In aggravation you were involved in this other matter for which you're currently serving time." Without further explanation, she imposed a thirty-month sentence with ten concurrent months and twenty consecutive. She ordered him to participate in psychiatric treatment "if the probation department deems it necessary."

Walker stood stunned, wordless. It is extraordinary for a judge to mete out more time than a prosecutor is fighting for and unheard of when the defendant is a cooperating witness. Nor was Whitacre a garden-variety informant. He was the most productive informant in the history of antitrust enforcement. Brutal criminals, even murderers who testify against mobsters, routinely win leniency. Whitacre's transgressions against ADM were paper crimes, and the victim had been repaid.

Seated among his three lawyers, Mick Andreas blanched when he heard the sentence. The hammering of the snitch did not augur well for the principals.

The judge asked Whitacre if he had questions. He failed to answer immediately, then asked her to repeat the sentence. She read it back, wished him well, and terminated the call. He would not hear the sentencing of his codefendants.

Manning took Andreas next. Griffin said the "volume of commerce" again had been underestimated in the presentence report and had to be raised $25 million to $193 million. But this was unlikely to increase the punishment since the guidelines gave seven points for all crimes over $100 million.

Well-pressed, coiffed, and relaxed, Bray took the podium. With massive self-assurance, he seemed to re-argue the case. His client had been entrapped. Andreas could be "the first person in America" to be convicted of an antitrust offense based on sales volume allocation. The FBI shrewdly had kept its informant from confronting him directly about fixing prices. The tapes inexcusably were incomplete, and conversations likely pointing to innocence were missing. Actually, the "consumers reaped a tremendous benefit" from ADM's lysine venture.

He had a strong bond with the judge. She followed every word. He told her about a decision in which another federal court had approved a "downward departure" from the guidelines at a sentencing due to law enforcement misconduct. He reminded her that she had called the lysine investigation "not the government's finest hour."

Bray described his client as, at most, a marginal participant in the scheme especially in comparison with the Japanese who were "profligate price-fixers." As with Whitacre, the probation department saw Andreas as a manager of the crime. He wanted her to reject the finding.

The government sought the maximum three-year sentence. Bray presented lavishly colored, high contrast, jumbo poster boards reflecting that half of convicted price-fixers did not even go to jail.

Moreover, his client was a good family man, who raised a foster child with his own children, and was a help to his aging parents, a philanthropist, and a pillar of the community. He asked the judge to recall the numerous stirring letters she had received on behalf of his client, especially those from Andrew Young and Robert Strauss, who were the most prominent of his supporters.

Young praised Mick and his family's strong financial backing of civil rights. Strauss pooh-poohed the crime:

Market fights between US companies attempting to deal with the potentially destructive competition of Asian companies are, in my experience, seldom a product of greed. Rather they are more often an attempt to find ways to survive the onslaught of foreign industries who have often been protected by their own governments and allowed latitude to compete unfairly in the United States.

The government, insisted Bray, was seeking such bitter medicine for his client "because of his name. If his name was Michael Andrews they wouldn't be asking for it."

Though never resorting to drama, Griffin wanted the maximum sentence. All of the issues that Bray raised "were rejected by the jury." It was "very unfortunate that Andreas masterminded one of the largest antitrust conspiracies in history, causing harm and damage to businesses throughout the world." The defendant deserved an "upward departure" from the sentencing guidelines as an "organizer of the conspiracy." Moreover, the $193 million represented only the illegal dry lysine profits domestically. The worldwide conspiracy had grabbed over a billion dollars.

Manning said she would deal with Andreas' and Wilson's sentencing after she heard from both defendants. Weingarten ambled forward. His tack differed from Bray's. His client, he offered, would admit full responsibility. But Weingarten also felt hamstrung about discussing the crime because a grand jury in San Francisco still was investigating citric acid. The lawyer did not want to say anything that would be used against Wilson or lead to another indictment.

Weingarten began the battle for the nonincarceration of his client. The first argument was equal treatment for Wilson. The lawyer told Manning, "I've never understood how the Japanese competitors were less culpable" in lysine. Since none of the Japanese had done time, neither should his client.

The next theme involved Wilson's health. Mary Jo Wilson came to the stand. She had been married to the defendant for forty years, and they had raised four children. A former nurse with a pleasant, strong face, she would not cry or become maudlin. With Hulkower gently leading, she described the difficulty of testifying in front of a full courtroom. She was a private person. She disclosed that her husband's medical condition was dire. Sixteen years before he had gone into full cardiac arrest. Hulkower noted that Wilson "had been paddled back to life like on ER." Also, he had had a bypass. Now he had only one artery open, but his lungs were too weak to endure more surgery. His wife said he had frequent chest pain and sometimes fainted.

Wilson's retirement plans had centered on golf. But now she lamented that he could muster only four or five holes. Their country club even let him drive his cart off the paved paths and onto the fairways because walking had become so labored.

The weakness was aggravated by advanced pulmonary fibrosis. Her husband had begun smoking at ten or eleven and was fiercely addicted. He had quit "forty or fifty times" trying every remedy from nicotine patches to Prosac, but it was hopeless.

Plus, he was "in denial" about his health. Often he refused to get treatment. With a nursing background she could recognize the signs of acute cardiac distress and would call the cardiologist "behind his back," or cajole him into going to the emergency room. In prison, she feared, he would be stoic, so no one could intervene, and he would die.

She and her husband had "a deep commitment." The "stress of separation alone" would worsen his heart condition.

Though her private nature restrained her, she alluded to a family matter more fully spelled out in the papers filed by Wilson's lawyers. The couple's retarded thirty-five-year-old son lived at home. He was violent towards himself and others. With her husband, she could manage him. Without Terry, she could not. The government had no questions for Mrs. Wilson. She walked with her head down from the stand.

Hulkower gave the court a long disquisition on his client's heart and lungs based on the examinations of a fleet of eminent physicians including the president of the International Society of Cardiologists. "At forty," argued the lawyer, Wilson "had the heart of a sixty year old. Now at sixty-two, he has the heart of an eighty year old." One of the specialists had given Wilson a "one in five chance of having a major event" in the coming year.

Hulkower told Manning that Wilson was his first case in private practice after working as an assistant US attorney. Former prosecutors often try to get this edge for their clients, which of course has nothing to do with justice. In his long career, he had argued every conceivable legal motion. "But there is one motion I haven't argued until today. It's a little overwhelming. It's a plea for person's life. Mr. Wilson," he added, "does not have a famous name. He's not a famous person. But he's in a famous case. That's why the government is trying to get the maximum sentence."

James Mutchnick rose to defend the government's experts' opinions that Wilson's condition could be managed in a federal prison. As for Wilson's son, the situation was unfortunate, but there was no showing that he could not be maintained in an institution or by Mrs. Wilson with the help of family and friends.

Scott Lassar approached the court. Since the trial, a frisson of barely suppressed anger charged the air between the lawyer and Manning.

Lassar asked for the maximum of thirty-six months for Wilson and Andreas since both had "coordinated and orchestrated the vast conspiracy" to rig a billion-dollar market. It was "a worldwide crime, a brazen crime. . . . Every day in the United States disadvantaged young people who sell a handful of crack on a street corner go away for longer. In a sense, Judge, it's unconscionable that [Wilson and Andreas] can get only three years given the size of the crime."

Manning wasn't buying. She thought Wilson may have been more "verbose" than other conspirators. But, she saw him and Andreas as among "equals" rather than as managers in the lysine racket. Under the guidelines, this pronouncement, which ran afoul of the probation department's finding, translated into a three-level decrease and to a substantial reduction in the potential sentence.

The notion rocked Lassar. He tried to fire back facts to show that the defendants warranted manager status, including Wilson's schooling of the group in Hawaii, and Andreas' meeting with Ajinomoto's Yamada in Irvine to carve up the market before extending the scheme to the smaller producers. Besides, Whitacre and the Japanese informants had pleaded guilty as managers. Andreas and Wilson were Whitacre's superiors and had crafted the conspiracy in accordance with ADM's citric acid experience.

But Manning's mind was made up. She would not designate them managers and gave each seventeen points, one less than Whitacre. Their permissible sentences under the guidelines would be in the range of twenty-four to thirty months. Politely, Jim Griffin asked for the latter, since the volume of commerce nearly doubled the $100 million plateau necessary to trigger the maximum level. When the prosecutors returned to their seats, Lassar rolled his eyes.

Weingarten retook the floor. Glaring, he wheeled on the government table and particularly Mutchnick. "I hope no heartless, faceless bureaucrat ever says to them that their child can be warehoused in an institution." Calming himself, he told Manning that "without fanfare," Wilson had made a "substantial contribution" to the foundation Weingarten had set up to help troubled youth in Washington, DC. "He's a good, decent, effective man." With a lump in his throat the lawyer pleaded, "Send him home. Send him back to Decatur. Home detention, Your Honor."

Manning wanted to hear from the defendants. Mick Andreas approached the bench. In his rich, deep voice, he began, "I'm truly sorry for everything this trial and its outcome have meant." But this was not to be an apology. "I love this country and I thought I knew its rules. I did not want to commit a crime. I did not think I did commit a crime. I meant no harm." He thanked the judge for her courtesy and fairness during the trial.

It was an unusual statement for a white-collar defendant, impudent in its way. For one thing, sentencing is not normally the time to maintain innocence, which in fact Andreas had done, since the antitrust crimes require intent that he claimed to lack. For another, his complaint of being a victim of shifting rules suggested that ADM had consistently played by other rules that he "knew," and that products besides lysine had been rigged. Ordinarily, if a criminal defendant denied guilt at sentencing and implied a pattern of similar behavior, a judge would probe. But Manning did not challenge the remarks.

Wilson walked to the well of the court. His gait and bearing were surprisingly firm. He stood tall and gave the judge a sad smile. His voice was low-key, warm, and engaging. He obviously had been a good salesman and speaker at business group functions.

"When you find yourself in a hole," he began, "you quit digging. I have no intention of making it deeper and wider. I accept total and complete responsibility for my actions." He grasped the irony of his plight. He recalled that once he had been a witness in a federal trial. Twice he had served as a jury foreman. Now he had seen the system from the vantage point of a defendant and was "humbled by it." He thanked the judge for her thoughtfulness when he was ill during the trial.

Manning refused to give a "downward departure" to Wilson for his health and family reasons. She sympathized, but dislocation was the result of criminal convictions. "They take people out of circulation. I see such situations on a day-to-day basis."

The usual white-collar sentencing becomes a pulpit for the judge to conduct a public object lesson on the socially corrosive effects of economic crimes committed by people who already have plenty of money. But Manning said nothing along these lines. Nor did she chastise the defendants for their greed. Instead, she viewed each as "a wonderful family man" and member of the community, and, as a result, sentenced at the "low end of the range" giving both twenty-four months in custody. However, they would not report to the Bureau of Prisons until the fall. She fined each $350,000. Once imprisoned they would have to serve about 80 percent of the time, assuming good behavior. The prosecutors sat poker-faced. Smiles and signs of relief broke out at the defense tables.

Jack Bray rose to make a motion for bail pending appeal. The lawyer planned to focus on prosecutorial misconduct. Another issue was whether the government had properly introduced the citric acid testimony. The defense had filed a 1996 letter in which a federal prosecutor in San Francisco had promised Aubrey Daniel that the government would not make "direct or indirect use" of the information that Cox provided at his interviews with the FBI against "ADM or its employees." If Cox's testimony from the stand breached the understanding, then the appellate court could toss the convictions. The government insisted that Wilson and Andreas were excluded from the deal.

In any event, Manning wanted briefs before the proposed incarceration date in September about whether the defendants should stay free on bond. She told Bray that if he "needed more time, to let me know." Prison would be put off at least until the briefs came in.

Afterwards Weingarten was in fine spirits. Any sentence was too long for his client, but it could have been much worse if the government had thrown the book at the defendants, including numerous counts of mail fraud, wire fraud, and related counts. The single Sherman Act charge was a "tremendous gift." He thought that his client had a good chance of staying out on bond during the appeal. How long would an appeal last? He grinned, "Forever."

Lassar was not in a great mood. "Whitacre really got whacked."

It astonished David Hoech that the convicts did not leave the court in custody. "'If you need more time let me know!'" boomed Hoech echoing Manning's words to Bray. "What kind of shit is that?" He had never heard of defendants effectively setting their own jail dates. "Mick and Terry will never serve a day," he assured. "And the whistleblower gets ten years?"

Afterwards, the Department of Justice held a press conference in its camera friendly media center on the eleventh floor. Griffin and Lassar stood at the microphone. Behind them, prosecutors and FBI agents on the case fanned out in a row. Brian Shepard, who had left court with his jaw set grimly, was not in attendance. No one seemed particularly overjoyed. To the extent the mood of G-men and women can be perceived, this was one of relief that a heroic four-year struggle was over, mixed with unsatisfying twinges about whether the result warranted the sweat.

Griffin tried to make the best of it. While not the maximum, Judge Manning's sentence "will send a very serious message to those who may consider engaging in this kind of criminal activity. This was a reprehensible crime." He conceded that some antitrust offenders actually had gotten longer sentences, especially when they also were charged with mail fraud and wire fraud.

Asked why Wilson and Andreas had not been sentenced as conspiracy managers, Lassar mused, "I'm not sure why the judge did that." Nor could he explain why Whitacre had gotten the enhancement, beyond noting that Walker hadn't objected to it.

The prosecutors disputed Manning's decision not to invoke the alternative fine provisions because of an alleged failure of the government to cooperate. Griffin was adamant, "we don't feel we thwarted attempts to obtain information."

Whitacre's punishment led to questions about whether it would deter informants from coming forward. Lassar felt that it would not because the mole's situation was unique. The US Attorney added that "probably his cooperation resulted from his embezzlement scheme."

Fielding final questions, the prosecutors revealed that the grand jury in Atlanta, investigating criminal activity in high fructose corn syrup, had been shut down without indictments. But, the one in San Francisco probing citric acid still was active.

As for Yamada, the government failed to explain why he had not been extradited. But Griffin assured that he would not be fixing prices here. "Unless he goes to trial, it would not be in his best interests to come to the United States."

Later the sentences led to controversy in the media. While one Chicago business columnist termed Whitacre a "pinocchio with a PhD" who got what he deserved, this was a minority view. In the *New York Times*, John Coffee, Jr., a Columbia professor of corporate law, said he could not find "any shred of explanation" for deeming Whitacre a coordinator of the conspiracy, but not his supervisors, and tagging the mole with a heavier penalty. "It doesn't bode well for future whistleblowers."

Alan Guebert, the trenchant syndicated farm columnist who had covered the case from the beginning, also objected:

> If ever you stand trial in federal court as the ringleader of a global ag price fixing cartel, pray your trial is held before Judge Blanche Manning in federal court in Chicago.
>
> And if you are convicted of price fixing in Judge Manning's court, don't acknowledge your crime. Instead, stick to your story and say, "I didn't think I had committed a crime."
>
> That way, despite the prosecutor's request to hit you with 36 months in jail and a $25 million fine, you'll receive 24 months and a $350,000 fine.
>
> But if you are the whistleblower who delivers the key evidence to convict the ringleader, beat feet to Bolivia rather than stand still before Judge Manning because she'll thump you. Hard.

Guebert doubted whether the penalties meted out to Wilson and Andreas—"if they ever see prison walls from the inside"—would cause a corporate honcho to veer from the path of price-fixing. With credit for good behavior, the two "could spend as few as twenty months perfecting their tennis serves or tending roses in Club Fed." Indeed, he questioned whether the convictions even had cleansed the lysine trade:

> And yet life in the ag markets goes on: On June 25, the three major US lysine makers—ADM, BioKyowa and Heartland—all raised bulk lysine prices from 44 cents per pound to 59 cents per pound.
>
> Within minutes of each other.

Four days after the sentencing, Manning filed a written opinion. Without explanation, she seemed to harden towards business criminals. This time she noted "the court's fundamental obligation to never implicitly or explicitly disregard the severity of the crime. That is an especially serious concern with 'white-collar' offenses in which there is a popular but absolutely erroneous perception that the violation is minor."

Probably she was responding to the stern warning her superiors on the Seventh Circuit issued in a decision the previous month. The appeals court ruling, which she cited, raked the double standard of punishment:

[W]e take this opportunity to emphasize to the district judges of this circuit that no "middle-class" sentencing discounts are authorized. *Business criminals are not to be treated more leniently than members of the "criminal class" just by virtue of being regularly employed or otherwise productively engaged in lawful economic activity . . . [i]t is natural for judges*, drawn as they (as we) are from the middle- or upper-middle class, to sympathize with criminals drawn from the same class. But in this instance we must fight our nature. Criminals who have the education and training that enables people to make a decent living without resorting to crime are more rather than less culpable than their desperately poor and deprived brethren in crime.

Nevertheless, regarding Wilson and Andreas, she conceded that "the simple truth is that in the long run they will fare far better than the typical criminal defendant that appears before this court."

In the opinion, Manning once again took the opportunity to tweak the prosecution for failing to obtain information on the size of the market from the foreign price-fixers. "It will be interesting to observe whether the government will revoke some of those cooperation agreements in light of some of the foreign coconspirators' unwillingness to produce documentation necessary to calculate the alternative fines."

However, the government still maintained that the required data was produced. "We don't know what she's talking about," said Randy Samborn, a spokesperson for the US attorney's office in Chicago.

Finally, Manning wrote about her unusual decision to hit the mole harder than the other defendants:

Needless to say, this court is not persuaded that Whitacre deserves any reduction in sentence for his "aid." Whitacre is the major exception to the basic rule that cooperating witnesses deserve lesser sentences. Time and time again, the government must often rely on the aid of crooks and snitches to convict the guilty.

She made no effort to conceal her wrath towards the imprisoned convict:

Whitacre complained that he has received no form of aid from the government since being indicted before this court. Well, quite frankly, he should never have expected any after trying to play both sides of the fence. Recall, Whitacre lied to everyone about his embezzlement of ADM funds and attempts to extort money from the biotechnology espionage affair commonly referred to as the "Fujiwara Incident." And who could possibly forget about Whitacre's attempts to derail the entire lysine prosecution and save his own neck by claiming that he destroyed exculpatory evidence and/or hid it by sending it to his associate David Hoech.

Manning also minimized the impact of Whitacre's cooperation:

> But for the testimony of the other coconspirators and the videotapes which captured Andreas and Wilson in the act, the court is thoroughly convinced that the jury would have acquitted the defendants. Whitacre helped nobody but himself and prolonged this case to the detriment of the government and this court and now suffers a fate created by his own misguided greed, deceit, and outright theft!

The judge did not explain how Whitacre had prolonged the case. Neither his lawyer nor the government had sought delays due to his behavior. Moreover, the trial surely was shortened by his indictment, which resulted in his choice not to testify. If he had taken the stand, the cross-examination could have stretched the case by weeks.

In court, Manning had stated that the probation department could determine whether Whitacre needed mental treatment. Now, she directly ordered him to "seek assistance of psychiatric/psychological counselling." Why the defendant with mental problems would be punished more severely than someone without them is another lingering question.

The judge also dealt with the seeming discrepancy of giving Whitacre but not Wilson or Andreas the enhancement for being a conspiracy manager. It hinged on Whitacre's failure to object to the designation that appeared in the presentence report. She took special pains to insulate Walker from blame, finding "it incredibly important to note for the record that [he] diligently represented the best interests of his client."

She also wrote that "the court previously allowed Whitacre to ride on the coattails of Andreas and Wilson and gave him the benefit of favorable rulings that arguably should apply to all three defendants. That practice stops immediately!"

Her stewardship of the case had spanned almost three years and innumerable motions, hearings, court days, and rulings. Sentencing was the court's last and arguably most important chore. It was an odd time to be changing the rules.

THE MOLE—PART TWO

"You say why didn't we fire [Whitacre] on the spot?
We wanted our money back, for one reason. Nothing wrong with that."
—Dwayne O. Andreas

Edgefield, South Carolina, lies fifteen miles north of the Georgia line. It has fragrant peach farms, neat suburban split-level homes, and a weathered, genteel courthouse square. Its most famous son is Senator Strom Thurmond, and the federal government has been generous. On the two-lane highway into town is an arms depot with tanks in orderly rows. Turn left at the Chevy dealer, drive a half mile through low pines, and come to a clear-cut swath the size of an airport. To the right is a stark gray fortress with thick perimeter walls topped with razor wire. This is maximum security. To the left are medium and minimum security facilities. One is low-slung and looks like a rural community college. Because it has no walls, it is designated a prison camp. After a year of bouncing among correctional sites in Missouri, North Carolina, and Mississippi, Mark Whitacre wound up here.

The low security is apparent in the light, airy visiting room, where no one searches you and you can use real money to buy snacks and sodas rather than exchanging it at the entrance for tokens. You can stroll with an inmate out to the picnic area, which is pleasant enough except for the views of the neighboring lockups where the time is harder. The guards are friendly and helpful to children who need a bathroom. The couples hold hands or play cards. The atmosphere is relaxed. But for a first time visitor, it is nonetheless terrifying because these people seem like you, and you can see yourself here, your plans in smoke, your life irrevocably changed.

Three weeks after his sentencing by Judge Manning, Whitacre, forty-two, looked younger than he had on television following the raid in 1995. Losing the double-breasted tweeds, the tie, the job, and thirty pounds was part of it. He was ruddy from landscaping and fit from crunches, push-ups, weights, and a "veggie diet with a little tuna." His cholesterol was down more than a hundred points.

He wore a green shirt and matching trousers with a canvas belt, an outfit that looked like a boy scout uniform, without the merit badges, and immaculate white running shoes. His handshake was firm, and his smile quick and genuine. Lengthy meetings used to be a drag on his time. In prison he cherished them, not that he had languished in jail. Besides his landscaping job on the grounds, he had studied and acquired new degrees, pursued highly structured Bible study, tutored other inmates preparing for their general equivalency degree (GED) exams, and taken a correspondence course on becoming a writer.

With Judge Manning's sentence and without some mitigation from an appeals court or intervention by the Justice Department, he will be released in 2007, when he approaches fifty. Writing is just one possible career for when he gets out. He knows he has had an unusual life: international businessman, scientist, informant, defendant, and prisoner, which he might be able to convert into something readable. Another possibility that would draw upon his advanced degrees in law and psychology would involve becoming a jury consultant. Or, he could go back into business, but probably not for a large company like ADM. Sometimes he and his wife think about going abroad as missionaries.

A surprising result of prison has been that it has brought his family together. "When I was at ADM, work came first and I didn't see my kids enough. Now Ginger comes with them every Friday night, and also visits on Saturday and Sunday. We celebrate every holiday together. I think last Christmas was our best. We're a lot closer as a family now."

Ginger is the mainstay of the family. After her husband's firing, she went back to college and earned a degree in elementary education. In order to keep the family together, she moved to nearby Aiken, South Carolina, and took a job as kindergarten teacher.

He deeply regrets that his actions caused his family so much pain. "They're out there and I'm in here, but sometimes I think they're suffering more than I am." There were also things he regrets about the case. "My biggest mistake was not telling the FBI everything. I should have told them about the bonuses. It was also a big mistake for Brian Shepard not to push me harder about what was going on at ADM. But once the FBI had its antitrust case, they didn't seem interested in anything else."

Another nagging regret was that he had spoken to John Dowd, an ADM attorney, on the day after the raid. Whitacre believed that Dowd had been assigned to advise him confidentially and protect his rights. Dowd never told him that he would disclose his role as an informant. Whitacre also said that he liked Dowd and was impressed because the lawyer had investigated Pete Rose for major league baseball. But Dowd also did not tell him that he was a partner at Akin Gump. "That was Robert Strauss's law firm. I never would have talked to Dowd if I knew he was in it because Mr. Strauss was a director of ADM." Whitacre never spoke to Dowd after their meeting. So how did he learn that Dowd had exposed him? "I remember my pager went off. The number calling me was 424-5413, Howard Buffett. I called him. Howard said, 'Dwayne knows. John Dowd told him everything.'"

Whitacre recalled that he and Buffett had been good friends at ADM, and they and their wives socialized as couples. The bond between the two men was natural. Both were relatively young in the company. Both were nondrinkers, family men, and committed Christians in an atmosphere known for carousing. Both enjoyed tending to land and animals.

Whitacre stated that he told Buffett about being an informer about a year before the raid. Buffett was threatening to quit over a "large campaign irregularity" involving cash for an Illinois senatorial candidate. (ADM's flouting the campaign finance laws actually became evident on a surveillance tape when Mick Andreas advocated such excesses because the only downside was paying a "small fine.") According to Whitacre, Buffett was encouraged by Whitacre's clandestine work and its potential to clean up the company and so stayed with ADM.

Whitacre remembered that Buffett also was disturbed by some of Randall's remarks. The ADM president bragged that Dwayne Andreas had carried $100,000 to Washington in a briefcase for politicians during the Watergate era. Plus, Whitacre recalled that Buffett had heard Randall saying that he had authorized Reinhard Richter's off-the-books bonus. Whitacre said that Buffett quit when it became clear that his job in public relations would require him to trash his friend.

For a time after the raid, Buffett remained supportive. The Buffetts and Whitacres socialized in public and went out to restaurants in Decatur, which was daring during the summer of 1995. According to Whitacre, Buffett's father Warren, the legendary investor, even interceded with *Fortune* to convince it to run the 1995 cover piece on the mole. His logic was that it was important for "me to get out my story before ADM did." But then Whitacre became too hot, too much of a pariah, and Buffett kept his distance. Whitacre remains pained by the separation.

Whitacre did not regret his conduct in the Fujiwara affair that had been detailed so devastatingly against him at the trial. If he had testified, a different version would have emerged.

Shortly after ADM began making spoiled lysine, Randall, Andreas, and Whitacre concluded that there was no sabotage. "But then Mick learned that his father and cousin Allen had contacted the CIA, which brought in the FBI." It was an inopportune time for a federal probe. According to Whitacre, Mick still wanted to misappropriate the Ajinomoto technology by buying it from one of the Japanese company's employees, which was how ADM had snatched bacitracin. Also, the price-fixing conspiracy was afloat. According to Whitacre, Mick was upset with his father, whom he called an "asshole" for causing law enforcement attention.

"Mick told me to tell two lies. First, Fujiwara had contacted us, not the other way around. Second, it was on my OPX line." This was the ADM corporate phone in his home. "We didn't want them to look at private phone records." By this time the bills included numerous calls with Japanese lysine producers in the conspiracy.

But what about the allegation that Whitacre had used the Fujiwara affair to extort ADM? "It's not true. I wasn't trying to get money. If I needed money, I'd just go to Randall with an invoice."

One highly confidential document—the transcript of the November 12, 1996 grand jury testimony of Mark Cheviron—has surfaced that lends support to Whitacre's view of the Fujiwara affair. Cheviron, ADM's vice president in charge of security, was probed regarding discussions between ADM and the FBI in early November 1992 about using an FBI undercover agent to buy Ajinomoto's lysine producing organism for three million dollars. The marked cash would be advanced by the FBI to trap the Japanese extortionist. Cheviron then was asked if Mick Andreas expected ADM to be able to keep "any enzyme or micro-organism that was purchased as a result of this undercover operation?"

Cheviron responded, "The way he talked, he expected it." It was a remarkable reply. It corroborated Whitacre's position expressed in prison that Mick Andreas saw the Fujiwara affair as an opportunity to obtain a stronger lysine bug. Even more important, it showed that Mick wanted to entangle the government in a scheme to misappropriate the technology of Ajinomoto.

The grand jury learned that the plan progressed to the extent that the government drafted a contract under which ADM would compensate the FBI for any cash lost during the sting. But the covert operation never was carried out. The reason has to be that the FBI soon independently knew from Whitacre that there was no saboteur.

To the grand jury, Cheviron recalled a statement by Randall on November 5, 1992, that there was no sabotage in ADM's lysine plant, just "start-up problems." However, Cheviron did not relate this finding to the FBI until December 16, 1992.

Cheviron's only explanation for the delay in telling the FBI was that Whitacre, who had made the allegation of sabotage, was higher than Cheviron on the corporate ladder. But that made no sense since Randall, who had ruled out sabotage, was Whitacre's superior. A better explanation for ADM's delay was that the powers-that-be at the corporation hoped that the Fujiwara goose chase would distract the FBI for over a month from focusing on the real ongoing crime—price-fixing.

Cheviron further confirmed that he stopped the company's cooperation with the FBI's Fujiwara investigation when he became aware that the bureau intended to tap Whitacre's private residential line as well as the company installed OPX line on which the extortionist supposedly called. In the grand jury room Cheviron did not explain why tapping two of an employee's lines was so much worse than one. But tapping both lines meant that the FBI also would intercept the price-fixing conversations on Whitacre's private line. Cheviron testified that Randall, Mick, and Dwayne Andreas knew of his withholding cooperation from the FBI. Oddly, Cheviron was not questioned at all about Dwayne Andreas' knowledge of the reason for the rupture with law enforcement.

Cheviron did say that Mick Andreas knew that the FBI's proposed tapping of both of Whitacre's lines was the problem. Mick's awareness reflected that he probably knew about the price-fixing communications to Whitacre at this juncture. Not surprisingly, the grand jury indicted Mick.

When Cheviron was asked what he had told Randall about ceasing to cooperate with the FBI, the witness took the Fifth Amendment. That was very strange since the company had pledged total cooperation in its plea agreement of less than a month before. However, the federal prosecutor did not press Cheviron, and he was allowed to remain silent about evidence that could have shown the ADM's president's knowledge of price-fixing operations.

Regarding the bogus bonus scheme, Whitacre said, "I see it as tax fraud and money laundering but not an embezzlement case." He was willing to plead guilty since he deemed the activity wrong, but part of an overall climate of immorality at ADM in which others were taking off-the-books bonuses. Like Bill Walker, he maintained that an unreleased spring 1994 audio tape included a passage in which Mick Andreas made reference to the fake pay-off scheme.

Judge Baker's fraud sentence astonished him. Early on, the government had told his lawyer James Epstein "that I could do some time, say six months, but less than the main antitrust violators."

He remembered his meeting with the Department of Justice's fraud section attorneys at Epstein's office in Chicago in September 1995. "They were really interested in what was going on at ADM. I thought I was going to have the same kind of working relationship with them that I had during the antitrust investigation. About a month later, it really changed. They were only interested in what I did and what a few other people in the BioProducts Division did. The FBI didn't want to look into anything outside the division. They didn't want to see it as a corporate problem, which is what it was."

The only active piece of litigation that Whitacre still had was his civil case with ADM that began in 1996 when ADM demanded up to $30 million from him for embezzlement and breach of his fiduciary employment duties. He counterclaimed for at least $700,000, plus interest for wrongful discharge based on his firing as a whistleblower. The case was scheduled for a fall 1999 trial.

When we spoke in July 1999, he reported that ADM had proposed to drop its suit if he would drop his counterclaim and remain silent about the case. The offer did not attract him. He had no money left besides his pension and really nothing left to lose. He believed he could prove that the invoices were part of a pattern at ADM and not the real cause of his demise.

He insisted that his bonuses were logical. They meshed with the price-fixing scheme. In early 1992 he made clear that he did not want to work for Terry Wilson and was thinking of leaving ADM. Wilson "was not well-liked. Plus, it was a control issue." Mick Andreas proposed a substantial bonus, $1.5 million, so that Whitacre would stay and hook up with Wilson, the price-fixer.

In 1993, the company realized that the conspiracy was working. ADM went from losing $5 million a month on lysine to making about $5 million. Whitacre said Mick Andreas decided to give him a bonus equal to two weeks of the lysine profit, or $2.5 million. The following year when the monthly profit climbed above $7 million, he again got another half month's payoff or roughly $3.75 million.

Whitacre planned to subpoena Andreas whom he expected to take the Fifth Amendment. Also he would subpoena Liz Taylor, his former secretary at ADM, whom he said personally took the bogus invoices to James Randall for his signature. He expected her to testify. Taylor declines to talk to reporters. When she retired in 1996 after ten years, ADM gave her a separation package with an agreement that prevented her from speaking about the company. Such agreements are extremely rare in situations where no claims are pending. Taylor had not sued ADM, although perhaps she could have. Government records reflect that after failing to provide evidence against her ex-boss, Taylor was assigned to a factory job. Rather than accept the transfer, the elderly secretary quit.

Whitacre also planned to subpoena Lou Rochelli, an ADM accountant and former friend. Now based at an ADM joint venture called Golden Peanut in Georgia, Rochelli had worked in the Decatur headquarters in 1995. Shortly after the raid, according to Whitacre, Rochelli called him at home to warn that Randall had told the accounting department precisely where to find the phony invoices.

Rochelli did not return my calls. If Rochelli would corroborate Whitacre's statements at trial, the impact could be great. His testimony could help prove that Randall knew plenty about the invoices and how they could be used to hurt the mole. In addition, it would call into question why the invoices had not been discovered until Whitacre had been exposed as an informant, and how ADM suddenly had known just where to find them in its ocean of largely legitimate purchasing paper, a search that under normal circumstances could have taken weeks, if not months.

Another potential witness was Thomas Frankel, the former treasurer of ADM.

He resigned suddenly in 1991, on the day ADM failed to file its annual report with the Securities Exchange Commission (SEC) because of unreported losses of $6.49 million in a series of trading transactions over the previous *four years*. In 1991, ADM refused to discuss the resignation except to say that the losses "may reflect a lapse in internal controls which has been remedied."

Whitacre maintained that Frankel and Mick Andreas were close friends and that the millions were covertly funneled to Frankel, who never was prosecuted but was merely let go when ADM could not meet SEC standards. He named Frankel to the fraud section in 1995. Frankel could not be reached for comment.

Then there was another top manager, referred to as K. According to Whitacre, ADM hired him away from another ag processing company. Then K was used to fix prices of compounds called soy isolates with employees from that company. Whitacre said Mick Andreas told him that K received so much money in phony bonuses from ADM that he was able to retire young. Whitacre also reported this to the fraud section. K, who has established a protein company in Kentucky, declined to return phone, fax, and e-mail messages.

How did Whitacre learn to make complex foreign financial transactions using offshore banks to park and launder money? Whitacre rejected any suggestion that he acquired the expertise while working for Degussa in Europe. "I only had a regular checking account in West Germany when I worked for Degussa. I never dealt with Swiss banks or anything like that." Support for his position comes from the fact that the FBI and IRS, which assembled all of Whitacre's offshore banking documents, do not seem to have found anything before 1991 when he already had been an ADM employee for almost two years. Whitacre viewed offshore banking as part of ADM's secretive corporate culture.

Whitacre claimed to have had two mentors in foreign finance. One was Ronald Ferrari, who had worked for ADM in Decatur, Rotterdam, and London, and reported to K. Whitacre described Ferrari as "a good friend and very ambitious marketing manager who told me about overseas bonuses." Ferrari incorporated a dummy company, Far East Specialists (FES). ADM paid a phony invoice from FES for $1.5 million. The money was run through a Swiss bank account in Hong Kong that Ferrari had set up. Also, Ferrari wired over a million dollars from the account to Whitacre's bank in the Cayman Islands and over a hundred thousand to Reinhard Richter's bank in Houston.

What did Ferrari get in exchange for his services? During his deposition on January 27, 1998, in the *ADM v. Whitacre* civil case, Ferrari was adamant that Whitacre had not paid him for the use of the Swiss bank account that Ferrari had opened on March 1, 1992. However, Ferrari was shown a check for $3,500 that he had deposited. It was made out to him by Mark Whitacre on February 27, 1992. Ferrari professed, "I don't remember this."

Perhaps more amazingly Ferrari swore that he did not know that $1.5 million that passed through his Swiss account had belonged to ADM. But his bank statement, also presented at the deposition, plainly indicated that the money came from "Archer Daniels Midland Company," that it was drawn on ADM's bank—National City Bank of Minneapolis—and that the amount was intended for "regulatory services." Ferrari knew that his company never provided any services. At the deposition he claimed that his Swiss bank did not send him his account statements, so he had no idea that ADM money was washing through the account. He also claimed that $25,000 in interest free loans that he received from Whitacre in 1993 (and did not repay until two years later) were totally unrelated to the Hong Kong machinations.

At the deposition, ADM had lawyers present from Williams & Connolly and from the company's local firm in Decatur. An aggressive attorney could have cross-examined Ferrari to a frazzle. But ADM's lawyers were content to let the witness' assertions of ignorance and innocence slide, preferring instead to allow Ferrari to portray himself as Whitacre's violated friend.

During his testimony, Ferrari revealed that he had never been called before the grand jury in central Illinois that had indicted Whitacre and Richter. Ferrari was part of the infrastructure of the money laundering and easily could have been indicted. Also, he could have answered questions about Kilburn or Randall. Not bringing him before the grand jury was inexcusable from a law enforcement standpoint and called into question the legitimacy of the fraud investigation.

Ferrari appeared to have had some sort of star status in Decatur. Once a football hero at nearby Moweaqua High, he later starred at the University of Illinois and played for the San Francisco 49ers. After getting an MBA and joining ADM, he became close to Jim Randall and seriously dated the ADM president's daughter, according to Whitacre.

The fact that Ferrari has remained unindicted and unsued buttressed Whitacre's contention that an ADM favorite could launder company money off-shore without being punished. My phone calls to Ferrari left with his secretary at his current employer, Household International, in Prospect Park, Illinois, went unreturned.

Another problem with Ferrari's deposition was that Bill Walker did not attend and therefore was not able to ask questions. Only ADM's lawyers, Ferrari, and his counsel were present. In fact, Walker did not depose any of the witnesses to the alleged fraud. Apparently, his and his client's low-budget strategy was to wing it at trial.

Whitacre said his second mentor was a Swiss named Beat Schweizer. "After I was at ADM for a couple of years, I went to a dinner at Dwayne Andreas' house. Mick said it was time that I started getting off-shore bonuses. But I didn't know any foreign bankers. Dwayne's brother Lowell was there. He lived part of the year in the Cayman Islands. He gave me Beat's name. I met with Beat when I was on vacation in the Caymans. He was very discreet. When I said I got his name from Lowell Andreas, he wouldn't say whether he knew Lowell or not. He was a good Swiss banker."

Holding a power-of-attorney from Whitacre, Schweizer incorporated a phony holding company called ABP Consulting, Ltd. and opened an account at the Union Bank of Switzerland. He also established an account at the Caledonian Bank and Trust Limited in the Cayman Islands. Over $6 million of the phony bonuses were invoiced under the APB name and went into these accounts. Government documents reflect that Schweizer personally profited. Schweizer transferred $100,000 of the invoiced funds into his own Swiss account on February 6, 1995. Like Ferrari, Schweizer never was charged by the government; nor was he extradited to appear before the grand jury. Indeed in the papers filed against Whitacre, the fraud section seemed extremely protective of Schweizer, referring to him only as "the Swiss financial advisor."

After Whitacre told the government about the bonuses, he began cooperating by taking steps to freeze his domestic and foreign bank accounts. To this end he called Schweizer and faxed him articles about the antitrust investigations. "Beat seemed surprised that I went against ADM in the price-fixing case. He made comments that it was better if we did not communicate anymore."

In addition, Whitacre hoped to subpoena Steven Mills, the controller, who was ADM's representative at the corporate guilty plea on lysine and citric acid in October 1996. Mills has an interesting corporate lineage. He worked under Thomas Frankel until the 1991 SEC filing fiasco and supervised Lou Rochelli at the time the bogus Authorization for Expenditures (AFE's) suddenly were "found" in July 1995 shortly after the raid.

As controller, Mills would have known the ADM invoice approval protocol. Whitacre had approval power only for expenditures up to $50,000 before November 1, 1992 and up to $100,000 afterwards. James Randall could approve expenditures up to $250,000. Above $250,000, an AFE required at least five signatures including that of the employee requesting payment, Randall and the chief financial officer or controller (Mills); and those of Dwayne, Mick, or G. Allen Andreas before submission to the board of directors. Approval by the board was shown by the signatures of Richard P. Reising, the vice president/general counsel and secretary/treasurer; and by that of a nonemployee board member such as Robert Strauss, Brian Mulroney, or F. Ross Johnson. Most of Whitacre's larger AFE's had five signatures. Randall has maintained that Whitacre photocopied his signature onto forms without the ADM president's permission. No one else in the company's authorization hierarchy has made similar claims.

Mills, as controller, allowed a $1.5 million wire transfer to Ferrari's Swiss bank in Hong Kong without any of the other necessary signatures besides Whitacre's.

Whitacre told me that Mills balked at first. "He said, 'we're too big a company for this; we're a public company.' I told him to ask Randall if he had any questions."

David Hoech, who has followed the AFE question closely, said, "Mills has a lot of explaining to do. There's no legitimate public company that simply wires a million dollars to a Swiss bank account." Whitacre expected that Mills would take the Fifth Amendment in a trial. Then there's Randall. In the bankruptcy petition filed with the assistance of Walker and Richard Kurth, another Southern Illinois attorney, Mark and Ginger Whitacre provided an intriguing entry in the schedule pertaining to "Creditors Holding Unsecured Non-priority Claims." Randall was listed as a creditor for "$500,000 of husband's debt." The money was "held initially in Hong Kong Account. Now in Palmer Bank, Danville, IL."

According to Whitacre, of the $1.5 million Far East Specialists bonus, "$500,000 was Jim's." This was a kickback to the then-president on a phony invoice that Whitacre said Randall had approved.

Making a false statement on a bankruptcy petition or one of its included schedules is a serious matter. In fact, it is a felony exposing the petitioner, and possibly his attorney, to five-years imprisonment and a $500,000 fine. Bankruptcy fraud is not a difficult offense to prove. Whitacre was not popular with ADM. It is fair to say that the corporation did its best to have the book thrown at him so he would go away for a long time. The indictment included forty-five charges but none for bankruptcy fraud or perjury. According to Whitacre and Walker, ADM also did not include the Randall entry in its many challenges to the petition. So Whitacre wanted to put his corporate father figure on the stand.

Whitacre stressed that the statements of Dwayne Andreas also supported his case. Andreas was famous for avoiding the press and letting others do his talking including farmers, loyal retainers, and politicians. But occasionally, he would give an interview and his brashness would come through.

For instance in "Dwayne's World," a thoughtful *Mother Jones* piece by Dan Carney that appeared shortly before the raid, Andreas joked about price-fixing in other countries and mocked free enterprise, "There isn't one grain of anything in the world that is sold in a free market. Not one! The only place you see a free market is in the speeches of politicians. People who are not in the Midwest do not understand that this is a socialist country."

Andreas became expansive for a 1996 profile by Peter Carlson in the *Washington Post Magazine*. When the talk turned to Whitacre, Andreas' long-time executive assistant Claudia Madding asked, "is this off-the-record?" The article continued:

"Well, no," Andreas says. "It's in the press, what I'm saying. It's in the press."

He continues his story. "We found that he had stolen millions and millions of dollars very, very cleverly. He made up elaborate contracts, forged our president's signature time after time. . . . And when we caught him, the first thing we saw was that he had a deal we thought was illegal—I thought was illegal—with the Japanese." It was "a deal for sabotage in the lysine business," he says. "We immediately went to the government and reported it. We went to the CIA because it was international."

The CIA called in the FBI. When Whitacre heard about the FBI's investigation, he panicked, Andreas says. "He had told us, for example, that the Japanese were going to kidnap his daughter. . . . So we immediately got our general counsel and director of security into his office, and he admitted that was all a fabrication." (Whitacre denies that he ever concocted a kidnapping plot.)

And so, Andreas says, he knew that Whitacre had stolen millions of dollars, conspired with the Japanese, and invented a bogus kidnap plot. And yet he did not fire him until nearly three years later. Why?

"After we found out he was a crook, we had to be very careful how we handled it," Andreas says, "because we had the FBI and we had to do whatever we thought was the right thing. We did all the things you're supposed to do. . . ." A few minutes later, he returns to this topic: "You say why didn't we fire him right on the spot? We wanted to get our money back, for one reason. Nothing wrong with that. As a result of that, we got $6 million frozen in Switzerland, and in Grand Cayman we have frozen one and one-half million dollars."

Andreas' explanation made no sense. The money that Whitacre moved offshore belonged to the shareholders. By late 1992, he already had taken $2.8 million. To allow him to hold it for three years meant he could spend it, invest it, or hide it in a hundred ways. Also, he could keep stealing. A prudent CEO who discovered embezzled money would have reported it promptly to the FBI so that it could be impounded immediately, and the thief could be stopped. There are only two logical explanations for Andreas' behavior: either he did not think the funds were stolen (in other words they were approved) or he didn't care. Like many who question the fraud section's hasty conclusion that ADM did not bless his bonuses, Whitacre found the *Post* interview "key."

"Dwayne admitted that he knew of the bonuses in 1992. If not approved, then why did he promote me to corporate vice president in November 1992, send a letter that I would be the next president of ADM in May 1995, give me 70,000 shares of stock options, the second most in the company after Mick, and increase my salary to $320,000? That's a lot to do for a guy that he was supposedly trying to get rid of." It was certainly an unprecedented way to punish a thief.

Thoughts of the corporate heights Whitacre had reached triggered memories of his importance to the FBI during the antitrust investigation. "I really felt like part of the team." The FBI even had relied on him to pick the night of the raid. "It had to be a time when Mick, Terry, Dwayne, Barrie Cox, and I all were in Decatur. Since we all travelled so much I had to check all of their schedules. June 27, 1995 was a good time because they were in town for a meeting."

He had performed countless other services large and small for the government. "When the Japanese government wouldn't let the FBI tape in Japan, Brian Shepard made his preferences clear. He said he would be disappointed if I didn't tape. I knew there was a chance that I'd get in trouble with the Japanese government, but I still decided to do it."

Not surprisingly, Whitacre felt unappreciated and at times devastated by his heavy sentences. He thought Judge Manning did a good job at the trial but unduly minimized his impact in her sentencing order when she credited the conviction to the coconspirators' testimony. "None of them would have cooperated with the government, if I hadn't gotten them on tape first."

Nevertheless he was quick to admit that he chose to plead guilty. "I shouldn't have taken shareholder money." He was willing to accept some punishment but he believed his was disproportionate and failed to account for his service. "Whistle-blowers," he sighed, "aren't all good. They make mistakes. They're human."

He returned to his own conduct. To Whitacre it was part of existing in a confusing moral vacuum after the straightforward business atmosphere at Degussa.

"It was very materialistic at ADM. I liked Jim Randall a lot. But he was always talking about his three Ferraris. He bragged to Ginger that 'we're going to make your husband a wealthy man.' This was early on. Once, we ran into him at a children's clothing store in Decatur. He said the same thing and that I would have the Ferrari parked outside. It seemed inappropriate in front of my son."

He revealed how close he came to not helping the FBI initially. On the night of November 4, 1992, as Shepard sat outside in the car, Whitacre asked Ginger what to do. "She convinced me to go through with it, to tell him about the price-fixing. She said it was the right thing. She talked to Brian that night, too. I knew it would be hard, but I didn't know how hard."

Even after days of intimate conversation with Whitacre, it was difficult to trust him a hundred percent. This was not because his explanations about Fujiwara and the off-the-books bonuses have altered over the years. (For instance, at his sit-down with the fraud section in September 1995, he did not say that Mick Andreas had tied his $2.5 and $3.75 million bonuses to half of monthly lysine profits. Rather, he stated that Andreas had explicitly approved only early kickbacks and permitted him to take others without informing the vice chairman in advance.) But, time can cause stories to shift.

ADM fixed markets on a worldwide basis. It cheated us all. The fact that Whitacre took advantage of such a company was not the block that kept me from believing him completely. Rather, it was the fact that he had broken faith with those on his side who had tried to help, his psychiatrist and his lawyers. I liked Mark Whitacre, applauded his contribution to antitrust law enforcement, and admired the way he coped with his broken life and disproportionate punishment. But I never entirely got past the fear that he might forge another piece of stationery, perhaps even mine.

Before visiting was over, the best-known informer in the annals of white-collar crime remembered a time early in the summer of 1995 when there were back channel phone calls with ADM about burying the hatchet and joining forces against the FBI. On July 13, 1995, he received a fax from Richard Reising, ADM's vice president, secretary, and general counsel, indicating that Aubrey "Daniel is on his way to meet with you at the office in the ADM Hanger (sic) at 1 PM for as long as necessary." The clandestine airfield rendezvous, which sounded like something out of *Casablanca*, was objected to by James Epstein, Whitacre's lawyer at the time, and never occurred. "Looking back," mused Whitacre, "I sometimes wish I had gone to that meeting. I wonder what would have happened."

THE SCORE

*"He's [Whitacre] one of the most productive informants in history
and one of the most courageous. He stood up to two eight-hundred-
pound gorillas—ADM with the Andreases and the federal government.
This was one of the most important antitrust cases of the century.
It certainly was the most important to agriculture."*
—Nicholas Hollis

Less than a week after I left Edgefield, federal judge Michael P. McCuskey, who had taken over *ADM v. Whitacre* when Judge Baker retired, issued rulings on the corporation's claims and Whitacre's counterclaims. On August 5, 1999, McCuskey announced his satisfaction that Whitacre's 1997 guilty pleas to thirty-seven counts proved that he had engaged in "fraudulent transactions beginning in 1991 and continuing into 1995, which caused ADM to pay a total of $9,538,694.00 for services it never received." At the criminal sentencing, Baker tacked $1,865,004.00 in interest on top of that for a total restitution order of $11,403,698.00.

Now McCuskey granted summary judgment to ADM on its civil claim against the prisoner. Since Whitacre had been a "fiduciary employee" and "a corporate officer in a position of trust," he was entitled to compensation only for the "faithful performance of his duties." Therefore, McCuskey ordered Whitacre to reimburse ADM additionally for his salary and benefits during the period of his criminal conduct, which totaled $1,174,167.52.

However, McCuskey failed to do ADM's bidding on a novel issue. The corporation remained apoplectic about the tapes and their potential release. It therefore proposed a sweeping injunction to prevent

Mark E. Whitacre, his agents, his servants, his employees, his attorneys, and any person in active concert or participation with him or them who receives actual notice of this order, from using, disclosing, or divulging or endeavoring to use, disclose, or divulge the tapes made by Whitacre of internal ADM conversations, copies of the tapes, information stored on the tapes or copies thereof, or any information derived directly or indirectly from the tapes. The Court further commands Mark E. Whitacre, his agents, his servants, his employees, his attorneys, and any person in active concert or participation with him or them who receives actual notice of this order, to deliver any tapes, copies of the tapes, or other documents or things containing any intercepted information to the Court for placement under seal or destruction.

The order requested by ADM amounted to an end run around the First Amendment and a device allowing the company to control the flow of information. McCuskey found it ridiculous. Many of the tapes were in the public domain. Moreover, ADM "has failed to portray itself as the innocent victim of Whitacre's wrongdoing. The Court notes that, based in part on the tape recordings made by Whitacre, ADM pleaded guilty to price-fixing and paid a fine of $100 million." McCuskey likewise chided the corporation for trying to induce him to wield judicial power against unnamed people. "The Court reminds ADM that Whitacre is the only party defendant in this action."

Then McCuskey dismissed Whitacre's claim for wrongful discharge against ADM. The judge chastised Whitacre and his attorney for utterly failing to comply with court rules in the response to ADM's motion for summary judgment by providing "no statement of why any of the facts were in dispute and no citation to discovery material or affidavits" as well as "little reasoned analysis explaining why summary judgment should not be granted." The judge adopted ADM's logic that it should be allowed to fire an employee whose conduct resulted in a conviction on thirty-seven counts.

Probably ninety-nine out of a hundred American judges would have granted summary judgment to ADM on Whitacre's discharge case. For Whitacre and Walker to believe that they could prosecute such a claim after a guilty plea was peculiar at best. But, to think they would be permitted to go to trial in such a novel case without making a showing to a judge that they had strong evidence in the form of depositions and affidavits was legal lunacy. McCuskey was a new judge inheriting a caseload. He probably saw an old, unprepared claim on his desk and decided to pitch it. No appeals court would fault him for it.

Afterwards, Walker made self-justifying remarks to the press that ADM had blocked discovery, the formal pretrial investigation process. "There's a stone wall put up. They [ADM] had all the guns and all the bullets." In fact, Walker had subpoena power and had not used it to take depositions. Whitacre never would have a chance to prove to a jury that the company allowed off-the-books bonuses.

Nevertheless, the notion of wider fraud will not go away. In a case that lasts for years, embroils a company as controversial as ADM, and includes rival factions of the government, there are bound to be leaks. A confidential government document, the presentence investigation (PSI) of the US Probation Office, gave some credence to Whitacre's claim of high-level company approval.

Whitacre and Walker long had insisted that Randall had approved Reinhard Richter's shady start-up cash. Richter denied the allegation in 1997 before he pleaded guilty in exchange for a small fine and nonreporting probation. However, the PSI reflected that Richter initially told a far different story to federal agents:

> During an interview with the FBI on November 8, 1995, Reinhard Richter provided a copy of an ADM memorandum that indicated his compensation package with ADM included a $50,000 start-up bonus. According to Richter, the question of a bonus was discussed at a meeting at which Dr. Whitacre and ADM president James Randall were present and which took place in Randall's office. According to Richter, Dr. Whitacre and Randall agreed Richter would receive a start-up bonus that would be in addition to the $50,000 bonus listed in an ADM memorandum dated November 8, 1991. Richter further stated that James Randall advised that the additional bonus would be paid in a "special way" so that other ADM employees would not be aware of it. Randall indicated that Dr. Whitacre would handle the details of the bonus.
>
> Richter further indicated that he eventually negotiated a $240,000 start-up bonus and that $190,000 of that amount would not appear on ADM's books. Ultimately, Dr. Whitacre devised a plan to pay the bonus through the creation of bogus invoices which Richter prepared at Dr. Whitacre's direction.

However, the document went on to explain Richter's change of heart in 1997.

> Randall was unaware of the bonus. According to Richter, Dr. Whitacre contacted him prior to his interview with the FBI in November 1995 and had directed Richter to make it appear that Randall was aware of the bonus so that Dr. Whitacre alone would not be responsible for diverting funds.

On October 17, 1995, more than three weeks before his FBI interview, the *Wall Street Journal* carried Richter's comments, including that Randall "absolutely" had approved of the off-the-book bonus. Whitacre either coached Richter in time for the interview, or Richter changed the facts later.

Other evidence that Richter felt the money was properly approved appeared on his tax return. He reported the entire amount, including the laundered portion, to the German government, suggesting that at the time he believed the money was legitimate corporate income.

Probably the most meaningful early evidence was Richter's letter of December 4, 1990, accepting a position with ADM in Mexico. Writing on the stationery of Aminac, his purported consulting firm, Richter noted earlier discussions involving himself, Whitacre, and Randall in Decatur. After confirming his salary and February 1, 1991 starting date, Richter wrote:

> Furthermore, you and Mr. Randall stated that it will cost you about US $150,000 to get bacitracin approved in Mexico. During my two days in Decatur, we agreed that my company, Aminac Mexico S.A. de C.V. will take the project over and that you will cancel the other contractor that you were about to agree with to do this. I agreed that I can get approval for ADM in Mexico for about US $95,000 to 100,000. (1/3 cheaper). and to get approval also quicker (by end of 1991 instead of 1992).

Aminac never performed any service for ADM. The idea was merely a ploy to let Richter send phony bills to ADM that produced his off-the-books bonuses. Obviously, the German felt that it was important before taking the job to confirm in writing Randall's role in the hiring negotiations. In the end, Richter switched to the story that won him freedom and safe passage back to Mexico. It was the one that implicated Whitacre alone rather than Randall and Whitacre.

Did the fraud section improperly use sticks and carrots to obtain guilty pleas? It is an open secret that former ADM BioProducts vice president Sidney Hulse, who also received a signing bonus from Whitacre involving fake invoices, long held himself out to be innocent in the belief that management had approved the money. He felt squeezed to plead guilty.

When Hulse was balking at a plea deal, the government offered Whitacre a shorter sentence if he would testify against Hulse, but Whitacre and Walker refused because they believed the prosecutors wanted false testimony. Whitacre got the longer sentence. Richter, however, agreed to testify against Hulse. Facing the possibility of a long sentence if convicted, Hulse pleaded guilty on May 29, 1998 to ten months confinement and $995,000 in restitution.

The charge of embezzlement was particularly odd in Hulse's case because he was still in friendly contact with Randall after he was fired but before he was indicted. On April 2, 1996, Hulse mailed a letter to Randall stating that his off-the-book compensation "had approval by ADM's top management." Nevertheless, the cloud of alleged misconduct was keeping him from getting a new job. Hulse concluded with a request:

> If you could find it in your heart to drop me a note that will give me some peace of mind that the funds I received were not embezzled, it would be deeply appreciated. Your thoughts, recommendations, and leads toward any future employment would be appreciated, as well.

On Saturday, April 6, 1996, Randall called Hulse and invited him to meet the next time Hulse was in Decatur to discuss the letter. No date was set. Nine days later on Monday, April 15, 1999, David Hoech was on the phone with FBI agent Michael Bassett. (Hoech later would accuse Bassett of being in ADM's pocket because of earlier cooperation between the agent and the company during the Chicago Board of Trade sting. But for now the relations between the activist and Bassett were civil.) Hoech knew about the Hulse-Randall contacts and mentioned them to Bassett, along with the fact that Hulse had given him a copy of the letter to Randall. The FBI agent insisted upon obtaining Hulse's letter immediately and threatened to have fraud section attorney Donald Mackay subpoena it. Hoech said that was unnecessary and faxed it to Bassett.

The next day, April 16, 1996, Hulse received a stiff letter from Randall that was carbon copied to Aubrey Daniel (who may have written it) and to Hulse's attorney Sheldon Zenner. Randall accused Hulse of "misconduct" involving "embezzled funds" told him to make restitution and stated that any future discussions would involve ADM's lawyers. There would be no further informal contacts.

Ultimately, one other ADM employee defendant, Marty Allison, a BioProducts vice president who had drawn off-the-books payments with Whitacre's help, was punished with probation. Besides Whitacre, none of those prosecuted was hit with a heavy sentence. Significantly, Whitacre was the only whistleblower among the group.

More evidence of officially sanctioned fraud has come from a former ADM employee who spoke on the condition of anonymity. Despite a long career and good work record, the source remained terrified of the company. This individual saw AFE's circulate for signatures among executives, including Randall. In addition, this person recalled Randall's signature in ink on an AFE form for technology that ADM never received. However, Randall has insisted that his actual signature did not appear and that Whitacre had photocopied it from another document and inserted it onto the authorization form.

Why is this so important? Randall was integrally involved with new ADM technology. He would be aware of which large bills from vendors were legitimate and which were invoiced for nonexistent services and products. As he has indicated in court papers, this was because he knew all the major purveyors. So, for example, he has admitted that the "Applied Biotechnology Products" invoice for $3.75 million that was wired to a Swiss bank for vitamin C technology made no sense, since there was no such company in that field. Yet, his signature appeared on the copy of the AFE in court records. Randall insisted his signature was xeroxed.

It is no mean trick to photocopy a signature from one document and line it up precisely on another. Moreover, such chicanery can be readily discovered by modern digital document analysis. Unfortunately, court records do not reflect that the FBI performed any such tests.

The anonymous source was interviewed briefly by the FBI in 1995 but inexplicably never called before the fraud grand jury operating in central Illinois. Yet, the individual's evidence was sufficiently significant that the Justice Department issued an invitation for the person to come to Washington to discuss it. The source claimed that ADM learned of the proposed Washington trip, although it was unclear how. Nevertheless, after ADM found out about it, the invitation was cancelled without explanation, and the source never went to Washington.

Lack of interest at Justice about the approval of fraud at the highest levels in ADM was suggested by another internal government document that surfaced in a 1999 court filing. This was the FBI 302 memorandum of the interrogation of Barrie Cox on October 12, 1996.

The document had an interesting origin. In October 1996, corporate guilty plea negotiations heated up between the Department of Justice and ADM, whose principal negotiator was Aubrey Daniel. The company was attracted by the possibility of a highly discounted fine on citric acid and sweeping immunity for the acts of all but two employees, Terry Wilson and Mick Andreas. The government naturally wanted to know if ADM would be candid about price-fixing involving itself and its competitors. Justice would not sign off without assurances that ADM's "cooperation" would be complete.

In order to make the deal, the government required a litmus test. Since before the search, it had known that Barrie Cox was a knowledgeable actor in the upper echelons of international price-fixing. Now it wanted to hear from him. If his singing were satisfactory, ADM could have the deal.

ADM was skittish about the arrangement. As the final negotiations were under way, it refused to tell the FBI precisely where Cox was, except to say that he was in the San Francisco Bay Area. Finally, the last details were nailed down on Friday evening, October 11, 1996. Cox met with the FBI that night and the following day. He informed extensively and in the government's view candidly. "He certainly wasn't happy about it," said Jim Griffin, "but he was truthful." The result was a twenty-five page, single-spaced FBI 302 form that made ADM's guilty plea and immunity deal fly the following Tuesday in Judge Castillo's Chicago courtroom.

Nearly all of Cox's information dealt with antitrust issues. The 302 mentioned only a single unrelated situation with possible criminal overtones:

> On one occasion, Cox talked with Mick Andreas about some "strange payments" on MSG technology. This occurred at the time the Whitacre embezzlement came to light. Andreas said he'd look into it. It was later decided that the payments were not improper.

ADM's conclusion that the payments were clean was highly suspicious. The paper trail for Richter's invoice involving MSG contained dead giveaways that it was phony. First, ADM received nothing in return for paying for it. Second, MSG was not even a product that Richter handled. Was Richter's bogus MSG payment among those that Mick Andreas looked into and later decided was not improper? If so, then the fraud had the blessing of upper management as Whitacre claimed.

More fundamentally, it appears that the Justice Department did not go beyond Andreas' blithe comments about the expenditures. The government already believed in 1996 and would later prove that Andreas was a felon. Who was he to judge whether "strange payments" were proper?

Other charges of government laxity surfaced in the spring of 1999 following hearings on agribusiness concentration and monopolization in St. Paul, Minnesota. By and large the discussions focused on the power of the few huge remaining shippers and processors, such as ADM, to strangle the producers. Many angry farmers and ranchers were present, as were officials of the Departments of Agriculture and Justice and two senators, Tom Harkin of Iowa and Paul Wellstone of Minnesota.

Joel Klein, the deputy attorney general and chief of the antitrust division, was introduced by Wellstone as the lawyer who "supervised and signed off on the ADM plea bargain." This was surprising since Klein declined to be interviewed in the fall of 1997. Saying "I really didn't have very much to do with it," he referred this reporter to Gary Spratling.

Klein told the audience in St. Paul that he was there "to listen." But his introduction spurred questions about the ADM guilty plea. A spectator asked why ADM had not been "debarred" or cut off from USDA contracts following its felony convictions for citric acid and lysine in 1996.

Debarment from government funding is fairly standard, especially after proven criminal conduct. Twenty years before ADM had been debarred after it engaged in bid rigging of products for the Food for Peace program. Sun-Diamond Growers, a big California fruit and nut growing cooperative convicted in 1996—three weeks before ADM's plea—for giving "improper gifts" to then-agriculture secretary Mike Espy, was debarred. So was Mark Whitacre in 1997 following his guilty plea to tax fraud, money laundering, and related counts.

Financially and politically ADM was close to the USDA. At the time of its plea, it held $83.5 million in annual federal contracts in programs ranging from school lunches, to nutrition for Native Americans, to Food for Peace, (where ADM had 31.5 percent of the total business) to grain storage. It was banned from none of them.

Another St. Paul panelist, Undersecretary of Agriculture Michael Dunn, entered the fray, saying he might "need Joel's back-up on this."

What we do is we have an opportunity to debar industries or companies that are found guilty of criminal wrongdoing. In this particular case, that was part of the plea bargain that they came forward with. . . . One of the things ADM asked for was they would not be debarred. So in lieu of debarment, what we put to them was the types of ethical actions that they have to follow, and we're doing an ongoing monitoring of these ethical actions.

Dunn's statement and Klein's apparent tacit agreement set off a firestorm of criticism. The $100 million fine now looked more like $16.5 million since the government would continue to subsidize $83.5 million of it. Justice and ADM had represented to Judge Castillo that the plea "agreement constitutes the entire agreement between the United States and the defendant." But, nothing had been disclosed in the courtroom about the lucrative avoidance of debarment, which gave credence to a cover-up.

The Justice Department still maintained that its negotiators on the plea were Lassar, Griffin, and Spratling. Lassar convincingly denied that they had any discussion on debarment with their negotiating partners at William & Connolly. Moreover, he conceded that if such an understanding were reached outside of the official plea agreement, it would constitute "dirty pool."

However, evidence emerged that there had been a second negotiating team from Akin Gump, and that the debarment matter received the direct attention of Secretary of Agriculture Dan Glickman, a former Kansas congressman and major beneficiary of campaign support from ADM. The failure to lift ADM's government contracts remains a touchy matter in both Justice and Agriculture, which steadfastly have resisted Freedom of Information Act inquiries on the plea negotiations and debarment issues. However, if a judge decides that the true nature of the plea agreement was not revealed, the guilty plea could be negated. That could cause ADM to go to trial, its employees to lose immunity, and the antitrust and fraud investigations to be re-opened.

There is another odd wrinkle that calls into question the testimony of ADM's corporate guilty plea to lysine and citric acid price-fixing. The ADM special board committee's representative at the plea hearing on October 15, 1996, before Judge Ruben Castillo was Steven Mills, the corporation's controller. During the plea hearing, the judge asked Mills about the controller's "investigation into these matters as the designee of the special committee, does it show that the company did participate in the [illegal] actions?" Mills answered, "Yes." However, less than a year later at his deposition in a civil class-action suit alleging high fructose price-fixing, Mills admitted that actually he "did not conduct an investigation" into lysine or citric acid despite what he had sworn to Judge Castillo.

Hence, it seems unlikely that ADM's October 1996 guilty plea was "knowing, intelligent, and voluntary" as required by law. The main unanswered question is why would the corporation plead guilty through a representative who wasn't knowledgeable about the charges? Since lawyer Aubrey Daniel, who handled the plea, refused to respond to an interview request, one can only speculate. But, it seems logical to conclude that ADM chose to present someone who was ignorant of price-fixing in case Judge Castillo tried to interrogate him about the true nature, scope, and damages flowing from the corporation's antitrust behavior before imposing punishment. Regardless of its reason, ADM's use of a witness who actually wasn't knowledgeable about its crimes and who allowed the court to be misled about his participation in an investigation is a serious breach that also could unravel the guilty plea.

As a practical matter, there is still too much official secrecy in this case. Although the main events occurred five or more years ago and convictions have been obtained, the government declines to comment or disclose a good deal of public information. It drags its feet and obstructs FOIA requests. Indeed, it sometimes treats the case as if it pertained to national defense, terrorism, or nuclear secrets, rather than business swindles. Here are some of the issues it refuses to explain.

First, it declines to comment on how and why it permitted Dwayne Andreas and James Randall to avoid even being interviewed by the FBI during an investigation in which ADM had agreed to provide full cooperation. Likewise, despite the common knowledge and admission that Mick Andreas reviewed everything of importance with his father and much with Randall, who was on some of Whitacre's tapes, neither was targeted in the search warrant executed on June 27, 1995.

Similarly, the government refuses to explain why it went to the trouble of investigating and indicting Kazutoshi Yamada, the managing partner of Ajinomoto, but then failed to extradite him for trial. This action allowed the defense to seize on a supposed double standard for Asian versus American cartelists that played into the trial and the sentencing of Mick Andreas and Terry Wilson. Also, customary Japanese business protocol would require that an executive at Yamada's level would talk with those of equivalent stature, in other words Dwayne Andreas, Mick Andreas, and James Randall. Had Yamada appeared at trial, his peers at ADM might have been implicated.

Nor will the government disclose why it shut down the federal grand jury investigating price-fixing in the nearly $3 billion high fructose corn syrup (HFCS) market dominated by ADM with a 32 percent share. This commodity is worth more to ADM than lysine and citric acid put together. The potential fine for manipulation of the HFCS market by ADM, if convicted, could have exceeded a billion dollars.

Perhaps because high fructose was ADM's most valuable product, it merited the direct attention of multiple Andreases. In the fall of 1993, Whitacre recorded a session involving Mick Andreas, his cousin Martin, the senior vice president in charge of HFCS, and Terry Wilson, where they discussed raising the price. Knowing that Coca-Cola would be angered, they wondered how to explain the increase to the soft drink maker. Mick Andreas joked, "What are you gonna tell [Coca-Cola] that we got to deal with two, our two biggest competitors, to fuck ya over?" His cousin and Terry Wilson laughed heartily.

Other evidence showed that the importance of HFCS may have warranted the full focus of Dwayne Andreas. The information emerged at a deposition in the huge civil class-action case alleging price-fixing in the HFCS market. The witness was James House, head of commodity procurement at Kraft Foods. Because high fructose was a major commodity to Kraft, House's job involved locating sufficient supplies at favorable prices.

Kraft came to believe that the major HFCS makers (ADM, Cargill, CPC, and A.E. Staley) fixed prices. In 1994, House learned that a new producer called Pro-Gold was building a wet corn milling plant that could produce HFCS in North Dakota on the Red River border with Minnesota.

ProGold was a joint venture of various sugar beet cooperatives. One of the cooperatives was American Crystal. Its president, Joe Famalette, told James House that ADM had invited him to Decatur. At ADM headquarters Famalette met with Dwayne Andreas.

At his deposition, House described his conversation with Famalette:

> Well, as Joe related to me, that Mr. Andreas was interested in what it would be worth to the participants in the ProGold venture to not build the facility; that is, more specifically, that ADM was willing to make a payment to the participants in ProGold to not build that facility, to not bring that volume on line.
>
> Joe described to me that he joked back to Mr. Andreas, that if a sufficient quantity of money were to be deposited in Joe's personal Swiss bank account, then they could probably have a meaningful discussion and come up with an agreement.

Later Famalette admitted to a reporter that he had met with Andreas but refused to reveal the contents of their discussion. However, former North Dakota governor George Sinner disclosed that Famalette told him that Andreas tried to pay Pro-Gold not to produce high fructose.

According to House, Famalette related to him that Andreas also had spoken somewhat ominously. "There was an impression on my part that there was a suggestion that they [ADM] would make it very difficult for ProGold to succeed."

House testified that Famalette also told him that Cargill's president of corn milling, Mike Urbanic, had suggested a payoff to ProGold for staying out of the market. The ADM and Cargill overtures were both rejected.

ProGold built the plant but could not run it profitably as prices fell marketwide. In 1996, the cooperative allowed Cargill to take over operations.

House also testified to another disconcerting experience in the HFCS trade. It occurred when Kraft tried to give additional business to A.E. Staley, ADM's crosstown neighbor. "We made an overture to Staley and offered them significantly increased volume. Our assumption was that Staley would be very happy to have that increased volume. But we were shocked that they took no additional volume." In addition, House said that none of the major suppliers priced as competitively as it could have if it wanted to increase sales to Kraft.

Attempting to bribe a competitor to keep it out of a market, driving a company from the market with collusive low prices, and allocating customers among competitors all violate antitrust laws. On two occasions Justice Department officials met with Kraft executives. However, James House was not called to testify before the Atlanta-based high fructose grand jury, which later disbanded without issuing indictments.

For Justice to pass up a prosecution is not necessarily evil or even unusual. Rather, the culture of the department is such that it mainly chooses to prosecute only the strongest and most winnable cases. Defense attorneys who square off against the department know its penchant for slam dunks.

A much criticized aspect of the department's competitiveness has been its handling of informants. This is especially true in the wake of the "war on drugs." Seamy deals with snitches have emerged during trials. Besides their freedom or light sentences, informants have been given drugs to peddle or large amounts of cash with which to buy them, resident alien status when they were wanted on foreign charges, and carte blanche to continue committing crimes, including contract killing.

These are extreme situations, but it is not an exaggeration to say the department often protects, nurtures, and even coddles those who cooperate by testifying against their fellows. The situation was exacerbated by the Thornburg memo, a departmental policy issued by Reagan-Bush Attorney General Richard Thornburg, that released federal prosecutors from the ethical standards that prevent other lawyers from compensating witnesses. Worse, appellate courts have extended the "harmless error" doctrine to the extent that they will affirm a conviction despite perjured testimony from an informant if they find that the jury would have convicted without it.

To some extent there has been a backlash. Bills, some popular, emerge in Congress to curb prosecutorial misconduct, but the department lobbies effectively against them. The Tenth Circuit Court of Appeals' decision that attacked leniency for snitches as inconsistent with the federal antibribery statute, and with which Judge Manning had to deal, was a frustrated judicial response to the problem.

It was expected that ADM's attorneys would savage the snitch. What was highly bizarre in the world of criminal law was the way the Justice Department joined in the frenzy to destroy Whitacre. This was an aberration. The informant was impure. There was nothing new about that. But the perpetrator was a politically wired corporation whose law firm—the president's law firm—had unbridled entrée and influence at Justice. The mole's lawyer had none.

Whitacre accused his corporation of a gamut of crimes. Those handled by the antitrust team involving lysine, citric acid, misappropriation of technology and prostitution have been exposed. Those entrusted to the fraud section including campaign violations, misuse of the corporate jet, self-dealing in real estate by officers and directors, environmental breaches, bribes of foreign governments, drug trafficking, and widespread invoice fraud and money laundering have been squelched by the corporate plea agreement.

The fraud section of the Department of Justice was even more tight-lipped about its work in the ADM case than was the antitrust division. For instance, fraud's chief attorney Mary Spearing flatly declined to be interviewed while Gary Spratling commented extensively for Antitrust.

There also seemed to be a rift between the fraud section and the FBI. In September 1999, the FBI permitted me to review its investigative file from the fraud investigation.

The ground rules were that the documents could not be copied. The file was kept in an unmarked, highly-secured FBI office suite in the Chicago Loop. The custodian of the file was Anthony D'Angelo, an affable, broad-shouldered FBI agent who had been assigned to the fraud case at its inception in the summer of 1995.

The basic division of labor in a federal crime probe is that the FBI investigates and the Justice Department lawyers decide whether to prosecute. According to D'Angelo, "When the investigation started, the FBI told Aubrey Daniel we wanted access to ADM employees and files. They [Williams & Connolly] provided us with one little notebook of documents and insisted on being present for interviews with ADM employees." This had a chilling effect on the individuals. "It was tooth and nail to get anything out of ADM."

Eventually the government took the dramatic step of subpoenaing documents from the company even though it was the complaining victim, which was ironic. "I've never been in a case like this," said D'Angelo. "It was bizarre." Finally, a court ordered ADM to produce the documents, but D'Angelo had no confidence that the company had turned over everything.

In the fraud investigation he maintained that "Williams & Connolly held a lot of power. They basically ran the show." He recalled being stunned by the Justice Department's announcement in October 1995 "that there was no evidence of wrongdoing by ADM. It was early. We had just gotten involved in the investigation. That had to be driven by Williams & Connolly."

Among other things, Williams & Connolly threatened that it had evidence including a letter showing that FBI agents in the antitrust investigation had been aiding Whitacre in moving the ADM money offshore. The letter, which was anonymous, proved to be "nothing" according to D'Angelo. But the firm's accusations led to "a little bit of acrimony" between the FBI's fraud and antitrust teams and produced a wall that blocked information from flowing between them.

One key piece of evidence that never crossed the wall was the lengthy October 1996 antitrust interview of Barrie Cox in San Francisco. The resulting FBI 302 report contained Cox's reference to his discussions with Mick Andreas about suspicious MSG invoices. Because of the wall, D'Angelo said he never saw this 302 during the fraud probe. Hence, the MSG documents that it referenced were not reviewed, Andreas was not questioned, and a key opportunity to probe whether ADM's top management had approved the off-the-books bonus scheme was lost.

D'Angelo conceded that the investigation never looked into any of Whitacre's allegations such as foreign bribes and environmental offenses. This was because the fraud section "issued a directive not to look at peripheral issues."

Additionally, D'Angelo insisted that ADM did not even want any of the individuals such as Sidney Hulse, who had been involved with Whitacre in the offshore bonuses, to be prosecuted. Through its lawyers, ADM made clear that it sought the indictment of only one person (Whitacre) and wanted him charged only for the $2.5 million transfer to ABP.

The implications of D'Angelo's comments that ADM did not want to prosecute anyone but Whitacre—and indeed only to prosecute him only for a single $2.5 million transaction out of over $9 million taken—are staggering. It is reasonable to conclude that the corporation's leadership did not wish to ruin anyone except the whistleblower and did not care about the rest of the money.

In order to limit the investigation and "wrap it by Thanksgiving [1995], Aubrey Daniel raised hell with DOJ." Daniel argued that he had given DOJ a case against Whitacre "that a first-year law student could prosecute successfully."

D'Angelo said the Justice Department accepted the "urgency of getting the investigation wrapped up as quickly as possible." However, he indicated that the FBI fought a bureaucratic battle with the fraud section to have at least some of the others in Whitacre's circle prosecuted, that the FBI won in terms of indicting Hulse, Richter, and Marty Allison. Allison caused $220,000 in bogus foreign invoices to be sent to ADM, shared the proceeds with Whitacre, and later was sentenced to a term of probation. Also, a Missouri consultant named Milos Covert sent $81,000 of phony invoices to ADM, from which he gave kickbacks to Whitacre and Allison. After pleading guilty to one count of misdemeanor tax evasion, Covert received probation.

At some point the FBI's dissatisfaction with how the investigation was being run from Washington became so great that the bureau pressed for appointment of a cocounsel in the Chicago US Attorney's office. The FBI lost this battle although fraud's Donald Mackay was assigned to Chicago.

Reading the documents, which were organized into three binders, each an inch thick, also was a revelation. For one thing, Aubrey Daniel expected and received immediate attention on demand at the highest levels of the Justice Department, including from the chiefs of the criminal division and the fraud section. One file entry reflects him calling Spearing on August 4, 1995 at 7:10 AM to say that he and his partner would show up at the department in fifteen minutes. On August 19, 1995, Spearing wrote Daniel to protest his pressure and declared that the Department of Justice "does not represent ADM and should not be viewed as acting on behalf of ADM."

While Daniel pushed Justice very hard, the FBI records show that he sometimes pulled his punches. For instance, he declined to be straightforward about how and when ADM learned of Whitacre's embezzlement. A file entry from August 16, 1995 noted that Daniel "fidgeted" and said that he "believed [the discovery] was after the search of ADM," by the FBI. According to the file, Daniel also reportedly indicated that Whitacre's fraud scheme was "detected by an [ADM] attorney who was reviewing documents relating to ADM's patent litigation with Ajinomoto." Why the unnamed corporate lawyer would come across phony invoices involving matters not pertaining to a patent or to Ajinomoto was not explained. According to the FBI file, "Aubrey agreed later that we are not getting the whole story of the events surrounding the discovery of the alleged misconduct."

While ADM resisted giving the government the evidence it wanted, the file showed that the corporation on its own initiative turned over information through Williams & Connolly to the FBI about David Hoech and Bonnie Wittenburg, the Dain Bosworth analyst who had issued the "sell" recommendation on ADM stock. No investigation apparently was conducted of Wittenburg. Hoech, however, was vetted by the FBI after Williams & Connolly accused him of making threats. The bureau found nothing illegal involving the activist or at least nothing appeared in the file. D'Angelo angrily disputed a published charge by Hoech that the agent had surreptitiously videotaped him. Also, D'Angelo questioned the stability of the activist, "Sometimes I don't think that all of [Hoech] made it back from Vietnam." But the two were uncannily united in their views that Aubrey Daniel and his team had dominated the investigation and that ADM had held back evidence. "Williams & Connolley," said the agent, "did everything they could to impede the investigation."

One ADM witness who cooperated fully with the FBI was James Kirk Schmidt who had been the controller of the BioProducts Division when Whitacre had been its president. Schmidt revealed that invoices above $250,000 required approval by the board of directors. Indeed $6.5 *million* of the phony invoices received board approval.

Also, curiously, at least one false Whitacre expenditure for only $11,000, which was far below the board's usual limit, nevertheless was approved by the board. Why the board took it up remains unexplained.

In the ordinary course of business at large publicly held companies, major expenditures for capital equipment, contractual services, real estate, and the like are discussed by the board before they are paid. It is difficult to know for sure if this was the process at ADM because the company declined my questions, and with one exception—Howard Buffett, who was not asked about board procedure—its directors were not formally interviewed by the FBI. Regardless, the ADM board that included a host of members who were highly knowledgeable about world agriculture, and knew or should have known which expenditures were real and which were fakes, signed off on the bulk of the money that flowed offshore. Corporate governance expert Nell Minow, who followed the crises at ADM, took a dim view of the board's performance regarding the authorizations for phony payments. "The board was either responsible or it was irresponsible. They [the directors] were either crooks or they were negligent."

When the ADM board did not sign off on other phony payments, poor audit controls nevertheless enabled them to be put through. The $1.5 million wire transfer to Ferrari's Swiss bank account in Hong Kong bore no board signatures but nevertheless won the approval of Schmidt and Steven Mills, the controller. One of Richter's false payments went through even though its paperwork was inconsistent. The check request referred to a bonus, but the backup documentation indicated it was to pay for services. In his FBI interview, Schmidt could not explain the discrepancy. Moreover, the "services" supposedly related to monosodium glutamate, a product that Richter did not even handle.

In his deposition in the high fructose civil case, Steven Mills touched on the money that landed offshore. Mills insisted that he had the responsibility to review all AFE's over $100,000, that he had the support of an internal audit staff of thirty. Plus ADM's outside auditor, Ernst & Young, had access to the AFEs.

The scrutiny must not have been very intense. It is hard to believe that the audit controls confronting Whitacre were any better than they had been during the

Frankel/SEC flap. A high-ranking executive still could loot the company. Neither Mills nor Schmidt, nor anyone else from the financial side of ADM has yet explained why Whitacre was not taken to task for his illicit activities until after his exposure as a mole.

The FBI file also showed that Howard Buffett was interviewed by the government on October 13, 1995 about three months after he had left ADM. When he was at ADM, his office was on the sixth floor near those of Dwayne and Martin Andreas. Buffett corroborated Whitacre on certain points, including that Whitacre had disclosed his FBI role to Buffett before it became public in order to persuade Buffett not to resign from the company.

According to the file, besides Buffett, Whitacre also gave various lower-level managers and his secretary advance notice of the raid, so they would not be frightened. Remarkably none appears to have tipped off ADM to the search, which suggested that the employees felt no great loyalty to the company or desire to help it head off legal trouble. Buffett said he remained in contact with Whitacre for about a month after both ceased to be employed at ADM.

Buffett spoke in general terms about his reasons for resigning from ADM. He mentioned that he felt uneasy about putting out information that was not completely accurate in his public relations role, uncomfortable with Mick Andreas, whom people feared, and with Dwayne Andreas who had stated that competitors were ADM's friends and customers were the enemies. Also, he told his interviewers that a continued role on the board would have forced him to become involved in coping with the criminal case in ways that he could not tolerate. He did not offer specifics.

Buffett also had befriended Reinhard Richter while at the company and helped the German to open the ADM office in Mexico. After Buffett resigned, Richter phoned him twice and Buffett called Richter once. During the conversations Richter said he had a problem and would need an attorney. Then Richter flew up to Decatur to meet Buffett for dinner. Richter told Buffett about the $190,000 in phony invoices. According to the FBI interview sheet, Richter told Buffett that Whitacre received authority for the invoices from someone higher at ADM "perhaps Randall." Buffett was troubled by this conversation and mentioned it to his wife and father.

According to his interview record, Dwayne Andreas also put Buffett on the spot on the day after the FBI search. Andreas knew Buffett had been contacted by the FBI during its sweep and wanted to know what Buffett had said. He told Buffett that the FBI never would prove price-fixing.

That morning at 9:30, Buffett observed Dwayne Andreas' assistant, Claudia Madding, and another employee taking a box of documents out of the back door of Dwayne's office. It should be recalled that the FBI search warrant had not targeted the sixth floor. Later, Buffett learned that Martin Andreas had organized a team of five employees to remove documents from other employees' offices as well.

On July 29, 1995, Dwayne Andreas confronted Buffett again. Andreas accused Buffett of being Whitacre's friend, said he knew that Whitacre was the informant, and mused that it was "interesting what an attorney will tell you."

On July 2 or 3, 1995 Buffett observed a "tub" full of shredded documents near the back entrance to Dwayne Andreas' office. At the interview Buffett said that he may have mentioned this sight to Whitacre.

Claudia Madding came to Buffett's office on the day after the raid seeking all documents pertaining to the proposed promotion of Mick Andreas to the new position of managing director of ADM, which would have put him a step closer to being chairman. Recently, Buffett had begun writing the announcement. Now Madding even fished a draft out of Buffett's wastebasket. The promotion was never announced. Madding's avidity to halt the information on the day following the raid was not explained. However, one explanation might be that she and her boss Dwayne Andreas already knew the depth of Mick's involvement in the price-fixing conspiracy and thus did not want to risk the announcement of his promotion.

In accordance with the corporate guilty plea deal of October 1996, the government agreed not to interview Dwayne Andreas. The FBI records contain no indication that he was interviewed in the period of over fifteen months between the raid and the plea.

The guilty plea deal did not prevent Andreas from being called before the antitrust or fraud grand juries investigating crimes at ADM. If he had appeared, he could have been forced to explain under oath whether he was aware of price-fixing, what was removed from his office following the raid, and what if anything he knew about the off-the-books bonuses. Obviously, that would have included questions about his 1996 interview with the *Washington Post*, in which Andreas said that the company had known of Whitacre's thefts for three years without taking action.

According to D'Angelo, Justice Department attorneys made the decisions about whom to subpoena to the grand juries. While Andreas was not called, Claudia Madding testified. D'Angelo said she was asked about Andreas' remarks to the *Post* and said that her boss was "just rambling" at the time.

Madding's testimony strained credulity. In 1996, Andreas was very much in control of his company and sharp as a razor. Of course, grand jurors would not have known these facts unless the federal prosecutor subpoenaed Andreas to appear, cross-examined Madding hard about her boss, or presented other witnesses on the issue—none of which apparently occurred.

In his interview, Buffett also revealed that while at ADM he tried to steer clear of conversations involving high fructose corn syrup pricing and operations because he was on the board of Coca-Cola, a major HFCS customer, and wanted to avoid a conflict of interest. Nevertheless, Buffett heard a few things that disturbed him. After an ADM corn plant manager resigned to join crosstown HFCS competitor, A.E. Staley, Buffett heard someone "possibly Randall" say, "ADM had to send someone over there to straighten out the plant." Understandably Buffett found the remark unusual. What did Randall (or whoever) mean by "straighten out the plant?" If the phrase meant to control the output in order to affect the price, or not to take orders from potential customers such as Kraft, an antitrust conspiracy could have been proven. But Randall never was interrogated due to the deal that Justice made with ADM for its guilty plea on lysine and citric acid.

Buffett also reported that Randall bragged about telling A.E. Staley's president "how to do things." Was Randall commanding his competitor on HFCS price setting, production, or customer allocation? Again, the Justice Department apparently did not follow up due to the plea deal.

The file revealed that the FBI interviewed Ronald Ferrari on October 9, 1995. Ferrari described himself as an ingenue who became a pawn of Whitacre's. Ferrari admitted it was his own idea to incorporate Far East Specialists and claimed he learned how to do it through an ad in an in-flight magazine. He said he chose to set up a Swiss bank account for it in Hong Kong although it had no assets, stationery, or business. He opened the account at the Swiss Bank Corporation, a bank he said he selected simply because it was in the same Hong Kong office building where he met once with a protein distributor. Of the numerous offshore banks where one could enjoy account secrecy, the Swiss Bank Corporation coincidentally was the same institution for which Beat Schweizer worked. It was only after setting up the shell company and the account that Ferrari said Whitacre coincidentally asked the ex-football star if he had an account abroad. Ferrari said yes, absorbed $1.5 million from Whitacre, and distributed over a million to the Swiss bank's branch on Grand Cayman Island. The file entry reported that Ferrari maintained that Whitacre gave him a "currently unrecalled explanation" for the deposit, and that Ferrari had declined any payment from Whitacre though he received a $25,000 interest free loan that he insisted was not related to his banking favors. Mysteriously, Ferrari also said that he kept $25,000 in cash in a safe deposit box because he and his wife were very conservative and always saved cash.

Ferrari mentioned that while working in London for ADM he had heard "through the grapevine" that ADM executives received overseas compensation in the form of "kickbacks." The fact that Ferrari had been alerted to unkosher ADM payments abroad was significant, particularly since the source was not Whitacre. But the records contained no indication that the government took the elementary steps of tracing and questioning those who comprised Ferrari's ADM "grapevine" at the time he worked in London, including his office mates and other company contacts.

Similarly, the file reflected that the FBI went through the exercise of learning the locations of some of the murkier figures mentioned by Whitacre, including Frankel, and determining whether they had lawyers. But they never were brought before grand juries.

In his second interrogation on December 6, 1995 Ferrari somewhat changed his story. For one thing, he said he repaid the $25,000 loan from Whitacre in installments and not with one payment as he previously related. In the second session, he claimed his $25,000 in cash was from "unofficial" bonuses from the San Francisco 49ers. Now, he recalled that Whitacre had offered an explanation for the $1.5 million—it came from a consulting deal in Nigeria. Interestingly, Ferrari also stated that he had heard evidence from Whitacre as early as August or September of 1991 about price-fixing activities at ADM. If true, this revelation came more than a year before Whitacre started informing to Brian Shepard and could have involved information new to the government. But the bureaucratic protocol was so rigid that fraud section attorney James Nixon, who was present, did not explore the subject, saying it was within Scott Lassar's jurisdiction.

D'Angelo did not know why Ferrari was not prosecuted for his role in the money laundering. "We [the FBI] thought he should be indicted. We had plenty of evidence." Also, he was surprised to learn that Ferrari had not even been called before the grand jury, but that decision was made by the fraud section in Washington.

Besides Milos Covert, none of the non-ADM employees who participated in the phony transfers including lawyers, bankers, their spouses, and assorted others, was indicted or sued. Perhaps the most blatant case concerned David Page, a distributor from central Pennsylvania. In 1994, Whitacre put through paperwork for Page to join ADM as a full-time employee at a salary of $120,000 and bonus of $30,000. But Page actually stayed back in Pennsylvania running his own business and performing few if any services for ADM. Yet, he received ADM payments of $240,000 and kicked back a third of the money to Whitacre. Of Page, D'Angelo asked with frustration, "How could he *not* be indicted?" But indictments were not the FBI's call, and ADM was interested only in destroying the snitch.

The records reflected that Reinhard Richter was interviewed first on November 8, 1995, at which time he implicated Randall in his off-the-books payment. Richter recanted the charge when he next met with the FBI in Mexico City on May 13, 1997 as he was approaching trial. But the record of the original meeting also contained significant information that Richter did not retract. For instance, he told the FBI that on August 3, 1995 he was summoned to Washington for a meeting at Williams & Connolly. It surprised Richter that ADM's Washington lawyers already knew about his two phony invoices. Richter informed the company lawyers that Whitacre *and* Randall knew about the off-the-books money.

At his initial FBI interview, Richter reported that he called Buffett from Mexico on August 5, 1995 and told him that ADM could have found about the invoices so quickly only because Randall and others at the company already knew about the bonuses. Buffett named others in the company who may have received such phony payments, including ADM representatives in Hong Kong and Australia. The files contained some names and phone numbers of individuals in Australia and the Far East, but showed no efforts to interview them. According to Richter, Buffett also told him that Dwayne Andreas destroyed paperwork at ADM headquarters on the day following the raid.

Richter informed the FBI that he had received correspondence from Williams & Connolly stating that *he did not have to talk to the FBI,* an extremely odd position for a victim's attorney to take. During his next meeting with Williams & Connolly in September 1995, Richter brought his own attorney and refused to answer the firm's questions about fraudulent transactions. Richter's eventual guilty plea for probation, according to D'Angelo was "a fabulous deal" for the German, considering his involvement in the racket.

The FBI also had the opportunity to interview Beat Schweizer when he was in the United States on May 13, 1996. Schweizer had ceased to work for the Swiss Bank Corporation and was employed by the Zurich Life Insurance Company. He corroborated Whitacre's story that the two had met while the banker was assigned to the Cayman branch and continued the association when he moved to Switzerland. He admitted to taking 50,000 Swiss francs and expenses for handling the ABP account, but declined to answer questions on various wire transfers. The government neither subpoenaed him to appear before a grand jury nor arrested him. D'Angelo reiterated that such decisions were the province of DOJ attorneys not the FBI.

At his FBI interview Schweizer offered something amazing. He said that Swiss law required that an accountant be involved in the incorporation process related to ABP Consulting, Ltd. Then he reported that Whitacre insisted on using the accounting firm Ernst & Young *since it also represented ADM.*

For Whitacre to chose ADM's accountant to help set up a shell company to defraud ADM was bizarre. The ordinary embezzler would not take the risk that the accountant would detect something amiss—say the fact that the ABP Consulting performed no services and produced nothing but bogus bills—and report it to its major corporate client. It would have made more sense for Whitacre to engage an obscure European accountant who couldn't spell ADM. But Whitacre insists that ADM already knew about his bogus bonus ploy. Thus, he had nothing to fear from Ernst & Young or anyone reporting it to Decatur—until he became a whistleblower.

Anthony D'Angelo does not believe conventional behavioral norms can be applied to Whitacre whom he calls a "pathological liar." But Whitacre's pathology (if that's what it is) did not emerge until his middle and late thirties when he scaled the heights at ADM.

But a different assessment of the jailed former super-achiever was supplied by Nicholas Hollis, president of the Agribusiness Council, a Washington-based watchdog group with affiliates in farm states. "He's one of the most productive informants in history and one of the most courageous. He stood up to two eight-hundred-pound gorillas, ADM with the Andreases and the federal government. This was one of the most important antitrust cases of the century. It certainly was the most important in agriculture.

"Before the case, Dwayne had it within his reach to achieve hegemony in the world food system. Now he's been knocked back. And his son Mick has been surgically removed from the chain of command. The credibility of ADM also has been damaged in Washington."

Within a week of Judge McCuskey's summary judgment order in favor of ADM, Judge Manning issued a surprisingly quick decision on the motions of Wilson and Mick Andreas to remain free during their criminal appeals. In the Seventh Circuit a judge must deny bond after a conviction at trial unless there is an issue "that very well could be decided the other way" on appeal. Manning had been thorough at the trial. She again fielded the attacks on her rulings and with one exception found them wanting.

The defendants reiterated that prosecutorial misconduct during Lassar's closing argument had cost them a fair trial. Manning ruled that the government "only just barely avoided being smacked with a mistrial." But the jury's verdict had been fair:

> While the government crossed the line, the overwhelming videotaped evidence (particularly the Irvine videotape) and the court's strong admonishment to the jury to disregard the inflammatory nature of the government's closing argument completely purged the taint, if any, created by the unfortunate fiasco created by the government's momentary lapse of judgment. Having had the opportunity to assess all of the evidence adduced at trial, the court is thoroughly satisfied that the verdict was influenced solely by the evidence and not the government's misconduct. Accordingly, the government's misconduct—under these very limited circumstances—is no basis for the granting of bond pending appeal.

She ordered Andreas and Wilson to report to the Federal Bureau of Prisons on September 10, 1999, which later was extended until October 5, 1999, when they surrendered. Federal prosecutors were elated. Incarceration time was the coin of their kingdom. That the two targets would see the inside of a prison proved that all the jury, grand jury, and surveillance work had not been an existential exercise.

Jim Griffin reflected back to his dealings with the Japanese, Korean, and French during the case. "The international business community thought the Department of Justice never would prosecute the individuals and especially not the son of the chairman because of ADM's political influence." Now the sentences of the inform-ant hopefully would "speak volumes" in terms of deterrence.

David Hoech took no joy in the imprisonments. At least, he said, Mick had stayed in this country to face the trial, unlike his father, who had run to Europe during his Watergate prosecution.

Once among the world's most powerful companies, ADM was different, weaker. It had dodged the bankrupting bullets of huge fines for citric acid and high fructose. But now it was under constant scrutiny by Justice, Agriculture, and the Securities Exchange Commission (SEC). Its annual reports and SEC filings con-tained pained disclosures of criminal convictions, class-action settlements, pend-ing litigations, and mounting millions for legal fees.

The 1999 report listed the amount set aside to deal with such problems at $269 million. It was a staggering sum especially considering that it exceeded ADM's most recent net earnings by $4 million.

ADM employees now knew that they could be forced to cough up information at any time by the government. The company's business partners and competi-tors, likewise, were aware that ADM could funnel their words back to the feds. In a climate of surveillance and mistrust, ADM's once cozy strategy of entering mar-kets with few players, fixing prices, and allocating shares was a fool's paradise.

The corporation's other habitual tactic, "greasing politicians," would continue to work but less well since ADM and its executives had been branded as felons. Plus, in Washington the wind was shifting against corporate welfare, and Dwayne, the magician, now was offstage.

Wall Street did not like what it saw. ADM completely missed the bull market of the late nineties. In 1996 with the Dow Jones Index at about 6,000, ADM shares traded at almost $22. After the 1999 sentencing, with the Dow at 11,000, ADM slipped below $13.

Even the EPA's criticism of MTBE, ethanol's methane-based competitor, failed to boost ADM's stock. In 1999, rumors abounded that G. Allen Andreas' days as CEO were numbered, and that ADM, once a mighty acquirer of companies, could become a takeover target perhaps of DuPont. But it was hard to imagine any cor-poration wanting to swallow ADM, with its baggage of post-conviction red tape, enduring litigation, and aroma of corruption. There were rays of sunlight even in fortress Decatur. In the past, the *Decatur Herald & Review* rarely had taken ADM to task. The paper did not even assign a reporter to cover the raid of 1995, choos-ing instead to rely on wire services. Now it investigated the company's deals, fines, crimes, and jailings, and gave space to its critics.

ADM finally was training its employees *not* to fix prices. It developed a "Corporate Code of Conduct" called "The ADM Way." One of its precepts showed how profoundly the company had been shaped by Whitacre's activities:

> All relations with competitors should be conducted as if they were completely in the public view, and it should be assumed that any conversation with a competitor may later be the subject of testimony.

In addition, ADM created a toll-free hotline for employees and others who wished to report anticompetitive acts. The company passed out plastic wallet cards embossed with the 800 number to employees "as a future reminder of their link."

Not everyone was impressed. A letter writer to the *Herald & Review* scoffed:

> Hurray for ADM for setting up a hot line for whistleblowers! I'm sure they will have to add additional phone lines to accommodate the huge numbers of ADM employees who will be calling in to report ADM violations, given Whitacre's reward for doing so.

Nevertheless, the imprisonment of Andreas and Wilson in the fall of 1999 concluded a grueling seven years' war that began in an FBI agent's car on November 4, 1992. As with most epic struggles, blood had been let on both sides. Predictably, ADM had won major rounds in Washington. But ultimately, it lost the war in the heartland when an American jury saw its methods through the eyes of a mole.

APPENDIX 1
ADM—TIME LINE OF MAJOR EVENTS

10/19/89	Mark Whitacre, thirty-two, begins career at ADM as a president of the BioChem Division.
02/1992	Mark Whitacre meets Terry Wilson.
04/1992	Wilson and Whitacre fly to Tokyo to meet with major competitors Ajinomoto and Kyowa Hakko Kogyo to discuss forming a trade association.
06/1992	Wilson and Whitacre meet with Japanese producers in Mexico City.
08/19/92	Dwayne Andreas hears of alleged plant sabotage and has it reported to the CIA.
11/04/92	Whitacre tells the FBI of price-fixing at ADM.
12/22/92	Whitacre admits to FBI that there is no sabotage plot in the lysine plant.
01/09/93	Whitacre signs his confidential cooperating witness agreement with the FBI.
5/14/93	In Tokyo, Wilson advocates that lysine producers form a trade association.
10/25/93	Mick Andreas and Mark Whitacre meet in Irvine, California, with two senior executives of Ajinomoto, to fix world lysine markets.
12/08/93	Lysine conspirators in Tokyo agree to share their monthly sales figures and submit them centrally to Ajinomoto.
03/10/94	Hawaii meeting of lysine conspirators
05/03/94	Phony invoice of ABP Consulting submitted to ADM for $2.5 million. Whitacre authorized payment.

02/21/95	Whitacre authorized second payment of $3.75 million for another phony ABP Consulting invoice.
06/21/95	FBI agent Brian Shepard appears before the US Magistrate in Urbana, Illinois, to obtain a warrant to search ADM.
06/27/95	FBI raids ADM's Decatur headquarters.
06/28/95	Whitacre's role as a mole is revealed to ADM.
07/10/95	Whitacre's role as a mole is reported by the *Wall Street Journal*.
07/10/95	Whitacre and Howard Buffett are barred from ADM headquarters after Buffett resigns; Whitacre remains on payroll.
07/19/95	ADM forms a special committee of outside directors to organize its response to litigation.
07/28/95	ADM announces to the press that it is being investigated for antitrust violations.
08/02/95	Whitacre confesses role in bogus bonus scheme to federal investigators.
08/07/95	ADM fires Whitacre, accusing him of theft.
08/09/95	Whitacre attempts suicide with carbon monoxide.
09/04/95	*Fortune Magazine* runs "My Life as a Corporate Mole for the FBI" cover story.
09/05/95	Whitacre and his attorneys meet with representatives of the Department of Justice's fraud section.
09/21/95	ADM fires three executives, Marty Allison, Sidney Hulse, and Reinhart Richter, accusing them of being in the embezzlement scheme with Whitacre.
10/16/95	ADM sues Whitacre in a Swiss court for $6.25 million.
10/19/95	ADM's annual meeting is marked by shareholder discontent that is quieted by former Prime Minister Brian Mulroney of Canada.
01/15/96	ADM reorganizes its board of directors in response to shareholder concerns.
03/21/96	ADM president James Randall and ADM vice chairman Mick Andreas announce they will not stand for reelection to the board of directors.
07/19/96	ADM agrees to pay $25 million to settle civil lysine suits.
08/14/96	The *Chicago Tribune* reports that the Justice Department may be seeking a fine as large as $400 million against ADM.
08/27/96	ADM coconspirator companies Ajinomoto, Kyowa Hakko Kogyo, and Sewon, plead guilty as does one executive from each.
09/21/96	ADM sues Whitacre for embezzlement.
10/15/96	ADM pleads guilty to criminal antitrust violations involving lysine and citric acid and agrees to pay $100 million in fines.
10/24/96	Mick Andreas takes a leave of absence from ADM and Terry Wilson retires.

11/23/96	Whitacre countersues ADM for wrongful dismissal based on whistle-blowing.
12/03/96	Mick Andreas, Whitacre, Wilson, and Kazutoshi Yamada are indicted on criminal price-fixing charges.
01/13/97	Whitacre files a civil rights suit against Brian Shepard and the FBI.
01/15/97	Whitacre indicted on money laundering, tax fraud, and related offenses involved in misappropriating $9.5 million of ADM funds.
01/29/97	Haarmann & Reimer, a coconspirator to ADM in citric acid price-fixing, pleads guilty and pays a $50 million fine.
04/17/97	Dwayne Andreas retires as chief executive of ADM but remains as chairman.
06/23/97	Randall retires as ADM president.
09/25/97	Mark and Ginger Whitacre file for bankruptcy in North Carolina.
10/10/97	Whitacre pleads guilty to thirty-seven criminal charges in Urbana, Illinois.
10/28/97	Reinhart Richter, former president of ADM Mexico, pleads guilty to fraud.
11/03/97	Judge Blanche Manning conducts hearing on whether to suppress tape recordings made by Whitacre based on allegations that tapes were altered or destroyed.
02/26/98	Second Whitacre suicide attempt delays his sentencing.
03/04/98	Mark Whitacre is sentenced to nine years in prison on fraud, money laundering, and tax evasion counts.
04/16/98	Judge Blanche Manning approves the use of audio and video surveillance tapes in the forthcoming trial of Mick Andreas, Whitacre, and Wilson.
05/98	ADM drops Swiss law suit against Whitacre.
05/29/98	Former ADM vice president Sidney Hulse is sentenced to ten months in prison for fraud and income tax evasion.
07/09/98	Federal trial of Mick Andreas, Whitacre, and Wilson begins.
07/16/98	Federal jury hears the first of the tapes recorded by Whitacre.
09/02/98	Government and defense attorneys rest their cases.
09/10/98	Jurors begin deliberations.
09/17/98	Mick Andreas, Whitacre, and Wilson are convicted of antitrust violations involving lysine.
07/09/99	Mick Andreas, Whitacre, and Wilson are sentenced by Judge Manning.
10/05/99	Andreas and Wilson are incarcerated.

Allison, Marty — Former ADM vice president, charged with fraud

Andreas, Dwayne — Former chairman and CEO of ADM

Andreas, G. Allen — President and CEO of ADM; chief financial officer for European operations from 1989 through 1994

Andreas, Lowell — Brother of Dwayne, former ADM president

Andreas, Michael (Mick) — Former vice chairman and executive vice president of ADM, antitrust conspirator; son of Dwayne Andreas

Bassett, Michael — FBI special agent in the fraud investigation

Bray, Jack — Attorney to Mick Andreas

Buffett, Howard — Former ADM vice president and publicist

Cheviron, Mark — ADM vice president and director of security

Cox, Barrie — ADM vice president who became a prosecution witness

Crouy, Alain — Executive of Eurolysine, antitrust conspirator and witness against ADM

D'Angelo, Anthony — FBI special agent on the fraud investigation

Daniel, Aubrey — ADM's lead attorney in civil cases; partner at Williams & Connolly

Dunn, Michael — Undersecretary of Agriculture

Ferrari, Ronald — Former ADM executive, established Swiss bank account in Hong Kong through which ADM funds were laundered

Epstein, James — Mark Whitacre's first attorney

Glotzer, Martin — ADM shareholder activist

Griffin, James — Lead federal antitrust prosecutor

Herndon, Robert — FBI special agent in the antitrust investigation

Hoech, David   Dissident ADM shareholder and critic; writer of *Shareholders Watch* newsletter

Hoech, Carol   Wife of David Hoech, editor of *Shareholders Watch* newletter

House, James   Executive of Kraft Foods, testified about alleged antitrust violations in the high fructose corn syrup market

Hulkower, Mark   Attorney to Terry Wilson

Hulse, Sidney   Former ADM vice president, fired for receiving off-the-books money

Ikeda, Hirokazu   Former executive of Ajinomoto, testified against ADM

Johnson, F. Ross   Member of the ADM board of directors

Kim, Jhom Su   President of Sewon America, price-fixing coconspirator and federal witness

Lassar, Scott   United States attorney for the Northern District of Illinois and lead prosecutor in the Chicago criminal price-fixing trial

Mackay, Donald   Federal fraud prosecutor

Mann, Robin   Federal antitrust prosecutor

Manning, Blanche   Federal judge in the criminal price-fixing trial in Chicago

Mills, Steven   ADM controller

Mimoto, Kanji   Executive of Ajinomoto, coconspirator, and federal witness

Mulroney, Brian   Former Canadian prime minister, ADM board member

Mutchnick, James   Federal antitrust prosecutor

Nixon, James   Federal fraud prosecutor

Randall, James   Former ADM president

Reising, Richard   ADM vice president and general counsel

Richter, Reinhard   Former president of ADM Mexico, pleaded guilty to fraud and conspiracy

Schweizer, Beat   Swiss banker, established accounts and a corporation for Mark Whitacre's use in money-laundering scheme

Shepard, Brian   Lead FBI special agent in the antitrust investigation

Spratling, Gary   Former chief of criminal prosecutions for the Justice Department's antitrust division

Strauss, Robert   ADM board member and friend of Dwayne Andreas; sometime attorney to ADM; partner at Akin, Gump, Hauer & Feld

Walker, Bill   Attorney to Mark Whitacre

Weingarten, Reid   Lead attorney to Terry Wilson

Whitacre, Mark   Former president of the ADM Bioproducts Division, FBI informant, money launderer

Wilson, Terry   Former president of the ADM Corn Processing Division, anti-trust conspirator

Yamada, Kazutoshi   Managing partner of Ajinomoto, indicted antitrust conspirator, and fugitive

Yamamoto, Masaru   Executive of Kyowa Hakko Kogyo, antitrust coconspirator; federal witness

Young, Andrew   ADM board member and friend of Dwayne Andreas; former US ambassador to the United Nations

APPENDIX 3
SOFT MONEY* DONATIONS
FROM ADM 1995-1999**

DATE	AMOUNT	RECIPIENT
02/08/1995	$10,000	National Republican Senatorial Committee (NRSC)/Non-Federal Account
02/10/1995	$50,000	Republican National Committee (RNC)/Republican National State Elections Committee
02/14/1995	$25,000	RNC/Republican National State Elections Committee
02/23/1995	$15,000	RNC/Republican National State Elections Committee
03/22/1995	$50,000	1995 Republican Senate/House Dinner Committee
05/01/1995	$15,000	Democratic Congressional Dinner Committee (DCDC)/ Non-Federal Account
05/17/1995	$30,000	DCDC/Non-Federal Account
05/17/1995	$15,000	DCDC/Non-Federal Account
06/01/1995	$25,000	NRSC/Non-Federal Account
10/12/1995	$50,000	NRSC/Non-Federal Account
02/15/1996	$15,000	RNC/Republican National State Elections Committee
05/10/1996	$50,000	Democratic Senatorial Campaign Committee (DSCC)/ Non-Federal Corporate Account
06/12/1996	$40,000	RNC/Republican National State Elections Committee
06/28/1996	$25,000	NRSC/Non-Federal Account
07/26/1996	$50,000	Democratic Congressional Campaign Committee (DCCC)/Non-Federal Account
08/30/1996	$25,000	DSCC/Non-Federal Corporate Account
09/06/1996	$25,000	RNC/Republican National State Elections Committee

DATE	AMOUNT	RECIPIENT
09/17/1996	$25,000	National Republican Congressional Committee (NRCC)/ Non-Federal Account
09/18/1996	$25,000	DSCC/Non-Federal Corporate Account
10/08/1996	$20,000	NRSC/Non-Federal Account
11/08/1996	$25,000	DSCC/Non-Federal Corporate Account
05/02/1997	$15,000	RNC/Republican National State Elections Committee
06/06/1997	$25,000	NRSC/Non-Federal Account
06/30/1997	$45,000	1997 Republican Senate/House Dinner Committee
07/07/1997	$15,000	NRCC/Non-Federal Account
10/14/1997	$14,000	DSCC/Non-Federal Corporate Account
11/25/1997	$50,000	DCCC/Non-Federal Account 1
02/27/1998	$35,500	RNC/Republican National State Elections Committee
02/27/1998	$4,500	RNC/Republican National State Elections Committee
03/23/1998	$5,000	DSCC/Non-Federal Corporate Account
03/24/1998	$30,000	DSCC/Non-Federal Corporate Account
04/30/1998	$50,000	DSCC/Non-Federal Corporate Account
05/04/1998	$25,000	NRSC/Non-Federal Account
05/15/1998	$20,000	1998 Republican Senate/House Dinner Committee
06/19/1998	$15,000	NRSC/Non-Federal Account
08/14/1998	$10,000	RNC/Republican National State Elections Committee
09/30/1998	$10,000	RNC/Republican National State Elections Committee
10/08/1998	$100,000	Democratic National Committee (DNC)/Non-Federal-Corporate Account
10/29/1998	$15,000	NRCC/Non-Federal Account
11/12/1998	$10,000	RNC/Republican National State Elections Committee
03/05/1999	$50,000	RNC/Republican National State Elections Committee
03/10/1999	$75,000	NCRR/Non-Federal Account
03/10/1999	$25,000	NRCC/Non-Federal Account
05/20/1999	$20,000	1999 Republican Senate/House Dinner Committee
06/17/1999	$50,000	DCCC/Non-Federal Account 1
07/26/1999	$25,000	NRSC/Non-Federal Account
TOTAL:	$1,349,000	

* Soft money involves political donations that are not regulated by federal election laws and Federal Election Commission (FEC) regulations. The donations are intended to benefit political parties but not specific candidates. Soft money contributions are mainly used for state and local political activities and for supporting national Democratic and Republican efforts. Soft money is considered by many to be the most lucrative and largest loophole in the federal elections laws.

** Through December 1, 1999, according to the Federal Election Commission (FEC).

ADM POLITICAL ACTION COMMITTEE*

CONTRIBUTIONS TO FEDERAL CANDIDATES, 1993-1999**

Presidential Candidates

Bush, George W. (R)	$2,000	(1999-2000 election cycle)
Dole, Bob (R)	$6,000	(1995-1996 election cycle)
Dole, Elizabeth (R)	$5,000	(1999-2000 election cycle)
Hatch, Orrin G. (R)	$1,000	(1999-2000 election cycle)
Wilson, Pete (R)	$5,000	(1997-1998 election cycle)

Total to presidential Democrats: $0

Total to presidential Republicans: $19,000

Senate Candidates

Akaka, Daniel K. (D-HI)	$1,000	(1993-1994 election cycle)
Andrews, Thomas H. (D-ME)	$1,000	(1993-1994 election cycle)
Ashcroft, John (R-MO)	$6,500	(1993-1994, 1997-1998 and 1999-2000 election cycles)
Baucus, Max (D-MT)	$3,000	(1995-1996 election cycle)
Bayh, Evan (D-IN)	$3,000	(1997-1998 election cycle)
Bennett, Robert F. (R-UT)	$1,000	(1993-1994 election cycle)
Bond, Christopher S (R-MO)	$6,000	(1997-1998 election cycle)
Boschwitz, Rudy (R-MN)	$4,200	(1995-1996 election cycle)
Boxer, Barbara (D-CA)	$4,000	(1993-1994, 1995-1996 and 1997-1998 election cycles)
Breaux, John B (D-LA)	$3,000	(1997-1998 election cycle)
Brennan, Joseph E. (D-ME)	$1,000	(1995-1996 election cycle)
Brock, William (R-MD)	$5,000	(1993-1994 election cycle)

Brownback, Sam (R-KS)	$5,000	(1995-1996 and 1997-1998 election cycles)
Bryan, Richard (D-NV)	$500	(1993-1994 election cycle)
Bunning, Jim (R-KY)	$2,000	(1997-1998 election cycle)
Burns, Conrad (R-MT)	$5,500	(1993-1994, 1997-1998 and 1999-2000 election cycles)
Campbell, Ben Nighthorse (R-CO)	$3,000	(1997-1998 election cycle)
Chafee, John H. (R-RI)	$2,000	(1993-1994 election cycle)
Conrad, Kent (D-ND)	$15,000	(1993-1994, 1997-1998 and 1999-2000 election cycles)
Coverdell, Paul (R-GA)	$4,000	(1997-1998 election cycle)
Craig, Larry E (R-ID)	$4,000	(1995-1996 and 1997-1998 election cycles)
Crapo, Michael D (R-ID)	$1,000	(1997-1998 election cycle)
D'Amato, Alfonse M (R-NY)	$8,000	(1997-1998 election cycle)
Daschle, Tom (D-SD)	$7,000	(1993-1994 and 1997-1998 election cycles)
DeConcini, Dennis (D-AZ)	$620	(1993-1994 election cycle)
DeWine, Mike (R-OH)	$1,000	(1993-1994 election cycle)
Didrickson, Loleta (R-IL)	$1,000	(1997-1998 election cycle)
Dorgan, Byron L. (D-ND)	$3,500	(1997-1998 election cycle)
Durbin, Richard J. (D-IL)	$14,000	(1995-1996, 1997-1998 and 1999-2000 election cycles)
Durenberger, Dave (R-MN)	$2,000	(1993-1994 election cycle)
Faircloth, Lauch (R-NC)	$5,500	(1993-1994, 1995-1996 and 1997-1998 election cycles)
Feinstein, Dianne (D-CA)	$4,000	(1999-2000 election cycle)
Fitzgerald, Peter G (R-IL)	$5,000	(1997-1998 and 1999-2000 election cycles)
Frahm, Sheila (R-KS)	$5,000	(1995-1996 and 1997-1998 election cycles)
Frist, Bill (R-TN)	$1,000	(1997-1998 election cycle)
Furman, Hal (R-NV)	$1,000	(1993-1994 election cycle)
Glenn, John (D-OH)	$3,000	(1993-1994 election cycle)
Graham, Bob (D-FL)	$8,000	(1995-1996 and 1997-1998 election cycles)
Gramm, Phil (R-TX)	$2,000	(1997-1998 and 1999-2000 election cycles)
Grams, Rod (R-MN)	$2,000	(1997-1998 and 1999-2000 election cycles)
Grassley, Charles E (R-IA)	$10,000	(1995-1996 and 1997-1998 election cycles)
Gregg, Judd (R-NH)	$2,000	(1993-1994 and 1997-1998 election cycles)
Hagel, Chuck (R-NE)	$2,000	(1997-1998 election cycle)
Harkin, Tom (D-IA)	$12,000	(1993-1994, 1995-1996 and 1999-2000 election cycles)
Hatch, Orin (R-UT)	$8,000	(1993-1994 election cycle)
Haytalan, Garabed (R-NJ)	$2,000	(1993-1994 election cycle)

Helms, Jesse (R-NC)	$2,000	(1997-1998 election cycle)
Hollings, Ernest F (D-SC)	$2,000	(1995-1996 and 1997-1998 election cycles)
Hutchison, Kay Bailey (R-TX)	$5,000	(1993-1994 election cycle)
Hyatt, Joel (D-OH)	$4,000	(1993-1994 election cycle)
Jeffords, James M. (R-VT)	$2,000	(1993-1994 and 1999-2000 election cycles)
Johnson, Tim (D-SD)	$10,000	(1995-1996 and 1997-1998 election cycles)
Kennedy, Edward M (D-MA)	$10,000	(1997-1998 and 1999-2000 election cycles)
Kerrey, Bob (D-NE)	$14,000	(1993-1994, 1997-1998 and 1999-2000 election cycles)
Krueger, Robert (D-TX)	$3,500	(1993-1994 election cycle)
Kustra, Robert W. (R-IL)	$1,500	(1995-1996 election cycle)
Kyl, Jon (R-AZ)	$1,000	(1999-2000 election cycle)
Levin, Carl (D-MI)	$1,000	(1995-1996 election cycle)
Liebman, Joseph I. (D-CT)	$2,000	(1993-1994 election cycle)
Lincoln, Blanche Lambert (D-AR)	$2,000	(1997-1998 and 1999-2000 election cycles)
Lott, Trent (R-MS)	$4,500	(1993-1994 and 1997-1998 election cycles)
Lugar, Richard G. (R-IN)	$10,000	(1993-1994, 1995-1996 and 1997-1998 election cycles)
Mack, Connie (R-FL)	$1,000	(1997-1998 election cycle)
McConnell, Mitch (R-KY)	$3,000	(1993-1994 and 1995-1996 election cycles)
McCurdy, Dave (D-OK)	$1,500	(1993-1994 election cycle)
Moseley-Braun, Carol (D-IL)	$10,000	(1995-1996 and 1997-1998 election cycles)
Moynihan, Daniel Patrick (D-NY)	$3,000	(1993-1994 election cycle)
Nelson, Ben (D-NE)	$10,000	(1995-1996 election cycle)
Oberly, Charles M. III (D-DE)	$1,500	(1993-1994 election cycle)
Pressler, Larry (R-SD)	$7,500	(1993-1994 and 1995-1996 election cycles)
Riegle, Donald W. Jr. (D-MI)	$1,000	(1993-1994 election cycle)
Riggs, Frank (R-CA)	$500	(1997-1998 election cycle)
Robb, Charles S (D-VA)	$12,000	(1993-1994, 1995-1996 and 1999-2000 election cycles)
Roberts, Pat (R-KS)	$6,000	(1995-1996 election cycle)
Rockefeller, Laurance (R-NY)	$5,000	(1995-1996 election cycle)
Roth, William V. Jr. (R-DE)	$1,000	(1999-2000 election cycle)
Santorum, Rick (R-PA)	$1,000	(1993-1994 election cycle)
Sarbanes, Paul S. (D-MD)	$1,000	(1993-1994 election cycle)
Sasser, Jim (D-TN)	$1,000	(1993-1994 election cycle)
Shelby, Richard C. (R-AL)	$2,000	(1993-1994 and 1997-1998 election cycles)
Simpson, Alan K. (R-WY)	$1,000	(1995-1996 election cycle)

Thomas, Craig (R-WY) $1,000   (1999-2000 election cycle)
Thompson, Fred (R-TN) $2,000   (1993-1994 election cycle)
Torricelli, Robert G. (D-NJ) $20,000   (1995-1996, 1997-1998 and 1999-2000
                                         election cycles)

Thurmond, Strom (R-SC) $3,000   (1995-1996 election cycle)
Voinovich, George V. (R-OH) $2,000   (1997-1998 election cycle)
Warner, John W. (R-VA) $8,000   (1995-1996 election cycle)
Wheat, Alan (D-MO) $2,000   (1993-1994 election cycle)
Wilder, L. Douglas (D-VA) $2,000   (1995-1996 election cycle)
Wofford, Harris (D-PA) $6,000   (1993-1994 election cycle)
Wynia, Ann (D-MN) $5,000   (1993-1994 election cycle)

Total to Senate Democrats: $208,620
Total to Senate Republicans: $176,200
Total to Senate candidates: $384,820

House Candidates

Armey, Dick (R-TX) $1,000   (1997-1998 election cycle)
Baker, Bill (R-CA) $1,000   (1995-1996 election cycle)
Baker, Mark (R-IL) $5,500   (1995-1996 and 1997-1998 election cycles)
Barca, Peter W. (D-WI) $1,000   (1993-1994 election cycle)
Barlow, Tom (D-KY) $1,000   (1993-1994 election cycle)
Barrett, Bill (R-NE) $1,000   (1995-1996 election cycle)
Bereuter, Doug (R-NE) $2,500   (1993-1994 and 1995-1996 election cycles)
Berg, Jerry Ray (R-IL) $2,000   (1997-1998 election cycle)
Berry, Marion (D-AR) $5,000   (1995-1996 election cycle)
Bevill, Donald H. (D-AL) $500   (1997-1998 election cycle)
Bishop, Sanford D. Jr.(D-GA) $1,000   (1993-1994 election cycle)
Bliley, Thomas J. Jr. (R-VA) $1,000   (1995-1996 election cycle)
Blunt, Roy (R-MO) $2,000   (1997-1998 election cycle)
Bonior, David E. (D-MI) $2,500   (1993-1994 election cycle)
Bono, Sonny (R-CA) $500   (1995-1996 election cycle)
Boswell, Leonard L. (D-IA) $5,500   (1995-1996 and 1997-1998 election cycles)
Brownback, Sam (R-KS) $1,350   (1993-1994 election cycle)
Bryant, Ed (R-TN) $500   (1995-1996 election cycle)
Camp, Dave (R-MI) $500   (1997-1998 election cycle)
Clement, Bob (D-TN) $1,500   (1993-1994 and 1995-1996 election cycles)
Coleman, Tom (R-MO)   -$1,000   (1993-1994 election cycle)
Combest, Larry (R-TX) $1,000   (1997-1998 election cycle)
Cooley, Wes (R-OR) $500   (1995-1996 election cycle)
Coopersmith, Jeffrey (D-WA) $2,000   (1995-1996 election cycle)
Costello, Jerry F. (D-IL) $500   (1993-1994 election cycle)

Crane, Philip M. (R-IL)	$1,500	(1995-1996 election cycle)
Crapo, Michael D. (R-ID)	$1,000	(1995-1996 election cycle)
de la Garza, F. "Kika" (D-TX)	$7,000	(1993-1994 election cycle)
Delauro, Rosa L. (D-CT)	$500	(1993-1994 election cycle)
DeLay, Tom (R-TX)	$9,000	(1995-1996, 1997-1998 and 1999-2000 election cycles)
Derrick, Butler (D-CT)	$500	(1993-1994 election cycle)
Dicks, Norm (D-WA)	$2,500	(1993-1994, 1995-1996 and 1997-1998 election cycles)
Doolittle, John T. (R-CA)	$2,500	(1995-1996 and 1997-1998 election cycles)
Dorman, Robert K. (R-CA)	$500	(1993-1994 election cycle)
Durbin, Richard J. (D-IL)	$6,000	(1993-1994 election cycle)
Emerson, Bill (R-MO)	$1,500	(1993-1994 and 1995-1996 election cycles)
Emerson, Jo Ann (R-MO)	$4,500	(1995-1996, 1997-1998 and 1999-2000 election cycles)
English, Karan (D-AZ)	$500	(1993-1994 election cycle)
English, Phil (R-PA)	$500	(1995-1996 election cycle)
Espy, Henry (D-MS)	$3,000	(1993-1994 election cycle)
Ewing, Thomas W. (R-IL)	$12,750	(1993-1994, 1995-1996 and 1997-1998 election cycles)
Fazio, Vic (D-CA)	$1,500	(1995-1996 and 1997-1998 election cycles)
Fish, Hamilton, Jr. (R-NY)	$500	(1993-1994 election cycle)
Flanagan, Michael Patrick (R-IL)	$250	(1995-1996 election cycle)
Foley, Thomas S. (D-WA)	$4,000	(1993-1994 election cycle)
Furse, Elizabeth (D-OR)	$2,000	(1995-1996 election cycle)
Ganske, Greg (R-IA)	$1,500	(1995-1996 election cycle)
Gephardt, Richard A. (D-MO)	$23,000	(1995-1996, 1997-1998 and 1999-2000 election cycles)
Gibbons, Sam M. (D-FL)	$6,000	(1993-1994 and 1995-1996 election cycles)
Gilman, Benjamin A. (R-NY)	$1,250	(1993-1994 and 1995-1996 election cycles)
Glickman, Dan (D-KS)	$1,500	(1993-1994 election cycle)
Grandy, Fred (R-IA)	$1,000	(1993-1994 election cycle)
Gunderson, Steve (R-WI)	$500	(1993-1994 election cycle)
Gutknecht, Gil (R-MN)	$1,000	(1993-1994 and 1997-1998 election cycles)
Hahn, Janice K. (D-CA)	$500	(1997-1998 election cycle)
Hall, Tony P. (D-OH)	$500	(1997-1998 election cycle)
Hamilton, Lee H. (D-IN)	$5,000	(1993-1994 and 1995-1996 election cycles)
Harman, Jane (D-CA)	$500	(1995-1996 election cycle)
Hastert, Dennis (R-IL)	$1,500	(1993-1994 and 1997-1998 election cycles)

Heard, B. Keith (R-MS)	$4,500	(1995-1996 election cycle)
Hoagland, Peter (D-NE)	$3,000	(1993-1994 election cycle)
Hoffman, Jay C. (D-IL)	$5,000	(1995-1996 election cycle)
Holden, Tim (D-PA)	$500	(1993-1994 election cycle)
Hottinger, John C. (D-MN)	$2,000	(1993-1994 election cycle)
Houghton, Amo (R-NY)	$1,000	(1997-1998 election cycle)
Hoyer, Steny H. (D-MD)	$3,500	(1993-1994, 1995-1996 and 1997-1998 election cycles)
Hulshof, Kenny (R-MO)	$500	(1997-1998 election cycle)
Hyde, Henry J. (R-IL)	$1,500	(1995-1996 and 1997-1998 election cycles)
Inslee, Jay (D-WA)	$1,000	(1993-1994 election cycle)
Jackson, Jesse Jr. (D-IL)	$1,000	(1997-1998 election cycle)
James, Steve (D-NY)	$10,000	(1995-1996 election cycle)
Jesernig, James M. (D-WA)	-$150	(1993-1994 election cycle)
John, Chris (D-LA)	$1,000	(1997-1998 election cycle)
Kennedy, Joseph P. II (D-MA)	$6,500	(1993-1994, 1995-1996 and 1997-1998 election cycles)
Kennedy, Patrick J. (D-RI)	$2,500	(1993-1994 and 1997-1998 election cycles)
Kildee, Dale E. (D-MI)	$2,000	(1993-1994 and 1997-1998 election cycles)
Kline, John P. Jr. (R-MN)	$1,000	(1997-1998 election cycle)
Klug, Scott L. (R-WI)	$500	(1993-1994 election cycle)
Knollenberg, Joe (R-MI)	$500	(1999-2000 election cycle)
Kolbe, Jim (R-AZ)	$1,500	(1997-1998 election cycle)
LaHood, Ray (R-IL)	$500	(1997-1998 election cycle)
Lancaster, H. Martin (D-NC)	$2,500	(1993-1994 election cycle)
Latham, Tom (R-IA)	$500	(1995-1996 election cycle)
Levin, Sander M. (D-MI)	$3,500	(1993-1994, 1995-1996 and 1999-2000 election cycles)
Lightfoot, Jim Ross (R-IA)	$500	(1993-1994 election cycle)
Lindar, John (R-GA)	$500	(1995-1996 election cycle)
Lipinski, William O. (D-IL)	$1,850	(1993-1994 election cycle)
Livingston, Robert L. (R-LA)	$3,500	(1997-1998 election cycle)
Long, Jill L. (D-IN)	$500	(1993-1994 election cycle)
Luther, William P. "Bill" (D-MN)	$500	(1993-1994 election cycle)
Manzullo, Donald (R-IL)	$500	(1995-1996 election cycle)
Margolies-Mezvinsky, Marjorie (D-PA)	$1,000	(1993-1994 election cycle)
Matsui, Robert T. (D-CA)	$2,000	(1993-1994 and 1995-1996 election cycles)
McCrery, Jim (R-LA)	$1,000	(1993-1994 election cycle)

McGovern, Jim (D-MA)	$12,000	(1993-1994, 1995-1996 and 1997-1998 election cycles)
Minge, David (D-MN)	$11,500	(1993-1994, 1995-1996, 1997-1998 and 1999-2000 election cycles)
Morella, Constance A. (R-MD)	$1,000	(1993-1994 election cycle)
Murphy, Austin J. (D-PA)	$500	(1993-1994 election cycle)
Neubauer, Jeff (D-WI)	$500	(1993-1994 election cycle)
Nussle, Jim (R-IA)	$5,000	(1993-1994, 1995-1996 and 1997-1998 election cycles)
Ortiz, Solomon P. (D-TX)	$500	(1995-1996 election cycle)
Palmer, Brian Paul (R-MI)	$1,000	(1997-1998 election cycle)
Pease, Ed (R-IN)	$500	(1997-1998 election cycle)
Petterson, Collin C. (D-MN)	$500	(1993-1994 election cycle)
Phelps, David D. (D-IL)	$8,500	(1997-1998 and 1999-2000 election cycles)
Pomeroy, Earl (D-ND)	$6,000	(1993-1994, 1995-1996, 1997-1998 and 1999-2000 election cycles)
Rangel, Charles B. (D-NY)	$6,000	(1995-1996 and 1997-1998 election cycles)
Redmond, Bill (R-NM)	$500	(1997-1998 election cycle)
Reynolds, Mel (D-IL)	$1,000	(1993-1994 election cycle)
Richardson, Bill (D-MN)	$500	(1995-1996 election cycle)
Roberts, Pat (R-KS)	$1,000	(1993-1994 election cycle)
Rostenkowski, Dan (D-IL)	$10,000	(1993-1994 election cycle)
Roth, Toby (R-WI)	$500	(1993-1994 election cycle)
Royce, Ed (R-CA)	$500	(1997-1998 election cycle)
Schaefer, Dan (R-CO)	$500	(1995-1996 election cycle)
Sessions, Pete (R-TX)	$500	(1993-1994 election cycle)
Shimkus, John M (R-IL)	$2,500	(1997-1998 election cycle)
Smith, Adam (D-WA)	$500	(1995-1996 election cycle)
Smith, Neal (D-IA)	$5,000	(1993-1994 election cycle)
Spratt, John M. Jr. (D-SC)	$1,000	(1999-2000 election cycle)
Stenholm, Charles W. (D-TX)	$7,250	(1993-1994, 1997-1998 and 1999-2000 election cycles)
Thune, John (R-SD)	$500	(1997-1998 election cycle)
Torricelli, Robert G. (D-NJ)	$500	(1993-1994 election cycle)
Towns, Edolphus (D-NY)	$1,000	(1997-1998 election cycle)
Verticchio, Rick (D-IL)	$2,500	(1997-1998 election cycle)
Walsh, James T. (R-NY)	$500	(1999-2000 election cycle)
Walsh, Michael Patrick (U-NC)	$500	(1993-1994 election cycle)
Weldon, Dave (R-FL)	$500	(1995-1996 election cycle)

Weller, Gerald C. (R-IL)	$3,500	(1993-1994, 1995-1996, 1997-1998 and 1999-2000 election cycles)
Wicker, Roger (R-MS)	$1,000	(1997-1998 election cycle)
Williams, Pat (D-MT)	$500	(1993-1994 election cycle)
Winters, Brent (R-IL)	$3,000	(1993-1994 and 1997-1998 election cycles)
Wyden, Ron (D-OR)	$1,500	(1993-1994 election cycle)
Young, Don (D-OR)	$1,500	(1993-1994 election cycle)
Zeliff, Bill (R-NH)	$276	(1995-1996 election cycle)

Total to House Democrats: $211,950

Total to House Republicans: $102,876

Total to House candidates: $315,326

* A PAC or Political Action Committee raises and spends money for the purpose of electing candidates. PACs can donate $5,000 to a candidate's committee per election, $15,000 annually to any national party committee, and $5,000 annually to any other PAC. PACs may receive up to $5,000 from any one individual, PAC, or party committee per calendar year.

** 1999 contributions are based on data released by the FEC from the ADM PAC's July 28, 1999 Mid-Year Report.

The data was assembled from databases from the FEC and the Center for Responsive Politics.

The Department of Justice investigated international price-fixing conspiracies involving citric acid, high fructose corn syrup ("HFCS"),[1] and lysine. Numerous companies and individuals were charged in either the lysine conspiracy or the citric acid conspiracy.[2] The criminal investigations led to lawsuits (class and nonclass) for civil remedies for antitrust violations. Numerous shareholder derivative suits were also filed in response to the investigations. Recently, the lawsuits have spread beyond the United States.

On November 12, 1999, ADM reported to the SEC on the status of federal investigations into antitrust violations:

> Federal grand juries in the Northern Districts of Illinois, California and Georgia, under the direction of the United States Department of Justice ("DOJ"), have been investigating possible violations by the Company [Archer Daniels Midland, Co.] and others with respect to the sale of lysine, citric acid and high fruc-

1. Although ADM was investigated in connection with price-fixing HFCS, it and its executives were never charged with anything related to HFCS.

2. As of February 1998, the investigation had resulted in criminal charges against ten companies and fifteen individuals. *See* February 26, 1998 Statement of Joel I. Klein, Assistant Attorney General Antitrust Division of the United States Department of Justice, before the Antitrust, Business Rights and Competition Subcommittee of the Committee on the Judiciary of the United States Senate in Washington, DC.

tose corn syrup, respectively. In connection with an agreement with the DOJ in fiscal 1997, the Company paid the United States fines of $100 million. This agreement constitutes a global resolution of all matters between the DOJ and the Company and brings to a close all DOJ investigations of the Company. The federal grand juries in the Northern Districts of Illinois (lysine) and Georgia (high fructose corn syrup) have been closed.

The Company, along with other domestic and foreign companies, was named as a defendant in a number of putative class action antitrust suits and other proceedings involving the sale of lysine, citric acid, sodium gluconate, monosodium glutamate and high fructose corn syrup.... The Company has made provisions of $21 million in fiscal 1999, $48 million in fiscal 1998 and $200 million in fiscal 1997 to cover the fines, litigation settlements related to the federal lysine class action, federal securities class action, the federal citric class action, the federal sodium gluconate class action, and certain state actions filed by indirect purchasers of lysine, certain actions filed by parties that opted out of the class action settlements, certain other proceedings and the related costs and expenses associated with the litigation described above.[3]

The following is a summary of the major criminal and civil cases that have arisen out investigations into price-fixing lysine, citric acid, and HFCS.

ARCHER DANIELS MIDLAND COMPANY AND ITS OFFICERS

Criminal Investigations

CITRIC ACID AND LYSINE
Archer Daniels Midland Company

In the criminal case filed on October 15, 1996, under criminal no.96-CR-00640, Archer Daniels Midland Company was charged with two violations of the Sherman Act, 15 U.S.C. § 1, et al. Count One charged that ADM conspired to restrain trade in lysine in violation of 15 U.S.C. § 1. Count Two charged that ADM conspired to restrain trade in citric acid in violation of 15 U.S.C. § 1. In both counts, the coconspirators remained unnamed (*Criminal Information*, No. 96-CR-00640, 12/15/96).[4]

---

3. ADM's quarterly report pursuant to Section 13 or 15(d) of the Securities Exchange Act of 1934 for the quarterly period ending on September 30, 1999.

4. *Criminal Information, United States v. Archer Daniels Midland Company*, Criminal No. 96-CR-00640 (October 15, 1996, N.D. Ill.) (Castillo, J.).

Citric acid is a 1.2-billion-dollar industry worldwide (DOJ, 3/26/97).[5] Lysine is a 600-million-dollar industry worldwide (DOJ, 8/27/96).[6] According to Purdue University Professor John M. Connor, ADM controlled 50 percent to 54 percent of the United States lysine market between 1991-1995. Similarly, ADM controlled between 37 percent to 49 percent of the United States-Canadian market in citric acid between 1990 and 1995 (Connor, January 1998).[7]

On October 15, 1996 ADM pleaded guilty to both charges, and it was granted immunity from prosecution in the HFCS investigation. ADM was sentenced to pay a $100 million fine for its convictions of the two conspiracies, $70 million was allocated to the lysine conspiracy, and $30 million was fined for its participation in the citric acid conspiracy (Connor, August 1998).[8]

LYSINE

Michael D. Andreas, Terrance S. Wilson, Mark E. Whitacre, and Kazutoshi Yamada

Michael D. Andreas was the executive vice president of ADM. Terrance S. Wilson was the group vice president and president of ADM's corn processing division. Mark E. Whitacre was the president of ADM's BioProducts Division. Kazutoshi Yamada was the managing director of Ajinomoto Co. Inc. in Tokyo, Japan.

In an indictment filed on December 3, 1996, they were charged with violating Section One of the Sherman Act, 15 U.S.C. § 1, by fixing the price of and allocating the sales volume of lysine, which was offered for sale to customers worldwide and by conspiracy with ADM, Ajinomoto Co., Inc., Kyowa Hakko Kogyo Co. Ltd., Sewon America, Inc., and others to suppress competition in the lysine market worldwide.[9]

On September 17, 1998, a jury convicted Andreas, Whitacre, and Wilson. On

5. United States Department of Justice (1997), *Justice Department's Ongoing Probe into the Food and Feed Additives Industry Yields $25 million More in Criminal Fines,* DOJ press release #97-123:03:26-97.

6. United States Department of Justice (1996), *Justice Department Takes Action Against International Food and Feed Additive Price Fixers,* DOJ press release #96-411:08-27-96.

7. Connor, John M., *Archer Daniels Midland: Price-Fixer to the World,* staff paper 98-1, Department of Agricultural Economics, Purdue University, dated January 1998, pp. 2-4.

8. Connor, John M., *What Can We Learn from the ADM Global Price Conspiracies?* staff paper 98-14, Department of Agricultural Economics, Purdue University, dated August 1998, p. 9 n.6.

9. United States Department of Justice (1996), *Former ADM Executives, Japanese Executive, Indicted in Lysine Price Fixing Conspiracy,* DOJ press release #96-573:12-03-96.

July 9, 1999 the three codefendants were sentenced. Whitacre received a thirty-months sentence without a fine. Wilson and Andreas were each sentenced to twenty-four months and a $350,000 fine. To date, Yamada has not been extradited or tried.

Civil Lawsuits

Under federal and some state laws, victims are entitled to recover injunctive relief to stop the antitrust activities, as well as compensatory damages, treble damages, attorneys fees and costs. Often these cases are pursued by groups of plaintiffs called putative classes, who attempt to have the suits certified as class actions, for purposes of the litigation.

HIGH FRUCTOSE CORN SYRUP (HFCS)

As of September 30, 1999, ADM, along with other companies, has been named as a defendant in thirty-one antitrust suits involving the sale of HFCS. Thirty of these actions have been brought as putative class actions.[10]

Twenty-two of the cases were consolidated in United States District Court for the Central District of Illinois as *In Re High Fructose Corn Syrup Antitrust Litigation*, MDL No. 1087 and Master File No. 95-1477. These cases allege federal antitrust violations, including that the defendants agreed to fix, stabilize, and maintain at artificially high levels the prices of HFCS.

On January 14, 1997, a lawsuit begun against ADM and its officials under the caption *Gray & Co. v. Archer Daniels Midland Co., et al*, No. 97-69- AS. It was filed in Oregon and alleges state and federal antitrust violations, and claims that defendants conspired to fix, raise, maintain, and stabilize the price of corn syrup and HFCS.

ADM and its officials also have been sued in seven California state antitrust lawsuits. The suits allege that defendants violated California antitrust and unfair competition laws by agreeing to fix, stabilize and maintain at artificially high levels the prices of HFCS. The first case *Kagome Foods, Inc. v Archer Daniels Midland Co. et al.*, Civil Action No. 37236 (October 17, 1995, Superior Court for the County of Stanislaus, California), was removed to federal court and consolidated with the federal class actions described above. Five of the cases were combined into one class action under the caption *Food Additives (HFCS) cases*, Master File No. 39693 (Superior Court for the County of Stanislaus, California). The five cases were *Borgeson v. Archer Daniels Midland Co., et al.*, Civil Action No. BC131940 (July 21, 1995, Superior Court of the County of Los Angeles, California); *Goings v. Archer Daniels Midland Co., et al.*, Civil

---

10. ADM's quarterly report pursuant to Section 13 or 15(d) of the Securities Exchange Act of 1934 for the quarterly period ending on September 30, 1999.

Action No. 750276 (July 21, 1995, Orange County Superior Court, California); *Rainbow Acres v. Archer Daniels Midland Co.*, et al., Civil Action No. 974271 (November 22, 1995, San Francisco County Superior Court, California); *Patane v. Archer Daniels Midland Co., et al.*, Civil Action No. 212610 (January 17, 1996, Sonoma County Superior Court, California); and *St. Stan's Brewing Co. v. Archer Daniels Midland Co., et al.*, Civil Action No. 37237 (October 17, 1995, Stanislaus County Superior Court, California). In 1997, after the five cases were coordinated, Varni Brothers Corp. filed a complaint to intervene in the action.

On March 18, 1996, ADM and certain officials were sued for alleged violations of antitrust practices regarding HFCS under state and federal law. The suit was filed in the Circuit Court of Coosa County, Alabama and it is captioned *Caldwell v. Archer Daniels Midland Co., et al.*, Civil Action No. 96-17. On April 23, 1997, the court severed the claims and dismissed all non-Alabama claims. Discovery is ongoing.[11]

LYSINE

ADM, over the past several years, has been named a defendant in twenty-three putative class-action suits involving the sale of lysine. The majority of these lawsuits have been settled. Two key lawsuits remain open, and one motion to certify a class is pending.

The first lawsuit was filed in Alabama state court. On August 17, 1995, ADM and other companies were sued for violating Alabama antitrust laws in the lysine trade in *Ashley v. Archer Daniels Midland Co., et al.*, Civil Action No. 95-336 (Circuit Court of DeKalb County, Alabama). The plaintiff alleged that defendants agreed to fix, stabilize, and maintain at artificially high levels the prices of lysine. Plaintiff sought to have this case certified as a class-action. This request was denied. The complaint was subsequently amended to include approximately 300 individual plaintiffs.

The second lawsuit originated in Ontario, Canada. On June 11, 1999, ADM and other companies were served with a putative class-action lawsuit captioned *Rein Minnema and Minnema Farms Ltd. v. Archer Daniels Midland Company, et al.*, Court File No. G23495-99. This case alleges that defendants fixed prices and fixed volumes on lysine sold to customers in Ontario in violation of Sections 45 (1)(c) and 61(1)(b) of Canada's Competition Act. According to ADM, the plaintiffs seek $25 million for violations of the Competition Act, and $10 million in punitive, exemplary, and aggravated damages, interest, and costs of the action.

ADM also was named as a respondent in a putative class-action involving alleged

11. ADM's quarterly report pursuant to Section 13 or 15(d) of the Securities Exchange Act of 1934 for the quarterly period ending on September 30, 1999.

violations of Section 45(1)(c) of Canada's Competition Act. A motion is filed at *Option Consommateurs, et al v. Archer Daniels Midland Company, et al.*, Court No. 500-06-000089-991, in which the plaintiffs seek permission to file a class action. The case is in the Superior Court in the Province of Quebec, District of Montreal.[12]

CITRIC ACID

As of the quarter ending September 30, 1999, ADM, along with other companies, has been named as a defendant in fourteen antitrust suits and two nonantitrust lawsuits involving the sale of citric acid. Three cases remain open. The remaining cases have either been settled or dismissed.

ADM and other companies have been named as defendants in two Canadian-based putative class-action lawsuits charging violations of Canada's Competitive Act with respect to the sale of citric acid:

1. *Ashworth v. Archer Daniels Midland Company, et al.*, Court file No. 53510/99, (Superior Court of Justice, in Newmarket, Ontario, Canada); and

2. *Fairlee Fruit Juice Limited v. Archer Daniels Midland Company, et al.*, Court File No. 32562/99, (Superior Court of Justice, in London, Ontario, Canada).

The first lawsuit seeks $30 million and punitive and exemplary damages in the amount of $30 million, interest, costs and fees, while the later case seeks general damages in the amount of $300 million, punitive and exemplary damages in the amount of $20 million, interest, costs and fees. The actions involve the sale of citric acid in Canada.

The remaining United States-based lawsuit is *Seven Up Bottling Co. of Jasper, Inc. v. Archer Daniels Midland Co., et al.*, Civil Action No. 95- 436 (July 27, 1995, Circuit Court of Walker County, Alabama). This action alleges violations of the Alabama antitrust laws, including that the defendants agreed to fix, stabilize, and maintain at artificially high levels the prices of citric acid. ADM, and the other defendants, filed a motion to dismiss on the legal basis that Alabama's antitrust laws apply only to intrastate commerce. The trial court denied the motion. However, on June 25, 1999, the Alabama Supreme Court reversed this decision and held that Alabama antitrust laws apply only to intrastate commerce. On October 22, 1999, the Alabama Supreme Court denied plaintiff's request for reconsideration.

ADM is also a named respondent in a putative class action involving alleged violations of Section 45(1)(c) of Canada's Competition Act. A motion is filed at *Option Consommateurs, et al. v. Archer Daniels Midland Company, et al.*, Court No.500-06-

12. ADM's quarterly report pursuant to Section 13 or 15(d) of the Securities Exchange Act of 1934 for the quarterly period ending on September 30, 1999.

000094-991 (Superior Court in the Province of Quebec, District of Montreal). The plaintiffs in this action seek general damages in the amount of $300 million, punitive and exemplary damages in the amount of $20 million, interest, costs, and fees.[13]

HFCS/CITRIC ACID ACTIONS

ADM and other companies have been sued in five class actions alleging violations of the antitrust laws, including charges that the defendants agreed to fix, stabilize, and maintain at artificially high levels the prices of both HFCS and citric acid. The first two cases were filed in California under state antitrust and unfair competition laws: *Gangi Bros. Packing Co. v. Archer Daniels Midland Co., et al.*, Civil Action No. 37217 (October 11, 1995, Stanislaus County Superior Court, California) and *MCFH, Inc. v. Archer Daniels Midland Co., et al.*, Civil Action No. 974120 (November 20, 1995, Superior Court of San Francisco County, California). Subsequently, the California actions were split into citric acid and HFCS cases. The cases were then coordinated with existing cases on those products. The citric acid portion of these cases was settled on September 30, 1998.

ADM was also sued for violations of West Virginia's antitrust laws, including allegations that the defendants agreed to fix, stabilize, and maintain at artificially high levels the prices of both HFCS and citric acid. The case is *Freda's v. Archer Daniels Midland Co., et al.*, Civil Action No. 95-C-125 (October 26, 1995, Circuit Court for Boone County, West Virginia).

A similar case was filed in the District of Columbia, *Holder v. Archer Daniels Midland Co., et al.*, Civil Action No. 96-2975 (April 12, 1996, Superior Court for the District of Columbia). This case has been certified as a class action.

Alleging violations of Kansas antitrust laws, including that the Defendants agreed to fix, stabilize and maintain at artificially high levels the prices of HFCS and citric acid, Plaintiffs filed suit in Kansas City, Kansas in *Waugh v. Archer Daniels Midland Co., et al.*, Case No. 96-C-2029 (May 7, 1996, District Court of Wyandotte County, Kansas).[14]

Case:HFCS/Citric Acid/Lysine Actions

ADM and other defendants were sued in six putative class-action suits in California alleging violations of state antitrust and unfair competition laws, including that the defendants agreed to fix, stabilize, and maintain at artificially high levels the prices of HFCS, citric acid, and/or lysine. The cases are *Nu Laid Foods, Inc. v.*

13. ADM's quarterly report pursuant to Section 13 or 15(d) of the Securities Exchange Act of 1934 for the quarterly period ending on September 30, 1999.

14. ADM's quarterly report pursuant to Section 13 or 15(d) of the Securities Exchange Act of 1934 for the quarterly period ending on September 30, 1999.

Archer Daniels Midland Co., et al., Civil Action No. 39693 (December 18, 1995, Superior Court for Stanislaus County, California); *Batson v. Archer Daniels Midland Co., et al.*, Civil Action No. 39680 (December 14, 1995, Superior Court for Stanislaus County, California); *Abbott v. Archer Daniels Midland Co., et al.*, No. 41014 (December 21, 1995, Stanislaus County Superior Court, California); *Noldin v. Archer Daniels Midland Co., et al.*, No. 41015 (December 21, 1995, Stanislaus County Superior Court, California); *Guzman v. Archer Daniels Midland Co., et al.*, No. 41013 (December 21, 1995, Stanislaus County Superior Court, California) and *Ricci v. Archer Daniels Midland Co., et al.*, No. 96-AS-00383 (February 6, 1996, Sacramento County Superior Court, California). As with the other actions based upon more than one product, the court bifurcated the cases so that each antitrust action dealt with only one product. Some of the cases were settled while others were coordinated with similar actions in San Francisco County Superior Court and Stanislaus County Superior Court.[15]

SODIUM GLUCONATE

ADM was a defendant in three federal antitrust class actions involving the antitrust violations in the sale of sodium gluconate. The first and second cases are *Chemical Distribution, Inc, v. Akzo Nobel Chemicals BV, et al.*, No. C -97-4141 (CW) (December 2, 1997, United States District Court for the Northern District of California); and *Stetson Chemicals, Inc. v. Akzo Nobel Chemicals BV*, 97-CV-1285 RCL (December 31, 1997, United States District Court for the District of Massachusetts). Shortly afterwards, ADM was named as a defendant in a third, already existing class action for sodium gluconate antitrust practices. The three cases were transferred to the United States District Court for the Northern District of California for coordinated or consolidated pretrial proceedings. According to ADM the cases were settled on October 29, 1998. The settlement included ADM paying $69,600 to the plaintiff class. On May 28, 1999, the court granted final approval of the settlement and dismissed the action.[16]

Monosodium Glutamate Actions

ADM has been named as a defendant in four putative class-action antitrust suits involving the sale of monosodium glutamate and/or other flavor enhancers. The cases are

---

15. ADM's quarterly report pursuant to Section 13 or 15(d) of the Securities Exchange Act of 1934 for the quarterly period ending on September 30, 1999.

16. ADM's annual report pursuant to Section 13 or 15(d) of the Securities Exchange Act of 1934 for the year ending on June 30, 1999.

1. *Thorp, Inc. v. Archer Daniels Midland Company, et al.,* NoC99 4752 (VRW) (United States District Court for the Northern District of California);

2. *Premium Ingredients, Ltd. v. Archer Daniels Midland Co., et al.,* No. C 99 4742(MJJ)(United States District Court for the Northern District of California); and

3. *Felbro Food Products v. Archer Daniels Midland Company, et al.,* No.C99 4761 (MJJ) (United States District Court for the Northern District of California).

ADM and another company were also named as defendants in a state court putative class action involving the sale of sale of monosodium glutamate. This case, which was filed on June 25, 1999, is *Fu's Garden Restaurant v. Archer Daniels Midland Company, et al.,* Civil Action No. 304471 (Superior Court of San Francisco County, California).[17]

SHAREHOLDER DERIVATIVE ACTIONS

In June 1995, the DOJ publicly announced the grand jury investigations into alleged antitrust practices of ADM and its officials. Shortly thereafter, three (3) shareholder derivative suits were filed against ADM and some of ADM's then current directors and executive officers in the United States District Court for the Northern District of Illinois. Fourteen (14) shareholder derivative suits also were filed in the Delaware Court of Chancery, a special court dealing with companies incorporated in Delaware.

The three (3) Illinois cases were consolidated as *Felzen, et al. v. Andreas, et al.,* Civil Action No. 95-2279 (Central District of Illinois). It alleges breach of fiduciary duty, waste of corporate assets, abuse of control and gross mismanagement, and other wrongdoing.

The fourteen Delaware cases have been consolidated as *In Re Archer Daniels Midland Derivative Litigation,* Consolidated No. 14403.

On or about May 29, 1997, ADM entered into a settlement of all of these shareholder derivative suits for $8 million. In addition, certain changes in the structure and policies of the ADM's Board of Directors were to be made.

Foreign Investigations

ADM is being investigated by several foreign agencies to determine whether it has engaged in anticompetitive practices. According to ADM, the only outstanding investigations are with the Commission of the European Communities and the Mexican Federal Competition Commission.

17. ADM's quarterly report pursuant to Section 13 or 15(d) of the Securities Exchange Act of 1934 for the quarterly period ending on September 30, 1999.

COMMISSION OF THE EUROPEAN COMMUNITIES

In June 1997, ADM received notification that the Commission of the European (CEC) Communities had initiated an investigation into possible anticompetitive practices in the amino acid markets, in particular lysine, in the European Union. On October 29, 1998, the CEC initiated formal proceedings against ADM. ADM filed a response on February 1, 1999. A hearing was held on March 1, 1999. On August 8, 1999, the CEC filed documents expanding the scope of the investigation. The formal proceedings are still pending.

In September 1997, ADM was notified that the CEC also was investigating anticompetitive practices with respect to citric acid market.

In November 1998, a European subsidiary of ADM was put on notice that the CEC was probing activities in the sodium gluconate market in the European Union.[18]

MEXICAN FEDERAL COMPETITION COMMISSION

On February 11, 1999, an ADM subsidiary in Mexico was notified that the Mexican Federal Competition Commission had initiated an investigation as to possible anticompetitive practices in the citric acid market in Mexico.[19]

According to ADM, it may become the subject of similar antitrust investigations conducted by the applicable regulatory authorities of other countries.[20]

SELECT OTHER COMPANIES

Criminal Investigations: LYSINE

Ajinomoto Co., Inc; Kyowa Hakko Kogyo Co. Ltd.;
Sewon America, Inc.; Kanji Mimoto.; Masaru Yamamoto; and Jhom Su Kim

The above defendants were charged with violating Section One of the Sherman Act, 15 U.S.C. § 1, by fixing the price and allocating the sales volume of lysine, which was offered for sale to customers worldwide.

Ajinomoto Co., Inc. is a corporation with its principal place of business in Tokyo, Japan. It operates Heartland Lysine, Inc. (a wholly owned subsidiary) in Chicago, Illinois. Kanji Mimoto was the deputy general manager and later the general manager of the Feed Additives Division of Ajinomoto.

18. ADM's quarterly report pursuant to Section 13 or 15(d) of the Securities Exchange Act of 1934 for the quarterly period ending on September 30, 1999.

19. ADM's quarterly report pursuant to Section 13 or 15(d) of the Securities Exchange Act of 1934 for the quarterly period ending on September 30, 1999.

20. ADM's quarterly report pursuant to Section 13 or 15(d) of the Securities Exchange Act of 1934 for the quarterly period ending on September 30, 1999.

Kyowa Hakko Kogyo is based in Tokyo. It operates BioKyowa, Inc. (a wholly owned subsidiary) in Cape Girardeau, Missouri. Masaru Yamamoto was the deputy general manager and later the general manager of the Agricultural Products Department of the Bio-Products Division of Kyowa.

Sewon America, Inc. is a Delaware corporation with its principal place of business in Paramus, New Jersey. Jhom Su Kim was the president.[21]

In August 1996 Ajinomoto pleaded guilty and paid the statutory maximum fine of $10 million. Mimoto also pleaded guilty and paid a $75,000 fine. Kyowa pleaded guilty and paid the statutory maximum fine of $10 million. Yamamoto also pleaded guilty and paid a $50,000 fine. Sewon pleaded guilty, and the court was to determine its fine following the ADM trial. Kim also pleaded guilty and paid a $75,000 fine.[22]

CHEIL JEDANG LTD. AKA CHEIL FOODS & CHEMICALS, INC.

On December 3, 1996, Cheil Jedang Ltd. of Seoul, Korea pleaded guilty to participating in the lysine price-fixing and sales volume allocation conspiracy. The company agreed to pay a $1.25 million dollar fine in connection with its guilty plea.[23]

Criminal Investigations: CITRIC ACID

HAARMANN & REIMER CORP. AND HANS HARTMANN

Haarmann & Reimer Corp. is a New Jersey-based subsidiary of the German-based Bayer AG. Hans Hartman is a senior executive at the German-based Haarmann & Reimer Gmbh. Haarmann and Hartman both pleaded guilty to participating in the citric acid price-fixing and sales volume allocation conspiracy. Haarmann agreed to pay a $50 million fine. Hartman agreed to pay a $150,000 fine.[24]

---

21. *Criminal Information, United States v. Ajinomoto Co., Inc.*, et al., Criminal No. 96-CR-520 (August 27, 1996, N.D. Ill.) (Castillo, J.).

22. United States Department of Justice (1996), *Justice Department Takes Action Against International Food and Feed Additive Price Fixers*; DOJ press release #96-411:08-27-96; United States Department of Justice (1997), *Ongoing Probe into the Food and Feed Additives Industry Yields Second Largest Fine Ever*, DOJ press release #97-039:01-29-97.

23. *Criminal Information, United States v. Cheil Jedang Ltd., et al.*, Criminal No. 96-CR-00761 (December 3, 1996, N.D. Ill.) (Alesia, J.); United States Department of Justice, *Former ADM Executives, Japanese Executive, Indicted in Lysine Price Fixing Conspiracy* (1996), DOJ press release #96-573:12-03-96.

24. United States Department of Justice (1997), *Justice Department's Ongoing Probe into the Food and Feed Additives Industry Yields $25 Million More in Criminal Fines*, DOJ press release #97-123:03:26-97.

F. HOFFMAN-LA ROCHE LTD. AND
JUNGBUNZLAUER INTERNATIONAL AG

These chemical companies pleaded guilty on March 26, 1997 to participating in the citric acid price-fixing and sales volume allocation conspiracy. Hoffman-La Roche, of Switzerland, agreed to pay a $14 million fine. Jungbunzlauer, of Austria, agreed to pay an $11 million fine. Udo Hass, former managing director of SA Citrique Belge NV—a citric acid producing affiliate of Hoffman—also pleaded guilty and agreed to pay a $150,000 fine. Rainer Bichlbauer, the chairman and president of Jungbunzlauer, also pleaded guilty and agreed to pay a $150,000 fine.[25]

Cerestar Bioproducts BV and Silvio Kluzer

On June 23, 1998, Cerestar Bioproducts BV, a Dutch subsidiary of the French agribusiness giant, Eridania Beghin-Say SA, pleaded guilty to a single count charge of conspiring to fix prices and allocate market shares in the sale of citric acid worldwide. The company agreed to pay a $400,000 fine. Silvio Kluzer, an Italian citizen and Cerestar's managing director, also pleaded guilty and paid a $40,000 fine.[26]

SELECT OTHER INDIVIDUALS

SIDNEY D. HULSE

Sidney D. Hulse was a former vice president of the BioProductions Division of ADM. Hulse was charged with conspiracy, wire fraud, and money laundering in connection with the Whitacre fraud investigation. The twelve-count indictment was issued in US District Court in Springfield, Illinois.[27] On November 4, 1997, Hulse was indicted in Atlanta, Georgia, for filing false income tax returns for the years 1992 and 1993.[28] In March 1998, Hulse pleaded guilty to one count of filing a false income tax return in 1992 and one count of conspiracy.[29] On May 29, 1998, Hulse

25. United States Department of Justice (1997), *Justice Department's Ongoing Probe into the Food and Feed Additives Industry Yields $25 million More in Criminal Fines*, DOJ press release #97-123:03:26-97.

26. United States Department of Justice (1998), *Dutch Company Charged with Price-Fixing on Citric Acid: Agrees to Pay $400,000 Criminal Fine*, DOJ press release #98-298:06-23-98.

27. United States Department of Justice (1997), *Former ADM Official Indicted for Fraud*, DOJ press release #461:11-05:97.

28. United States Department of Justice (1997), *Former ADM Official Indicted for Fraud*, DOJ press release #97-461:11-05:97.

29. "Briefly," (March 7, 1998, business section, pp. 2, col. F) *Dallas Morning News*.

was sentenced to ten months in federal prison for defrauding ADM and ordered to pay ADM $995,500 in restitution.[30]

REINHARD RICHTER

In or early February 1997, Reinhard Richter, president of ADM's Mexican subsidiary, was indicted on eight counts for conspiring to swindle ADM out of $171,000 and federal tax evasion.[31] On October 28, 1997, Richter pleaded guilty to charges of conspiring to defraud ADM and assisting Whitacre in defrauding the IRS.[32] On January 30, 1998, Richter was sentenced to one year of probation and a $25,000 fine.

MARTY W. ALLISON

Marty W. Allison, a former vice president of ADM's BioProducts Division, pleaded guilty in US District Court in Chicago, Illinois, on February 25, 1997. He was charged with conspiring with others to obtain money and property from ADM from 1991 through September 1995[33] amounting to more than $300,000.[34] Allison pleaded guilty to conspiracy to commit wire fraud and to transmitting checks taken by fraud in interstate commerce.[35] On May 12, 1998, he was sentenced to three-years probation and ordered to make restitution in the amount of $75,000.

MILOS LEE COVERT

Milos Lee Covert was charged with a fraudulent tax return in violation of 26 U.S.C. § 7207. The criminal information alleged that he falsely reported having a business income of $81,250.[36] On September 9, 1997, he executed a plea agreement and was sentenced to two years probation, and a $720 fine.[37]

30. Gunset, George, "Former ADM Executive Sentenced," (May 30, 1998) *Chicago Tribune*.

31. AP, (February 7, 1997, § Business News), "Former Colleague of ADM Mole Indicted for Conspiracy, Money Laundering," *Associated Press*.

32. "Ex-ADM Executive, Richter, Pleads Guilty to Conspiracy Charges," (October 29, 1997, §B, pp. 8, col. 5), *Wall Street Journal*.

33. United States Department of Justice (1997), *Former Archer Daniels Midland Vice President Pleads Guilty in Fraud Probe*, DOJ press release #97-084.

34. "Allison, Former Official of ADM, Pleads Guilty in Case Involving Fraud," (February 27, 1997, §B, pp. 2), *Wall Street Journal*.

35. United States Department of Justice (1997), *Former Archer Daniels Midland Vice President Pleads Guilty in Fraud Probe*, DOJ press release #97-084.

36. *Plea Agreement, United States v. Milos Lee Covert*, Criminal No. 97-CR-0037 (September 3, 1997, N.D. Ill.).

37. *Criminal Information, United States v. Milos Lee Covert*, Criminal No. 97-CR-0037 (September 3, 1997, N.D. Ill.)

PART I: THE RAID

Preface

i-ii An excellent article on the political and media influence at ADM at the time of the raid is Scott Kilman, Bruce Ingersoll, and Jill Abramson, "Risk Averse: How Dwayne Andreas Rules Archer-Daniels by Hedging His Bets, CEO Works with Rivals, Gives to Both Parties and Invests in the Media," *The Wall Street Journal* (October 27, 1995). Since 1991, the company had given more than $800,000 to the Democratic party and more than $1.5 million to the Republicans. ADM spent $4.7 million to advertise on *Meet the Press*, $4.3 million for *Face the Nation*, and $6.8 million for the *MacNeil/Lehrer NewsHour*, between January 1994 and April 1995.

Chapter 1: The Mole

3-5 The facts pertaining to the issuance of the search warrant are derived from the search warrant and affidavit at Case No. 95-U-22 presented to the United States Magistrate David G. Bernthal in Urbana on June 21, 1995. Analysis of the strength of ADM and the prospect for Mark Whitacre to become its next president and Michael Andreas to become its next CEO is found in the Dain Bosworth research report of March 20, 1995 by Bonnie Wittenburg.

5-6 Information about the experience of the Lincoln family in Decatur, the 1860 Illinois Republican convention, the Lincoln courthouse, and the Lincoln homestead can be found in D. Ray Wilson in *Illinois, Historical Tour Guide* (Carpentersville, Illinois: Crossroads, 1991).

6 The descriptions of Dwayne Andreas' office at the time he was CEO are found in E.J. Kahn, Jr., *Supermarketer to the World, The Story of Dwayne Andreas, CEO of Archer Daniels Midland* (New York: Warner Books, 1991) hereafter "Kahn," on page 178. The description of ADM's headquarters including the trading floor is found in Ronald Henkoff, "Oh, How the Money Grows at ADM," *Fortune* (October 8, 1990). The raid also was reported in Ronald E. Yates, "Battle Lines Drawn at ADM; Midnight Raids in Decatur; Legion of Lawyers Muster Worldwide," *Chicago Tribune* (July 30, 1995).

6-7 Descriptions of the raid and the effect on ADM stock are found in Sharon Walsh, "Grain

Firms Target of Antitrust Probe; 4 Sweetner Makers Subpoenaed," *The Washington Post* (July 8, 1995) and William Smith, "Tight-Lipped ADM Keeps Own Board in Dark," *Chicago Sun-Times* (July 12, 1995). In addition, Mark Whitacre described his experience during the raid in interviews on May 22, 1999 and July 30, 1999, and during five hours of videotape for WAND-TV made on March 10, 1996.

7 The ADM connections to Robert Strauss and Edward Bennett Williams and their law firms are described by Kahn on pages 184 and 201-208. An interesting comment on the connection between private lawyering and the highest levels of government and the careers of Robert Strauss as well as other top Washington lawyers is Ruth Marks, "What Price Fame—and Who Pays It?" *The National Law Journal* (August 10, 1981). Strauss was interviewed on the ADM crises in *Business Week on Line* November 13, 1996.

The situations involving John Dowd and Howard Buffett were described in Ronald Henkoff and Richard Behar, "Andreas's Problem is Becoming a Mountain," *Fortune* (August 24, 1995).

8-14 Mark Whitacre's background, rise at ADM, and relationship to the FBI were described by Mark Whitacre to Ronald Henkoff, "My Life as a Corporate Mole for the FBI," *Fortune* (September 4, 1995), Mark Whitacre expanded upon these points in his interviews with me on May 22 and July 30, 1999.

8 The order banning Buffett was issued by Roger L. Davis, the president of Davis Security, ADM's contracting security vendor.

11 See John Greenwald, "The Spy Who Cried Help," *Time* (August 28, 1995); Kurt Eichenwald, "A Shareholder Rebellion," *New York Times* (October 19, 1995); and Harland S. Byrne, "Against the Grain: Price-Fixing Probe Puts Unwanted Spotlight on Archer Daniels," *Barron's* (July 17, 1995). The quotation about Dwayne Andreas regarding Whitacre as a second son appeared in John Greenwald, "Harvest of Subpoenas: A High-Level Spy Helps FBI Agents Probe Possible Price-Fixing at Archer Daniels Midland," *Time* (July 24, 1995). The article also contains a description of Whitacre's local philanthropy.

Attorney James McKown, described his crossed-telephone wire experience to me in an interview on January 23, 1998. For a reporter's similar experience, see Alan Guebert, "ADM Security, This is Betty," *Food and Farm File* for the week beginning Sunday, September 15, 1996. This column by Guebert on agribusiness issues is syndicated in newspapers throughout the Midwest.

12 The Whitacre resume fraud was reported in Joseph Menn and David Evans, "Archer Daniels Informant Has Inconsistencies in Academic Record," *Bloomberg News* (July 20, 1995). James Epstein was quoted by the *Reuter Business Report* of July 24, 1995.

12 The TV news interview was also reported in Michael Arndt and George Gunset, "FBI Mole Story about ADM Probe Mole; Executive Wishes He Had Quit; Firm Buying Shares," *The Chicago Tribune,* July 21, 1995. Whitacre was quoted in Ronald E. Yates, "Is He a Hero or a Traitor," *The Chicago Tribune,* (July 30, 1995), which also reported the civil suit against ADM. The allegation of embezzlement was reported in Joseph Menn, "Archer Daniels Seen Firing Informant Whitacre for Alleged Theft," *Bloomberg News* (August 7, 1995).

13 The demand figure in excess of $9 million was announced in the civil case of *ADM v. Whitacre* and in the criminal prosecution *United States v. Whitacre,* both of which were handled in the United States Federal Court for Central Illinois.

Various prosecutors reviewed the problem of having an informant who turned out to be an embezzler, including Scott Lassar (interviewed in Chicago on January 31, 1998), James Griffin (interviewed by telephone on August 13, 1999) and Gary Spratling (interviewed in Washington on December 19, 1997).

The actual cooperation agreement between Whitacre and the Department of Justice was signed by Whitacre and federal prosecutor Brian Cudmore on January 9, 1993.

14 In addition to the *Wall Street Journal*, August 14, 1995, Whitacre's suicide attempt and related challenge to reporters to dig deeper also appeared in Ronald Yates and William Gaines, "Suit Leads to Another ADM Probe; Food Processor, Several Other Firms Accused of Price Fixing," *The Chicago Tribune* (August 13, 1995). The dealings between Whitacre and the Department of Justice and FBI over his status following the exposure of his role in illegal wire transfers is set forth most fully in the extensive FBI 302 interview form of September 5, 1999. In a telephone interview on August 13, 1999, federal antitrust prosecutor James Griffin explained the fact that his division learned of the embezzlement on August 2, 1995 and thereafter turned the matter over to the criminal division of the Department of Justice and more specifically its fraud section.

14-16 The companies listed in conjunction with ADM all began receiving subpoenas at the time of the raid on June 27, 1995. Whitacre's suicide attempt and rescue was reported by Joseph Menn, "Archer Daniels Mole's Suicide Try Could Hurt People," *Bloomberg* (August 14, 1995). *Bloomberg* saw it as a possible ploy for "jury sympathy." *Bloomberg* also reported the rise in the stock and in trading of the stock in reaction to the news of the suicide attempt.

15 The pieces in *The Echo* were written by Michael Welner, MD, a New York City psychiatrist. In the articles Welner also analyzed Whitacre's personal financial transactions as a possible source of distress.

15 The effects of Whitacre's double life on himself and his family were reviewed in interviews with Whitacre, his wife, and three children at the Federal Prison Camp at Edgefield, South Carolina, on July 30, 1999.

15-16 In the FBI file log, Whitacre also is reported making highly emotional statements about not wanting to hurt people at ADM and at the same time fearing that they all were against him. The rule against Whitacre going to a doctor or a lawyer was set forth in his cooperation agreement with the Department of Justice.

15 Whitacre's new employment was provided by the company of an entrepreneurial former professor of his at Cornell. Information about this relationship is found in Whitacre's presentence investigation (PSI) by the United States Probation Office. In Chicago on September 17, 1999, FBI records were shown to me of an interview with the principal of the start-up company. Information about the position appeared in the bankruptcy petition of Mark and Ginger Whitacre filed on September 11, 1997 in North Carolina.

T. Nelson Campbell, the principal of Whitacre's new employer, also wrote to describe the company and Whitacre's financial relationship to it in a letter to the FBI on November 2, 1995. The allegations of Williams & Connolly pertaining to wrongdoing by the FBI and Whitacre's embezzlement began appearing in FBI files on August 16, 1995.

16-17 In his telephone interview of August 13, 1999, James Griffin, who headed the antitrust investigation, said the Chinese Wall began taking effect in early August 1995. Griffin recalled introducing Whitacre and Whitacre's lawyer to the fraud section attorneys and then he (Griffin) and Scott Lassar, who was also present, left the meeting. There was very little communication between the two wings of the Justice Department, although the assistant US attorney, James Mutchnik, in Chicago seemed to act as times as a go-between, furnishing information to the fraud investigators.

17-18 All of the Whitacre allegations were made on September 5, 1995. This interview occurred at Whitacre's attorney's office in Chicago. A subsequent FBI 302 form preserved a telephonic interview on related topics between Whitacre and the bureau on October 10, 1995.

17 Ronald Henkoff's *Fortune* piece appeared on November 27, 1995. The news that ADM was not being investigated appeared in Glenn R. Simpson, "US Says It Isn't Investigating ADM over Payments," *Wall Street Journal* (October 18, 1995).

18 Whitacre did not move until 1996. However, he placed his house on the market after recovering from his first suicide attempt in late August 1995 according to a report by David Evans, "ADM Whistleblower Whitacre Resurfaces, Defends Actions," *Bloomberg* (August 31, 1995). Whitacre described the abduction in his WAND-TV interview with Steve Delany on March 10, 1996.

Chapter 2: The Special Committee and the Gadfly

19 The composition of the ADM board as well as the equity held by the Andreas family was reported in Paul Merrion, "Cozy Board Ties Have ADM in Bind; Critics Charge Connections Hurt Credibility," *Crain's Chicago Business* (August 7, 1995). Similarly, *Crain's* reported the criticism of ADM governance by institutional investors.

20 The inception of the special committee and hiring of Cyrus Vance was reported by Joseph Menn and Kevin Price, "Archer-Daniels Said to Face Indictments Within a Week," *Bloomberg* (August 2, 1995). Another good piece about ADM governance is Kurt Eichenwald, "A Shareholder Rebellion: Investors Demand Answers from Archer Daniels," *New York Times* (October 19, 1995). Shreve Archer praised Dwayne Andreas to Kahn in *Supermarketer to the World* on pages 149-150. Kahn also profiled Happy Rockefeller and Ray Goldberg, as well as F. Ross Johnson. A more full profile of Johnson appears in Bryan Burough, *Barbarians at the Gate, The Fall of RJR Nabisco* (New York: Harper Collins, 1991). Sharon Walsh, "Large Investors Seek a Board Shakeup at ADM," *The Washington Post* (October 13, 1995), analyzed the board in relation to ADM's large institutional investors who were clamoring for change, according to the article.

21 F. Ross Johnson's September 13, 1995 "scum bags" speech at Emory University was reported in Ronald Henkoff, "Checks, Lies and Videotapes," *Fortune* (October 30, 1995). Henkoff provided some of the best early coverage of the scandal.

21-22 Brian Mulroney's role both in Canadian history and at ADM were reported in an article by Michael Posner, "At the Center of a Storm," *MacLean's* (October 23, 1995). A fine investigative account of Mulroney's years as Canada's prime minister is Stevie Cameron, *On The Take* (Toronto: Seal Books, 1995).

22-24 The remarks from the October 19, 1995 annual meeting, including those of Dwayne Andreas, Mulroney, and Richard P. Reising, were taken from ADM transcriptions of the meeting, as well as from the PR Newswire of the same day. The changes in the board were widely reported, including in the *New York Times* on January 16, 1996 and January 15, 1996. Tim Weiner, "Dwayne's

World," *New York Times* (January 16, 1996), was especially illustrative on the company's influence and was complemented by Kurt Eichenwald, "Big Board Room Shift Will Bring in Outsiders," *New York Times* (January 16, 1996). Sharon Walsh, "Battling Bloodlines on ADM's Board; Agribusiness Giant Seeks to End its Corporate Cronyism," *Washington Post* (January 21, 1996), predicted that the upshot of the board turnover would include choosing successors to top managers Andreas and Randall. The Goldberg praise of the change appeared in Eichenwald's piece.

Nancy Millman of the *Chicago Tribune* wrote some of the most aggressive and balanced reportage during this period. Her piece "Board Shift Weakens Andreas' Iron Grip; ADM Patriarch no Longer Able to Hand Pick Successor," *Chicago Tribune* (January 17, 1996), tempered the positive aspects of the reform with the reality that ethical issues still clouded the company. Nevertheless, Millman likewise reported that Wall Street was praising the change.

24-26 A set of the *Shareholders Watch* newsletters was given to me by David and Carol Hoech. David Hoech was the writer. Carol Hoech was an editor of these documents. The Chicago Board of Trade Scandal, "Operation Sour Mash," and FBI agent Michael Bassett's role undercover first as an ADM employee and then as an independent broker is described in David Greising and Lorie Morse, *Broker's, Bagmen & Moles; Fraud & Corruption in the Chicago Futures Markets* (New York: John Wiley & Sons, Inc., 1991). In addition to being a fine history of an epic sting, the book is one of the few that makes the archaic dealings of the future markets comprehensible to the average reader.

27-29 The comments on the surveillance tapes were made by Kenneth Adams, the Washington lawyer whom I interviewed on January 26, 1998 at his office. Adams handled several of the high profile civil class-actions against ADM and other antitrust conspirators. He was an incisive critic of price-fixing as well as a class-action lawyer who fought hard for his clients and never sold them out for a big fee. In addition, Adams was one of the first to recognize the connection between the Watergate era and ADM. My understanding of the *Lamed Vav*, sometimes spelled *Vov*, is derived from Philip Birnbaum, *Encyclopedia of Jewish Concepts* (New York: Hebrew Publishing Co., 1979). Several reporters later explained to me that the use of the term whet their interest for information about the dissident shareholders. David Hoech told me in an interview at his apartment in November 1998 that Ray Goldberg was the one who announced his identity to the company. This was confirmed in my review of FBI files in September 1999.

27-29 The information about the Hoechs came from my interviews with them and their sharing with me of their scrapbooks on the case. The fact that Hoech had been critical of Whitacre insofar as the former ADM executive took corporate money and even advocated jail time for him also was corroborated in FBI files.

29 Carol Rosenberg and Dan Keating, "S. Florida Donors Defray Clinton's Legal Bills," *The Miami Herald* (February 25, 1999), reported the $10,000 contribution by Dwayne Andreas to President Clinton's impeachment defense. Peter Carlson, "Dole Delivered on Methanol, But Who Will Help with the FBI?" *The Sacramento Bee* (August 4, 1996) ran a thorough story about Andreas' political influence, including his flight to Nixon's funeral with Clinton.

29-30 Hoech's letter to Yamamoto of January 8, 1996 is an extremely interesting piece of cross-cultural communication. Hoech also shared with me some of his recollections of their earlier business relationship and friendship, as well as correspondence. Notwithstanding Hoech's recommendation, Yamamoto politely declined to participate in this project.

30 The Dain Bosworth Bulletin about ADM was published on February 12, 1996. In addition to raising serious questions about ADM management, it accurately forecast a long downturn in the stock that probably was not apparent to most investors in light of the corporate governance reform.

31 David Hoech described the situation with the *New York Times* in a telephone call on March 22, 1999. He received a letter from Aaron Liptak of the *New York Times* on December 17, 1996. *New York Times* reporter Kurt Eichenwald's remark about a "setup" was made to Hoech on a taped phone call on December 18, 1996. David Hoech taped many of his phone calls regarding the ADM story and anyone who spoke with him knew that Hoech was likely to be taping.

32 Hoech's remarks about the losses of his business and of spending over $160,000 were made during a phone interview on August 16, 1999.

32 It was also during this interview that Hoech revealed the referenced threat.

Chapter 3: Skirmishing

33 The civil class-action settlement was reported by Nancy Millman, "ADM Okays Antitrust Settlement," *Chicago Tribune* (April 13, 1996).

33-34 I attended the unusual fairness hearing auction before Judge Shadur at the Chicago federal court on April 19, 1996.

34 The economic analysis for the probable market injury was performed by John M. Connor, professor, Department of Agricultural Economics at Purdue University. Connor also became an economic expert for the federal government in its prosecution of the individual defendants. The media criticism was picked up widely. See, e.g., "Archer Daniels Settlement May Be Low, a Judge Says," *New York Times* (April, 20, 1996) from the Associated Press. In addition, it drew international coverage. On April 20, 1996, *Bloomberg* published an incisive article about the legal bidding and also showing that the process had had a favorable effect on ADM shares, which went up 3/8 of a point. "Incentives," *National Law Journal* (April 29, 1996), also raised questions about the class-action lawyers taking a large fee and settling a case after little discovery had been undertaken particularly in light that of the fact that the case could have been won by the plaintiffs and was likely to have produced a large verdict. I met John Connor and heard him and other economists articulate their theories of the damages in this case during a meeting of the Industrial Organization Society, entitled, "Forensic Economics in Action: The Case of the Lysine Cartel" in New York City on January 4, 1998.

35-36 I interviewed James McKown by telephone on January 23, 1998. McKown furnished me with copies of documents from his poisoned cow case in Kansas City, including the affidavits of Whitacre and Bassett, as well as the deposition transcript of Gerald C. Weigel of January 4 and 5, 1996. The file of the case, which was known as *Moberly v. The Archer Daniels Midland Co.*, also contained the scholarship on the toxicological effects of gossypol to animals, as well as the references to human sterility studies in China.

The difficulties of individuals, including McKown, trying to reach WAND-TV and instead being put through to ADM security were detailed in the *Food and Farm File*, Alan Guebert, "ADM Security, This is Betty," (September 15, 1996).

34-37 The widespread nature of the harm is reflected in the cases filed throughout the United States and in Europe, Mexico, and Canada. See Appendix 4.

38 The fines and guilty pleas of ADM's coconspirators and their executives were announced by Michael J. Sniffen, "3 Companies to Pay $20 Million in Fines in Price-Fixing Case," Associated Press (August 27, 1996). Kenneth Adams was quoted in the Associated Press coverage. Thomas M. Burton, "Archer-Daniels Faces a Potential Blow as Three Firms Admit Price-Fixing Plot," the *Wall Street Journal* (August 28, 1996).

The possibility of ADM paying enormous fines was written by Nancy Millman, "US Raises Pressure on ADM: Foreign Firms' Cooperation Bolsters Case," *Chicago Tribune* (August 28, 1996).

The settlement of the citric acid suits was reported in Kurt Eichenwald "Archer's Settles Pricing Suits For $65 Million," the *New York Times* (September 28, 1996). Scott Kilman, "ADM Agrees to Settle Suits Over Products for $65 Million," the *Wall Street Journal* (October 1, 1996), calculated the long-term effect on the stock, a drop in value of a billion and a half dollars since July 1995. However, quoted analyst John McMillin correctly predicted that ADM's stock would exceed twenty dollars once the company became free of antitrust legal problems.

38-39 The remarks of the prosecutors, Aubrey Daniels, Steven Mills, and Judge Castillo were reported in the transcript of the court proceedings in Chicago on October 15, 1996. The transcript of the Justice Department press conference was obtained from documents filed by ADM in its civil case against Mark Whitacre in Urbana, Illinois. The effect on the stock prices was reported in Scott Kilman and Thomas M. Burton, "ADM's Guilty Plea Could Doom Andreas Reign," *The Wall Street Journal* (October 15, 1996).

38 Patricia Macht of the CALPERS was quoted in Sharon Walsh, "Agribusiness Giant Admits it Fixed Prices," *The Washington Post* (August 15, 1996).

39 John McMillin was quoted in the *Bloomberg News* account of October 15, 1996.

David Hoech's views were shared with me during a visit in November, 1998.

The December 3, 1996 indictment was reported by Nancy Millman, "Judge May Find ADM Case Trying," *The Chicago Tribune* (December 12, 1996).

The "honorable businessmen" remarks were attributed to Reid Weingarten in an excellent long piece forecasting the trial by Sharon Walsh, "4 Indicted in ADM Price-Fixing Case: Chairman's Son, Government's Informant Are Among Those Charged," *The Washington Post* (December 4, 1996).

39-40 Weingarten's remarks about the unusual nature of targeting the informant in a criminal prosecution were carried on *CNN Money Line with Lou Dobbs* on December 19, 1996.

Whitacre's assets and liabilities were derived directly from his bankruptcy petition. His educational attainments were stated in an affidavit dated February 22, 1998 that he submitted to the Federal District Court in the Central District of Illinois prior to pleading guilty.

40-41 The lawsuit between ADM and Whitacre was reported by Matt Kelley, "ADM's Lawsuit Against FBI Mole Will Stay in Federal Court, Magistrate Rules," Associated Press, December 12, 1996. The writer also discussed the maneuvering by ADM to attempt to try the case in state court in Illinois as opposed to federal court, which Whitacre favored since he was now a citizen of North Carolina. Whitacre's lawyers also thought that the local state court in Macon County, Illinois would be more favorable to ADM.

Whitacre's civil rights suit against the FBI and Bryan Shepard was filed on January 13, 1997 in Urbana. The representations about the "hard-sided brief case," are derived from the complaint. Two days later the fraud section filed criminal charges against Whitacre in Urbana on January 15, 1997.

41 Whitacre's forgeries on the stationery of his lawyer and psychiatrist were reported in Kurt Eichenwald, "Archer Daniels Informer Admits Recent Deception," *The New York Times* (January 15, 1997). The article was a landmark point in the case. Moreover, Whitacre's relations with Eichenwald seemed to chill after the printing of the article.

41 The citric acid criminal litigation was reported in Nancy Millman, "Another Guilty Plea, Fine From Price-Fixing Investigation," *The Chicago Tribune* (January 30, 1997).

41-42 The handling of the high fructose corn syrup consolidated class actions in Peoria was reported by Mark Fitton, "Judge Orders Tapes Turned over in ADM Price-Fixing Case," *Copley News Service* (June 19, 1997). The replacement of Dwayne Andreas by G. Allen Andreas, Jr., as CEO at ADM was reported by Kurt Eichenwald, "Andreas Retires as Chief of Archer-Daniels," *New York Times* (April 18, 1997). The *Chicago Tribune* reported the resignation of Lowell Andreas on April 18, 1997. The European Union's investigation of ADM was announced by the Associated Press on June 11, 1999 along with the ensuing fall in ADM share price. Randall's resignation and replacement as president by G. Allen Andreas was reported by Reuters on June 23, 1999. In addition, Richard P. Reising who had been general counsel was elevated to the position of senior vice president. The management changes were put into effect for July 1, 1997. Dwayne Andreas still remained as chairman of the board.

42-43 Judge Baker's ruling settling shareholder actions was the subject of an extended fairness hearing in Urbana at which some plaintiffs objected on the basis of the low value of the settlement and the lack of notice. Nevertheless, Judge Baker found the settlement to reflect important reforms and imposed it.

Tara Burghart, "ADM Whistleblower Pleads Guilty," Associated Press (October 10, 1997), covered Whitacre's guilty plea and the remarks of David Hoech. In addition, attorney Donald Mackay of the fraud section told the press at that time that there was no connection between the price-fixing case and the fraud case.

Chapter 4: Revenge

45 I attended pretrial hearings during the fall of 1997 in Judge Manning's courtroom in Chicago.

46 The judge shopping dispute was reported by Nancy Millman, "Judge May Find ADM Case Trying," *Chicago Tribune* (December 12, 1996). Specifically the allegation was made in court by Joseph J. Duffy, the local counsel to Mick Andreas.

46-47 Jack Bray was interviewed at his law firm in Washington, DC on January 14, 1998. In addition, he and his firm, King & Spalding, furnished biographical materials on Bray. Weingarten and his firm likewise furnished biographical materials. A front-page profile of Weingarten appeared in Harvey Berkman, "A Capital Defender," *National Law Journal* (December 15, 1997). I never had a formal interview with Weingarten, however, he was helpful in terms of answering questions throughout the court proceedings to this author.

47-48 Scott Lassar sat for a lengthy interview in his office on January 31, 1998. Also, he furnished biographical documents. With regard to all of these lawyers, as well as Judge Manning, I researched their prior cases on LEXIS and WESTLAW.

48-49 Lassar incidently was named as one of the "people to watch in 1998" by the *Chicago Sun Times* on January 5, 1998. Lassar also was helpful throughout the proceedings to this author. Similarly, Bill Walker took my questions throughout the proceedings. Judge Manning did not respond to a request for a discussion. Unlike other government officials, judges can make a strong argument for not discussing matters in which they were involved.

49-55 The materials are based on hearings that I attended and official transcripts of those hearings. Nancy Millman, "FBI Mole's Wife Cites Fifth Amendment; Taped Testimony Still Eludes ADM Judge," *Chicago Tribune* (December 18, 1997), also included excellent coverage of the immunity/tape dispute involving David Hoech.

55 The DC bar dispute involving David Hoech and Mark Hulkower produced a body of correspondence between Hoech and the DC bar, which I reviewed, including a letter to the DC Bar from Hoech dated April 1, 1998; a letter from DC bar regulation counsel, Keith J. Soressy, to Hoech, April 14, 1998; a letter from Michael S. Frisch, senior assistant bar counsel to Hoech on April 21, 1998; a letter from Hoech to Frisch dated June 9, 1998; and a letter to Hoech from Frisch dated June 4, 1998. Hoech and Hulkower also exchanged letters on December 18 and 19, 1997.

55-57 Hoech caustically criticized Bassett in a lengthy letter that he sent to Lassar on January 21, 1998 and carbon copied to federal judges Manning and Baker, among others, including reporters.

I attended the sentencing of Richter in Urbana on January 30, 1998 and reviewed the potential penalties in filed government documents. The presentence investigation was confidential. The references to it were made in open court. I interviewed attorney Gerald Goldstein by telephone on February 5, 1998.

57 I was in Urbana on February 26, 1988 for the scheduled sentencing proceedings that were cancelled due to Whitacre's suicide attempt.

57-59 The Whitacre suicide note was carried in the *Corporate Crime Reporter* of March 8, 1998. The *Reporter* is a Washington-based newsletter that capably covers corporate crimes, including price-fixing, other antitrust violations, environmental violations, and worker injuries, as well as political and electoral misconduct.

59-61 Whitacre's affidavit of February 22, 1998 and its supporting exhibits were recovered from federal court files in the case against him in Urbana, Illinois.

61 The story of ADM dropping its Swiss case against Whitacre appeared in Alan Guebert, "Meet the New Boss: ADM's Chief Following Game Plan of Dwayne Andreas," *Food and Farm File* (June 29, 1997). Guebert reported that the Swiss case had been dropped in mid-May. In the same outstanding column, Guebert reported some of ADM's other international moves, including spending about a half a billion dollars to corner the world market to control cocoa processing. Portions of the Swiss investigation also appeared in the civil case file of the $30 million claim by ADM against Whitacre. These documents also appeared to show that that investigation had ended without charges against Whitacre.

62-65 I attended Whitacre's sentencing on March 5, 1998. My interview with Gary Spratling occurred at his office in the Department of Justice on December 19, 1997.

The government identified forty-nine participating executives during the sentencing hearing of Whitacre, Andreas, and Wilson on July 9, 1999.

65-66 I attended the press conferences given by defense and government attorneys following Whitacre's fraud sentence on March 5, 1998 in the Urbana courthouse.

66-67 David Hoech provided his views on the Florida Court proceedings in an interview on March 18, 1998. John Kelso was interviewed by telephone on August 30, 1998. The course of the litigation involving Hoech, his family, his company, and their various financial records is set forth in correspondence between Kelso and Daniel, including a letter from Kelso to Daniel of March 19, 1997; a letter from Kelso to Hoech of March 27, 1997; a letter from Kelso to Daniel of March 27, 1997; letter from Laurie S. Fulton of Williams & Connolly to Kelso of April 21, 1997; correspondence and a memorandum of Archer-Daniels Midland in Opposition to Motion to Quash the Subpoena to Barnett Bank filed in the United States District Court of the Middle District of Florida on March 7, 1998; letters from Kelso to Hoech of March 18, 1998; from Kelso to Daniel of April 6, 1998. Also see the letter from Kelso to Mackay of April 16, 1998; from James J. Nixon to Kelso of April 17, 1998; John Stebbins, "ADM Says $2.5 Million Missing from Money Stolen by Former FBI Mole," *Bloomberg* (March 11, 1998), quoted Mackay indicating that there never was any indication that Hoech had acquired the $2.5 million. Hoech's accusation that the fraud section was "lying for ADM again," appeared in his letter to Donald Mackay of March 13, 1998.

Ajinomoto won its favorable decision on patent infringement in federal court in Delaware on March 13, 1998. See *Ajinomoto Co., Inc. v. Archer Daniels Midland Co.* Civil Action No. 95-218-SLR. The order of the Florida Court was written by United States Magistrate Judge John E. Steele in *Archer Daniels Midland v. Mark E. Whitacre*, Case No. 98-13-Misc-J-10B in the United States District Court for the Middle District of Florida, Jacksonville division on May 18, 1998.

PART II: THE ROOTS

Chapter 5: From Andy's Feed to the Supermarket to the World

71-73 An excellent overview of the development of ADM from the nineteenth century through World War II, including acquisitions, research, products, and organization is found in Thomas Derdak, editor, *The International Directory of Company Histories* (Chicago and London: St. James Press, 1994) See vol. I, pages 419-421.

73-75 Profiles of the members of the Andreas family including Dwayne, his parents, his brothers, sister, wife, and children, all are found throughout Kahn, *Supermarketer to the World*. Mick Andreas' childhood quotation is reported in Kahn on page 129. Dwayne Andreas' Cargill years are described by Kahn on pages 78-81, which also includes an explanation of Andreas leaving Cargill. A massive history of Cargill that also describes the post-war years and Dwayne Andreas' role at the company is Wayne G. Broehl, Jr., *Cargill: Trading the World's Grain* (Hanover, NH: University Press of New England, 1992). See especially pages 682-688 and 708-710. An excellent piece describing Andreas' transition from Cargill to ADM and his early years at ADM is "Dwayne Andreas' Affair with a Soybean," *Business Week* (June 2, 1973).

74 Dwayne Andreas' flamboyance in Minnesota was reported by Kahn and recounted to me in a discussion with his old neighbors, James and Richard Lindsay, in Idaho on January 1, 1998.

75 Michael Kinsey's quotation was reported in Kahn at pages 238-239, as was his comment about advertising.

76 James Randall and his early role in ADM likewise were reported by Kahn at 126-127.

76-77 The soybean focus of Andreas' early years was reported in "Dwayne Andreas' Affair with the Soy Bean," *Business Week* (June 2, 1973) and in Irwin Ross, "Dwayne Andreas's Bean Has a Heart of Gold," *Fortune* (October 1973).

77 The propensity to put Andreas' family members on the board of ADM after Dwayne Andreas took power as well as the practice of not printing pictures of these family members in the annual report was described by Kahn on pages 156-158.

77 The acquisitions of Columbian Peanut and Growmark were described in *The International Directory of Company Histories*. In addition, I followed the modern acquisitions and divestitures through the annual reports from 1980 through the present.

77 The importance of ethanol and high fructose corn syrup to ADM has been described in Charles Siler, "Weatherman," *Forbes* (February 22, 1988); Ronald Henkoff, "Oh, How the Money Grows at ADM," *Fortune* (October 8, 1990); and Marcia Berss, "Plowing Washington for Profit," *Forbes* (September 16, 1991). Also see Jeffrey H. Birnbaum and Viveca Novak, "The Corporate Dole," *Time* (September 23, 1996).

77 Marcia Berss, "Plowing Washington for Profit," touted ADM's outperformance of Cargill.

77-78 The relationship between Dwayne Andreas and Alfred C. Toepfer as well as the joint venture between their companies was described by Kahn on pages 278 through 279 and in ADM's 1993 annual report.

78 ADM's 70 percent market share in ethanol was reported in Ronald Henkoff, "Oh, How the Money Grows at ADM."

The Andreas quotation about "plans" and the information about the 1.4-billion-dollar capital spending program were reported in "Not a Kernel of Waste," *Forbes* (January 6, 1992).

78-79 The numbers pertaining to the capital assets of the company were derived from the 1999 annual report. The material about "nutraceuticals," was taken from the 1998 annual report.

Chapter 6: ADM: Politics, Money, and Trouble

81 ADM's recent soft money and PAC political contributions are detailed in Appendix 3. The quote from *Fortune* about the "most manipulated industry," and Dwayne Andreas' quote are found in Ronald Henkoff, "Oh, How the Money Grows at ADM." Henkoff also related the story of the acquisition of the Waldorf suite.

82 The story of the Andreas separation from Cargill is told in Broehl's *Cargill: Trading the World's Grain*, pages 762-764. In his magisterial history of Cargill, Broehl makes clear that Andreas was let go for insubordination. However, Kahn, in *Supermarketer to the World*, tries to make the situation seem like a true resignation and even suggests that Andreas' trip to Moscow was "grudgingly approved." See page 80. However, this appears to be baseless revisionism.

82 Andreas' experiences during the Eisenhower-McCarthy years was related by Henkoff, in *Fortune* (October 10, 1996), and Kahn, pages 81-85.

82-83 The contribution to Humphrey was related in Dan Carney, "Dwayne's World," *Mother Jones* (July-August, 1995). Kahn detailed the friendship between Humphrey and Andreas, especially on pages 38-48, 85-94, 144-49, and 181-86. For the blind trust, see Jeff Gerth, "Andreas, A Man in the Spotlight, Minnesotans Spur Controversy," *New York Times* (July 26, 1978).

83 The golfing relationship between Humphrey and Andreas was related to me by one of Andreas' former caddies, James Lindsay, in an interview on January 1, 1998.

83 Humphrey's role in the GTA was described by Kahn on pages 115-116. The Food for Peace program was described by Kahn on pages 90-115. Its criticism including antitrust implications was found in Henkoff in "On How the Money Grows at ADM." An incisive Cato institute report covering Food for Peace is James Bovard, "Archer Daniels Midland: A Case Study in Corporate Welfare," *Cato Policy Analysis No. 241* (September 26, 1995).

84-85 The Strauss, Rockefeller, and Humphrey election issues are in Kahn, page 159.

86 The Sea View is in Carney. The Andreas-Dewey connection is in Kahn on pages 38, 105-110, 160, 201, and 227.

85 The *Parade* listing is found in Kahn on page 181.

87-90 For the early Watergate information see Carney, "Dwayne's World"; Bernard Gwertzman, "G.A.O. Report Asks Justice Inquiry into G.O.P. Funds," *New York Times* (August 27, 1972), pages 1, 52; Henkoff; Walter Pincus, "The G.O.P. Money Scandal," *The New Republic* (April 21, 1973), pages 17-21; Walter Rugaber, "G.O.P. Aid Inquiry on Check in Study of Raid on Democrats," *New York Times* (August 24, 1972), page 1; Walter Rugaber, "Stans Asserts He Doesn't Know How Suspect Got G.O.P. Funds," *New York Times* (August 25, 1972), at page 1; "Republican Mystery" (editorial), *New York Times* (August 26, 1972), page 24; "Milk and Honey" (editorial), *New York Times* (August 26, 1972), page 24; Peter Nulty and Ronald Henkoff, "Can ADM's Andreas Escape the Judicial Mill?" *Fortune* (August 7, 1995), page 28; and Owen Ross, "Dwayne Andreas's Bean Has a Heart of Gold," *Fortune* (October 1973), page 137. Maurice Stans' statement about Andreas appeared in Stans' memoir, *The Terrors of Justice*, (Ontario: Beaver Books, 1978).

The cash from Andreas and his desire for anonymity was described by Fred Emery, *Watergate: The Corruption of American Politics and the Fall of Richard Nixon* (New York: Random House, 1991), page 188. Also see Frank Mankiewicz, *Perfectly Clear: Nixon from Whittier to Watergate* (New York: Quadrangle Books, 1973), pages 141-142.

88 The White House plan to use Andreas as an intermediary was detailed by John Dean in *Blind Ambition: The White House Years* (New York: Simon & Schuster, 1976), pages 145-146.

88 The Minnesota press was most active in terms of following the Andreas Watergate story. Erlichman's testimony was covered in Finlay Lewis, "Erlichman Links O'Brien, Andreas to Reported Try to Settle Suit," *Minneapolis Tribune* (July 28, 1973), page 3a.

88 The story of the Patman Committee, Andreas' bank charter, and the White House is told ably in Clark P. Mollenhoff, *Game Plan for Disaster: An Ombudsman's Report on the Nixon Years* (New York: W.W. Norton & Co., Inc., 1976), pages 226-233.

88-89 For coverage of the Andreas indictment, trial, and acquittal, "'68 Campaign Charge Upheld" UPI, *New York Times* (March 14, 1974), page 25; Anthony Riley, "Jaworski Moves to Help the IRS," *New York Times* (June 23, 1974), page 17; "Humphrey is Linked to Inquiry by Jaworski in Dairy Gifts," *New York Times* (July 6, 1974), page 6; "Humphrey Backer is Found Innocent in Loan of $100,000," Associated Press, *New York Times* (July 13, 1974).

For Minnesota coverage see Frank Wright, "Andreas Gifts to HHH Said to be Illegal," *Minneapolis Tribune* (October 20, 1973), page 1a; "Andreas's Court Appearance Set Back to November 23," Associated Press, *Minneapolis Tribune* (November 5, 1993), page 1a; Steven Dornfeld,

"Financier Andreas Pleads Not Guilty," *Minneapolis Tribune* (November 24, 1973), page 1a; Bob Lundegaard, "Andreas Attorney Asks Case Be Dropped," *Minneapolis Tribune* (January 24, 1974), page 4a; Harley Sorensen, "Judge Refuses to Drop Charges Against Andreas," *Minneapolis Tribune* (March 13, 1974), page 1b; Finlay Lewis, "Scope of Nixon Probe Reduced," *Minneapolis Tribune* (April, 26, 1974), page 1a; Frank Wright, "HHH: Andreas Advised Contribution," *Minneapolis Tribune* (June 30, 1974), page 1a; Linda Picone, "Judge Hears Andreas Case, Ponders Verdict," *Minneapolis Tribune* (July 9, 1974), page 1b; Paul Lights, "Andreas is Found Innocent," *Minneapolis Tribune* (July 13, 1974), page 1a; Linda Picone, "Andreas Never Materialized During the Legal Proceedings Against Him," *Minneapolis Tribune* (July 13, 1974), page 7a; Finlay Lewis, "Haldeman Says He Tried to Hide Andreas Gift," *Minneapolis Tribune* (December 4, 1974), page 1a; Finlay Lewis, "Colson, Mitchel Hinted at Bugging of HHH, Andreas," *Minneapolis Tribune* (December 6, 1974), page 1a.

The quoted passage by Humphrey defending Andreas was reported by Kahn on page 184.

89 For the Humphrey blind trust, see Jeff Gerth, "Andreas a Man in the Spotlight, Minnesotan's Actions Spur a Controversy," *New York Times* (July 26, 1978), at D1.

The Rosemary Woods allegation was reported by Peter Nulty and Ronald Henkoff, "Can ADM Andreas Escape the Judicial Mill," *Fortune* (August 7, 1995), page 28.

89-90 The July 25, 1972 White House conversation appeared in Stanley I. Kutler, *Abuse of Power, The New Nixon Case* (New York: The Free Press, 1997), pages 104-107. The August 1, 1972 tape appears in Kutler on pages 109-112.

90-91 For reporting on the Gartner scandal, see George Anthan, Gannet News Service (February 2, 1989); James L. Rowe, Jr., "Johnson Quits as Chairman of CFTC," *Washington Post* (January 19, 1983); Frank J. Prial, "More Questions Raised on Gartner—Andreas Tie," *New York Times* (June 28, 1978), page D2; "Gartner Insists He Won't Quit, Stock Gift Is Not a Violation Says Commodity Aide," Associated Press, *New York Times* (June 29, 1978); "David Gartner's Obligations" (editorial), *New York Times* (June 30, 1978). Also see Jeff Gerth, "Andreas a Man in the Spotlight, Minnesotan's Actions Spur Controversy," *New York Times* (July 26, 1978), D1.

91 Dwayne Andreas's remark about Gartner appeared in Kahn on page 189. Mick Andreas gloated to Kahn about his fine on pages 285-286. Kahn reported the sting operation on pages 286-289. In general, see Greising and Morse, *Brokers, Bagmen & Moles.*

92 The contributions were calculated from the Center for Responsive Politics' web site, which based its data available on-line from the FEC. Another source was Nancy Millman, "Subsidies Still Fuel Ethanol Debate," *Chicago Tribune*, business section page 1 (June 10, 1997). The dinner checks were reported by Carney in "Dwayne's World."

92-93 The gifts to Clinton's transition, GOPAC, and farm belt legislators were reported by Carney.

For relations to politicians and celebrities see Kahn; on Brinkley pages 11, 98, 124; on Carter pages 91, 185-186, 203-207, 243; the Doles, pages 39, 89, 98-99, 124, 243-247; and Tip O'Neill, pages 39, 86, 98-99, 124. Also see Cornelia Grumman, "Government Reform: Where the Candidates Stand," *Chicago Tribune* (August 8, 1996), news section 1; Hedrick Smith, "Sen. Dole Is Not Running, But He Is Hopeful," *Chicago Tribune* (September 6, 1985); David Jackson, "Soft Money Spins a Political Web: Foreign Cash a Likely Debate Topic," *Chicago Tribune* (October

16, 1996); Don L. Boroughs, "Reaping a Bitter Harvest (FBI Investigation of Archer Daniels Midland)," *US News and World Report* (July 24, 1995); "Politics Called a Giant Auction, Study Reveals How Patrons Back Candidates," Associated Press, *Chicago Tribune* (January 12, 1996).

92 The Brinkley situation stimulated a great deal of controversy among journalists over ethics. See Frazier Moore, "Brinkley Commercials Pulled by ABC," Associated Press (January 15, 1998); John Carmody, "The TV Column," *Washington Post* (January 14, 1998).

92-94 For subsidies, see Carney, Don L. Boroughs, "Reaping a Bitter Harvest," *US News and World Report* (July 24, 1995); John Bovard, "Corporate Welfare Fueled By Political Contributions," *Business and Society Review* (Summer 1995); Nancy Millman, "Subsidies Still Fuel Ethanol Debate," *Chicago Tribune* (June 10, 1997); Frank James, "Agribusiness Keeps It Clout in GOP's House," *Chicago Tribune* (November 6, 1995); "Tax Breaks for Ethanol Criticized: Lawmakers Call Subsidy to Producers Wasteful," *Chicago Tribune*, Associated Press (March 14, 1997); Rob Wells, "Government Study Hits Ethanol Subsidy," *Chicago Tribune*, Associated Press (March 23, 1997); Peter Nulty, "Ethanol Capers," *Fortune* (March 21, 1994); Ernest Holsendolph, "Sugar's New Rival: High Fructose Corn Syrup," *New York Times* (October 16, 1974).

Dwayne Andreas' rats story was reported by Kahn, pages 176-179.

94 On subsidies and interlocking see Marcia Beress, "Prowling Washington for Profits," *Forbes* (September 16, 1991).

94 For Andreas' free market views, see Kahn page 192 and as quoted in Carney.

94-95 For Andreas' ties to the Soviet Union, see Kahn pages 15-33, 81-84, 162-164, 203-204, 261-278, 288-289, 293-297, and 305-307. Klein's view was carried by Kahn on page 21; Buchanan's on page 265.

96-100 On ethanol, see "General Accounting Office, Tax Policy: Effects of the Alcohol Fuels Tax Initiatives," letter report (March 6, 1997); John Bovard, "Corporate Welfare Fueled by Political Contributions (Archer Daniels Midland's Ethanol Program)," *Business and Society Review* (Summer 1995); Nancy Watsman, Jay Youngclaus, and Jennifer Schecter, "Center for Responsive Politics, Money in Politics Alert" (March 17, 1997); Nancy Millman, "Subsidies Still Fuel Ethanol Debate," *Chicago Tribune* (June 10, 1997); John Bovard, "Archer-Daniels Midland: A Case Study in Corporate Welfare," *CATO Institute Report* (October, 1995); and Center for Responsive Politics, "The Year in Review, 1996 Campaigning Finance Highlights from A to Z" (December 18, 1996). The Reagan-Andreas connection is covered by Kahn, pages 14 (statue), 161, 178, 204, 203. For a good piece on ADM's involvement in another country's politics, see John Nicol and Jock Ferguson, "The Price Fixers: How Global Cartels Gouged Canadian Farmers," *MacLean's* (February 22, 1999).

Chapter 7: The Rise and Fall and Rise of Antitrust

101 Articles describing the ADM's antitrust litigation before 1990 include Henkoff, "Oh, How the Money Grows at ADM." Jeff Gerth, "Andreas, A Man in the Spotlight," *New York Times* (July 26, 1978), surveyed price-fixing activities in the Food for Peace program. The carbon dioxide case was covered in Ronald Yates, "ADM Rivals Cry Foul in Carbon-Dioxide," *Chicago Tribune* (September 9, 1995).

I reviewed the case files of the lengthy litigation over high fructose in which ADM eventually prevailed. See *US v. Archer Daniels Midland & Nabisco*. The decision was rendered by Judge Harold D. Vietor in Federal Court for the Southern District of Iowa on December 10, 1991.

101-102 The changes in American life in terms of industrialization and urbanization and the drive for reform were detailed in Richard Hofstadter, *The Age of Reform* (New York: Vintage, 1995). Hofstadter traced the number of millionaires in America between the 1800s and 1980s on page 136. Perhaps the best historian writing on antitrust and its meaning in American life, Hofstadter crystallized his ideas on these issues in the brilliant essay "What Happened to the Antitrust Movement?" (1964).

102-103 John D. Rockefeller's ideas on pools and trusts, as well as the formation of the standard oil trust were detailed by Alan Sampson, *The Seven Sisters* (New York: Viking, 1975). See particularly pages 18–32.

103 Rockefeller's American Beauty Rose metaphor is found in Sampson on page 18. Louis Brandeis' antimonopoly background is detailed by Philippa Strum, *Brandeis, Justice for the People* (New York: Schocken Books, 1984). In particular see pages 55-60, 147-153, and 212-222.

104-105 The story of John Sherman and the Sherman Antitrust Act is told well in Theodore E. Burton, *John Sherman, American Statesman* (Boston: Houghton Mifflin, 1906). See especially pages 356-364. Sherman's progressive racial and anti-imperial views are described on pages 414-427.

105 The history of the trust cases described was recorded by Samuel Elliot Morison, *The Oxford History of the American People* (New York: Oxford University Press, 1965), pages 817-823.

106 The quotes attributed to Theodore Roosevelt on this page were reported in Henry F. Pringle, *Theodore Roosevelt, A Biography* (New York: Harcourt Brace, 1931), on 360 and 368.

106 Pringle reported the relations between Roosevelt and Upton Sinclair and Roosevelt and Judge E.H. Gary, respectively, on pages 428 and 442-443. The Roosevelt-Taft split and the role that antitrust issues played in it was described by Gabriel Kolko, *The Triumph of Conservatism* (Chicago: Quadrangle, 1967), on pages 123-127, 167, and 177.

106 The productivity of the Taft administration in terms of antitrust prosecutions was described by Pringle on page 427.

106-107 The importance of the "per se" rule as decided by the Supreme Court in the Standard Oil case is described by Robert Bork, *The Antitrust Paradox; A Policy at War with Itself* (New York: The Free Press, 1997), on pages 33-41.

107 The relationship between Louis Brandeis and Woodrow Wilson and the role of antitrust policy in it was a major subject of Strum in her biography of Brandies. See pages 150-222. Brandeis argued against natural monopolies on page 148, likened Judge Gary's conspicuous consumption to the French revolution on page 150, helped articulate the New Freedom on page 198, proposed the FTC legislation on 213, disparaged "price cutting" on 213; and Kolko described Brandies' involvement in the initiation of the Federal Trade Commission on pages 267-268.

108 Richard Hofstadter has identified the connection between the fear of fascism and the new rise of antitrust in late 1930s. See *The Age of Reform*, page 254.

108 Thurman Arnold's years at Yale Law School and his friendship with William O. Douglas, who later became a justice of the United States Supreme Court, are described in Douglas' biography, *Go East Young Man* (New York: Dell, 1979), on pages 157-172.

108-109 Arnold's relationship to the Roosevelt administration is described by William E. Leuchtenberg, *Franklin D. Roosevelt* (New York: Harper and Row, 1963), on pages 258-259.

109 The effect of Arnold on the antitrust division was analyzed in the Nader report by Mark

Green, editor, *The Closed Enterprise System* (New York: Grossman, 1972) on pages 66-67, which is also where Arnold's quotes about the "big stick" and a "fight without a referee" appear.

109 Though written in 1940, the *Socony-Vacuum* case remains among the most significant of all Supreme Court antitrust decisions. It controlled the prosecutions both of ADM and its executives. The case citation is 310 US 150 (1940).

110 The I.G. Farben antitrust case was described with devastating effect in *The Seven Sisters* at pages 79-80 and 122. Arnold's resignation from the bench and establishment of his Washington law firm were described in Anthony Lewis, *Gideon's Trumpet* (New York: Vintage, 1989), at pages 48-49.

110 The Japanese views of and experiences with antitrust are described in Karel Van Wolferen, *The Enigma of Japanese Power* (New York: Vintage, 1990). See pages 125, 205, 301, and 391.

110 Postwar antitrust policy is described in the Nader group report edited by Mark Green at pages 68-73.

110-111 Justice Black's views and decisions on antitrust were reported in Gerald T. Dunn, *Hugo Black and the Judicial Revolution* (New York: Simon and Schuster, 1977) on pages 342-400. It is interesting to note that Justice Black's decisions on antitrust, which involved a literal reading of the Sherman Act, were akin to his decisions on the Bill of Rights, which also were quite literal. The *Herald Tribune* and *Fortune* were quoted by Dunn respectively on pages 343 and 400.

111 The "electrical cases" were covered in Anthony Lewis, "Seven Electrical Officials Get Jail Terms in Trust Case," *New York Times* (February 7, 1961). The paper listed all the sentences and printed photographs of the key conspirators.

112 Orrick's tenure was evaluated by the Nader group and his congressional testimony was quoted on page 21. In the *Antitrust Paradox*, Bork termed Nader nihilistic on page 4. He criticized Brandeis on page 17. Another very prominent member of the Chicago School is Judge Richard Posner of the Seventh Circuit Court of Appeals, who was designated on the mediator in the case brought by the Department of Justice against Microsoft.

112 Galbraith's comments on "controlled prices" appear in his book, *The New Industrial State* (New York: Signet Books, 1968) on page 206.

112-113 The views of William Baxter and Robert Pitofsky were reported in Roger Lowenstein, "Trust in Markets: Antitrust Enforces Drop the Ideology, Focus on Economics; From Sherman to Pitofsky, Attitudes about Bigness Have Come a Long Way," *The Wall Street Journal* (February 27, 1997).

The Bell Atlantic NYNEX combination was reported in "The Trust Buster Who Roared," *Time* (October 3, 1997).

114-117 I interviewed Gary Spratling in his office at the Department of Justice on December 19, 1997. He and his associate Thomas King also provided a raft of documents pertaining to the antitrust division's policies and procedures. These included the statistical reports of the division, as well as Spratling's speech of September 8, 1995, "The Experience and Views of the Antitrust Division"; department guidelines on "Sentencing of Organizations"; a speech by Spratling on March 7, 1997 entitled "The Trend Towards Higher Corporate Fines; It's a Whole New Ball Game"; a speech by Spratling on February 21, 1997, "Criminal Antitrust Enforcement

Against International Cartels"; the Memorandum of Understanding (MOU) between the Antitrust Division of the United States Department of Justice and the Immigration and Naturalization Service of the United States Department of Justice; the United States Department of Justice Corporate Leniency Policy, August 10, 1993; the department's individual leniency policy, August 10, 1994; and a form cooperation agreement for an antitrust informer. Good articles on the use of "blue-collar" methods include Harvey Berkman, "Justice Seeking Stiff Price-Fixing Sanctions," *National Law Journal* (October 20, 1997); and see James Lyons, "Tough Guys," *Forbes* (April 15, 1991).

PART III: THE TRIAL

Chapter 8: Shaping the Table

121-126 The rulings and remarks of Judge Manning granting and denying the motions of the government and defense are found in a comprehensive forty-page June 1998 pretrial order. Some of the significant motions leading up to these rulings were the government's Consolidated Motions in Limine, March 10, 1998; the government's Motion in Limine to Exclude Evidence of Reasonableness, Justification or Lack of Intent, March 10, 1998; the Motion in Limine of Defendants' Michael D. Andreas and Terrance S. Wilson to Exclude Statements of Co-Defendant Mark Whitacre, March 10, 1997; the defendants' Memorandum in Support of Their Motion to Exclude Any Evidence of or Reference to the Guilty Pleas of Alleged Co-Conspirators or to Related Civil Litigation; The Reply in Support of the Motion in Limine of Michael D. Andreas and Terrance S. Wilson to Exclude Tapes Created by Mr. Whitacre for Violation of Their Sixth Amendment Confrontation Rights, April 7, 1998; and the government's Proffer of Co-Conspirators' Statements, May 6, 1998. Also, see Defendant Michael D. Andreas' Opposition to the Government's Motion in Limine to Preclude Evidence or Argument Regarding Alleged Government Misconduct in the Course of the Investigation, June 23, 1998.

126 The position of the Dickstein firm is set forth in its Memorandum in Support of Motion to Quash Subpoenas Duces Tecum, June 23, 1998.

127 See the decision in *Unites States v. Singleton*, 144 F.3d 1443 (10th Cir. 1998).

129 The Japanese juror was examined on July 9, 1998.

Chapter 9: Spinning

133-134 The Griffin opening appears in the trial transcript of July 15, 1998, pages 703-752, including objections.

135-137 Bray's opening statement also was reported in the transcript of July 15, 1998. See pages 755-801.

137-138 Walker's opening occurred on the same day and ran in the transcript from page 882-821.

138-142 Weingarten's opening presentation and objections are in the transcript of July 16, 1998 on pages 827-864.

140 See Kurt Eichenwald, "Recordings Played in Trial of Three Ex-Archer Officials," *New York Times* (July 17, 1998) referencing the alleged bombing of the ADM plant.

142 Questions pertaining to the judge's niece are in the transcript in the pages 866-870.

Chapter 10: Mimoto

143 Alan M. Dershowitz, *Reasonable Doubts, The Criminal Justice System in the O.J. Simpson Case* (New York: Touchstone, 1996).

142-163 Mimoto's testimony on July 16-July 23, 1998 spanned trial transcript pages 892-1666.

160 Judge Manning's handling of the possible newspaper infection of the jury appears on pages 1294-1337 of the transcript. See, Greg Burns, "ADM Tapes Show Rival Mistrust," *Chicago Tribune* (July 20, 1998). The Burns piece also contained a reference to Wilson saying that someone would "rub out" anyone found cheating in the conspiracy. This could have been highly prejudicial if seen by the jury.

Chapter 11: Ikeda

165-179 The testimony of Ikeda began August 3, 1998 and concluded on August 10, 1998. It was covered in trial transcript pages 1670-2158.

Chapter 12: White Rats

181-185 Trial testimony of Alain Crouy occurred on August 10, 1998 through August 11, 1998, and is in transcript on pages 2161-2568.

185-187 The debate about whether to allow Cox to testify is in the transcript on pages 2522-2602.

187-193 Cox's testimony appears on pages 2603-2801 of the transcript.

Chapter 13: The Handler

195-218 Shepard's testimony began on August 12, 1998 and concluded on April 19, 1998 and was covered in the transcript at pages 2802-3611.

209-210 An FBI 302 form is a memorandum that records an interview by the bureau.

218 Wilson's absence from court appears in the transcript on pages 3613-3619.

Chapter 14: The Windup

219 The testimony of Allison Ebel appears in the transcript on pages 3620-3646.

219-220 Bruce Koenig's testimony is in the transcript on pages 3650-3758.

220-229 Herndon's testimony appears in the trial transcripts of April 19-20, 1998, on pages 3759-3897.

229-230 The evidentary and administrative matters occurred in the transcript on pages 4088-4099.

229-230 The lost court day and missing juror issues are found in the transcript on pages 4100-4115. On August 26, the court dealt with replacing the juror and with whether Whitacre would testify, transcript pages 4116-4132.

230-241 Yamamoto's testimony is in the transcript on pages 4132-4609. The matters handled outside the presence of the jury by the court on August 31, 1998 are in the transcript on pages 4612-4704.

241-243 The matters discussed in chambers on September 1, 1998 are in the transcript on pages 4705-4846.

243-245 Witnesses Tomlinson and Coppock testified on September 2, 1998. Their testimony and final exhibits were introduced into the transcript on pages 4850-5035.

Chapter 15: The Pitch

247-258 Judge Manning's instructions to the jury are in the transcript of September 8, 1998 on pages 5576-5600. Scott Lassar's closing is in the transcript of the same day on pages 5600-5727.

258-264 Bray's closing on September 9, 1998 is in the transcript on pages 5729-5838.

264-265 Bill Walker's closing appears in the transcript on 5840-5880.

265 Judge Manning's handling of the mistrial issue, remarks to counsel, and to the jury appear in the transcript on pages 5885-5901.

265-274 Weingarten's closing is in the trial transcript of September 9-10, 1998 on pages 5903-6052.

274-276 Lassar's rebuttle is in the transcript on pages 6068-6117.

276-277 The computer training occurred on September 11, 1998. That and the court's final administrative tasks are in the transcript on pages 6146-6172. Other technical issues were dealt with on September 15, 1998 in the transcript on pages 6175-6181.

277 The jury question of September 16, 1998 was covered in the transcript at pages 6184-6202.

277-278 The verdict was taken on September 17, 1998; the court individually polled the jurors and set the original sentencing date of January 7, 1999. See transcript pages 6205-6213.

278-279 Juror Fritz Dujour was interviewed by telephone on April 20, 1999. Juror Linda Heflebower was interviewed by telephone on April 19, 1999.

PART IV: THE COVER-UP

Chapter 16: The Hit

283-284 I attended the stockholders' meeting on October 22, 1999. Also ADM printed G.A. Andreas' remark. I interviewed Martin Glotzer at the meeting. Glotzer provided the background information on cumulative voting during a telephone interview on July 27, 1999. A profile of Glotzer as a shareholders' rights advocate appeared in Steven R. Strahler, "Confessions of a Corporate Gadfly," *Crain's Chicago Business* (May 5, 1986). ADM's opposition to cumulative voting was stated in its proxy statement distributed to shareholders before the 1998 meeting.

284 Dwayne Andreas' resignation as chairman of ADM was covered in Greg Burns, "ADM Chairman Andreas Steps Down," *Chicago Tribune* (January 25, 1998). Nell Minow spoke with Burns as did Robert Strauss. The quotation from Strauss was not actually printed in Burns piece. However, he related it to me. Also see Emily Kaiser, "ADM's Andreas, Friend of President, Steps Down" Reuters, (January 25, 1999); it reported the growth of ADM in terms of employees and capital assets under Andreas.

284-285 The alternative fine dispute is set forth in numerous court filed documents, including the April 2, 1999 letter from Assistant US Attorney James H. Mutchnick to James T. Phalen and the "Government's Redacted Supplemental Economic Submission Under the Alternative Fine Provision, 18 U.S.C. § 3571(b)."

285 Judge Manning's excerpt comes from her ten-page opinion in *United States v. Andreas* filed June 2, 1999 wherein she also recaps the dispute from the court's perspective.

285-293 I attended the sentencing in Chicago on July 9, 1999. Before court, I met with Bill

Walker, who expressed his confidence that his client's sentence would be concurrent. Greg Burns, the reporter for the *Chicago Tribune,* informed me before the hearing that his paper had to utilize the services of a lawyer in order to keep Whitacre's sentencing open to the public. The letters from Andrew Young and Robert Strauss were not read in open court but were found in the case files kept by the Clerk of Courts at the Chicago Federal Courthouse. Likewise, the information about Terry Wilson's son was found in these files that were placed before the judge during her consideration of sentencing.

293 After court, I spoke with Weingarten, Lassar, and Hoech.

293-294 Later that day I attended the Department of Justice's press conference where the remarks of the prosecutors were made.

The press coverage of the sentencing included David Greising, "There Were No Winners Here," *Chicago Tribune* (July 11, 1999). Greising, a business columnist, referred to Whitacre as a "pinocchio." Professor John Coffee's remark appeared in Kurt Eichenwald, "Clues to Sentencing Mystery in the Archer Daniels Case," *New York Times* (July 13, 1999). Alan Guebert's remarks appeared in "Ag Justice: Lysine Prices Go Up Just Before the Whistleblower Goes Down—Again," in his *Farm and Food File,* for the week beginning Sunday, July 18, 1999.

294-296 Judge Manning's Memorandum and Order in *United States v. Andreas, et al,* was filed on July 13, 1999. The Court of Appeals' decision that she referenced is *United States v. Stefonek,* a Seventh Circuit decision written by Judge Richard Posner and filed on June 3, 1999.

Chapter 17: The Mole—Part Two

297-309 I began interviewing Mark Whitacre on May 22 and 23, 1999 at the federal prison camp in Edgefield, South Carolina. The interview continued for a third day on July 30, 1999. The material represented herein was provided to me over the course of three days. In addition, on July 30, 1999 I met with Ginger Whitacre and their three children, Alex, Bill, and Tanya at the prison.

300-301 Mark Cheviron's grand jury testimony appears in a transcript in the case "In re Grand Jury Investigation," No. 95 GJ573 November 12, 1996. The FBI interview notes are preserved in an FD-302 form prepared by Michael D. Bassett and Anthony P. D'Angelo dictated on September 6, 1995 from an interview conducted on September 5, 1995.

302 An FBI 302 form indicated that Taylor was interviewed on January 18, 1996. A lawyer from Williams & Connolly was present.

302-303 The Frankel/SEC problem was reported "Lapse,' ADM Taking Loss of $6.5 Million on Accounting Error," Associated Press (September 15, 1991). Also, see, Bill Ruminsky, "ADM Official Quits When Loss Told," *Decatur Herald-Review* (September 17, 1991). The company's quote about audit controls appears in both stories.

303-304 The quotations attributed to Ronald Ferrari were taken from his deposition in *ADM v. Whitacre,* No. 962237, in Chicago on January 27, 1998. Ferrari's incorporation papers for Far East Specialists, his documents from the Swiss Bank Corporation branch in Hong Kong, the checks associated with the $3,500 from Mark Whitacre, and the interest free loan were exhibits attached to the deposition transcript.

304-305 The information pertaining to transactions involving Beat Schweizer and the reference to him as the "Swiss Financial Advisor," are found in the "Statement of Facts" filed by the Department of Justice in *United States v. Whitacre* on October 10, 1997. In addition to the $100,000 that Schweizer transferred into his own account on February 6, 1995, he also transferred $40,000 Swiss francs on May 18, 1995.

305-306 The AFE protocol at ADM was in the presentence investigation report submitted to Judge Harold Baker by the US Probation Office on February 20, 1998 for the sentencing of Mark Whitacre. In his deposition on July 22, 1997 in the high fructose corn syrup antitrust (civil) litigation, Steven Mills testified to having been supervised by Frankel and to supervising Rochelli.

306 The knowledge of Steven Mills that the $1.5 million was transferred is shown in an FBI 302, January 24, 1996 interview of ADM assistant controller James Kirk Schmidt, who discussed the matter with Mills before the money was paid. The bankruptcy information is taken from the voluntary petition, *In re Whitacre*, 97-1451, September 11, 1997 in the bankruptcy court of the Middle District of North Carolina. The petition form states the fines and penalties for falsehoods.

306 See Carney, "Dwayne's World."

306-307 See Peter Carlson, "Chairman Across the Board," *Washington Post Magazine* (July 11, 1996). Besides giving support to Whitacre's contention, the Carlson piece is valuable because it is the only in-depth interview of Dwayne Andreas since the FBI's raid of ADM in 1995.

308-309 A good study of how the lysine price-fixing hurt the pork and poultry producers, as well as consumers, is Professor C. Robert Taylor, "Indirect Damages from Price-Fixing: The Alabama Lysine Case," Department of Agricultural Economics, Auburn University, 1997.

I was unable to discuss the facts or other matters with Richard Reising, who declined to be interviewed.

Chapter 18: The Score

311-312 The order granting summary judgment to ADM was filed in *Archer Daniels Midland Company v. Mark Whitacre*, Case No. 96-CV2237 on August 5, 1999.

312-313 The presentence investigation of the US Probation Department, including the excerpted portions about Richter, was submitted to Judge Harold Baker in Urbana on February 20, 1998.

313-314 See Thomas M. Burton, "ADM's Chairman Says Auditor Found No Improper Payments to Executives," *The Wall Street Journal* (October 17, 1995). Burton also reported that Richter had paid his German taxes.

Richter's confirmation letter of December 4, 1990 was submitted by ADM as an exhibit to its Motion for Summary Judgment in *ADM v. Whitacre*.

314-315 See Ray Long, "Former ADM Executive Indicted On Federal Conspiracy Charges," Associated Press (November 9, 1997), wherein Hulse's attorney, Sheldon Zenner, indicated that he and his client had been maintaining Hulse's innocence to the Justice Department for three years.

Hulse's guilty plea and sentence respectively were reported by *Bloomberg* on March 6, 1998 and May 29, 1998. The letter from Hulse to Randall was dated April 1, 1996 but mailed April 2, 1996, according to the fax from David Hoech to Michael Bassett. Hoech also indicated that Randall had called Hulse on Saturday, April 6, 1996.

315 Randall's letter makes reference to "conversations with company counsel," and requests

that Hulse meet with the ADM lawyer. Hence it appears that the letter was at least reviewed with counsel before it was sent to Hulse. Regarding Allison, see Bill Ruminsky, "Former ADM Executive Admits Fraud: In Plea Agreement, Marty Allison Says He Helped Divert More than $300,000 from Firm," *Decatur Herald & Review* (February 25, 1997).

315-316 See declarations of James R. Randall dated July 27, 1995 and December 11, 1995, pertaining to photostatic forgery (for the Swiss investigation) dated August 14, 1995. Randall indicated that he knew the providers of Vitamin C technology and that ABP was not among them.

The defense view is that forgery has dropped out of the case. In a telephone interview on September 8, 1999, Bill Walker told me that ADM was equivocating about the matter. It had begun to not challenge that the Randall signatures were original, but insist that Mark Whitacre had duped him into signing the forms. Also, Walker said that the forms were on carbon paper and that signatures had to go through at least four additional sheets, but that ADM had never turned over the additional sheets. That was important to him because a photostatic signature only would appear on the top sheet. He wondered why ADM had not turned over the others.

316-318 Antitrust prosecutor James Griffin, in a telephone interview on August 13, 1999, related the story of the corporate guilty plea hinging on the Cox information. In addition, I obtained the FBI 302 summary of the Cox interview of October 12, 1996 from the court files in *United States v. Andreas, Whitacre and Wilson* in Chicago where the document had been submitted by the prosecution. It was also in this 302 form that the information about other price-fixing and Cargill appeared. See David Barboza, "Archer Daniels Executive Said to Tell of Price-Fixing Talks with Cargill Counterpart," *New York Times* (June 17, 1999). Also, Alan Guebert, "Truth Getting Lost in Cargill Spinning, Justice Sandbagging," *Food and Farm File* for the week beginning Sunday, January 27, 1999.

318-319 The debarment issue, including the involvement of Secretary of Agriculture Dan Glickman and the firm of Aiken Gump was first described in Roger Runningen "ADM's $83.5 Million in USDA Business at Risk in Review," *Bloomberg* (December 17, 1996). *Bloomberg* continued to follow the story. See Runningen, "ADM Keeps USDA Business, Avoids Ban in Agreement," *Bloomberg* (January 17, 1997); and see David Ward, "US House Coalition Targets Corporate Welfare," *Bloomberg* (January 28, 1997).

The St. Paul meeting was covered in John Nemo, "Feds Appeal for Farmers' Patience," Associated Press (April 18, 1999), and John Nemo, "Farmers Meet with Federal Officials," Associated Press (April 19, 1999). Also see Benno Groweneveld, "US Senators, Officials Hear US Farm Woes," Reuters (April 18, 1999). The quoted passage involving Michael Dunn was reported by Alan Guebert, "Justice Department, USDA Official at Odds Over ADM Plea Agreement," in his syndicated *Food and Farm File* (May 16, 1999). Guebert also reported the issue of the debarment of Sun-Diamond over the Espy gifts. In addition, I reviewed audio tapes of the meetings. Scott Lassar used the phrase "dirty pool," during a telephone interview on May 7, 1999. In a phone interview on August 13, 1999, James Griffin confirmed that these issues remained confidential. These were also the positions of the government at the press conference.

The long-standing national standards of "knowing, intelligent, and voluntary" for guilty pleas were reviewed most recently by the United States Supreme Court in *Bousley v. United States*, 523 US 614 (1998).

The colloquy between Judge Castillo and Stephen Mills occurred during the corporate guilty plea in *US v. ADM* in Chicago on October 15, 1996. See the transcript pages 19-20.

319-320 Mick Andreas told E.J. Kahn, Jr., that he and his father "talked about everything." Indeed they spoke three to five times daily. See Kahn, pages 132-133.

The elitist nature and customs of Japan's industrial leadership are described by Wolferen, *The Enigma of Japanese Power*.

The material about Coca-Cola comes from a government surveillance tape of September 28, 1993 involving Whitacre, Wilson, and Marty Andreas.

320-321 The deposition of James A. House was taken on video tape on October 28, 1997. The portions dealing with ProGold and the HFCS conspiracy including the alleged conduct of other producers was reported on pages 61-119 of the transcript. Also, see John Stebbins, "ADM Chairman Offered Money to Stop Rival Plant, Executive Says," *Bloomberg* (November 21, 1997). Stebbins reported the comments of former North Dakota governor George Sinner, as well as the contacts between James House and the Department of Justice and the fact that Cargill was taking over the wet milling facility on the Red River.

Also see Nancy Millman, "Documents: ADM Tried to Pay Off Rival, Andreas is Accused in Deposition for Suit," *Chicago Tribune* (November 22, 1997).

321-322 An outstanding investigative series of articles highlighting the Department of Justice's relations with informants, the Thornburg memo, and the congressional response to the abuses is Bill Moushey, "Win at All Costs," *Pittsburgh Post-Gazette* (November 23, 24 and 29, 1998) and (December 1, 6, 7, 8, and 13, 1998).

323-327 The notion of a rift between the fraud section and the FBI was my interpretation based upon the fact that the FBI turned over its investigative files when the fraud section had refused, that the FBI allowed interviews, and that Special Agent D'Angelo seemed incredulous that more people had not been indicted. However, D'Angelo never directly said that there was a rift.

323-326 I interviewed D'Angelo on several occasions. On two occasions we spoke by telephone, September 8, 1999, and September 13, 1999. Further, I met with him at his office on September 17, 1999. The quotations are from these sessions, as well as a follow-up phone call on November 15, 1999. All the quotations on pages 475-476, up to the material about Barry Cox, are from September 8, 1999. The comment on the Barry Cox material came from the in-person meeting on September 17, 1999. Unless otherwise noted, the remaining quotations in the text attributed to D'Angelo were from the telephone interview on September 8, 1999.

324-325 The files referred to are those that were presented to me by D'Angelo in his office. The file dates were listed in the documents.

324-325 In the files of February 1996, the FBI noted that the materials on Wittenburg and Hoech were turned over to fraud section attorney James Nixon, who passed them to the FBI.

D'Angelo's remark about Hoech and Vietnam was made during my visit to Chicago on September 17, 1999.

325 The file contained an FBI 302 form of Schmidt from January 24, 1996.

325 Nell Minow was interviewed by telephone on November 12, 1999.

325-326 Stephen R. Mills' deposition testimony on his AFE review responsibility was taken from the deposition transcript on pages 12-13. The fact that the outside auditor also had authority to review was taken from the transcript on page 75.

326-327 The dates of the Buffett-Reichter communications were not clarified in the FBI file on Buffett. However, Richter provided them in his first FBI interview.

328 In his deposition of January 27, 1998, Ferrari contradicted his explanation to the FBI on how he found a Swiss bank. In the deposition he said that he had gotten the name of the Swiss Bank Corporation from a reference book in a library before he went over to Hong Kong.

328-329 In general the government will not indicate who was called before the grand jury. My position that Kilburn and Frankel were not called is based on D'Angelo's representations that the fraud section articulated a strong directive not to investigate peripheral issues among which they were included.

Ferrari stated in his deposition that he had not been called before any grand jury.

330 D'Angelo's comment about a "fabulous deal" for Reichter was made on September 17, 1999.

331 Nicholas Hollis was interviewed by telephone on August 20, 1999. Hollis also received a subpoena from ADM in 1998. He has been a longtime critic of the ADM-Washington relationship.

331-332 Judge Manning's decision from which the excerpts are taken was filed on August 13, 1999 in *US v. Andreas, et al.*

James Griffin was interviewed by telephone on August 13, 1999.

332 David Hoech was interviewed by telephone on October 5, 1999.

The amount of corporate money set aside by ADM as well as the net earnings calculation were derived from the 1999 annual report.

333 The ADM corporate code of conduct and 800 number were reported by Paul Brinkmann, "ADM Focuses on Ethics in Wake of Price-Fixing Case," *Decatur Herald & Review* (July 13, 1999). Brinkmann has been one of the new breed of local reporters beginning to investigate agribusiness, including ADM, effectively.

333 Alice Marie Oyler, letter, *Decatur Herald & Review* (July 25, 1999).

SELECTED BIBLIOGRAPHY

Adams, Charles Francis. *An Autobiography*. New York: The Confucian Press, 1981.

Allen, Frederick Lewis. *The Lords of Creation*. New York: Harper & Brothers, 1935.

Antitrust Challenges in the 90s: Enforcement Reaches New Heights. Harrisburg, PA: Pennsylvania Bar Institute, 1995.

Atkin, Michael, *The International Grain Trade*. Cambridge, England: Woodhead Publishers, 1992.

Arnold, Thurman W., *The Bottlenecks of Business*. New York: Da Capo Press, 1973.

———— *The Folklore of Capitalism*. New Haven, CT: Yale University Press, 1938.

———— *The Symbols of Government*. New Haven, CT: Yale University Press, 1935.

Blair, Roger D. and Jeffrey L. Harrison. *Monopsony: Antitrust Law and Economics*. Princeton, NJ: Princeton University Press, 1993.

Birnbaum, Philip. *Encyclopedia of Jewish Concepts*. New York: Hebrew Publishing Company, 1964, 1975.

Bork, Robert H. *The Antitrust Paradox: A Policy at War with Itself*. New York: The Free Press, 1997.

Breit, William and Kenneth G. Elzivga. *The Antitrust Cookbook*. Chicago, IL: The Dryden Press, 1982.

Broehl, Wayne G., Jr. *Cargill: Trading the World's Grain*. Hanover, NH: University Press of New England, 1992.

Burbach, Roger and Patricia Flynn. *Agribusiness in the Americas*. New York: Monthly Review Press, 1980.

Burrough, Bryan. *Barbarians at the Gate: The Fall of RJR Nabisco*. New York: HarperCollins, 1991.

Burton, Theodore E. *John Sherman*, New York: Houghton Mifflin Company, 1906.

Cameron, Stevie. *On the Take: Crime, Corruption and Greed in the Mulroney Years.* Toronto, Canada: Macfarlane Walter & Ross, 1994.

Cramer, Gail. *Agricultural Economics and Agribusiness.* New York: Wiley Press, 1985.

Cramer, Gail L., ed. *Grain Marketing.* Boulder: Westview Press, 1993.

Connor, John M. *Archer Daniels Midland: Price-Fixer to the World.* West Lafayette, Indiana: Department of Agricultural Economics, Purdue University, 1998.

——— *The Global Lysine Price-Fixing Conspiracy of 1992–1995.* Storrs, CT: Food Marketing Policy Center, Department of Agricultural and Resource Economics, University of Connecticut, 1998.

——— *What Can We Learn from the ADM Global Price Conspiracies?* West Layfayette, IN: Department of Agricultural Economics, Purdue University, August 1998.

Dash, Samuel. *Chief Counsel: Inside the Ervin Committee–The Untold Story of Watergate.* New York: Random House, 1976.

Dean, John. *Blind Ambition: The White House Years.* New York: Simon and Schuster, 1976.

Derdak, Thomas, ed. *The International Directory of Company Histories.* Chicago and London: St. James Press, 1994.

Dershowitz, Alan, M. *Reasonable Doubts: The Criminal Justice System and the O. J. Simpson Case.* New York: Touchstone, 1997.

Dewey, Donald. *The Antitrust Experiment in America.* New York: Columbia University Press, 1990.

Douglas, William O. *Go East, Young Man.* New York: Dell Publishing Co., 1974.

Dunne, Gerald T. *Hugo Black and the Judicial Revolution.* New York: Simon and Schuster, 1977.

Emery, Fred. *Watergate: The Corruption of American Politics and the Fall of Richard Nixon.* New York: Random House, 1991.

Engler, Robert. *The Brotherhood of Oil: Energy Policy and the Public Interest.* Chicago and London: The University of Chicago Press, 1977.

——— *The Politics of Oil: Private Power & Democratic Directions.* Chicago, IL: The University of Chicago Press, 1961.

Galbraith, John Kenneth. *The New Industrial State.* New York: Signet Books, 1968.

Gardner, Nick. *A Guide to United Kingdom and European Union Competition Policy.* 2nd ed. Houndmills, UK: Macmillian, 1996.

George, Henry. *Progress and Poverty.* New York: Robert Schalkenback Foundation, 1981.

Gilmore, Richard. *A Poor Harvest: The Clash of Policies and Interest in the Grain Trade.* New York: Longman Press, 1982.

Grayson, David. *American Chronicle: The Autobiography of Ray Stannard Baker.* New York: Charles Scribner's Sons, 1945.

Green, Constance McLaughlin. *Washington: A History of the Capital, 1800-1950.* Princeton, NJ: Princeton University Press, 1962.

Green, Mark J., ed. *The Closed Enterprise System.* New York: Grossman Publishers, 1972.

Greenhut, Melvin L. *American Antitrust Laws in Theory and Practice.* Brookfield, VT: Avebury, 1989.

Greising, David and Laurie Morse. *Brokers, Bagmen & Moles,* New York: John Wiley & Sons, Inc., 1991.

Grennes, Thomas. *The Economics of World Grain Trade.* New York: Prager, 1978.

Guttman, Daniel and Barry Willner. *The Shadow Government: The Government's Multi-Billion-Dollar Giveaway of its Decision-Making Powers to Private Management Consultants, "Experts," & Think Tanks.* New York: Pantheon Books, 1976.

Hallam, Arne, ed. *Size, Structure, and the Changing Face of American Agriculture.* Boulder, CO: Westview Press, 1993.

Higgins, George W. *The Friends of Richard Nixon.* Boston: Little, Brown and Co., 1974.

Hilton, Stanley G. *Senator for Sale: Senator Bob Dole.* New York: St. Martin's Press, 1995.

Himmelberg, Robert F., ed. *Evolution of Antitrust Policy from Johnson to Bush.* New York: Garland Publishing, 1994.

Hofstadter, Richard. *The Age of Reform.* New York: Alfred A. Knopf, 1961.

Jaworski, Leon. *The Right and the Power: The Prosecution of Watergate.* New York: The Leon Jaworski Foundation, 1976.

Jorde, Thomas M. and David J. Teece, eds. *Antitrust, Innovation, and Competitiveness.* New York: Oxford University Press, 1992.

Kahn, E. J. Jr. *Supermarketer to the World: The Story of Dwayne Andreas, CEO of Archer Daniels Midland.* New York: Warner Books, 1991.

Kaplan, Justin. *Lincoln Steffens: A Biography.* New York, New York: Touchstone, 1974.

Kneen, Brewster. *Invisible Giant: Cargill and Its Transnational Strategies.* London, East Haven, CT: Pluto Press, 1995.

Kolko, Gabriel, *The Triumph of Conservatism.* Chicago, IL: Quadrangle Books, Inc., 1967.

Krebs, A.V. *The Corporate Reapers: The Book of Agribusiness.* Washington, DC: Essential Books, 1992.

Kutler, Stanley I. *Abuse of Power: The New Nixon Tapes.* New York: The Free Press, 1997.

Lasch, Christopher. *The New Radicalism in American 1889-1963: The Intellectual as a Social Type.* New York: Vintage Books, 1965.

Leuchtenburg, William, E. *Franklin D. Roosevelt and the New Deal.* New York: Harper and Row, 1963.

Lewis, Anthony. *Gideon's Trumpet*. New York: Vintage Books, 1989.

Lowenstein, Roger, *Buffett: The Making of an American Capitalist*. New York, New York: Main Street Books, Doubleday, 1996.

Lukas, J. Anthony. *Nightmare: The Underside of the Nixon Years*. New York: The Viking Press, 1976.

Margruder, Jeb Stuart. *One Man's Road to Watergate*. New York: Atheneum, 1974.

Mankiewicz, Frank. *Prefectly Clear: Nixon from Whittier to Watergate*. New York: Quadrangle, 1973.

———. *US v. Richard M. Nixon: The Final Crisis*. New York: Quadrangle, 1975.

Mollenhoff, Clark P. *Gameplan for Disaster: An Ombudsman's Report on the Nixon Years*. New York, W.W. Norton and Co., Inc., 1976.

Morgan, Dan. *Merchants of Grain: The Incredible Story of the Power, Profits, and Politics Behind the International Grain Trade*. New York: Viking Press, 1979.

Morison, Eliot Samuel. *The Oxford History of the American People*. New York: Oxford University Press, 1965.

Navasky, Victor S. *Kennedy Justice*. New York: Atheneum, 1971.

O'Connor, Richard. *Iron Wheels & Broken Men*. New York: G.P. Putnam's Sons, 1973.

Ouchi, William G. *Theory Z*. New York: Avon Books, 1982.

Peritz, Rudolph J.R. *Competition Policy in America, 1888-1992: History, Rhetoric, and Law*. New York: Oxford University Press, 1996.

Pringle, Henry F. *Theodore Roosevelt: A Biography*. New York: Harcourt, Brace and Company, 1931.

Ridgeway, James. *Who Owns the Earth*. New York: Collier Books, 1980.

Ross, Irwin. *Shady Business: Confronting Corporate Corruption*. New York: The Twentieth Century Fund Press, 1992.

Sampson, Anthony. *The Seven Sisters: The Great Oil Companies & the World They Shaped*. New York: The Viking Press, 1975.

Stelzer, Irwin M. and Howard P. Kitt. *Selected Antitrust Cases: Landmark Decisions*. 4th ed. Illinois: Richard D. Irwin, Inc., 1972.

Strum, Philippa. *Louis D. Brandeis: Justice for the People*. New York: Schocken Books, Inc., 1984.

Sullivan, E. Thomas, ed. *The Political Economy of the Sherman Act: The First One Hundred Years*. New York: Oxford University Press, 1991.

Sussman, Barry. *The Great Coverup: Nixon and the Scandal of Watergate*. New York: Thomas Y. Crowell Co., 1974.

Thompson, Fred D. *At That Point in Time: The Inside Story of the Senate Watergate Committee*. New York: Quadrangle, 1975

Vogeler, Ingolf. *The Myth of the Family Farm: Agribusiness Dominance of US Agriculture*. Boulder, CO: Westview Press, 1981.

Wamser, Frank. *Enforcement of Antitrust Law: A Comparison of the Legal and Factual Situation in Germany, the EEC, and the USA.* New York: Peter Lang, 1994.

Weinstein, James. *The Decline of Socialism in America 1912-1925.* New York: Vintage Books, 1969.

White, Theodore H. *The Making of the President: A Narrative History of American Politics in Action.* New York: Atheneum Publishers, 1973.

Wilson, Ray, D. *Illinois: Historical Tour Guide.* Carpentersville, IL: Crossroads Communications, 1991.

Wolferen, Karel van. *The Enigma of Japanese Power.* New York: Vintage Books, 1990.

Woodward, Bob and Scott Armstrong. *The Brethren: Inside the Supreme Court.* New York: Avon Books, 1979.

INDEX

exports. *See* agricultural exports
extortion allegations, 195–98, 252–54
   Cheviron's statement on, 300–301
   fabricated by Whitacre, 50–51, 137,
      199, 205, 217, 262, 269
   FBI investigation, 133–34, 195–98, 199,
      204–5, 215, 217, 253–54
   stipulated document, 196–97
   Whitacre's version of story, 299–300,
      308
Exxon, 110

Famalette, Joe, 320–21
FBI (Federal Bureau of Investigation)
   ADM raid (June 1995), 3–5, 6–8,
      155–56, 213–14, 308, 326
   agents in ADM offices, 225
   Behavioral Sciences Unit, 50, 124, 206
   Chicago Board of Trade investigation,
      25, 91–92
   extortion investigation, 133–34, 195–98,
      199, 204–5, 215, 217, 253–54
   file on fraud investigation, 322–25,
      326–30
   guidelines for informant use, 202, 206,
      263
   guidelines for undercover
      investigations, 202, 206, 217, 221,
      275
   lysine price-fixing investigation, 10–11,
      50, 199, 201, 205–7, 221, 224
   negotiations with Whitacre on immu-
      nity, 13–14
   Office of Professional Responsibility,
      241
   price-fixing investigations, 14
   sabotage investigation, 10–11, 50,
      195–98, 205
   Whitacre as informant, 10–11, 13–14,
      15–16, 198–200, 205–6, 216, 308,
      322
   See also video tapes

Federal Bureau of Investigation. *See* FBI
Federal Trade Commission (FTC), 107, 113
Ferrari, Ronald, 303–4, 305, 325, 328–29
Food for Peace program, 83, 101, 317
Forbes, 77
Fortune, 29, 78, 81, 111, 299
Frankel, Thomas, 302–3, 305, 329
fraud case
   ADM cooperation, 66, 322–23, 324
   FBI file, 322–25, 326–30
   grand jury, 304
   investigation by Justice fraud section,
      16–18, 23, 25, 66, 301, 304, 323, 324
   lack of prosecutions other than
      Whitacre, 329
   limits on, 17–18
   separation from antitrust case, 16–17,
      65, 322, 329
   Whitacre's guilty plea, 43, 52, 57, 60,
      63, 228, 308, 317
   Whitacre's sentence, 57, 59–61, 62–66,
      301
   See also embezzlement by Whitacre
Freeh, Louis, 275
FTC. *See* Federal Trade Commission
Fujiwara, Mr., 146, 197
   See also extortion allegations
futures markets, 90–92

Gartner, David, 90–91
gasohol. *See* ethanol
General Motors, 111, 112
Gingrich, Newt, 99
Glickman, Dan, 318
Glotzer, Martin, 283–84
Goldberg, Ray A., 20–21, 23, 24, 31
Goldstein, Gerald, 56–57
Gorbachev, Mikhail, 95–96
gossypol case, 34–35
grain alcohol. *See* ethanol
Grain Terminal Association (GTA),
   74, 83